P9-AQJ-206

WITHDRAWN

930.1028
Sp2

127742

DATE DUE			

Spatial
  Archaeology

Spatial
Archaeology

edited by

DAVID L. CLARKE

Peterhouse,
Cambridge, England

CARL A. RUDISILL LIBRARY
LENOIR RHYNE COLLEGE

1977

Academic Press
London   New York   San Francisco

A Subsidiary of Harcourt Brace Jovanovich, Publishers

ACADEMIC PRESS INC. (LONDON) LTD.
24/28 Oval Road,
London NW1

United States Edition published by
ACADEMIC PRESS INC.
111 Fifth Avenue
New York, New York 1003

930.1028

S P 2

12 7742

Feb, 1984

Copyright © 1977 by
ACADEMIC PRESS INC. (LONDON) LTD.

All Rights Reserved

No part of this book may be reproduced in any form by photostat, microfilm, or any
other means, without written permission from the publishers

Library of Congress Catalog Card Number: 76-55909
ISBN: 0-12-175750-1

Printed in Great Britain by
The Lavenham Press Ltd.
Lavenham, Suffolk, England

List of Contributors

David L. Clarke *Peterhouse, Cambridge, England*
Peter Danks *King's College, Cambridge, England*
Peter Dickens *School of Cultural and Community Studies, University of Sussex, Falmer, Sussex, England*
Roland Fletcher *Department of Anthropology, University of Sydney, Sydney, N.S.W., Australia*
Robert Foley *National Museum, Nairobi, Kenya*
Ian Hodder *Department of Archaeology, University of Leeds, Leeds, England*
R. A. Raper *31, Ayresome Avenue, Leeds, England*

For little Onie —
My daughter Leonie Stella Clarke

Preface

The tragedy of David Clarke's early death occurred before the proofs of this book had been produced. We are fortunate that, through this collection of papers, spatial archaeology is one of the areas in archaeology where we can see most clearly not only how his fertile mind was developing, but also in what direction he thought the subject itself was moving. Perhaps his most important contribution in the field of spatial studies was the work on Glastonbury (*Models in Archaeology*, p. 801), which will remain of considerable significance, both for Iron Age studies and for our ability to reconstruct past social organization. He was also early in identifying spatial studies as one of the main paradigms within archaeological research (*Models in Archaeology*, p. 7). Even earlier, in *Analytical Archaeology*, the spatial structure of archaeological "cultures" was, for the first time, examined in detail, and there are numerous other discussions in that book of the techniques and problems of spatial analysis. Thus, in this, as in so many other areas in archaeology, he provided an important stimulus and focus for research. It is our tragedy that he was not able to continue this line of work himself.

The book largely represents work carried out by David Clarke's students and collected together by him. The volume thus appears largely as he envisaged it. However, any errors in minor detail which should have been ironed out at the proof-reading stage are entirely due to my own failings.

The typescript of David Clarke's own introductory chapter was clearly intended by him to be finally revised. In a number of places small changes to the text, and in particular to the references, proved necessary. I hope the reader will bear this in mind when considering his important chapter.

It is perhaps only fair to the contributors to mention that the articles were written some while before this book went to press. It was the enthusiasm of Academic Press for the New Direction series, of which this was to be the first volume, that has made the production of this book possible, and their continuing assistance which has carried this volume through. I would like to thank the contributors for the speed with which they dealt with their proofs.

Finally, gratitude should be extended to Dr. N. Hammond, Dr. A. Sherratt and especially to Mrs. Stella Clarke, for their advice and help in the final stages of preparation.

Leeds
January 1977   *Ian Hodder*

Contents

Contents   xi

1

Spatial Information in Archaeology

DAVID L. CLARKE
Peterhouse, Cambridge

This essay is an attempt to pull together the implications of several levels of spatial studies outside archaeology and the momentarily miscellaneous and disconnected archaeological studies involving spatial analysis, at various scales, on diverse material in several different archaeological schools or traditions. The main claim will be that the retrieval of archaeological information from various kinds of spatial relationship is a central aspect of the international discipline of archaeology and a major part of the theory of that discipline wherever it is practised. Certainly, part of this archaeological spatial theory may be reduced to the existing spatial theories of human behaviour developed in economics, geography, architecture and ethology — it would be surprising if it were not so. However, although rightly emphasizing the significance of this body of theory for the archaeologist, this common ground is but a small part of archaeological spatial theory which must deal with a more comprehensive range of hominid behaviour patterns, using data with the special characteristics and sampling problems of the archaeological record. Within this paradigm, individual manifestations of archaeological spatial analysis, whether settlement archaeology, site system analyses, regional studies, territorial analyses, locational analyses, catchment area studies, distribution mapping, density studies, within-site and within-structure analyses or even stratigraphic studies, are all particular forms of spatial studies at particular scales and in particular contexts (Clarke, 1972a, p. 47).

1. Historical introduction

In essence, there is a very evident expanding and convergent interest in
archaeological spatial information in all the contemporary schools of
archaeology, from the Russian to the Australasian. This interest has of
course a respectable antiquity within each tradition, but there have
been marked differences in emphasis and only now is the full
significance and generality of archaeological spatial analysis being
grasped and disconnected studies integrated around this important
theoretical focus. In Europe, archaeology was from the first much
concerned with inferences from spatial distribution and the ties with
geography were strong, if intermittent. In particular, the important
Austro-German school of "anthropo-geographers" (1880-1900) developed the formal mapping of attributes and artefacts in order to
distinguish and explain culture complexes as well as extending this
approach to mapping correlations between prehistoric settlement
patterns and environmental variables; often publishing in the Geo-
graphisches Zeitung (Gradmann, 1898; Ratzel, 1896; Frobenius, 1898).
Certainly, by the turn of the century the comparative analysis of
archaeological distribution maps had become a standard if intuitive
procedure within European archaeology.

The same movements more or less directly affected British archaeology where they impinged on an existing tradition which taught that
ancient and historic settlement patterns were conditioned by landscape
and geography (Williams-Freeman, 1881; Guest, 1883; Green, 1967).
These various ideas were combined and developed further by Crawford,
an archaeologist who trained as a geographer at Oxford in 1909, and
also by Fleure, Professor of Geography at Aberystwyth, in a series of
archaeological papers to the Royal Geographical Society and elsewhere
(Crawford, 1912; Fleure, 1921). It was from this background that Fox
later elaborated a technique combining series of archaeological and
environmental distribution maps to cover a region or a country
changing over several millenia, in a remarkable contribution which
was widely followed in the 1930's (Fox, 1922, 1932; Childe, 1934;
Grimes, 1945; Hogg, 1943; Woolridge and Linton, 1933). After an
interval in which "economic" interests dominated British prehistory,
the "spatial" approach reappeared in a revised form ultimately
stemming from the direct stimuli of the Cambridge School of New
Geography (Haggett, 1965; Chorley and Haggett, 1967) and the
neighbouring research centre of the School of Architecture (Martin *et*

al., 1974) — in one respect as a development in theoretical models in archaeology (Clarke, 1968, 1972a) and in another as the development by Vita- Finzi and Higgs (1970) of the "catchment area" concept from Chisholm (1968).

The American approach to spatial archaeology also shared something of the nineteenth-century tradition of the "anthropo-geographers" but it increasingly emphasized social organization and settlement pattern rather than artefacts and distribution maps; the anthropological dimension became stronger and the geographical aspect diminished. Jeffrey Parsons (1972) suggests that Steward's key studies on prehistoric regional and community patterns in the North American Southwest (1937, 1938) are distantly related to the earlier studies of Morgan (1881) and Mindeleff (1900) on the sociology of architectural remains and settlement development. Steward's work certainly stimulated a series of major field researches concerned with locating and mapping archaeological sites on a regional scale with the express purpose of studying the adaptation of social and settlement patterns within an environmental context: notably the lower Mississippi Valley survey carried out by Phillips *et al.* between 1940-1947 (1951) and the more influential Viru Valley survey undertaken by Willey (1953). Willey's project was so full of innovations that, rather like Fox's "Archaeology of the Cambridge Region" (1922), it had widespread repercussions and tended to fix the form of spatial interest in settlement pattern studies (Parsons, 1972).

The proliferation of archaeological settlement pattern studies in America culminated with the publication in 1956 of "Prehistoric Settlement Patterns in the New World" (Willey, 1956) by which point large numbers of archaeologists in America and elsewhere had slowly become more fully aware of the significance of settlement pattern and settlement system analyses (Winters, 1967, 1969). Field projects multiplied on the regional settlement survey model of the Viru Valley — Adams' project in the Diyala region of Iraq, 1957-58, Sanders' in the Teotihuacan Valley of Mexico, 1960-74 and Willey's Belize Valley and British Honduras project, 1954-56 (Parsons, 1972). At the same time, investigations into spatial patterns and social organization began to move from conventional categorization (Chang, 1958, 1962) to new analytical approaches and spatial variability in archaeological data (Binford and Binford, 1966; Wilmsen, 1975; Longacre, 1964; Hill, 1966; Cowgill, 1967; Wright, 1969). However, in most of these studies the sociological, economic or ecological objectives remained the dominant archaeological consideration and the role of spatial information, spatial structure and spatial variability was merely ancillary; spatial archaeology remained a secondary consideration.

Related developments in the spatial aspects of archaeology are equally to be found in most of the other schools of archaeology, with an anthropological and exchange system emphasis where "primitive" populations have survived (Chagnon, 1967; Campbell, 1968), and a geographical, marketing or economic emphasis in "developed" areas (Skinner, 1964; Stjernquist, 1967). In France, the older geographical approach has been joined by a swiftly-growing interest in spatial distributions, especially at the micro-level, exemplified by the work of Leroi-Gourhan (1972), at the Magdalenian open site of Pincevent, and similar studies elsewhere. Russian archaeology, with its early Marxist emphasis on settlement and social structure, pioneered many aspects of detailed large-scale settlement excavation and regional settlement pattern study, from Gravettian open sites to complete Medieval cities — a lead which certainly had direct repercussions in western European settlement studies (Biddle, 1967). In Oceania, Australasia and Africa there has also been a particularly stimulating interaction between local anthropological approaches, American settlement pattern archaeology and British ecological catchment area studies with very promising developments (Parsons, 1972, 134; Buist, 1964; Green, 1967, 1970; Groube, 1967; Shawcross, 1972; Bellwood, 1971; Cassells, 1972; Schrire, 1972; Parkington, 1972).

This expanding interest in archaeological spatial information in all the contemporary schools of archaeology has become an increasingly explicit but fragmented common development. Attention has been strongly focused on only limited aspects developed within each school — notably distribution analysis, locational analysis, catchment studies, exchange and marketing systems and regional settlement pattern projects. These specializations clearly relate to local interests and local school histories and, in particular, several complementary developments can be noted in which, for example, integrated settlement pattern studies were an early focus in the United States, whereas an interest in the formal extraction of information from detailed distribution mapping and the full impact of modern geographical methods first emerged in European studies.

It has, therefore, been as characteristic of this area of archaeological disciplinary development as any other that important steps in the retrieval of information from spatial relationships in archaeological contexts have been dispersed, disaggregated and dissipated: dispersed regionally and lacking developed cross-cultural comparisons; disaggregated by scale and context, severing within-site studies from between-site analyses, Palaeolithic spatial studies from Medieval and catchment studies from locational analyses; dissipated by slow communication between schools of archaeology at a general theoretical level and aggravated by a persistent reluctance to see beyond parochial manifestations of problems to their general forms throughout archaeology. In addition, the analyses of spatial information in archaeology for a long time tended to remain either inexplicit, intuitive, static and typological, or at best a secondary aspect of studies devoted to other objectives. However, it is not argued here that spatial studies in archaeology are more important than other objectives but merely that it is time that the major role of archaeological spatial information was recognized and its common assumptions, elements, theories, models, methods and problems explicitly investigated and systematized.

2. Past, present and future states

Although every archaeological study, past and present, has some spatial component, nevertheless the archaeological discovery and conquest of space has only recently begun on a serious scale. Of course, spatial archaeology was one of the twin pillars of traditional Montelian archaeology — the central pillars of the typological method and distribution mapping; the study of things, their classification into categories and the study, interpretation and explanation of their distributions (Clarke, 1973, pp. 13-14). However, as with artefact typology and taxonomy, it can now be seen that the intuitive analysis of spatial both "by inspection" or "eyeballing" is no longer sufficient nor an end in itself. It has slowly emerged that there is archaeological information in the spatial *relationships* between things as well as in *things* in themselves.

Spatial relationships are of course only one kind of relationship for archaeologists to investigate and the current interest in spatial relationships is thus merely part of the current ideological shift from the study of things (artefacts) to the study of the relationships between things (variability, covariation, correlation, association, change and process) (Binford, 1972). It is also part of the wider realization that archaeologists are engaged in information retrieval and that which constitutes archaeological information depends on a set of assumptions combined with some theories or hypotheses as well as some observations; archaeological observations are not only theory-laden but they only provide information at all in so far as they are constrained by assumptions and led by ideology. The collection and ordering of information, therefore, presupposes a theoretical frame of reference whether tacit or explicit — "all knowledge is the result of theory, we buy information with assumptions" (Coombs, 1964). The clear implications of this for spatial archaeology are that assumptions are honourable and necessary and theory is intrinsic and essential, with the reservations that assumptions and theory must be explicitly brought out, they must be flexible and not dogmatic and they must be subject to continual reappraisal against reality. To conceal or deny the role of archaeological assumptions and theory is merely to remove the possibility of gaining fresh information as well as to delude ourselves.

So the explicit scrutiny of spatial relationships and the sources of spatial variability in archaeology, together with their underlying assumptions and alternative theories, are all part of the current reformation in archaeology. Every archaeological school has long realised in its own intuitive and tacit manner the information latent in archaeological spatial relationships — this much is clear from the otherwise unwarranted precision of many maps and groundplans going back into the eighteenth century and the early intuitive manipulations of distributions or the meticulous three-dimensional location of artefacts in some early excavations. This mass of unliberated information, information gathered at a level more refined than the capacity for explicit analysis at the time, signals the intuitive recognition of the information hidden in spatial configurations, whilst at the same time these studies still present us with the valuable possibility of recycling old observations, maps, plans or reports for the extraction of new information (see Glastonbury, Clarke, 1972). Perhaps problem focused research and rescue excavation should bear in mind the possible capacities of future techniques and make some altars of observations to unknown technological gods. The choice is, after all, not between the impossibility of recording everything for unspecified purposes and recording only observations relating to specific problems but a skilful gamble somewhere in between, recording as many supplementary observations as time, money and primary objectives will allow.

To summarize, then, at the present time it is widely realised that there is archaeological information embedded in spatial relationships and there is much scattered individual work on settlement patterns and settlement archaeology, site systems and activity patterns, catchments and locations, exchange and marketing fields and population areas and territories. But with honourable exceptions, these projects still tend to be static, disaggregated studies involved in typologies of sites, patterns, distribution, as things; we get bits of individual clocks but no account of working systems and their structural principles. The only major books available are either confined to restricted archaeological aspects (Willey, 1956; Ucko *et al.*, 1972; Chang, 1958) or come from other disciplines (Haggett, 1965; Chorley and Haggett, 1967; Abler *et al.*, 1971; Martin and March, 1972). With the exception of the important and complementary research work by Hodder and Whallon, spatial analyses in archaeology are still either largely intuitive or based on an inadequately discussed statistical and spatial theory and unvoiced underlying assumptions (Hodder, herein and 1974; Whallon, 1973-4). Thus archaeology has accumulated many scattered individual spatial studies at particular scales, usually with narrowly limited horizons and employing only single spatial techniques; in very few studies are the mutually essential within-site and between-site levels integrated and the many appropriate techniques brought together in an harmonious analysis (for sketches in this direction see Moundville and Peebles, 1975; Glastonbury and Clarke, 1972b; Hammond, 1972).

Spatial archaeology, therefore, needs the elaboration of a common range of useful elements, assumptions, theory, models, methods and problems to be tested, reassessed and extended in dynamic and integrated case studies. Only now is the full significance of archaeological spatial analysis being grasped and a common integration of theory and methods beginning to emerge from slow internal development and scattered contacts with territorial ethology, regional ecology, locational economics, geographical studies, ekistics, architectural theory and proxemics — the spatial social sciences. Certainly, these theories and methods represent an ill-assorted ragbag of miscellaneous and abused bits and pieces but this is to be expected on the boundaries of archaeological research where the exercise is not the retrospective description of a completed field of perfected enquiry but rather the exploration of a difficult uncharted and expanding dimension. Equipped with a growing amalgam of spatial theory and methods, integrating small scale and large scale aspects, and appropriately transformed for the special problems of our data, archaeological spatial exploration can move forward and accurate mapping can commence.

The integration of archaeological spatial theory is, therefore, an enterprise which has hardly begun in a formal manner. The archaeologist must develop his own models and theories where possible or adopt and adapt suitable models and theories from the spatial sciences wherever they may prove appropriate. An early step towards this end should therefore include some appraisal of the common assumptions, theories and methods of the spatial techniques in other fields, in order to see how appropriate or inappropriate they are for archaeological purposes and how they may be adapted, modified and translated for archaeological data. Another early requirement must be to seek clarification about which spatial assumptions, theories and methods are appropriate at particular levels of study, within-structures, within-sites and between sites, and which have a powerful generality at several levels or a special restriction to more limited scales and forms of problem.

However, this fresh expansion of archaeological theory is not just important in itself, for it is interlinked with implications for field techniques, analyses and interpretation. These theoretical developments have, after all, been partly brought about by and inevitably imply a revision of field techniques and excavation ranging from field research strategies (Struever, 1968, 1971), to the more general three-dimensional recording of excavation data (Brown, 1974; Biddle, 1967) and detailed physical analyses of raw materials and artefacts to trace sources and movements as well as the increasing use of sophisticated surface and aerial surveys of all kinds. Spatial information comes not only from knowing the locational relationship of various items but also from tracing their relative movements and flow — the dynamic aspect. These sorts of requirements in turn necessarily focus attention on basic archaeological assumptions about the deposition and disposition of items in the archaeological record and in particular on sampling and simulating their spatial movements and spatial significance at every scale (Binford, 1972; Clarke, 1972a). This feedback between theory and practice, practice and theory, is an important reminder of the interactive nature of disciplinary development in archaeology.

Archaeology needs integrated and dynamic spatial studies because information comes from the interplay of different fields of observation and because, in archaeology, systems have no existence except in their proximity, flow and contact pattern: the restricted flow of activity within and between structures, sites and resource spaces—the clock-working. This gives us the basis for a rough definition of spatial archaeology and at once specifies its clear links with behavioural studies and the analysis of activity patterns. In the section that follows a purely preliminary and tentative attempt will be made to outline spatial archaeology, some of its common elements, relationships, theory, models and methods as well as highlighting the underlying assumptions and problems in practice.

3. Spatial archaeology

Spatial archaeology might be defined as—the retrieval of information from archaeological spatial relationships and the study of the spatial consequences of former hominid activity patterns within and between features and structures and their articulation within sites, site systems and their environments: the study of the flow and integration of activities within and between structures, sites and resource spaces from the micro to the semi-micro and macro scales of aggregation (Fig. 1). Spatial archaeology deals, therefore, with human activities at every scale, the traces and artefacts left by them, the physical infrastructure which accommodated them, the environments that they impinged upon and the interaction between all these aspects. Spatial archaeology deals with a set of elements and relationships

The elements principally involved are raw materials, artefacts, features, structures, sites, routes, resource spaces and the people who ordered them. The sites selected for study are *not* confined to settlements and include cemeteries, megalithic tombs, caves, shelters, mines, quarries and centres of resource extraction, indeed any centres of human activity; spatial archaeology, therefore, englobes but is not synonymous with settlement archaeology. The technical term "resource space" is introduced here as a valuable recognition that one area of space may be a resource in its own right and much used, whilst another neighbouring space may not have been used or visited at all—at the micro-level the areas around a fire or cooking range or in the lee of a house are resource spaces and so are zones of good agricultural soil, grazing pastures or mineral resources, at a different scale.

An important additional step is the recognition that archaeological maps, plans or section drawings are all "graphs" and that archaeolo-

gical elements on maps or plans have all of the qualities which are
more familiarly associated with graphical displays:

    Elements on maps have distributions which may be statistically
    summarized

    Elements on maps have qualitative and quantitative values

    Elements on maps may have structure (statistical non-randomness
    or geometrical regularity)

    Elements on maps may have associations or correlations with other
    sets of elements within and beyond the system at hand.

The next step is to identify the principal elements at a selected scale
of study and the particular relationships between them. By definition,
we are interested in the spatial structure of the system — the way in
which the elements are located in space and their spatial interaction.
The analysis of the spatial structure of the system of elements is the
stage at which appraisal by a swift intuitive glance must in most cases
be replaced by the surprisingly complex search for distribution shapes,
significant trends and residuals in quantitative and qualitative values,
patterns of association and correlation and locational structure or
geometrical regularity. Having discovered the strength and nature of
any significant distribution patterning, trends, correlation or spatial
structure within the elements in the system, other information from
the system can be brought in to try to model, interpret and explain the
activity patterns involved and their relationship to the dynamics of the
system under study.

Spatial structure at the levels of the site system, the site and the built
structure can then be described as the non-random output of human
choice processes which allocate structural forms, activities and artefacts
to relative loci within sites and within systems of sites and environments.
The aim of this kind of study is the search for and explanation of
spatial regularities and singularities in the form and function of
particular patterns of allocation, in order to gain a fuller understanding
of the adaptive role of particular systems at work and a better
knowledge of the underlying causes of archaeological spatial variability
in general.

The level of resolution of these studies, sometimes called the level of
aggregation, can and should be deliberately varied. Each element in
the system can be considered itself to be a subsystem which contains a
new set of elements (Fig. 1). Each level aggregates the output of the
levels below and above as internal and external inputs and, therefore,
no elements can be understood without investigating the competing

requirements of its individual compound structural units and the constraints imposed by the wider system of which it is merely a part. Three main levels or scales of spatial structure in this continuum of spatial relationships can be arbitrarily defined, each level with its appropriate scale of assumptions, theory and models. However, as we have already pointed out, the three levels are not separate and one of the attractive possibilities of spatial archaeology is that the problem, theory, models and methods of one level may be found useful at others within a spatially unified field theory (Echenique, 1971).

4. Levels of resolution of spatial archaeology (Fig. 1)

A. MICRO LEVEL

The micro level is within structures; proxemic and social models are mainly appropriate (Hall, 1944, 1966; Fast, 1970; Watson, 1972). At this level of personal and social space, individual and cultural factors largely dominate economic ones. Locational structure here comprises the non-random or reiterative allocation of artefacts, resource spaces and activities to particular relative loci within the built structures. A structure is any small scale constructed or selected unit which contained human activities or their consequences; "structures" may therefore include, for example, natural shelters, rooms, houses, graves, granaries or shrines (Fig. 2).

B. SEMI-MICRO LEVEL

The semi-micro level is within sites; social and architectural models are mainly appropriate (Lévi-Strauss, 1953; Sommer, 1969; Douglas, 1972; Alexander, 1964; Martin and March, 1972; March and Steadman, 1971). At this level of communal space, social and cultural factors may outweigh most economic factors but economic location looms larger. Locational structure is again the non-random or re-iterative allocation of artefacts, resource spaces, structures and activities to particular relative loci within the site. A site is a geographical locus which contained an articulated set of human activities or their consequences and often an associated set of structures; sites may be domestic settlements, ceremonial centres, cemeteries, industrial complexes or temporary camp locations (Fig. 3).

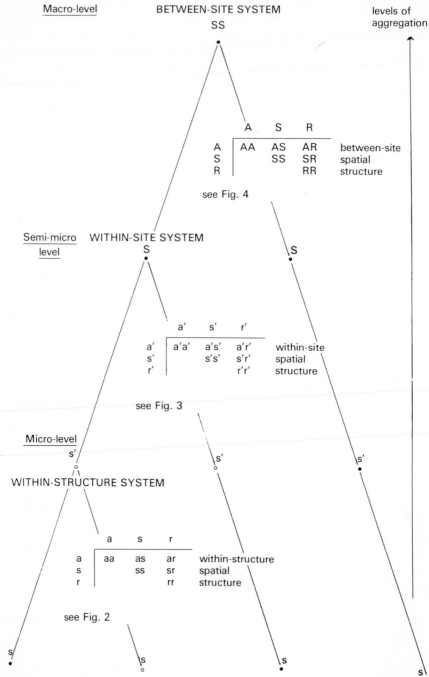

FIG. 1. Levels of resolution of archaeological spatial systems. Each level aggregates the output of the levels below and above as internal and external inputs into that system level. See Figs. 2, 3, 4 for key to the symbols.

Within structure

Spatial relationships
between

	Artefacts a	Features s	Resource spaces r
Artefacts a	aa	as	ar
Features s		ss	sr
Resource r spaces			rr

FIG. 2. Matrix of the spatial relationships which must be searched for archaeological information at the within-structure micro level.

C. MACRO LEVEL

The macro level is between sites; geographic and economic models are largely relevant at this level (Haggett, 1965; Chisholm, 1968; Chorley and Haggett, 1967; Clarke, 1972, 705-959; Renfrew, 1974). Because of the scale involved and the friction effect of time and distance on energy expenditure, economic "best-return-for-least-effort" factors largely dominate most social and cultural factors at this level. Locational structures here comprise the non-random or reiterative allocation of artefacts, resource spaces, structures and sites to particular relative loci within integrated site systems and across landscapes.

Within site

Spatial relationships
between

	Artefacts a′	Structures s′	Resource spaces r′
Artefacts a′	a′a′	a′s′	a′r′
Structures s′		s′s′	s′r′
Resource r′ spaces			r′r′

FIG. 3. Matrix of the spatial relationships which must be searched for archaeological information at the within-site, semi-micro level.

A site system is a set of sites at which it is hypothesized that the interconnection between the sites was greater than the interconnection between any individual site and sites beyond the system; the flow or flux between the sites embracing reciprocal movements of people, commodities, resources, information and energy. Studies at this scale embrace all large-scale archaeological distributions dispersed across landscapes as well as the integrated site systems that generated them (Fig. 4).

Between site

Spatial relationships
between

		Artefacts A	Sites S	Resource spaces R
Artefacts	A	AA	AS	AR
Sites	S		SS	SR
Resource spaces	R			RR

FIG. 4. Matrix of spatial relationships which must be searched for archaeological information at the between-site, macro level.

It will immediately be apparent that these levels of resolution are arbitrary horizons determined by the scale at which we wish to conflate related phenomena in a continuum of related phenomena; the levels and entities are merely summarizing terms-of-convenience and may be altered at will in particular studies by further subdivision or the choice of other specific scales and criteria. In the limiting case, the "structure" converges with the "site" and the "site" with the "site system"; the large rock shelter moves from the status of a structure to that of a site, the Minoan palace is a structure at a scale which converges upon the properties of sites of village or factory calibre, and a large settlement site may resemble and may even once have been a closely spaced system of smaller separate sites. The scale of definition and resolution is a matter of choice for the purposes of the particular study in hand.

It may also be noted that any partition of factors into personal, social, cultural, economic or geographic is similarly arbitrary, a modern retrospective separation of aspects of a whole into subsystems of convenience. It is, therefore, a truism that personal, social, cultural and economic factors count in spatial patterning and variability at every level. However, one utility of this truism is the realization that, at the small scale, the "cost" of being uneconomic is negligibly small and may therefore be overruled by the factors which we distinguish as personal, social, cultural or religious factors. At the large scale, the converse becomes true, although social and cultural factors always remain present, they may be dominated by economic and geographic constraints. A large religious or ceremonial centre with a permanent population must be sited so that its "cost" is tolerable to the supporting society, in relation to the expenditure of human energy involving other sites already in existence, as well as local resources and environment. However, the tolerable "cost" in energy expenditure is relative to particular societies and is obviously in part a culturally conditioned threshold as much as a purely economic one (viz. the cost of the Pyramids, Stonehenge, Avebury or Teotihuacan).

5. The matrix of spatial relationships

Spatial archaeology is especially concerned with the information latent within the spatial relationships between elements—the spatial structure. A large range of classes of archaeological elements is potentially involved and there exists, therefore, a vast number of possible mutual spatial relationships to explore for information; so vast that the archaeologist is often unaware of all but a few. The aim of spatial archaeology is to make the archaeologist aware of the vast matrix of spatial relationships and the many kinds of information which it contains for recovery by the proper methods. In real studies, this vast matrix of potential information-niches is only partially filled for recovery—the particular archaeological situation may preserve few artefacts, no structures and sparse external information. But this dilemma only emphasizes more clearly the need for the systematic extraction of what information there is and the greater priority that ought to be given to situations and sites which are known to be more richly endowed in this sense; if we are seeking more and new information we should not squander our limited resources on sites with little or only redundant information to yield, with certain exceptions.

It is impossible to illustrate the potential scale of the matrix of archaeological spatial relationships because the number of classes or elements is infinitely variable within alternative classifications, but using the arbitrary elements that we have already distinguished, we can

at least sketch its outline (Figs 1, 2, 3, 4). At each of our three
arbitrary levels of resolution, the need to search for information in the
spatial structure, the non-random reiterative or geometric spatial
relationships has to be indicated.

(a) At the within-structure level   Spatial relationships between
artefacts and other artefacts (aa), artefacts and features (as),
artefacts and resource spaces (ar), features and features (ss) and
resource spaces and other resource spaces (rr) (Fig. 2).

(b) At the within-site level   Spatial relationships between artefacts
and other artefacts (a′a′), structures and structures (s′s′), structures
and resource spaces (s′r′) and resource spaces and other resource
spaces (r′r′) (Fig. 3).

(c) At the between level   Spatial relationships between artefacts
and other artefacts over landscapes (AA), artefacts and sites (AS),
artefacts and resource spaces (AR), sites and other sites (SS), sites
and resource spaces (SR) and resource spaces and other resource
spaces (RR) (Fig. 4).

This arbitrarily simplified and terse matrix identifies six sets of
different spatial relationships for examination and search at each of
three levels, outlining eighteen coarse information niches which are
potentially rich in archaeological information in any area with sites,
structures and artefacts (Fig. 1). All of the existing studies in spatial
archaeology can be identified as sitting within some of these individual
niches — activity pattern analysis (aa, as, ar), structural module
analysis (a′s′, s′s′), locational analysis (SS), market and exchange
analysis (AR), catchment area analysis (SR), etc. The point is that
existing studies tend, with exceptions, to explore only one or two such
information niches ignoring the others which are not only present but
essentially and reciprocally interrelated.

However, the position has already been taken here that the
archaeological information within our spatial matrix is not simply a
collection of raw observations but rather a selection of observations
which will only yield information when arranged in terms of a
theoretical background, given certain assumptions (Coombs, 1964).
What, then, are the theories in terms of which the archaeologist
tackles his spatial analyses? Well, most spatial archaeology rests either
upon unstated but implicit archaeological spatial theory, as in the case
of the great studies by Fox (1922, 1932) and Willey (1953), or upon
theory borrowed from the spatial sciences (Clarke, 1968, 1972a; Vita-
Finzi and Higgs, 1970). The contemporary dilemma for the archaeol-

ogist is the choice between an archaeologically appropriate but inexplicit theoretical foundation for his analyses, or an explicit theory derived from another field, based on assumptions that may or may not be reasonable for the archaeological context. However, the solution is in the archaeologists hands and the gap between the individual theories of the spatial social sciences is not so great that particles of common or potentially common theory and dependent common models and methods are not already visible, however unsatisfactory they may be. Let us look briefly at some of the main theoretical approaches to spatial problems, noting in particular the archaeological acceptability of their assumptions and their ideological and metaphysical background. In this way, we can hope to see the way in which ideological and metaphysical assumptions directly affect our theories, explicit or implicit, and thence filter through to our common models and techniques, finally colouring the information we draw from our observations.

6. Common spatial theories

A theory, in this sense, may be defined as a system of thought which through logical, verbal or mathematical contents supplies an explanation of archaeological spatial forms, variability and distributions — how they arise and function, their basic structure and how they develop in processes of growth and change. It is usual to distinguish between "complete" and "incomplete" theories. Complete theories are those formal and comprehensive networks of defined terms or theorems which may be derived from a complete set of primitive and axiomatic sentences by deduction and tested against reality (e.g. Euclidean geometry). However, most theories in the social and behavioural sciences belong to the group of incomplete theoretical networks and they are often only "quasi-deductive" or "non-formal" theories. Archaeological theory in general, and spatial archaeological theory in particular, is in the main only quasi-deductive and largely non-formal. The theories are quasi-deductive in the sense that there are difficulties, some of them intrinsic, in establishing precise primitive terms in the initial stages of theory formation and thus a consequent weakness in the deduction process. The same theories are also non-formal since there are often difficulties in testing the theory and its models empirically because of vagueness and ambiguity, limited data, limited capacities for controlled experiment, severe sampling problems and a general lack of suitable evaluation techniques (Harvey, 1969, pp. 96-99; Riquezes, 1972, p. 83). However, this state of affairs makes it the more important for archaeology to move as far as possible in reforming its theories towards as complete, formal and deductive a form as may be possible, together with appropriate modelling and experimental testing in order that we may be clearer about the size and nature of any archaeological residue, if any, which cannot be treated in this way.

So archaeological spatial theory is represented by some loose, informal general theories, ultimately extended from anthropology, economics, biology or statistical mechanics, and by an incomplete series of localized and fragmentary subtheories and their dependent models, mainly derived from the spatial sciences and social sciences. The explicit subtheories are firmly linked to the general theories but the entire network is invisibly completed by important areas of yet unspecified archaeological subtheory, implicit in what many archaeologists do.

Four general theories underlie most of the detailed spatial archaeological studies that have attempted to move beyond description to the explanation of the relationships which occur in archaeology. These theories are not mutually exclusive alternatives but related and intersecting approaches whose differences arise from differing underlying assumptions and often a preoccupation with a particular scale of study. The four theories may be loosely labelled as follows.

1. Anthropological spatial theory.
2. Economic spatial theory.
3. Social physics theory.
4. Statistical mechanics theory.

Anthropological spatial theory has long been the traditional background for archaeological speculations and it has taken many changing forms over the years—from the direct equation of archaeological spatial relationships with social, tribal and ethnic ties to the more recent structural and behavioural approach (Lévi-Strauss, 1973; Binford, 1972). The essence of the more recent versions of this theory rest on the proposition that archaeological remains are spatially patterned as the result of the patterned behaviour of the members of an extinct society, thus the spatial structure is potentially informative about the way the society organized itself. The deep structure of social grammar is believed to generate different spatial surface manifestations and spatial moieties; elements of social structure are present in spatial structure, especially at the micro level. In practice, this approach has concentrated upon the functional interpretation of spatial clusterings of artefacts and the social interpretation of spatial patterning amongst ceramic attributes (Longacre, 1968; Speth and Johnson, 1974). The first step is usually to define the spatial patterning of the archaeological remains by quantitative methods and then to offer testable hypotheses based on anthropological or mathematical analogy as to the organization of the society and the associated patterns of individual and group behaviour behind the spatial patterning observed.

Economic spatial theory is perhaps the most common theoretical approach to spatial problems, especially at the macro scale. This theory makes the assumption that over a span of time and experience, people move to choices and solutions which minimize costs and maximize profits; originally conceived in economic and monetary terms, the theory is now seen as a special case of the general ecological theory of resource exploitation and usually interpreted in terms of choices which minimize energy and information expenditure and maximize energy and information returns. The theory underlies many geographic subtheories, notably the "least cost" location theories of Von Thünen, Weber, Christaller and Chisholm and archaeological extensions of these, e.g. the catchment area and territory approach of Vita-Finzi and Higgs (1970). The underlying theory has been criticized as too ideal in its disregard for non-economic factors and the fact that "cost" is at least in part a culturally conditioned and relative threshold, as noted earlier.

Social physics theory goes back to nineteenth-century speculations that although individual human actions may be unpredictable, nevertheless the resultant of the actions of large numbers of individuals may form predictable empirical regularities which the researcher may utilize. Here the analogy is being drawn between the behaviour of large numbers of human beings and large numbers of physical particles, with successful early physical laws, such as the Gas Laws, providing the stimulus. In its spatial form the researcher does not ask why archaeological spatial patterns occur but merely observes them and tries to find some empirical regularity in the process which will enable him to simulate their occurrence (Echenique, 1971). In trying to describe these empirical regularities, physical and electrical analogies have proved very helpful in formulating models, as in the case of the "gravity models" for predicting the interaction between places and populations — an analogy based on Newton's theory of gravity which had already been developed in the nineteenth century and appearing in several archaeological studies (Hodder, 1974; Tobler and Wineburg, 1971; Clarke, 1972a, p. 49). While the social physics approach has produced surprisingly good results for the simulation of spatial phenomena, it has been conceptually unsatisfactory because of its essentially descriptive flavour (Harvey, 1969, p. 110).

Statistical mechanics theory, in its spatial context, represents an interesting elaboration of the missing statistical and stochastic background behind the social physics approach and the analogy between the behaviour of large numbers of people and particles. This statistical theory of spatial distributions is largely the work of Wilson (1967, 1971) extended by subsequent development; the theory represents a limited but significant breakthrough by linking the social physics approach with the logic of statistical inference and the Likelihood Law (Hacking, 1965). In its original form, the theory was expressed using the intermediate concepts of statistical mechanics, thermodynamics and information theory but it may now be reduced to more fundamental Likelihood terms.

The basis of this statistical theory is that the most probable state of any system at a given time is the one which satisfies the known constraints and which maximizes its entropy, where maximum entropy is achieved by that state which can be arrived at in the maximum number of ways. The advantage of Wilson's approach is that the system can successfully be described as a whole without having to know or describe the detailed behaviour of individuals. This follows the pattern of the statistical solution to the mechanics of gases which the Newtonian approach, attempting to sum the coordinates and velocities of each particle, found insoluble. Statistical theory gives the probable state of the gas by simpler means: by maximizing its entropy where the concept of entropy may be given as the expected log probability of the states of a thermodynamic system. In the case of human spatial behaviour, it is similarly impractical to determine all the factors which governed individual decisions and dispositions, especially prehistoric ones, but it is possible, by means of this theory, to describe an overall system of spatial structure and to explain why particular equation models should be applicable to spatial structures for which certain assumptions are valid (Martin and March, 1972, pp. 175-218; Echenique, 1971).

In the practical approaches to particular spatial problems, the

informal general theories which we have just outlined are usually
expressed in the form of a subtheory restricted to a limited class of
phenomena. There are many of these scattered subtheories and their
dependent models, but the most important are the macro-location
subtheories of Von Thünen, Weber and Christaller and their within-
site applications to site spatial structure (Haggett, 1965); all of these
have now been applied in archaeological situations. It will be noted
that many of these subtheories originated in nineteenth-century
economics before their later elaboration in geography and subsequently in architecture, anthropology and archaeology, cascading
from the senior social science down to those with less developed
theoretical underpinnings. In the same way, the classical pattern of
development can be observed, in which descriptive models based on
broad analogies and empirical regularities may be upgraded to
mathematical models of deterministic form but with deeper powers of
explanation, eventually themselves being replaced by more comprehensive statistical and stochastic theoretical models (social physics
models, gravity models, Wilson's statistical models). However, from
the narrow archaeological point of view the current application of
models and subtheories from this limited background has certain
inherent dangers and drawbacks, especially at the micro-level of
within-site studies.

A. VON THÜNEN'S LOCATION SUBTHEORY

In his major work *Der isolierte Staat* in 1826, the economist Von
Thünen developed a model recognizing the relationships between the
spatial distribution of activities and landuse around a centre and the
law of diminishing returns with distance. The underlying theory of this
model states that concentric zones of landuse and activity pattern tend
to develop around "isolated" site centres. Although originally
expressed in monetary terms the theory is most powerfully developed
in terms of time and energy input and maximizing the returns for least
effort, given the friction effect of distance. The concentric zones of
landuse and activity pattern may then be directly derived from the
competing rate of increase in energy expenditure for particular
activities with increasing distance from the centre: the less intensive
the landuse, the further away from the centre.

Von Thünen's basically descriptive and limited model was extended into a normative theory by Lösch and Chisholm (1968) and developed for archaeological use by Vita-Finzi and Higgs (1970) as the catchment area approach to agrarian and hunter-fisher-gatherer sites. At the same time the theory has been successfully applied to concentric zone patterns at the within-site level in archaeology and geography and even at the micro level the concept of interacting concentric activity zones around artefacts (artefact association spheres) and structures (structural catchment areas) also has clear potential (Raper, this volume; Hammond, 1972). It is important to recollect that von Thünen specifically considered the case of the idealized, *isolated* agrarian site and therefore made important assumptions about:

1. The site considered in isolation from its network with no resources coming in and no produce going out to other sites or markets
2. Uniformity of surrounding land and one main means of transport
3. Rational (i.e. modern economic) behaviour to maximize returns from the application of minimum efforts (economic spatial theory).

These assumptions make it clear that the subtheory is very useful but unsatisfactory when extended beyond its simple limits. In archaeology its weaknesses are fairly apparent when foodstuffs and commodities appear to have moved between sites in significant quantities certainly from the beginning of the neolithic and in hunter-fisher-gatherer contexts there is a clear need for more appropriate special expressions of the subtheory.

B. WEBER'S LOCATION SUBTHEORY

In his economic text *Uber den Standort der Industrien* (1909), Alfred Weber put forward a model in part complementary to that of von Thünen. Instead of considering the pattern of landuse around an isolated site, Weber considered the location of a site in terms of its outward connections and the movement of resources. The central propositions of Weber's theory, further developed by Isard, was that sites would be selected so as to minimize unnecessary movement; sites represent minimum-energy least-cost locations. The location of a site will, therefore, depend on the distance to and from external resources, the weight of the material to be moved, and the effort or competitive cost of all movements (see Foley, this volume).

Weber's subtheory of optimum site location clearly rests upon the acceptance of the underlying economic spatial theory combined with some particular assumptions.

1. The sites mainly in mind were modern industrial sites at which methods of "rational" economic planning might be assumed.

2. The sites are considered purely in terms of their outward locational constraints, ignoring internal factors.

3. Weber took the limiting cases of stable, unchanging resources, sources, transport and technology. Isard has pointed out that transport costs are convex and increase with distance (Haggett, 1965, pp. 142-152).

Weber's subtheory has a number of theoretical and practical drawbacks but still provides a useful starting point. The subtheory has largely been ignored in explicit archaeological discussions although its ideology clearly underlies many archaeological discussions of "optimal site locatior., '. With modifications the technique could be applied to hunter-fisher-gatherer site locations in relation to resources but an obvious and better fitted case would be its use to explain the pattern of locational development of the major European Bronze and Iron Age workshop traditions in relation to their metal or clay sources, markets and distribution areas — a changing situation which Weberian analysis fits quite closely and upon which it throws many insights. The technique can also be applied to "optimum locations" of structures at the within-site semi-micro level of aggregation where it clashes interestingly with social models derived from anthropological spatial theory, the Garin-Lowry activity location model from social physics and the stochastic models derived from statistical spatial theory (Echenique, 1971, pp. 279, 293, 306; Clarke, 1972a, p. 48). Once again the weaknesses of the underlying assumptions for archaeological cases are readily apparent but may be met by the development of more appropriate archaeological and anthropological developments of the subtheory.

C. CHRISTALLER'S CENTRAL PLACE SUBTHEORY

Walter Christaller, a German geographer was the first to success-fully model the relationships between the area served by sites, the sites' functions and the network of sites, moving from the isolated site level of von Thünen, through the sites and resources level of Weber to the level of aggregation of site systems as a whole. Christaller

started by considering a network of sites packed in an undifferentiated
landscape and introduced the notion of a hierarchy of sites in which
some sites provide resources or services for others; clearly referring to
relatively sophisticated communities. Assuming static sites and
circulating resources, Christaller employed an analysis of demand to
determine the "range" of goods, resources and services in terms of
distance distributions from sites, in order to define an optimal
least-cost organizational structure of sites within the network. From
these assumptions and this analysis, Christaller showed that the sites in
the network are likely to adopt a hexagonal territorial tessellation of
space which may be varied by changing the orientation of the
hexagonal net, the size of each territory and thus the number and
variety of sites served by each central site; he also showed that some
solutions were much more likely to occur in reality than certain others
(Haggett, 1965, pp. 118-125).

In 1941, Lösch exploited the problem of site location within a wider
scope and produced a synthesis of Christaller's central place hierarchies,·
industrial location networks and the distribution structure of service
areas. The basic features of this developed model are listed.

1. Concentration of sites into sectors separated by less dense sectors.

2. Sites increase in size with distance from central large sites.

3. Small settlements are located about halfway between larger ones.
The subtheory has been further strengthened by later workers and
there has been some convergence of marketing "spheres of influence"
work with movement studies to develop areas of subtheory on general
patterns of element dispersal in diffusion, exchange, trade, marketing
and migration situations, with the emphasis on the pattern dynamics
rather than upon individual locations (Haggett, 1965).

Central place models have been very widely developed in
archaeology, especially in urban contexts with sophisticated
economies, for example in Hodder's (1974) work on Romano-British
towns and Johnson's (Ucko *et al.*, 1972) study of early dynastic
Mesopotamian settlement patterns in Iraq. Whether the assumptions
about site hierarchies may be wilfully extended backward with tombs,
temples and camps beyond the urban threshold and quite how the
central place model can be reorganised to cope with less "optimising"
societies has yet to be explicitly worked out. As with the preceding
subtheories, central place models may also be used at the within-site
level and certainly Lösch's sector model has interesting settlement
applications, notably in urban sector development (Hoyt, 1939).

D. SITE SPATIAL STRUCTURE SUBTHEORY

The subtheories which have tried to cope with the spatial structure of elements within sites have a much more miscellaneous background. At each stage it has been noted that the macro-location models of von Thünen, Weber and Christaller can have a micro application at the within-site level but with only moderate success, and that mainly at the largest micro scale possible with the greatest economic constraints — in urban sites. Architectural models too have concentrated on urban sites with the same large scale and economic qualities, either using the Lowry within place location model or statistical and stochastic models (Echenique, 1971, pp. 279, 293, 306). Anthropological models of site spatial structure ought to provide a major contribution for non-urban sites at this scale, dominated by social and proxemic factors but, alas with the anthropological neglect of explicit spatial theory, we are only provided with the retrospective analyses of particular sites (Douglas, 1972). Indeed, it seems probable that an awakening interest in the general importance of spatial patterning as opposed to kinship calculi may first reach anthropology from the trials and errors of the archaeologists in this area. In the meantime, the archaeologist is driven back to argument from selected ethnographic spatial analogies to support his archaeological inferences in the absence of the necessary general spatial theory in anthropology, or to developments of the most appropriate economic, geographic or architectural spatial models.

The Lowry within-site location model, for example, starts with the tasks which have to be performed to maintain the site and shows the relationships by which the correlated quantity of adult workers themselves generate a number of dependents (families, children, old people, domesticates) who in turn generate an additional number of service tasks and workers. Potentially, the new service and maintenance employment may generate more residents who in turn demand more services and so on. The iterative structure, however, approaches a state of equilibrium for a given input of adult worker-residents in a given environment. Garin improved this structure by explicitly representing the relationships within the site as flows thereby taking into account the between structure traffic. The Garin-Lowry model shows that the relationship between primary tasks and residents is the collective distribution of the journeys to the service areas. These models have been largely developed for architectural studies in urban contexts but once again they illustrate the general shape that analogous anthropological models might take and identify some of the positive and negative analogies between these different situations (Echenique, 1971, pp. 278-9).

The remaining within-site spatial structure subtheories represent micro-location extensions of the von Thünen, Weber and Christaller theories to underpin otherwise purely descriptive models. The concentric zone model put forward by Burgess in 1927 suggests that a site will develop a series of concentric zones of residence type, up to five in a large urban site, and each zone will migrate outwards into the territory of the next in a radial expansion through time (Haggett, 1965, p. 178). The main features of the Burgess models are based on von Thünen's theory of radial solutions to competing land use and costs; the model assumes an expanding population and that accessibility declines with equal regularity in a radial manner. Nevertheless, the Burgess model or an analogous concentric zone model approaches the archaeological structure at sites as diverse as the Mayan ceremonial centre at Lubantuun and the Graeco-Roman city of Pompeii (Hammond, 1972; Raper, this volume).

Alternatively, Hoyt put forward a "sector model" in 1939 which suggested that internal site structure tends to organize itself in wedges of different usage radiating from the centre with the main routes (Haggett, 1965, p. 178). The model is largely descriptive but appears to rest on the micro-application of Lösch's sector development of Christaller's central place theory (Haggett, 1965, p. 123); the approach improves on the concentric model by considering the direction of locations from the centre as well as the distance.

A more elaborate "multiple nucleus" model was put forward by McKenzie (1933) and developed by Harris and Ullmann (1945). This in effect constitutes a multiple Burgess approach with a number of competing growth centres within the individual site, with the consequent interference of their radial repercussions. These inlying centres may have begun as neighbouring small sites. When the areas in between later become occupied with intensive settlement, then the whole unit is restructured in order to function as a higher order site; an interesting possibility for the agglomerated temple mounds of many Meso-American centres and historically documented for a number of early urban centres elsewhere (e.g. Rome). However, the multiple "ward" or "tribal" centres can also arise or elaborate after the initial growth by virtue of the many locational forces which cluster some functions but scatter others (Haggett, 1965, p. 180).

   The four alternative within site spatial structure models (Lowry, Concentric Zone, Sector, Multiple Nucleii) and their underlying theory are not mutually exclusive; they select different aspects to model, at different scales, making different but related theoretical assumptions. In Raper's study of Pompeii, for example, the concentric zone and radial expansion model fits quite well for the town as a whole, but at the level of individual building blocks a multiple nucleii pattern accounts for many of the residuals (this volume, Chapter 5).

   The archaeological drawback with most of the spatial models drawn from the "economic" background, even at the macro-level, is that they are largely based on spatial theory generalized from consciously optimizing, post-industrial revolution European and American case studies; most of these are large scale settlement systems with urban components. These models and theories, therefore, make assumptions that rarely fit the archaeological situations very closely, although they still remain useful tools, pointing to the kinds of model and theory which must replace them and at the same time suggesting important information by the very deviations of the archaeological cases from the "economic" ideals. Nevertheless, there clearly is and has been a far wider variety of archaeological and anthropological spatial patterning than these models and theories comprehend, of which not the least important and most intractable are those traces of extinct systems which became maladaptive and nowhere survived into the recent ethnographic or geographic sample.

   The theory and models that should be most useful to the archaeologist, especially at the within-site level, are those to be developed from anthropological spatial theory. However, as we have seen, anthropological spatial theory has been even more neglected than archaeological spatial studies. There are many scattered, individual studies and insights but the determination with which anthropologists have resolutely mapped all the variability of their data onto the arbitrarily selected dimension of kinship relations has reduced spatial patterns of individual and group behaviour to the level of mere dependent variables, rather than the complex resultant of interaction between spatial, kinship and many other relationships. After all, distance is equally likely to affect economic and blood relationships and vice versa. When general anthropological spatial theory is contrasted with the limited but explicit theories of the economic, social physics or statistical approaches no comparably explicit models, mathematical or empirical, are found but only vague generalizations and inexplicit insights. Indeed hopefully, it is likely that the incompetent and naive attempts of the archaeologists to model "primitive" human spatial behaviour will be a primary stimulus towards creating a greater interest in theories of anthropological spatial variability, as well as making a direct contribution to the elaboration of that theory.

In conclusion, archaeologists may make considerable use of existing spatial theories, subtheories and models derived from ethology, sociology, architecture, geography, economics and anthropology. But in the end, archaeology must develop its own related range of spatial theory, capable of simulating extinct situations, suitable for dealing with the difficult but not impossible spatial characteristics of archaeological samples and, in its various branches, able to embrace non-settlement site data from linear, sectored, spiral, multiple nucleii cemetery spatial patterns to three-dimensional stratigraphic spatial clusters. We are certainly only just beginning to explore the possibilities of archaeological spatial theory at a sufficient level of generality to make it cross-cultural, cross-time and cross-specialization to the degree necessary for a respectable international set of disciplinary theory. New developments in methodology, from computer pattern recognition procedures to the source analysis of raw materials, now provide us with new kinds of information on spatial relationships, movements and connectivity, whilst even old observations may with care be pressed to new purposes. The interdependence of theory and method, method and practice is constantly ensuring that new possibilities in spatial archaeology are continuously developing for widespread use, but the archaeologist needs to be able to perceive the wider field to which particular spatial examples may relate, as well as a capacity to integrate amend and systematize these developments within an explicit body of spatial archaeological theory.

Bibliography

Abler, R., Adams, J. S. and Gould, P. (1971). *Spatial Organisation: the Geographer's View of the World*. Englewood Cliffs, New Jersey.

Adams, R. M. (1965). *Land Behind Baghdad: A History of Settlement on the Diyala Plains*. University of Chicago Press, Chicago.

Alexander, C. (1964). *Notes on the Synthesis of Form*. Harvard.

Bellwood, P. (1971). Fortifications and economy in prehistoric New Zealand. *Proceedings of the Prehistoric Society, London,* **XXXVII,** Pt. I, 56-95.

Biddle, M. (1967). *Some new ideas on Excavation.* Research Seminar Paper, London Institute of Archaeology, December 15th 1967.

Binford, L. R. and Binford, S. R. (1966). A preliminary analysis of functional variability in the Mousterian of Levallois Facies. *American Anthropology,* **68,** 238-295.

Binford, L. R. (1972). *An Archaeological Perspective.* Seminar Press, London and New York.

Binford, L. R. (1973). Interassemblage variability—the Mousterian and the "functional" argument. *The Explanation of Culture Change* (C. Renfrew, Ed.), p. 242. Duckworth, London.

Brown, J. A. (1974). Stratigraphy and regression analysis. *Proceedings of the XLI International Congress of Americanists, 1974.* Mexico.

Buist, A. (1964). *Archaeology in North Taranaki, New Zealand. New Zealand Archaeology Society Monograph* 3.

Campbell, J. M. (1968). Territoriality among ancient hunters: interpretations from ethnography and nature. *Anthropological Archaeology in the Americas* (B. Meggers, Ed.), pp. 1-21. Anthropol. Soc. Washington.

Cassells, R. (1972). Human Ecology in the Prehistoric Waikato. *The Journal of the Polynesian Society,* **81,** No. 2, 196-248.

Chagnon, N. (1967). Yanomamo social organisation and warfare. *War: The Anthropology of Armed Conflict and Aggression* (M. Fried, M. Harris and R. Murphy, Eds), pp. 109-159. Natural History Press, Garden City.

Chang, K. C. (1958). Study of Neolithic social groupings: examples from the New World. *American Anthropology,* **60,** 298-334.

Chang, K. C. (1962). A typology of settlement and community pattern in some circum-polar societies. *Arctic Anthropology,* **1,** 28-41.

Childe, V. G. (1934). Neolithic settlement in the west of Scotland. *Scottish Geographical Magazine,* **50,** 18-25.

Chisholm, M. (1968). *Rural Settlement and Land Use* (2nd edn.). Hutchinson, London.

Chorley, R. J. and Haggett, P. (1967) (Eds). *Models in Geography.* Methuen, London.

Clarke, D. L. (1968). *Analytical Archaeology.* Methuen, London.

Clarke, D. L. (1972a). Models and Paradigms in Archaeology. *Models in Archaeology* (D. L. Clarke, Ed.), pp. 47-52. Methuen, London.

Clarke, D. L. (1972b) (Ed.). A provisional model of an Iron Age society and its settlement system. *Models in Archaeology,* pp. 801-870. Methuen, London.

Clarke, D. L. (1973). Archaeology: the loss of innocence. *Antiquity,* **XLVII,** 6-18.

Coombs, C. H. (1964). *A Theory of Data.* Wiley Interscience, New York.

Cowgill, G. (1967). Evaluacion preliminar de la aplicacion de metodos a maquinas computadoras a los datos del mapa de Teotihuacan. *Teotihuacan: Onceava Mesa Redonda,* 95-112. D. F. Soc. Mex. de Antro, Mexico.

Crawford, O. G. S. (1912). The Distribution of Early Bronze Age settlements in Britain. *The Geographical Journal,* August and September 1912, 184-217.

Daniel, G. E. (1952). *A Hundred Years of Archaeology.* Duckworth, London.

Douglas, M. (1972). Symbolic orders in the use of domestic space. *Man, Settlement and Urbanism* (Ucko, Tringham and Dimbleby, Eds), pp. 512-521. Duckworth.

Echenique, M. (1971). A model of the urban spatial structure. *Models of Environment: Architectural Design*, May, 277-280.

Fast, J. (1970). *Body Language*. Evans, New York.

Fleure, H. J. (1921). *Geographical Factors in History*. Macmillan, London.

Fox, C. (1922). *The Archaeology of the Cambridge Region*. Cambridge University Press, Cambridge.

Fox, C. (1932). *The Personality of Britain*. Nat. Mus. Wales, Cardiff.

Frobenius, L. (1898). *Der Ursprung der Kultur*. Forschungsinstitut für Kulturmorphologie, Berlin.

Gradmann, R. (1898). *Das Pflanzenleben der Schwäbischen Alb*. Badischen botanischen Vereins, Stuttgart.

Green, J. R. (1881). *The Making of England*. Macmillan, London.

Green, R. C. (1967). Settlement patterns: four case studies from Polynesia. *Asian Pacific Archaeology Series*, 1, 101-132.

Green, R. C. (1970). Settlement pattern archaeology in Polynesia. *Studies in Oceanic Culture and History*, 1, 12-32.

Grimes, W. F. (1945). Early man and soils of Anglesey. *Antiquity*, 19, 169-174.

Groube, L. M. (1967). Models in prehistory: a consideration of the New Zealand evidence. *Archaeology in Physical Anthropology*, 2, 1-27.

Guest, E. (1883). *Celtic Origins and Other Contributions*. Macmillan, London.

Hacking, I. (1965). *Logic of Statistical Inference*. Cambridge University Press, Cambridge.

Haggett, P. (1965). *Locational Analysis in Human Geography*. Arnold, London.

Hall, E. T. (1944). Early stockaded settlements in Governador, New Mexico. *Columbia Studies in Archaeology and Ethnology* 2(i). New York.

Hall, E. T. (1966). *The Hidden Dimension*. Bodley Head, London.

Hammond, N. D. C. (1972). Locational models and the site of Lubantuun: a Classic Maya centre. *Models in Archaeology* (D. L. Clarke, Ed.), p. 757. Methuen, London.

Harris, C. D. and Ullmann, E. L. (1945). The Nature of Cities. *Annals of the American Academy of Political and Social Science*, 242, 7-17.

Harvey, D. (1969). *Explanation in Geography*. Arnold, London.

Hill, J. N. (1966). A prehistoric community in eastern Arizona. *Southwest Journal of Anthropology*, 22, 9-30.

Hodder, I. (1974). *Some Applications of Spatial Analysis in Archaeology*. Unpublished Ph.D. thesis, Cambridge.

Hodder, I. and Orton, C. (1976). *Spatial Analysis in Archaeology*. Cambridge University Press, Cambridge.

Hogg, A. H. (1943). Native settlements of Northumberland. *Antiquity*, 17, 136-147.

Hoyt, H. (1939). *The Structure and Growth of Residential Neighbourhoods in American Cities*. Federal Housing Administration, Washington.

Leroi-Gourhan, A. (1972). *Fouilles de Pincevent*. Gallia Préhistoire Supplement VII.

Lévi-Strauss, C. (1953). Social Structure. *Anthropology Today* (A. Kroeber, Ed.), pp. 524-553. University of Chicago Press.

Longacre, W. A. (1964). Archaeology as Anthropology: a case study. *Science*, 114, 1454-1455.

Longacre, W. A. (1968). Some aspects of prehistoric society in east-central Arizona. *New Perspectives in Archaeology* (S. R. and L. R. Binford, Eds), pp. 89-102. Aldine, Chicago.

McKenzie, R. D. (1933). *The Metropolitan Community*. McGraw-Hill, New York.

March, L. and Steadman, P. (1971). *The Geometry of Environment*. R.I.B.A. Pubs., London.

Martin, L. and March, L. (1972). *Urban Space and Structures*. Cambridge University Press, Cambridge.

Martin, L. *et al.* (1974). *Land Use and Built Form Studies;* Working Papers 1-70. 1967-1974. University of Cambridge School of Architecture.

Mindeleff, C. (1900). Localization of Tusayan clans. *19th Annual Report of Bureau of American Ethnology*, 639-653.

Morgan, L. H. (1881). *Houses and House Life of the American Aborigines*. Contributions to North American Ethnology, U.S. Department of the Interior, 4.

Parkington, J. (1972). *Seasonal Mobility in the Late Stone Age*. Circulated Research Paper. University of Cape Town, South Africa.

Parsons, J. R. (1972). Archaeological Settlement Patterns. *Annual Review of Anthropology*, **1**, 127.

Peebles, C. S. (1975). *Moundville: The Organisation of a Prehistoric Community and Culture*. University of Windsor (in press).

Phillips, P., Ford, J. A. and Griffin, J. B. (1951). Archaeological survey in the Lower Mississippi Aluvial Valley, 1940-1947. *Paper of the Peabody Museum on Archaeology and Ethnology, Harvard University*, **25**.

Ratzel, F. (1896). *Anthropogeography—the Application of Geography to History*. J. Engelhorn, Stuttgart.

Renfrew, C. (1974). *Before Civilisation: The Radiocarbon Revolution and Prehistoric Europe*. Cape, London.

Riquezes, J. (1972). *Operational Research and the Social Sciences: With Special Reference to Urban and Regional Planning*. L.U.B.F. research thesis, Cambridge.

Sanders, W. T. (1965). *Cultural Ecology of the Teotihuacan Valley*. Pennsylvania State University Department of Sociology and Anthropology.

Schrire, C. (1972). Ethno-archaeological models and subsistence behaviour in Arnhem Land. *Models in Archaeology* (D. L. Clarke, Ed.), pp. 653-670, Methuen, London.

Shawcross, W. (1972). Energy and Ecology: thermodynamic models in archaeology. *Models in Archaeology* (D. L. Clarke, Ed.), pp. 577-622, Methuen, London.

Sommer, R. (1969). *Personal Space*. Englewood Cliffs, New Jersey.

Speth and Johnson (1974). Problems in the use of correlation for the investigation of tool kits and activity areas. *Proceedings of the XLI International Congress of Americanists*, Mexico City.

Skinner, G. W. (1964). Marketing and social structure in rural China, Part 1. *Journal of Asian Studies*, **24**, 195-228.

Steward, J. H. (1937). Ecological aspects of Southwestern society. *Anthropos*, **32**, 87-104.

Steward, J. H. (1938). *Basin-Plateau Aboriginal Sociopolitical Groups*. Bureau of American Ethnology Bulletin 120.

Stjernquist, B. (1967). Models of commercial diffusion in prehistoric times. *Scripta Minora* 1965-66, **2**, 5-44.

Struever, S. (1968). Problems, methods and organisation: a disparity in the growth of archaeology. *Anthropological Archaeology in the Americas* (B. Meggers, Ed.). Anth. Soc., Washington.

Struever, S. (1968). Woodland subsistence-settlement systems in the Lower Illinois Valley. *New Perspectives in Archaeology* (L. R. and S. R. Binford, Eds), pp. 285-312. Aldine, Chicago.

Struever, S. (1971). Comments on archaeological data requirements and research strategy. *American Antiquity*, **36**, 9-19.

Tobler, W. R. and Wineburg, S. (1971). A Cappadocian speculation. *Nature*, **231**, 39-41.

Ucko, P. J., Dimbleby, G. W. and Tringham, R. (1972) (Eds). *Man, Settlement and Urbanism.* Duckworth, London.

Vita-Finzi, C. and Higgs, E. (1970). Prehistoric economy in the Mount Carmel area of Palestine: site catchment analysis. *Proceedings of the Prehistoric Society, London,* **36**, 1-37.

Watson, O. M. (1972). Symbolic and expressive use of space. An introduction to proxemic behaviour. *Current Topics in Anthropology,* **4.**

Whallon, R. (1973-4). Spatial analysis of occupation floors, I (1973) II (1974). *American Antiquity,* **38**, no. 3, 266-278 and **39**, no. 1, 16-34.

Willey, G. R. (1953). *Prehistoric settlement patterns in the Viru Valley, Peru.* Bureau of American Ethnology Bulletin 155.

Willey, G. R. (Ed.) (1956). *Prehistoric settlement patterns in the New World.* Viking Fund Publications in Anthropology, **23.**

Willey, G. R. *et al.* (1965). *Prehistoric Maya settlements in the Belize Valley.* Paper of the Peabody Museum of Archaeology and Ethnology, Harvard University, **54.**

Williams-Freeman, J. P. (1881). *An Historical Geography of Europe.* Macmillan, London.

Wilmsen, E. N. (1975). Interaction, spacing behaviour and the organisation of hunting bands. *Journal of Anthropological Research,* **29**, 1-31.

Wilson, A. G. (1967). Disaggregating elementary residential Location Models. *Centre for Environmental Studies Working Paper No. 37.* London.

Wilson, A. G. (1971). *Entropy in Urban and Regional Modelling.* Pion, London.

Winters, H. D. (1967). *An archaeological survey of the Wabash Valley in Illinois.* Illinois State Museum Report and Investigation, **10.**

Winters, H. D. (1969). *The Riverton Culture.* Illinois State Museum Monograph, 1.

Woolridge, S. W. and Linton, D. L. (1933). The loam-terrains of southeast England and their relation to its early history. *Antiquity,* **7**, 297-310.

Wright, H. T. (1969). *The Administration of Rural Production in an Early Mesopotamian Town.* Anthropology Paper 38, University of Michigan Museum of Anthropology.

2

An Analysis of Historical House-plans:
A Study at the Structural Level (Micro)

PETER DICKENS

*School of Cultural and Community Studies,
University of Sussex,
Falmer, Sussex*

This is a pilot study in two parts, the purpose of which is to examine certain characteristics of observed house-plans.[1] In the first part, the range of plan-forms that could theoretically exist and the probabilities of different forms occurring by purely random processes are studied. This range is then examined in relation to the range of forms that have been observed. In the second part of the study, house-plans are examined in more detail with a view to discovering which plans are common to a number of historical time-periods, and which are more closely associated with particular periods.

1. Theoretical and observed plans

A. NOTATION

A house-plan can be drawn in graph notation, where each room is represented by a point and the connections (or adjacencies) by lines. Thus a 3-cell plan (ignoring rotations) can be:

---

[1] The houses examined in this study are in Burwell, near Cambridge. The original data were provided by the Royal Commission on Historical Monuments. The study is of 74 house-plans.

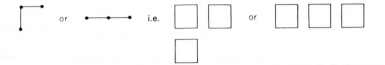

If the possible permutations for 1, 2, 3 and 4 cells are listed, then the combinations are:

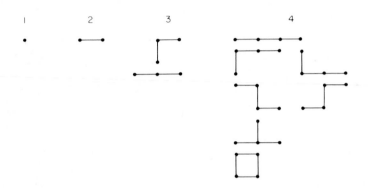

From this can be seen that when 4 (or more) rooms are considered then as well as rotational symmetry there is also reflective symmetry.

One way to look at the probability of each type occurring is to give each shape an equal probability. In the 1 and 2-cell plans, each will have a probability of 1.0 since only one basic shape exists. In the 3-cell case, each will have a probability of 0.5. In the 4-cell situation, each will have a probability of 0.2 or 0.1429 (approx.) depending on whether the reflections are regarded as being the same or distinct.

An alternative way of assessing the geometrical probability of different types of plan is to start off with one room and then to add another room to it. This can be done in four ways, each one rotationally equivalent. To any one of these a third room can be added in one of six places,

```
         2   3
    1 •——————• 4
         6   5
```

Of these, two result in,

•——————•——————•

namely 1 and 4. Using this system we can say that a right-angle is twice as common as a straight line. When a fourth room is added then the proportions of each kind of plan are

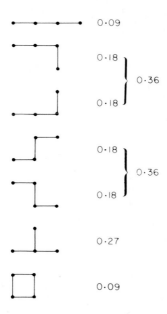

There is a third way of regarding the problem. Taking a grid such as

26	27	28	29	30	31	32
49	10	11	12	13	14	33
48	25	2	3	4	15	34
47	24	9	1	5	16	35
46	23	8	7	6	17	36
45	22	21	20	19	18	37
44	43	42	41	40	39	38

we then count the number of times each type of plan includes the square 1. For the 3-cell situation we get

For the 4-cell situation we get

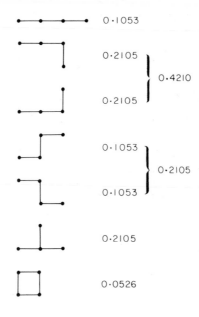

These different methods for assessing the probabilities of different plans occurring randomly result in somewhat varying values and rankings. Yet, a comparison between the ranges of theoretical and observed plans shows that in practice the range is very limited. Furthermore, the plans which are geometrically more probable are frequently those which are least commonly observed.

If the ranges of observed plans cannot be attributed to chance, the question then arises why one set of arrangements should occur with such regularity. It could be hypothesized that two main tendencies are restricting the number of theoretical alternatives. First, a tendency towards compactness of plan—relating to a reduction in the ratio of external surface to floor area and a minimization of distances within the plan. Second, a tendency for those forms to be selected which are the most economical to construct. Forms with more than the minimum four angles to their external surfaces (assuming a rectangular geometry) tend to involve more complex structural solutions, particularly in their roof-construction. An obvious further extension of this work would be to examine the extent to which certain forms are associated with certain types of construction.

With these considerations in mind, certain overall indices of shape can be used to evaluate our theoretical range of plans. One such measure is that used by Haggett and Chorley (1969) in measuring compactness of the form:

$$S = (1.27A)/L^2$$

where A = area of plan and L = dimension of long axis. The multiplier (1.27) adjusts the index so that a circle would have an index of 1.00 with values ranging down towards zero.

This index, when applied to our theoretical range of 4-cell plans results in the following values; the four-square form having the highest value, being nearest to the circular, and the linear plan having the lowest value.

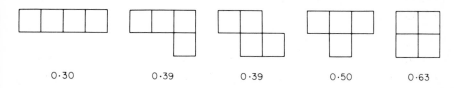

| 0·30 | 0·39 | 0·39 | 0·50 | 0·63 |

This type of index can be further extended to include a measure of a plan's complexity:

$$S = A/L^2V(R+1)$$

where A = area of plan, L = dimension of long axis, V = no. of vertices to plan and R = no. of re-entrants to plan.

This measure further orders our theoretical ranges to correspond more closely with those observed; though the number of 4-cell plans available is too small for the formula to be tested against actual frequencies. The next stage of this study will concentrate on examining the plans in an enlarged geographical area. This will multiply the sample about three times.

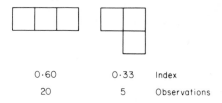

| 0·60 | 0·33 | Index |
| 20 | 5 | Observations |

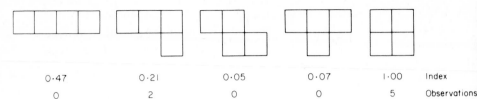

0·47	0·21	0·05	0·07	1·00	Index
0	2	0	0	5	Observations

2. The X^2 (chi-square) goodness of fit test[2]

In this test observed frequencies are compared with expected frequencies, giving a table of the sort:

Cell no.	1	2	3	i	n
Observed	0_1	0_2	0_3	0_i	0_n
Expected	E_1	E_2	E_3	E_i	E_n

As an example, the cells can be differing time-periods, and the observations can be the number of houses of the type under consideration. To find out whether or not X^2 indicates significant deviation of the observed from the expected frequencies, X^2 tables must be used and X^2 compared to the X^2 values corresponding to $n-1$ dfs (n = no. of cells; in all cases n was 6, giving 5 dfs). If X^2 is greater than the upper 5% point of the X^2 value with appropriate degrees of freedom then the X^2 value is said to be "significant at the 5% level". If it is bigger than the 1% point, then it is said to be significant at the 1% level, etc. Significance at the 5% level casts doubt on the observed

[2]The test statistic is

$$X^2 = \sum_{i=1}^{n} \frac{(0_i - E_i)^2}{E_i} = \sum_{i=1}^{n} \frac{0_i^2}{E_i} \quad N$$

where N = the total number of observations (and expected values).

$\sum_{i=1}^{n}$ is the sum over all values of i from 1 to n,

i.e. $\sum_{i=1}^{3} a_i$ is equivalent to $a_1 + a_2 + a_3$.

values being equal to the expected values and significance at the 1% point makes it fairly certain that the observed are in fact different.

This test is a large sample test and care should be exercised in using it when small expected values occur in the table. In each case the expected values used are the total number of houses still standing from each time-period suitably weighted so that there total is equal to the total of the observed values. It is recognized that systematic demolition of one or more types of house may have occurred (all one-room houses, for example, are likely to have been destroyed), but these expected values are the best available in the absence of evidence of differing rates of building and rates of demolition in different time-periods.

A. THE RELATIONSHIP BETWEEN HOUSE—SIZE AND PARTICULAR PERIODS

1. 2-cell houses

A chi-square test gave a value of 5.31. This is an insignificant value, meaning that such houses are equally likely to occur in any particular time-period.

2. 3-cell houses

A chi-square test for all 3-cell houses gave a value of 10.6, again an insignificant value meaning that such houses are equally likely to occur in any period. 3-cell houses in a linear plan only, however, i.e

gave a value of 18.6 (significant at the 1% level). This reflects the large number of houses of this plan in the time-period 1650-1700.

The number of houses of 1 and 4 cells was too small for reliable statistical tests to be made.

B. THE RELATIONSHIP BETWEEN TYPES OF GRAPH AND DIFFERENT TIME-PERIODS

We turn next to graphs representing the relationships between the rooms and the circulation elements of a plan. The graphs are all coded as follows: L, living room; S, service room; K, kitchen; B, bedroom; C, circulation; O, outside area.

1. 2-cell houses

A chi-square test for the following graph gave a value of 2.2:

This means that this graph is equally likely to occur in any timeperiod.

A chi-square test for the following graph, however, gave a value of 13.3 (significant at the 5% level). This reflects the large number of houses with this graph in the period 1750-1800.

Combining the following two graphs into one category, a chi-square value of 4.3 is found. This is insignificant, indicating that this graph too may be found to the same extent in any period.

The remaining graphs for 2-cell houses were in too small numbers for reliable tests to be made.

2. 3-cell houses

Most graphs of the 3-cell houses were also in too small numbers for statistical tests to be carried out. The following two graphs, however, were combined into one category and a chi-square test gave a value of 3.1 (significant at the 5% level), reflecting the large number of houses with these graphs in the time-period 1650-1700.

For all 3-cell houses the form

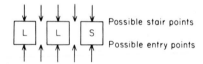

is present for every house. The positions of the entrance and stairs varies within this basic format. The theoretical possibilities for a 3-cell house with two adjacent living rooms and a service room with an entrance and a stair are:

This gives 25 possible permutations for this type of house, but in fact only six of these permutations occur in practice.

3. Conclusion and future work

For this study, there have been only a relatively small number of house-plans available, but for both house-forms and house-plans, certain types consistently emerge. Furthermore, they emerge independent of the probability that might be expected from purely random processes. In the case of house-plans, certain types emerge independent of the time-period in which they were constructed, while a few appear to be more closely associated with particular periods.

This type of study relies on sufficiently large numbers of each sample being available for analysis; many of the types have been in too small numbers for reliable statistical tests to be made. Future studies, therefore, should be based on more extensive information—both in

terms of an increased population of plans as well as further characteristics which may help to explain the regular recurrence of certain
forms.

APPENDIX

The following is a complete list of the observed graphs. It is subdivided
into houses of 1, 2, 3 and 4 cells. To the right of each graph is the total
number in each time-period. This is listed in the following order:

1551 — 1600
     — 1650
     — 1700
     — 1750
     — 1800
     — 1850

The rooms are coded as follows: L, living room; S, service room; K,
kitchen; B, bedroom; C, circulation; O, outside area.

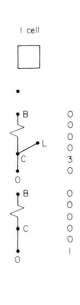

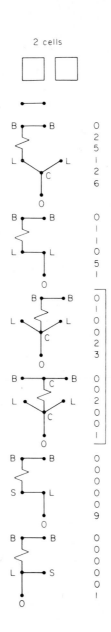

3 cells

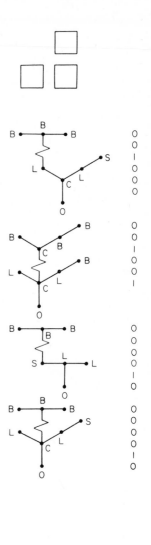

4 cells

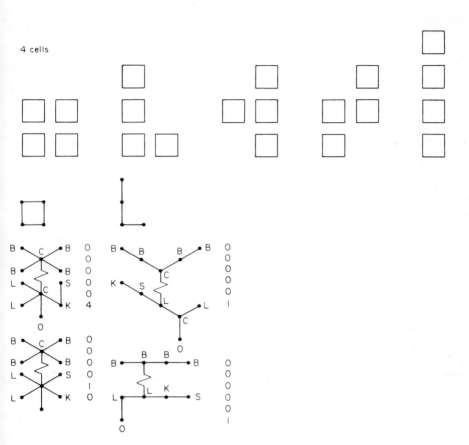

Bibliography

Haggett, P. and Chorley, R. J. (1969). *Network Analysis in Geography.* Edward
  Arnold, London.

3

Settlement Studies (Micro and Semi-micro)

Roland Fletcher

Dept. of Anthropology,
University of Sydney,
Australia

Part I. Introduction

1. Introduction

A settlement provides a framework of spaces and boundaries for the locational activities of the community it contains. The framework has obvious functional characteristics which are dominated by requirements of structural stability, manpower supply for construction and the general limitation of resources in the environment. There has been extensive analysis and discussion of the functional relationship between all these factors in social studies and by archaeologists. But there is also a substantial literature on what may be termed the formal analysis and description of the spatial arrangements of people and structures.

A functional study assesses the relationship between a number of factors in terms of the operating effect they have on each other. Does the social system provide communal labour groups large enough to build a viable residence unit? What effort is needed for the community to obtain the raw materials for its buildings? A formal study is concerned with the classificatory relationships in conceptual and visually perceived patterns, for instance; the various parts of a myth (Leach, 1967); the animals within the concern of a human group (Lévi-Strauss, 1963, 1966); the various types of space in a settlement or the signals used by human beings in their social interaction. From such

For notes see pp. 153-157.

47

a study, it might then be possible to assess the functional application or inadequacy of the classifications used by a community in its social activities and in response to the world around it.

Various combinations of functional and formal analysis are, therefore, possible and necessary, as is reflected in the tangle of structural functional and structural formal analyses (Harris, 1969). In this chapter, a method will be proposed for describing the locational organization in small scale settlements as a coherent visual context for the activities of its occupants. The study is a formal analysis of spatial order, followed by a functional interpretation of the relevance of visual contexts to the adaptive capacity of the community.

In the first part, the case for a formal analysis is presented. This is divided into two sections; a description of the approach so far pursued in social studies, archaeology and architecture; and an assessment of the relevance of formal order to human locational behaviour.

The second part is a preliminary presentation of research procedure and results from a study carried out in a small Konkomba settlement in Ghana. Data collection and presentation are described in two appendices.

The third part discusses the characteristics and adaptive consequences of formal spatial arrangements using data from an abandoned Hopi pueblo in Arizona (U.S.A.) as an illustration.

In this chapter, the general aim is to show that the human use of space is not only directed by immediate and material, functional or environmental controls, but it is also patterned by the human brain's need for signals specifying the similarities or differences between various parts of its context and by the use of classifications of space as an adaptive mechanism for coping with the environment.

2. Formal order in human spatial behaviour—studies in anthropology

A. PROXEMICS

The character and purpose of proxemic analysis is well stated by the title of O. M. Watson's summary of the subject, the *Symbolic and Expressive Use of Space* (Goffman, 1969; Sommer, 1969; Watson, 1969). Essentially, it is the analysis of space being used to signal information about human situations and status. The crucial point is that the human treatment of space is not regulated purely by physical requirements of effort expenditure. It is also affected by the need to consistently differentiate between different categories of activity and between people of different social status. The behaviour involved produces a classification of space. There are major static divisions, e.g. "a parents' room" that children do not enter. Within the frame, there are mobile divisions and signals which each individual carries about. These are the spacing distances they prefer or tolerate when engaged in intimate response, general conversation or an official discussion. Associated with these spacings are the multitude of body gestures and facial signals that specify a person's accessibility, approval and disapproval, or the degree of confidence a person possesses in a particular situation. This complex of messages is the subject of kinesics (Fast, 1972; Goffman, 1972) and is closely involved with proxemic analysis.

For my purposes, the important features of human locational behaviour were defined in *The Hidden Dimension,* the basic general introduction to proxemics by Hall (1966). In it he showed that societies each have their own characteristic spacing distances for locating personnel. In each society there are specific distances, ranging from small to large, which are successively applicable to private conversations, official encounters and public occasions. These differ from society to society, but in all cases people demonstrate a preference for particular distances. They are plainly capable of estimating distances without being deliberately aware of the actual distance[1] used and without the aid of any concrete measuring standard. Regularities in the spaces between people or within and around structures need not, therefore, depend either on conscious recognition of order, or on the use of any measuring device other than visual estimation.

B. ARCHAEOLOGY AND ARCHITECTURE

Structures should in consequence be able to provide some indication of the dimensions preferred by their builders even if no actual metrical standard, defined by a ruler of some kind, was used. There have been a number of archaeological studies of structural dimensions but these have often contended that the identified regularities reflect the conscious use of such a standard. Some, however, have argued for the occurrence of harmonic series of dimensions, with less certainty that the pattern was consciously recognized by its users.

The idea of a standard unit represented by a ruler of some kind has its basis in contemporary planning practice and the knowledge of standards in earlier civilisations, e.g. the use of the Royal cubit in Egypt (Edwards, 1967; Pochan, 1933).

Graham has presented the case for a Minoan "foot" used in the design of major structures in Crete in the second millenium B.C. (Graham, 1960, 1962). The "megalithic yard" proposed by Alexander Thom is supposed to have been used in the third and second millenia B.C. for the planning of the stone circles and rows erected in the British Isles (Thom, 1967). In both cases the basic contention is that the structures were deliberately planned engineering projects. We have the intellectual satisfaction of a mental rapport with rational architects, and feel a sense of familiarity with the structures they are supposed to have created.

A number of suggestions have been made in architectural studies that a harmonic order might occur in structural form or could be used to create structural order. The most famous proposal is the Modulor scale of measurement designed by Le Corbusier (1959). It was often described by Le Corbusier as if it was a method of designing façades though he intended that it should be used for the entire structural format of a building. His famous created example is the Unité d' Habitation in Marseilles (Le Corbusier, 1959) which he designed entirely on the Modulor standard. Modulor is derived from the mathematical qualities of the Golden Rectangle, imposed on the schematized form of a six foot man (Le Corbusier, 1959). The dependence of the Modulor values on the six foot man suggests that other series descriptions of structural order may be possible. Le Corbusier never studied existing structures stringently to discover whether the spatial dimensions of the Modulor had already been used in architectural design. There are many hints that its values do occur but these are never organized as members of the total population of dimensions in a building (Le Corbusier, 1959).

In archaeology, claims for harmonic sets of dimensions have been made more cautiously and have received more severe criticism than the cases for familiar standard units. In the report on Aichbuhl and Reidschachen, Schmidt (1930) suggests that there was a consistent use of particular dimensions. From the study of Lepenski Vir, Srejović (1972) notes that the various dimensions of the houses appear to form a series. He would like to explain this as a product of ritual foundation ceremonies carried out by a shaman or priest with knowledge of the pattern (Srejović, 1972).

In work on Minoan structures, Previosi has suggested that the overall dimensions of the buildings can be organized on a Fibonacci series (Previosi, 1967). To achieve this he has generalized the ground plans and used the overall limits of the area occupied by the structure as well as the concrete distances which are actually present. He also faces a severe problem of population size and its significance since very few spacing categories and dimensions can be extracted from any one structure, and relatively few structures are known in any one site. Assessment of the relative status of structures within a site must be carefully considered before comparing structures which might not be classificatory equivalents. In the main, Previosi's work is used as a description of the formal order in structures though he has also edited a study of functional order in room arrangements within the formal framework (Previosi, 1970). Graham (1968) has been extremely critical of Previosi's work.

Badawy has described the structure of Egyptian temples in terms of a Fibonacci series. The series is proposed as a description of the sides of the triangle which can be fitted inside the ground area of the temple (Badawy, 1965). This study is of interest because he argues that the builders were not aware of the order and that the successive extensions of a temple, by transforming the series, are a tacit description of cosmic order through time (Badawy, 1965).

The suspicion with which harmonic regularities are treated, and the disregard to which they are subject appear to have three sources. The primary cause is of great critical importance. Evidence needed to justify the case for a standard unit must inevitably be less than that needed to show the presence of a succession of consistently related dimensions. There is a simple doubt that sufficient quantified evidence has been provided to justify the claim for any harmonic series in an archaeological context. In many cases only one house has been used as an illustration, or the dimensions used have been generalized from the less tidy actual form of the buildings in question. This combines with the feeling that without a precise definition of the specific classes of dimensions to be used, absolutely any case could be proven by a judicious selection of examples.

For this reason, many studies of dimensional order whether in buildings or whole landscapes reside in the lunatic fringe of archaeology. The study of building dimensions in archaeology has an unfortunate ancestry. There is a close historical connection between precision surveys and the arbitrary use of measurements to justify any conceivable belief. The connection and divergence between the two analytic procedures is well illustrated by studies of the Pyramids of Giza. Petrie first visited Egypt to try and confirm for his father the beliefs of the "Pyramidiots" about the historical significance of the dimensions of the Pyramids. He remained to make a detailed survey of the Pyramids and to obtain the first information on the engineering methods involved in their construction (Casson, 1939).

The second reason is that there is a frequent attitude that order in structures can only be derived from deliberate and conscious planning. This is emphasized by the proposals that standard units were used or that there were specialists present to design the structures. Any construction that seemed "irregular" to the cultural preferences of the observer has been classed as a haphazard agglomeration of structures. This was the initial judgement on the Minoan palaces (Graham, 1962) and on most settlements in the "primitive" world. That the settlements of subsistence farmers and the temporary or permanent sites occupied by hunter-gatherers possess an intricate order, has been repeatedly pointed out. The case is encapsulated by Douglas Fraser (1968) in *Village Planning in the Primitive World.* There is both deliberate planning and formal order in these settlement patterns. A belief that structural order can result only from deliberate procedure must be considered an insufficient explanation of the regularities in settlement form.

The final reason is that while the functional relevance of a standard unit is quite apparent, the possible significance of a harmonic series is not; especially when the pattern is ascribed to tacit judgement by the builders.[1] However, a standard unit does not in itself explain why the particular multiples of its length are used. An explanation is required which regards material factors as the primary determinant of the lengths used. On such a basis, it is unlikely that the multiples would have any coherent association simply as lengths.

The notion of a harmonic series clashes very severely with this view since it claims that man succeeds in imposing rather more order in his transformations of the environment. Yet it has general similarity to the proposals that human beings and human groups organize the information on their environment into coherent patterns. It is this behaviour which enables them to handle the real world and to transmit consistent information about it (Douglas, 1973).

It cannot be contended that the case for harmonic dimensions has yet been fully demonstrated using archaeological evidence, but the already mentioned studies do show that the possibility of using structural data to understand how man tries to organize space is accepted. The interest in considering the harmonic arrangement further, is that it can subsume the conscious use of a standard unit because the multiples could form an ordered sequence of dimensions. It also constitutes an internally consistent system for describing the spatial aspect of reality, with every community having its own, different description of space. In these characteristics it would closely resemble the verbal classifications used by many different societies for describing the various components of reality such as space, animals and personnel.

C. SOCIAL ANTHROPOLOGY AND ETHNOGRAPHY

Analyses of formal order in the verbal classifications related to settlement form have covered the entire spectrum from the arrangement of residence units to the position of the settlement in its universe. Eliade in *The Myth of the Eternal Return* (Eliade, 1954; Moholy-Nagy, 1969) provides a general assessment of the relationship between cosmologies and settlement form. The connections between cosmologies, social rules, settlement form and environment are discussed in a convenient collection of information by Rapoport (1969) in *House Form and Culture.*

The basic theme of all these studies is that settlement and house form are closely connected to the internally consistent categories and rules used by human communities. Structures are in effect standing representations for the consistent classifications of other categories in the same cultural milieu. Two studies of house form, by Cunningham (1964) and Tambiah (1969), describe the connection to categories of wild and cultivated food and to order in the social hierarchy. Moving from house arrangements to the overall plans of settlements there are formal interpretations ranging from the extreme cosmological models of Griaule (1965) and Lebeuf (1962), to the more positional, social interpretation of several settlements by Lévi-Strauss (1963a). Stauder's analysis of the Majangir homestead illustrates the location of structures in a relatively simple frame of polarities connecting topography with male and female distinctions (Stauder, 1971; Rapoport, 1969). In more functional terms, Goody (1956) provides an interesting illustration of a community's attitude to house size and social behaviour in *The Social Organization of the Lowilli.*

They were formerly housepeople (*yidem*) living in one vast homestead which became so large that some of the many inhabitants might be gaily dancing to the xylophones without realising that a funeral had taken place in another courtyard. So they split (Goody, 1956).

But a settlement is also located in the total context of its environment. The community has to define boundaries separating the different portions which in its belief are distinct, and relate to the separate yet paradoxically connected orders of "nature" and "culture". It is this framework which encases among other factors; the location of the community's dead; decisions on the location of crops and domestic animals within the settlement area and response to the behaviour of wild animals. Placing of the dead (Bloch, 1971) varies considerably from society to society but in each case is coherent with the community's attitude to social order. Each Tallensi household keeps its dead close by the entry as befits the unity of a residence unit being contrasted to the marked segmentation of the community (Fortes, 1945, 1949). In a more specifically formal interpretation, the relationship of a community's concepts of "nature" and "culture" to the settlement and social order is beautifully presented by Mary Douglas in a study of the Lele belief system (Douglas, 1957, 1963, 1966).

Human communities appear to devise coherent verbal classifications to impose order on their environment. Their statements and behaviour also connect these regularities to concrete structural features of their settlements. It would be rather surprising if the structures themselves did not also possess some formal order as aggregates of shapes and dimensions. Dimensions, colours (Forge, 1970) and building sequences are also products of human action and are just as likely to form a possible classification of structures or space (Wooldridge, 1963; Whorf, 1956).[2] Conversely, criticisms of the models of formal order suggested for verbal descriptions of settlement form are a matter of linguistic and conceptual dispute. They are not to be critically judged by differing classifications based on other features.

The ideal Dogon settlement for instance does not have any obvious reflection in the close packed residence units that cover the basal slopes of the Bandiagara scarp (Fraser, 1968). The ideal might be incorrect as a linguistic analysis of the informant's opinions, but is not invalid because the ideal diverges from actuality (Ardener, 1971). What is lacking, however, in the description of the ideal is any information about the possible variation and deviance that may be recognized by the community. Harris emphasizes that an index of variation should be an essential feature in the description of a human group's behaviour and concepts (Harris, 1969). To relate concepts to the actuality of daily life, the degrees of tolerable divergence from ideal rules must be comprehended. An internal criteria of variation is also needed to appreciate the degree of clarity available in a concept system.

Human beings divide reality into discontinuous and manageable elements (Leach, 1966). The variation tolerable for each component will relate to the degree of difference required for the system to function coherently using a consistent set of categories. It is in this coherent context that ambiguous cases show up and can be utilized for ritual and classificatory purposes (Leach, 1966). Variation should be crucially connected to the degree of possible overlap between categories and so to the number and character of the alternative statuses available for any given entity.

D. CONSEQUENCES

It is recognized that the dimensions of structures might be used to gain an insight into the regularity desired by their creators. Studies of verbal classifications of house and settlement form emphasize that the patterns involved possess coherence. This regularity is connected to the everyday requirements of the community. Structures are important not only for their material function in providing shelter and storage but also because they form the coherent frame for community life and reflect its regularities.

It should, therefore, be possible to describe the horizontal dimension of space in a settlement in formal terms, as a coherent visual context for its occupants. But to do this a precise definition of the dimensions relevant to the pattern must be given; a method of describing the variation occurring in them; and an interpretation that integrates the variation into the description of spatial order.

3. Formal order and settlement structure

Formal order should occur in the structure of a settlement since consistency in the behaviour of the community will in part depend on regularity in the structural framework of individual's activities. If sizes of entities are consistent throughout the settlement and use a limited range of dimensions, response to that context will be facilitated because each individual's brain could predict the probable size of an entity and its separation from any other entity (Vernon, 1962). An individual could react without extending effort on exact estimations except in circumstances requiring high accuracy. Economy of effort as well as coherence of response could be achieved in a consistent visual context. At any given level of settlement detail such as within house arrangements, or at the general level of the entire settlement form, it should therefore be possible to identify a formal order in the dimensions of entities. The detail and character of activities relevant to each residence unit alone, cannot be regarded as identical with general locational activity in the entire settlement. A consistent relationship between the dimensions of all entities can only be expected if the source of the data on each entity is identical. All the post spacings in a settlement can be compared to all the doorwidths but not to the doorwidths from one residence unit. These can only be compared with the dimensions of another type of entity in the same or another residence unit.

The human brain has a finite storage and analytic capacity. The information on its environment passing through conversion processes is transformed into a form usable by the mechanism of the brain (Baddeley, 1971; Wooldridge, 1963). These two characteristics limit the brain's capacity to organize all the available data on its environment. The brain does not perceive the actual form of its context, only a version of that context sufficient to the effectiveness of the brain/body relationship (Bateson, 1973). In some cases the eye and brain can be fooled by the visual character of their context and perceive an illusion. Richard Gregory has argued that the illusion results from the brain's expectation about the meaning of the feature concerned (Gregory, 1966). In effect, the brain can be regarded as a mechanism which uses models of its environment as a method of handling situations (Young, 1964). We might therefore expect the visual form of a settlement to possess an order related to the operation of the human brain, since it is human activity which has drawn the settlement's structural identity from the environment. There can be no assumption about the degree to which the environment constrains this process. The order in settlement form must first be identified before the degree of influence can be decided.

If human beings can locate personnel at constant distances without using any concrete measuring standard, we would also expect them to produce a similar regularity in the structural framework of their daily lives. In communities which do not use a recognized measuring standard but where individuals both build and occupy the structures of the settlement, there should be a formal order of design based on consistent spacings.

It is expected that people prefer specific distances for particular purposes when locating personnel, since each individual is likely to have a personal attitude about distances used in interpersonal relations. By extension, it can be contended that people also prefer particular distances in the dimensions of their structures. The difficulty with this extension is that preference implies a considerably positive intent to obtain and maintain the preferred condition. This may be an acceptable description of the human attitude to interpersonal situations where the entities being located are the conscious beings themselves, but it is rather less acceptable as a description of peoples' attitudes to structures, which are less easily altered. Other factors, as well as human attitudes, are considered to influence the location of inanimate entities. We are, therefore, less sure with structures than with personnel that the members of a community actually prefer the product of their actions.

It can be argued however, that a community tolerates the visual form of the frame in which it lives. The people generally tolerate the spacings which occur, to the degree that they do not demolish or alter the structures containing the spacings. This applies regardless of the source of the tolerated values because the impact of the shape of entities on the human eye/brain can be considered independent of the origins of the entity. Instead of invoking human choice and preferences in terms of control on the productive mechanisms, we can ask, what form the visual context has and what effect it will have on consistent response by the community. If the context displays spatial order independent of the particular materials necessary to the existence of each component then that order will greatly facilitate the operations of human beings, because the brain can depend upon a consistent source of information about its context.

If the brain could assist in creating an environment, it might be expected to produce order. Human activity is plainly involved in the creation of settlement form. Therefore, if order of the type specified does occur, it can be regarded as a correlate to the operations of the human brain. That the order relates to a consistent patterning, in the brain, of information on structural forms is implicit in the relationship between the perceived entity and the transformation of its image to the biochemical and electrical patterns used in the brain. Since the behaviour which built the structures was in part regulated by the brain, the structures should be returning signal contributions which provide, at least, a partial confirmation of any intent involved in their creation. There should, therefore, be a consistent transformation from the bits of information as they will exist in actuality to the code representation of those bits in the brain's internal processes. A description of formal order using perceived units such as a wall form and room size should be a partial transformation of the order which the brain uses to handle the signals from those sources. The locations of the entities are not the order itself, only a description of it; in the same sense that a word is not the entity it specifies (Bateson, 1973).

But even if the form of the settlement were defined exactly in accord with an ideal consistent pattern, the conversion to material structures would inevitably involve distortion due to the influence of the environment. Men do not build in hypothetical space. For instance, a mode in a distribution of dimensions may occur because a builder has introduced a batch of standard thresholds or roof beams. Nor can it be presumed that the consistency needed will be adequately described by a single point, unique value. The members of a community must be able to expect consistently occurring amounts of variability as well as consistent, specific locations for entities. A possible basis to their behaviour would, therefore, be a specification of a range of variability defined in an absolute spatial frame. For convenience this could be understood as a range of variation around a central value.

4. Analytic context

Settlement structure can obviously be studied in functional terms. It would be absurd to contend that entities do not have functions and do not form part of functioning systems. On the other hand, this does not mean that a formal approach is unnecessary or meaningless (Leach, 1973). There should be no clash because each general class of analysis approaches the study of settlement structure from a different viewpoint, using different aspects of the same entities. Only a functional analysis which has to assume that the brain is a passive transmitter of data clashes with a formal analysis. The former would regard all acts and products of acts as direct results of environmental stimuli. Deterministic functional models regard the regularities in human activities as a result of the order in the environment and are, therefore, in contradiction to a formal approach which regards the order as a partial derivative of human behaviour. The formal view does not need to presume that the environment has no influence. It can be regarded as a constraining condition within which a variety of responses are possible (Forde, 1934, 1970). Furthermore, once the nature of the formal order is known, its functional relevance to human adaptive response can be considered. There is no *a priori* reason why the function of classifications should not be as relevant a functional study as any other: except that the long process of identifying the classification precedes its functional analysis.

It should not be imagined that a formal analysis of settlement structure can immediately describe a model in the human brain which either defined the form of the settlement or handles the information from it. The relationship between individual brains to produce the overall pattern of the community's behaviour would first need to be assessed. Any patterning in the brain will require a symbolic description using units independent of the structures perceived. This cannot be attained until some familiarity with the data has been gained. The initial purpose of this formal style is merely to show that the consistent patterning of settlement structure required by human behaviour can be identified and is derived as much from the activities of human beings as from the constraints of the environment.

Any functional criticism must therefore, either show that the order does not occur or that it can be explained entirely in functional terms. A demonstration that a separate functional explanation can be provided for each structure is not sufficient as a criticism of the formal case. I do not dispute that doors are the width they are because in general, human beings are narrow enough to pass through them! The case being made is that the particular doorwidths used in any one settlement can also be understood as a consistent part of the total spacing pattern of that settlement. If it is claimed that order of this kind is unnecessary in a study of human behaviour then a functional justification must be provided to explain why the functional relevance of classification systems can be discounted.

5. A personal observation

In the Dagomba settlement of Gbambaye, there was a blind, presumably effectively, mature girl who was able to move around her own house, to negotiate her way through the settlement into other houses and reach the functional location she was seeking. Though she was not as quick as her friends, she did not require and did not receive their guidance. Her sense of hearing was very good, and she had identified my presence in the courtyard, but her family had to tell her who and what I was and where I stood. As a child she may have seen the settlement, but its particular form is continually changing. If, consciously or otherwise, she recognized that there was a consistent locational order to the settlement and to each residence unit, then her effectiveness in moving about the structures would be readily explicable. Familiarity with her locational environment would demand the retention of a vast amount of information if the settlement form lacked regularity. It seems to have been the order in her general categories of space which aided her movement. Any specific gap such as a doorway was checked by hand before she attempted to pass through.

Part II. Ethnographic Example

1. Research procedure

The purpose of this study is to show that a small community behaves as if it uses a model of the horizontal dimension of space to aid its response to the environment. Settlement structure will be presented as a consistent formal context for the locational activities of a small community.

A. INTRODUCTION

To minimize uncertainty about the nature of locational pattern in settlements and their relationship to human behaviour, I have studied subsistence economy communities which occupy small-scale settlements. Greater coherence of behaviour can be expected in small communities than in large ones. Moreover, since the builders of the settlement are also its users, it would be natural to assume that the activities and intentions of the group are closely related to the form of the structures. Uncertainty about the locational pattern can be limited by collecting all the available data in any one settlement, avoiding complications caused by sampling procedures.

Consistency in the description of locational order is also aided by limiting the study to the overall character of the settlement. In this way, the largest possible populations of spacings can be obtained while the idiosyncracies of individual builders are classified as a topic relevant to the study of the locational order within each residence unit.

The description proposed is based on the relationship between adjacent entities and does not attempt or claim to describe the position of an entity in a field of locational influences (Harvey, 1969; Bondi, 1967). This approach has been selected because a unified field description would demand a vast amount of data on interrelations of entities; a method of organizing that data; and a symbolic logic to handle and describe it. None of these facilities can be easily achieved in the early stages of research because of lack of familiarity with the data. The simpler type of description should provide some familiarity, from which further research may be carried out and a more inclusive description produced.

In this study of the locational order in a settlement, this chapter includes a description of the variation which occurs and the indeterminacy in human distance estimation which in part produces it. Variation cannot merely be regarded as an inconvenience in the search for order. It may be an integral element of that order since variation in the dimensions of structure is as much part of the visual context of the community as any regularities. A relevant description should, therefore, relate variation to consistencies in the locational organization of a settlement.

B. VALUE OF SMALL-SCALE SETTLEMENTS

The data are restricted to spacings for structures in small-scale settlements. Several convenient and valuable research conditions can be satisfied in this restricted case because of the character of the data and its context.

Small settlements are used because the behaviour of the community concerned is likely to display consistency. In a small community most of the adult population will be familiar with most, if not all the structures around them. The total visual form of the settlement will, in consequence, be partially coincident with the image of it accepted by most of the population. Because the members of the community are continuously interacting, their behaviour must of necessity attain a consistency sufficient to maintain the group and ensure continued communication and physical interaction. If the visual context familiar to each is very similar, then consistency of behaviour is aided because a basic concensus will exist about the character of the frame to their interaction. Only in such a situation would it be possible to expect to clearly identify a human group's model of the horizontal dimension of space.

The model apparently used by a community should possess internal coherence since it has to provide a viable basis for daily life and enable members of the group to judge each other's acts and creations. Essentially a model can only form a unifying feature for a community if individuals in that group recognize as legitimate the judgements expressed by their peers and elders about acceptable behaviour and normal ideas (Gluckman, 1963). The most useful group to study is, therefore, the small-scale community, with its limited occurrences of subcultures, which might refuse to accept each other's judgements about matters of everyday life. A small community may be divided into a variety of groups which differ in their social and ritual roles, but in a subsistence economy context they have to interact coherently if their existence as a group is to be maintained. Though closely related people tend to live near each other, frequent interaction for the whole community is provided by the main routes and open spaces.

The study of a small-scale settlement also enables us to assess the locational behaviour of one group of human beings. There is no claim in this study that the order identified in one settlement also applies to other settlements whose communities are in the same major social group. Consistency in locational behaviour throughout the Konkomba communities is a different topic and problem to the order occurring inside any one community. The amount of social interaction involved decreases rapidly outside the settlement limits. Social procedures for maintaining coherence between communities are of a different order to those used within a community (Abrahams, 1967). My concern is the coherence in locational behaviour within a community. Tackling the problem of locational organization from this direction of community behaviour, makes it possible to limit confusion at the beginning of the study because the information available can initially be handled without using sampling procedures. With the small populations of spacings for structures, it is possible to identify the actual distribution type for those populations rather than specifying their form from a standard statistical assumption.

In general, there is no problem in defining the limits of a small-scale settlement because zones without structures separate the settlements, but in some areas like the Upper Region of Ghana there are dispersed settlements where the farm land used by the community separates the residence units of the settlement. In the Tallensi area and among the Lodagaba, the occupants of a residence unit will state which community they belong to, but the adjacent and nearest residence unit may be occupied by members of another community. The community connection, rather than the areal factor, has been chosen here as the criterion for a settlement since it is the social/economic interaction of a community which is affected and maintained by locational behaviour. The locational organization of dispersed residence units may differ from that of agglomerate or "adjacent residence unit" settlements but this can only be tested by seeking the same data and comparing the descriptions obtained.

The methods and results obtained from studying small-scale settlements should have a wide relevance in anthropological research. From the basis of single settlement studies, it should be possible to devise procedures for analysing consistency in locational organizations in groups of communities. More important, the small-scale settlement has been one of the most common frames for community life used by *Homo sapiens* (Klein, 1969). A study of small-scale settlements should, therefore, have relevance for both archaeological and contemporary settlement research.

Because the study concentrates on small-scale settlements and refers only to the behaviour of the community in the settlement studied, it is possible in a relatively short period of time to collect all the relevant data. It can be assumed that no radical changes in the general, locational organization of a community will occur over a short time range unless a major social-political upheaval disrupts the community. Restricting the data collection to a period of four to five weeks ensures that any change that might occur will be either avoided or only a very small part of the shift will be involved. In the Ewe settlement, some of the small huts for animals were rebuilt in the course of two months and a few shade stands for kitchens were altered. No major structure was rebuilt but the prospective fieldworker **should beware;** in one building season as many as six residence units out of sixty or seventy may be rebuilt and rearranged.

If any attempt is to be made to describe a model of locational organization in a settlement, it is necessary to obtain data on as many spacing categories as possible. Otherwise the study is open to a criticism of restricted relevance and that further examples of spacings from the settlement would not confirm the proposed model. Obviously, it is always possible for a critic to argue that there are further spacings to be considered, but at least data collection in small-scale settlements restricts the freedom of that criticism.

C. COMMENT

The theoretical and practical advantages of the proposed study are therefore complementary; not only is the small-scale settlement theoretically the most likely place for one to find a community behaving as if it uses a model of the horizontal dimension of space; it also offers many practical advantages for data collection, which helps provide the basis of a worthwhile test for the idea.

The fundamental problem in the study of small-scale settlements is the small populations of attributes that are involved. Since much human behaviour is carried out in a visual context composed of these small populations a method of handling them and relating them to the daily life of man will be essential to any further progress in this field.

D. SELECTION OF SPACINGS

The basic problem in describing the locational organization of a settlement is to decide which spacings between entities should be considered. At any one instant in time, the position of each entity could be defined in terms of the distances separating it from every other entity, but more economical criteria are suggested by the characteristics of the spacings used in proxemic studies. As well as helping to link the studies of personnel and structural location, they also have several, practical analytic attributes which are of relevance to a study of order in human locational behaviour.

The dimensions to be used are spacings between similar entities which are linked in some way either functionally or directly in the horizontal dimension of space. Two people having a conversation are similar entities linked by the topic of the conversation and by the gestures associated with it. But the two people are always separated by a short distance. Each person can be imagined as occupying the centre of their own bubble of space which keeps the other individual away (Fast, 1972; Kinzel, 1959). In normal social circumstances, this area should not be penetrated by anybody except with that person's special approval. To enter the space otherwise would be aggression or ignorant rudeness. When two people are talking together, each can therefore, be regarded as standing at the edge of the other's bubble of space. In a very simplistic description the separation of the two people represents the radius of each individual's personal area.

The measurement rules this suggests for structures are very simple. Between discrete entities like posts, the spacing is measured between their centres. For cases such as doorwidths, where the entities have only one finite edge, that boundary represents the limit of the spacing. When dealing with spaces, the dimensions should describe the enclosed area; in reference to its linear boundaries if rectangular; but in reference to its centre if the area is circular. In the Konkomba settlement, entities such as ovens and round huts are therefore described by their interior radial dimensions.

E. RELEVANCE OF THE SPACINGS BETWEEN SIMILAR, LINKED ENTITIES

1. Practical

The selection of a finite population of spacings solves the practical difficulty of handling all the available descriptions of the location of an entity. However, it may be that the position of an entity is defined by the location of every other entity in the settlement. If this is the case, the description of the pattern will not remotely resemble the obvious and familiar order that can be identified in proxemic behaviour, where people behave as if their immediate associates define the available positions.

One of the major problems in considering all the available data is that a hierarchy of spacings would have to be set up, based on the particular characteristics of the entities and the relationship between them. One cannot presume that the spacings between pots and walls form one set, since the functional relationship is not constant in every case. Huge water jars and small containers for food remain at any one place for differing lengths of time. Though a water jar may occupy a larger area at one point in time, the food containers which are being moved frequently across an area are involved throughout their journeys in a locational relationship to their structural frame. The spacings between food containers and walls at any one instant are therefore only part of an extensive time/space entity and need not be equivalent to the locational pattern for the large jars. Nor can it be presumed that the locational relationship between pots and walls has the same status as the association of people with walls. Once a hierarchy has been defined, how does one relate the spacings at different levels? Plainly, an approach in terms of all the spacings would demand either an extensive taxonomic procedure or a reassessment of the relevance of the actual form of an entity.

2. General

Concentration on similar, linked entities simplifies procedure and has several other positive qualities. In every settlement similar, linked entities occur from which sets of spacings can be obtained. Consistency in the locational organization of any one settlement, described in terms of spacings for similar, linked entities can therefore be compared with the order occurring in other settlements. Furthermore, this category of spacings, because it was originally derived from the tacit criteria of proxemic studies will enable us to relate personnel and structural spacings, using data from an adequate sampling procedure for studying proxemic behaviour outside the laboratory.

3. Social

Such a classification of spacings also coincides with the manner in which human beings apparently perceive the location of personnel and structures. Though individuals rarely if ever recognize the specific distances preferred in their society for particular activities, they none-the-less express attitudes about locational situations. The spacings used for any given activity or entity is not seen as a value independent of its context. In your own society people will complain if the proxemic rules are infringed not because they consciously know what distances are used, but because they expect and prefer a consistent response to a particular situation. Moreover, judgements about the acceptability of an action or a design also depend upon the degree to which a community tolerates variation. When people criticize and say "that house is too big" or "why has he built so far away", they indicate that the particular case lies outside the limits acceptable for its class. Amounts of variability are, therefore, perceived in terms of classes of acts or entities and not in reference to some abstract standard. Conversely, children are likely to learn about the variability acceptable to their community by perceiving how much variation occurs in categories of acts or entities such as the greeting behaviour of their elders or in the structures of a settlement.

Human beings behave as if their immediate responses relate to categories of acts and entities for which they recognize and possibly prefer, particularly spatial attributes. The similar, linked entities in a settlement form categories which are familiar to the every-day life of the community. A description of the locational organization of their spacings should therefore be useful in an understanding of human locational behaviour.

4. Theoretical

The topic of a formal locational study is the relationship between the *spacings* of entities, not of the relationship between the entities. Put another way: it is the study of the relationship between locational relationships. The posts forming part of the support for a platform are related to each other by their function and by the distance which is spanned by the beam linking them. The spacings between the uprights can be compared to all the other spacings in the settlement. The spacings between the entities and not the entities involved are being compared.

As has been pointed out, comparisons of this kind must be made between equivalent cases which can be consistently defined, otherwise confusion will result. Just as entities can be classified, so it is also possible to define types of spacings. In theory, one could study the relationship between the spacings of dissimilar, linked entities or even spacings of dissimilar, unlinked entities. But the category of spacings for similar, linked entities has several interesting characteristics, mentioned above which suggest that we may ultimately derive from it a more general model for the locational organization of the horizontal dimension of space in any given settlement.

The spacings for similar, linked entities form a relatively small proportion of the available spacings in a settlement and a description based upon them will, therefore, have the desirable attribute of being succinct. As well as being an economical description in terms of the amount of data used, the construction of the description is also simple. Although there are many different entities in a settlement, the situation considered for each spacing is the location of similar linked entities. The description depends on spacings which are of the same status, because in all cases the same basic locational situation is involved.

There is no claim however that the proposed pattern *is* the only determinant of location in the settlement. My purpose is simply to show that a community behaves as if it uses a locational model, and that the model can be described in a particular way.

2. Source of data

A. INTRODUCTION

The Konkomba settlement (Tait, 1961; Gil *et al.*, 1964; Prussin, 1969; Figs 1, 2 and 3) which will be used here for a detailed study was selected because of its smallness and isolation. Isolation ensures that there has been as little adverse effect by external, dominating influences as is possible in a rapidly developing country. Any "new" features such as rectangular structures and corrugated sheet roofing represent a positive choice and effort on the part of the owners.

The variety of structural types in this small settlement is a useful feature. The occurrence of locational consistency despite differences in the form of residence units would be a valuable indication that the hypothesis is applicable and that locational consistency is important to a community. If a settlement with a short history can be found, the influence of external political and economic factors can also be minimized. In Ghana, for instance, settlements in the north west, which are more than a hundred years old, were affected by the activity of the forces of Samori and Babatu (Dickson, 1969).

B. THE SETTLEMENT AND COMMUNITY

I studied a southerly settlement near Kpandai situated in woodland savanna on one of the long, broad ridges extending out towards the Oti river. Because there were only nine occupied residence units to study, I could work with speed yet concentration and ensure that my data covered a short period of time. I was allowed willing access to all the residence units in the settlement and my presence in the courtyards was freely tolerated. As a result the survey was completed in two to three weeks in November, 1971, following a visit in September.

The community operates a subsistence economy, based on the main carbohydrate crops of yams, maize and guinea corn. Ground-nuts are grown in the area as well as a range of vegetables (Tait, 1961).

A visually impressive feature of the settlement is the small herd of cattle owned by the eldest man of the community.[3] This herd was tied up in the evening outside the residence unit where I lived. The cattle were taken out to graze early in the morning a few hours after most of the men had gone to farm. Goats, pigs, chickens and guinea fowl, and the occasional cat and dog complete the domestic range of animals. I was told that the men occasionally liked to hunt, but I never saw such activity and it was not apparently a major part of the economy.

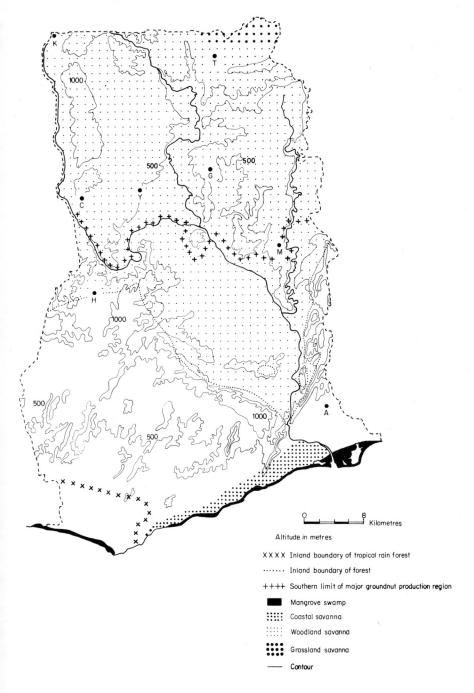

FIG. 1. Settlements and general environments (Ghana). A. Ewe; C. Vagala; G. Dagomba; H. Brong; K. Lodagaba; M. Konkomba; T. Tallensi; Y. Dagati.

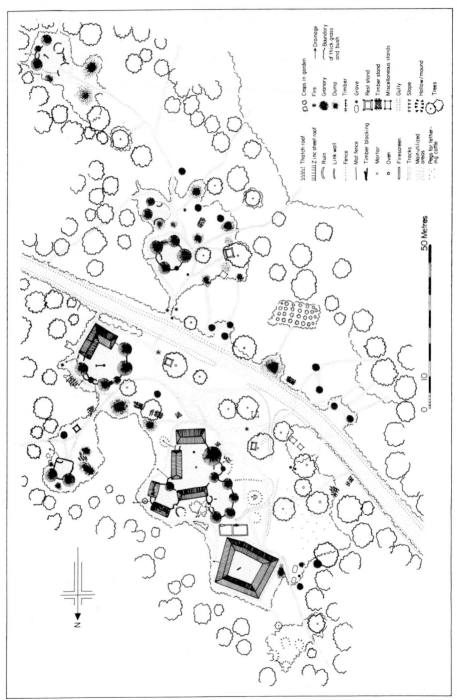

FIG. 2. Konkomba settlement plan in 1971.

Crops in garden
Fire.
Granary
Dump
Timber
Grove
Rest stand
Timber stand
Miscellaneous stands
Gully
Slope
Hollow/mound
Trees

Drainage
Boundary of thick grass and bush

Thatch roof
Z inc sheet roof
Ruin
Link wall
Fence
Mat fence
Timber blocking
Mortar
Oven
Firescreen
Tracks
Main utilized areas
Pegs for tethering cattle

0   10   50 Metres

N

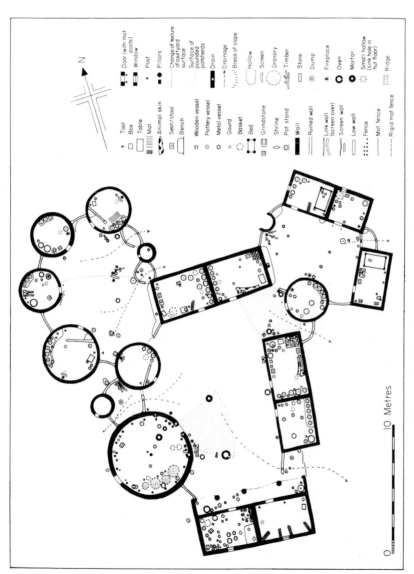

FIG. 3. Residence units II, III, IV of the Konkomba settlement. Structures and object location.

Four basic natural materials are used in the structures of the settlement. The red earth of the area provides the material for the walls, and floors of the huts and courtyard; also for the platforms in residence units, and over the graves. Cattle dung, mixed with earth, is the main material used in the plaster surfacing of walls, floors and courtyards. The thatch for roofing huts and granaries is made from

FIG. 4. Residence unit II, Konkomba settlement. (a) Courtyard viewed from N.E. corner. (b) Courtyard viewed from South.

the local grasses. In three of the residence units the rectangular structures have corrugated aluminium sheet roofs (Fig. 4). **Heavy duty mats** of the local grass are used to block doorways (Figs 4 and 5) **and** are the basic structural element in the walls and floors of the large granaries (Fig. 6). Timbers of varying sizes provide the structural members for roofing and for three types of stands. Stands for storage

FIG. 5. Konkomba settlement. (a) Residence unit VIII and (b) residence unit IX, courtyard viewed from the West.

or seating basically consist of timber uprights with cross-beams laid in
the forked tops of the uprights. A rough platform of timber is then laid
over the cross-beams. The largest of these stands are used to support
the granaries. Because the walls of the granary basket itself are made
of matting, they cannot support their own weight and require a circle
of tall uprights to prevent the mats sagging outwards. The tops of the
mats are attached to these poles which in turn are linked to each other
around the circumference of the granary. All roof thatch is laid over a
frame of thick branches bound by cables made from grass.

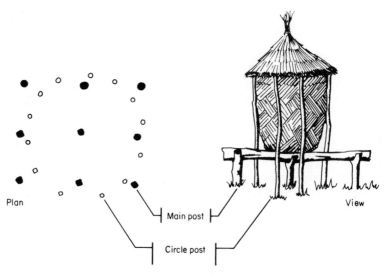

FIG. 6. Form of the granary structure.

The primary structural unit of the settlement is a courtyard
delimited by huts and walls linking those huts. There is a clear
distinction between the courtyards and the area outside. Access from
one to the other is limited to a single doorway. This usually involves
passing through one of the huts or rooms of the residence unit. Only in
cases where the unit consists only of two, large huts is the doorway
located in a wall or fence. The two basic hut or room types are used,
one for living/sleeping and the other for bulk storage and cooking.

The residence units may also aggregate into a group of interconnected courtyards. This only occurs in one case and the pattern
retains the character of the basic residence unit (Fig. 3). The three
courts are linked so that access to the two smaller courts is obtained

through the entrance hut of the large court. There is no direct access, however, between the two satellite courtyards. In the settlement, each residence unit, when fully operative, is occupied primarily by a man, his wife or wives and children. The two satellite residence units belong to the sons of the head of the community. Both sons are married and have children. When a man's sons are married they ideally build their courtyards attached to their father's court, through which they gain access to the outside world (Tait, 1961).

There are many structural components to the basic residence unit. The dominant feature is the hut or room of which there are several variants in the settlement. Floor areas enclosed by walls and roofed over, are either round or rectangular. Round rooms are never found directly juxtaposed without a link wall between them. Rectangular rooms are either single, double or combined into a large structure of several rooms. In one case the entire residence unit consists of juxtaposed rectangular rooms enclosing a roughly trapezoid court. In purely visual terms, there are two main types of each enclosed roofed area. Rectangular rooms are either fully enclosed or form verandahs. The round rooms used by human beings are all very similar except for the entrance hut in the head man's residence unit which vastly exceeds the dimensions of all the other round huts (Figs 3 and 4.). It is the only representation of a possible class of very large entrance huts. The main internal distinction in round huts is the presence of a screen wall, in the living/sleeping huts, which blocks direct view from the courtyard.

Two types of animal hut are present. One form is incorporated in the arrangement of huts around the courtyard. Interior diameters do not exceed 1.60 m and they may be roofed with thatch or smoothed off to a peak. The other animal used spaces are cavities built into the thickness of the hut walls with access provided through a small, approximately circular opening (Fig. 3).

Some of the gaps between huts are delimited by two walls to form a bath area. Entry to the area is obtained through a gap between the hut and the end of the link wall that faces onto the court or more rarely through the narrow gap between two huts. Drainage for the courtyard is directed through the bath areas.

The settlement was founded by the man who built the rectangular residence unit. When he died, his brother took over as the head of the community which currently has a population of 30-35 adults.[4] Kinship connections between the owners of the residence units are presented in Fig. 7. Through its entire development the community

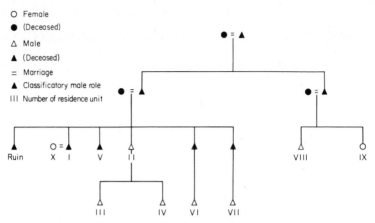

FIG. 7. Kinship between owners of residence units of the Konkomba settlement.

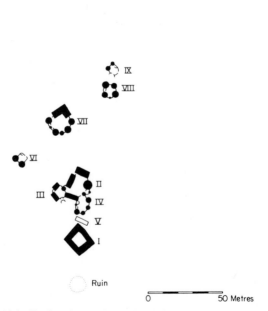

FIG. 8(a). Konkomba settlement. Residence unit numbers.

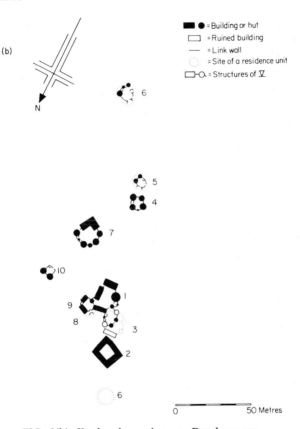

FIG. 8(b). Konkomba settlement. Development.

has produced eleven residence units, one of which at the north end of the settlement has been abandoned and is almost completely eroded away (Fig. 8). The ruined rectangular buildings and some of the huts in IV are remnants of an older residence unit which has been partly demolished and, in part, incorporated in the residence unit owned by one of the sons of the headman.

3. Analysis and results (Fig. 9) (Table 1)

A. ORDER IN VARIATION

Order in the visual form of a settlement is indicated by the consistent variation which occurs for the actual dimensions. A comparison of the means and standard deviations for the distributions,

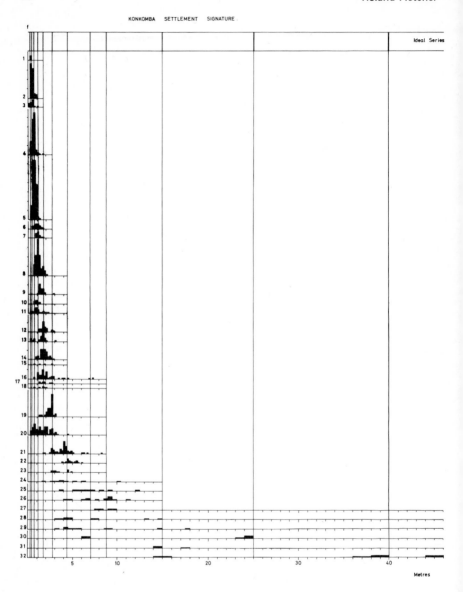

FIG. 9. Distributions of spacings, Konkomba settlement. On the frequency axis 1 unit represents 10 examples except for: (17), (18) where f axis represents 5 examples; (17) represents edge separations; (28), (29) set 1 description. Values absent are (31), 49 m and (32), 61 m.

with populations of more than eight examples, shows that there is a trend towards increasing variation with the increase in the length being used (Fig. 10). The standard deviation and mean can be used as an index of variation because they provide a range which will encompass a given percentage of the examples of one category of spacing (68% for 1 S.D.; 95% for 1.96 S.D.), and can be referred to a description of the central tendency for the distribution. The increasing standard deviation describes a wider and wider range within which a constant percentage of examples will occur. Although there can be no assumption that the community's behaviour depends upon the percentage expectation to which the standard deviation refers, the description can be used as one expression of the variation they actually tolerate.

The trend of variation can be used as an absolute description independent of the population sizes for the distributions. Population size does not simply decline as the lengths increase (Fig. 11) and there is, therefore, no direct correlation between variation and population size. Variation appears as a coherent factor in its own right, not as a derivative value!

Analysis of the distributions from seven other settlements[5] used by different social systems in Ghana, shows that there is a general tendency towards increasing variation as the lengths increase. The degree of variation and the rate of change with length differs in every settlement (Fig. 12). There is an overall connection between settlement size, defined by the number of residence units, and the steepness of the trend of variation (Fig. 13),[6] but a precise prediction of variation cannot be made from settlement size alone. Other factors such as availability of access and the degree of intervisibility are also involved. Within the broad zone of possible values the trend for any given settlement is a community specific feature not a direct consequence of settlement size.

The trend, referred to here as the drop-off rate, may therefore be a general characteristic of the interaction between human beings and distance in small scale settlements. This decrease of coherence should relate to the decreasing accuracy with which the human eye estimates increasingly large lengths (Vernon, 1962; Gregory, 1966). Since the trend occurs for several different settlements and is independent of materials or structural type concerned, its overall regularity must be connected to the behaviour of the human beings who located the various entities.

TABLE 1. Distribution populations by cluster (see Fig. 9)

Index	Spacing	N					Clusters (m descriptive convention.)								Excluded values
			.28	.40	.60	1.10	1.70	2.80	4.40	7.00	8.80	15.00	24.00	40.00	
1	Bench diameters	5	—	5	—	—	—	—	—	—	—	—	—	—	—
2	Bench widths	79	—	79	—	—	—	—	—	—	—	—	—	—	—
3	Fence link spacings	19	—	19	—	—	—	—	—	—	—	—	—	—	—
4	Doorwidths	109	—	—	109	—	—	—	—	—	—	—	—	—	—
5	Circle P/S	185	—	—	185	—	—	—	—	—	—	—	—	—	—
6	Fence main spacings	25	—	—	—	25	—	—	—	—	—	—	—	—	—
7	Zoh. II. P/S	17	—	—	—	17	—	—	—	—	—	—	—	—	—
8	Granary platform P/S	118	—	—	—	118	—	—	—	—	—	—	—	—	—
9	Stand short sides	27	—	—	—	(26)	—	—	—	—	—	—	—	—	2.80 m stand in Zoh II
10	Mat P/S[a]	10	—	—	—	10	—	—	—	—	—	—	—	—	—
11	*Bath, end widths	22	—	—	—	—	—	—	—	—	—	—	—	—	—
12	Stand, long sides	29	—	—	—	—	26	3	—	—	—	—	—	—	—
13i	Round room radii	28	—	—	5	—	22	—	—	—	—	—	—	—	3.10 m Zoh II
13ii	Oven radii	3	3	—	—	—	—	—	—	—	—	—	—	—	—
14	Granary platform T/D	60	—	—	—	9	51	—	—	—	—	—	—	—	—
15	*Firescreen wall lengths	4	—	—	—	—	—	—	—	—	—	—	—	—	—
16	*Link wall lengths	56	—	—	—	—	—	—	—	—	—	—	—	—	—
17	Pillar spacings	9	—	—	—	—	7	2	—	—	—	—	—	—	—
18	Screen wall lengths	6	—	—	—	—	5	—	—	—	—	—	—	—	—
19	Rectangular room, short walls	58	—	—	—	(4)	—	54	—	—	—	—	—	—	—
20	*Bench lengths, inner (arc benches)[c]	78	—	—	—	—	—	—	—	—	—	—	—	—	—
	*Bench lengths, outer (arc benches)	15	—	3	12	—	—	—	—	—	—	—	—	—	—
21	Rectangular rooms, long walls	58	—	—	—	—	2	14	41	—	—	—	—	—	8.30 m[f] Verandha VII.

TABLE 1—*continued*

No.	Category	N	C1	C2	C3	C4	C5	Isolated values
22	Round hut, centre separations along edge of residence unit	—	23	—	—	—	—	—
23	Rectangular building, exterior widths[d]	—	23	—	—	—	—	—
24	Granary, edge separations	12	8	—	4	8	—	10.00 m[f]
25	Granary, central separations	9	8	—	—	—	—	3.50 m, 12.00 m[f]
	1.	—	—	7	7	—	—	—
	2.	—	—	5	5	2	—	—
26	Rectangular building, exterior lengths 1.	14	—	2	2	12	—	11.50 m[f]
	2.	—	—	2	3	8	—	—
27	Courtyard I dimensions	4	—	—	—	4	—	—
28	Residence unit widths 1.	10	—	5	2	2	—	—
	2.	—	—	5	3	2	—	—
29	Residence unit lengths 1.	10	—	6	2	2	—	—
	2.	—	—	6	2	2	—	—
30	Residence unit, edge separations	7	—	—	—	—	4	49.00 m[f]
31	Residence units II, III, IV, centre separations	—	—	—	—	—	3	—
32	Residence unit, centre separations	7	—	—	—	—	5	15.00 m, 61.00 m[f]

Key: P/S = Post spacings. T/D = Total dimensions. ( ) = Aberrant median, N = Total Population and * = Excluded category. [a]For posts on either side of door to hold a mat in position (see Figs 4, 5). [b]Edge separations used. Centre separations also give values within the clusters. [c]Arc benches population included in bench length totals. [d,e]V values excluded because lengths not visible to present occupants of settlement.

If added: (23) m = 3.05   (26) 1. m = 9.00
           40% = 50   40% = 1.60
                            2. m = 9.20
                              40% = 0.60

[f]Isolated values. (Rounded) No median possible.

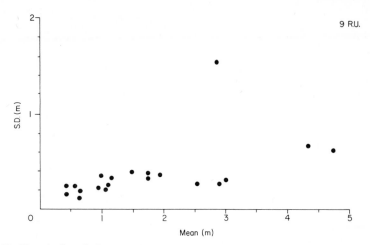

FIG. 10. Trend of variation, Konkomba settlement. For trend of large separations: correlation at $P = 0.05$. Note: anomaly M $= 3.88$ SD $= 1.53$ and Set 1 M $= 8.46$ SD $= 1.41$ Set 2 M $= 8.99$ SD $= 0.52$.

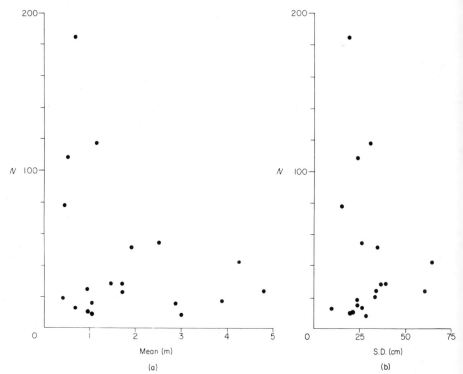

FIG. 11. Dimensions and population sizes for distributions, Konkomba settlement. (a) Population size and mean. (b) Population size and standard deviation.

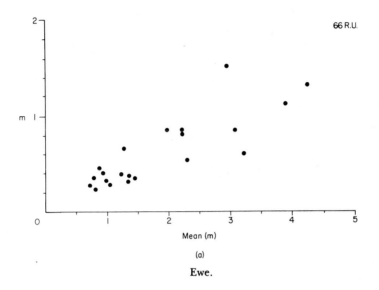

(a)

Ewe.

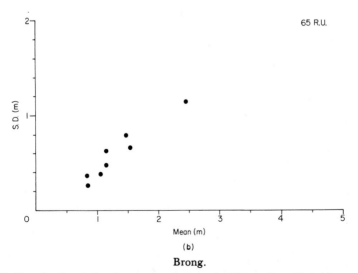

(b)

Brong.

FIG. 12. Trends of variation for some settlements in Ghana. For all trends excepting Lodagaba case, correlation at $P = 0.05$. R.U. = residence unit.

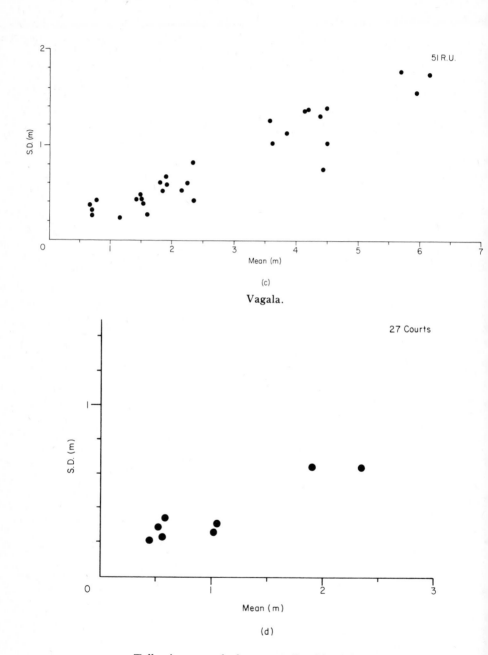

(c)

Vagala.

Tallensi composed of many small residential units.

FIG. 12. (continued).

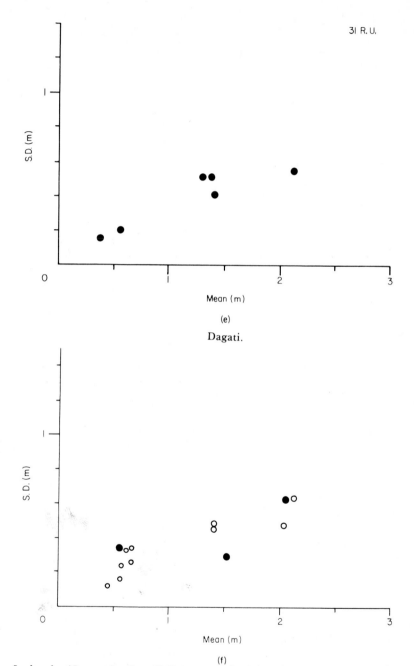

(e)

Dagati.

(f)

Lodagaba (O = value from R.U.; no meaningful correlation can be obtained).

FIG. 12. (continued).

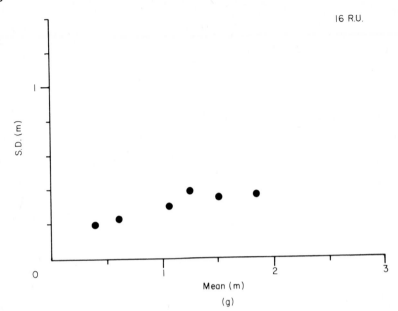

FIG. 12. Trends of variation for some settlements in Ghana. For all trends excepting Lodagaba case, correlation at $P = 0.05$. R.U. = residence unit. (a) Ewe (b) Brong (c) Vagala (d) Tallensi composed of many small residential units. (e) Dagati (f) Lodagaba (o) value from one R.U.; no meaningful correlation can be obtained (g) Dagomba.

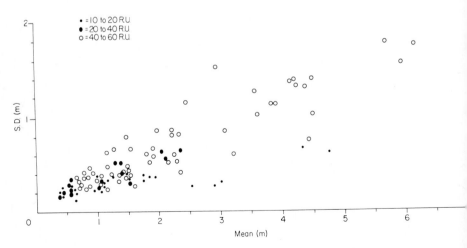

FIG. 13. Overall trend of variation, Konkomba settlement.

Variation for the large spacings, if it continues at the rate for the first 5 m is plainly very considerable for dimensions over about 10 m. The rate of increase may even exceed the linear trend. In the Vagala settlement, the increasing variation can be fitted to an upward curving trend. As will be seen later, the variation in the Konkomba settlement appears to increase in abrupt steps.[7]

The distributions for lengths above 5 m cannot therefore be regarded as meaningless scatters because their form can be seen as an extension of the variation occurring for the shorter spacings. Since the positive skew of the distributions also increases as the mean becomes larger (Fig. 14), the distributions for large spacings, such as the width and length of residence units are unlikely to show a distinct mode if the

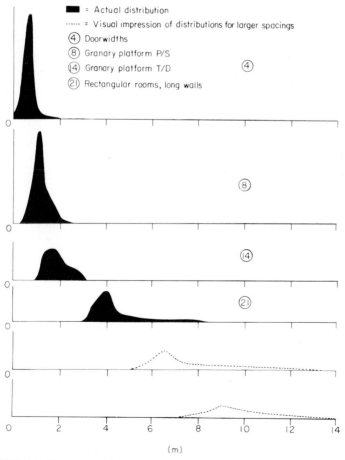

FIG. 14. Illustration of skew on distributions, Konkomba settlement.

populations are small. The variation allows a wide scatter and the skew sets up a substantial distortion away from any central tendency. In the visual presentation (Fig. 9), larger class intervals are used to keep above the survey error (see Appendix B). This is an incidental aid for visual presentation because though the spacings are more scattered, the perceptual mechanism that produced them is less capable of accuracy for larger distances. Large spacings may therefore seem more scattered in absolute terms but still appear to the observer in the settlement as similar distances.

The decrease of perceptual accuracy that is apparently affecting the form of the distributions will also influence any coherence there might be between them. If for instance the community was wishing to use identical lengths for different large entities, its ability to achieve this will decline as the dimensions become larger because the ability to judge similarity declines. Added to this, the greater the dimensions, the more influence external factors will have on the end product. Distortion increases as the capacity to recognize it declines.

B. ORDER IN THE CENTRAL TENDENCIES OF THE DISTRIBUTIONS

The trend in the variation suggests that a coherent pattern might also occur in the relationship between the central tendencies of all the distributions of spacings. So far we have connected variation to the absolute values of the central tendencies, but anyone moving about a settlement must also be able to expect some order in the relationship between the dimensions themselves.

The regularity that might be expected can be suggested by a simple illustration. In designing a machine which could find its way about a given area, the main task would be to instruct it about the distances which can be expected. If every feature of the area has different dimensions then an elaborate search model would be required. At the opposite extreme, if every length of an entity it will meet is the same, then the instruction becomes relatively simple. The same would apply to the brain of a human being moving about a settlement. There is a continual need to judge and predict distances to entities and to anticipate their actual size. But settlements are formed from more than one length. The simplest solution is then, that wherever possible the same length should be used for as many different purposes as possible; and that the different lengths should be simply related to each other so that a parsimonious mathematical description could cover them all. An obvious possibility would be to have all the dimensions as simple multiples of one basic length. In this way, a discontinuous use of space, with each dimension distinct from its adjacent values, will be formed. The continuum of all possible lengths will have been cut up into consistent, classificatory units.

Therefore, frequently used dimensions might be expected to occur in clusters, with the cluster consistently related by their actual values. Due to the drop off rate, however, the clusters should become more internally scattered and less consistently related as the dimensions increase. The pattern is familiar: we often divide things into categories of small, medium and large, and we accept less size similarity for the large objects than for the small ones.

1. Discontinuous occurrence of dimensions

When the medians[8] for all the available distributions are plotted on a linear scale, it appears that bunches of values do occur, with an increasing separation between values and a decline in the tightness of the clusters as we progress up the scale (Figs 15 and 22).[9]

The relationship between the central tendencies in terms of the separation between adjacent values, when correlated to the absolute dimensions, now has to be considered. This will indicate whether or not the relationship between the central tendencies is also regularly related to the increase of the dimensions.

The medians can be arranged in order from the smallest to largest and the separations between adjacent medians can then be plotted against the smaller median (Fig. 16). If there is any consistent trend to the separations it will then specify the next largest value in a succession of values, provided the length of the value is shown from which the prediction starts.

Several possible cases may occur. To provide a basis for testing the presence of order, it is necessary to predict the probable form of the pattern. If the central tendencies are unrelated, with no consistent separation between them, then a diagram of separation against absolute length would show a general scatter of values (Fig. 17a). If, however, values concentrate repeatedly in clusters and with consistent separations between clusters, then two distinct zones of values will appear. If for instance the clusters are separated by a constant length, a roughly horizontal zone of large separations will be found, well above the groups of very small separations describing the relationships within

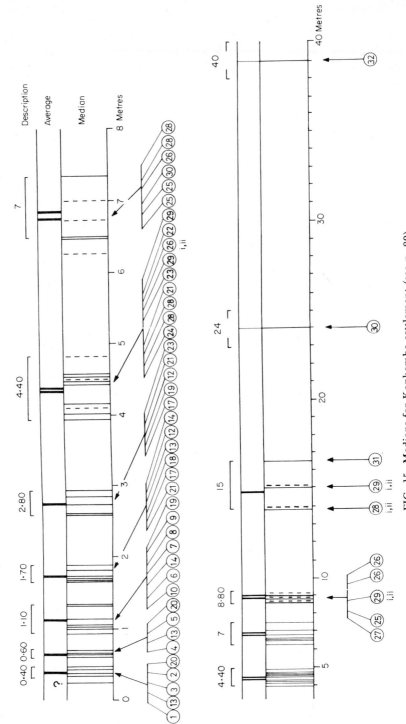

FIG. 15. Medians for Konkomba settlement (see p. 89).

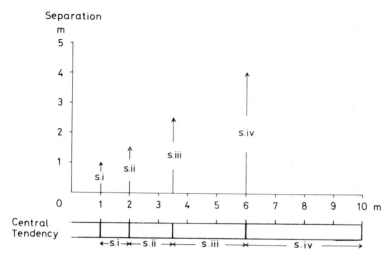

FIG. 16. Arrangement of separations, Konkomba settlement.

the clusters (Fig. 17b). Alternatively, the large separations may steadily increase or decrease with the increasing length of the descriptions of central tendency. The pattern need only be described for a steady increase (Fig. 17c), since the decrease is simply the image reversed. The relationship between the separations can be described by the regression of the separations against the lengths to which they refer. As can be seen from the examples, the slope for the larger separations will become steeper with the increasing difference between the successive separations. These successive values in effect form a mathematical series. The steepness of the slope can be compared to standard descriptions of such series, to find a convenient description of the pattern of separations (Fig. 17d). It is unnecessary to argue that any order which may appear is a particular series or relates to some specific comprehension of that series by the community. The description is merely a convenient method of referring to the pattern. But it may also suggest further characteristics to be considered by references to other circumstances where the same series description has been applied.

2. Separations for medians

When the separations of the medians are plotted against the smaller median of an adjacent pair, it can be seen that there are two zones of large and small separations. But there is also a severe anomaly to the

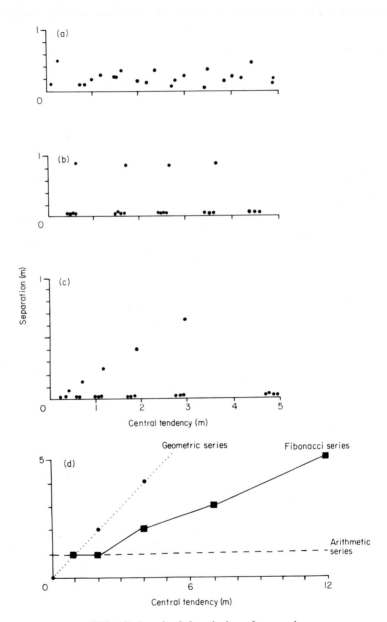

FIG. 17. Standard description of separations.

predicted pattern occurring around 7 metres (Fig. 18a). Initially, therefore, any study of the pattern must divide the data into two blocks on either side of 7 metres (Fig. 18b). The size of the separation allocated to the values around 4 m indicates that the median values near 7 m are associated with the trend of large separations commencing somewhere around 0.5-1 metres. The separations from 7 m onwards cannot be so included.

A further check on the existence of the group of large separations for dimensions from 5 to 7 m can be obtained by using three other possible descriptions of central tendency. These are the mean, mode and the average of the mean, mode and median. When combined they provide a general picture of separations for lengths of up to 7 metres (Fig. 19). The numerous points on the diagram do not then represent new values but merely show whether or not the alternative descriptions are in agreement. They appear to confirm the hypothesis that the values can be divided into groups. These will be referred to here as the large and small separations.

(*a*) *Large separations* It can be seen that the large and small separations apparently merge around the 1 m median but that there appears to be a ceiling to the small separations. This can be used to provide a more precise description of the large separations, because an extrapolation of the ceiling across to the *y* axis defines the points above it which can be used to describe the trend of large separations. Two descriptions are possible depending on the inclusion or exclusion of the separation values, just above the line, which refer to the separations between 1.20-1.40 m central tendencies.

The two alternative regressions are possible descriptions of the trend and indicate that separations between central tendencies of less than 60 cm could also form part of the trend. These further values must be the largest separations which can occur between absolute lengths of less than 60 centimetres. For the medians and in the average description, a relatively large separation occurs between values around 40 and 60 centimetres. When this separation is added the coherence of the upper trend is maintained, suggesting that a cluster of values around 40 cm can also be considered. This cluster is submerged in the blurring effect of the general description but can be recognized in the succession of median values.

A more problematic cluster could be identified between 1.00 and 1.50 metres. The overall trend would suggest that a separation of

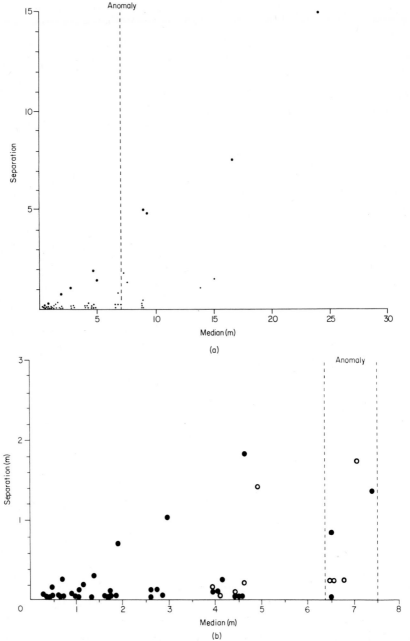

FIG. 18. Median separations, Konkomba settlement. For trend of large separations; correlation at $P = 0.05$. (a) Separations 0-40 m. ● = large, • = small separations. (b) ● = set 1 and O = set 2.

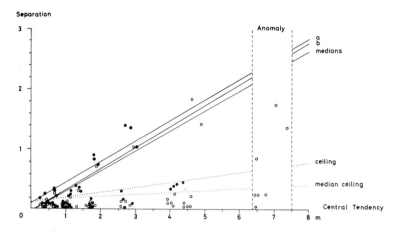

FIG. 19. Central tendency separations; 0-8 m. For large separation trends; correlation at $P = 0.05$. a = all large tendencies for central tendencies of 60 cm or more; excluding the 1-1.50 m C.T. values, b = all large separations for central tendencies of 60 cm or more. Medians = large separations for medians only.

40-70 cm could be related to a central tendency value in this zone. It is clear that there is a cluster around 1.70 m because it provides a platform for the next major increase up to the cluster around 2.80 metres. The regression, therefore, predicts a cluster preceding the 1.70 m group at about 1.00-1.30 metres. But such a cluster can only be clearly defined by eliminating, in particular, the description of the short sides of stands (9) which lies between 1.30 and 1.40 metres. There is no clear reason why this category should be anomalous. Although the distribution describes the short sides of several types of timber-built platform, variously used for rest and general storage, this cannot effectively be claimed as the cause of the anomaly. The same would have to apply to the dimensions of the long sides (12) but they conform neatly to the 1.70 m grouping. The best explanation of the anomaly is that it results from an extreme example of the positively skewed distribution pattern that generally applies in the settlement. Instead of sloping gradually away from the mode, there is an abnormal platform of values and an abrupt drop in the frequency of occurrence at about 2 metres. The discussion of this problem must be left to the later analysis of the clusters in relation to each other. It cannot be clarified in the relationship between their component values.

(*b*) *Small separations*   When we look at these separations for each of the possible descriptions, it is plain that the more values are added, the more they cluster, so that the ceiling becomes lower as the separations become smaller. The median separations provide the largest number of examples and the tightest pattern. But the correlation of median separations to the central tendencies is not significant at the 5% probability level. As a visual group, therefore, the small separations have very little coherence. The statistical description is stating that, given the absolute size of the values, the scatter is too great for a confident statement of correlation to be possible.[10] This is how the human eye would also assess the pattern in the settlement. It suggests that the separations may be related within each cluster but that there is no correlation between values in different clusters other than the ceiling restriction on their size.

C. VARIATION AND COHERENCE

How the trend of variation might be integrated with the consistent pattern of separations has now to be decided. The degree to which dimensions are recognized as similar or different by a community will depend upon its tolerance of variation. The more variation it will accept, the less certainly can distinctions be made about it. The degree of variation defines the degree to which two dimensions must differ in order to be recognized as different in the "rules" of the community's spatial game. If, therefore, there are two distinct degrees of separation between dimensions, they should relate to the community's perception of similarity and difference. The large gaps will mark difference, and the small separations will lie within the range of variation acceptable for entities to be classed as similar.

1. 40% range

According to this model the ceiling to the small separations will be set by that acceptable range of variation. It is noticeable that the trend to this ceiling and the regression for the index of variation based on standard deviations have very similar slopes. We need to assess what happens with the variation for large dimensions. For analytical purposes, a definition which provides a large number of values is also needed, particularly for dimensions above 4 metres. An index variation is, therefore, needed which can be related to the medians. It was found, by chance, that the range within which 40%[11] of the examples in a distribution occur, when plotted against the relevant median, provides a trend partially coincident to the ceiling (Fig. 20a). It also emphasizes that a group of substantially higher variations occur for dimensions above 4 m in length.[12] The trend of the 40% ranges can either be separated into an upper and lower set of values or can be described as a single trend.[13] The pattern will be discussed in terms of an upper and lower trend of 40% ranges.

The characteristics of the upper trend are of considerable interest when plotted against the large median separations from 7 m upwards (Fig. 20b). A marked break in the trend of large separations occurs around 7 m and is coincident with the zone where the large separations and the upper 40% range values overlap. The trend of large separations then continues beyond this break with three more separations, the final one being between a cluster of medians at about 24 m and a median near 40 metres. Just as the lower 40% range appears to define a ceiling for the small separations up to the 7 m cluster, so the upper 40% range marks a ceiling for "small" separations too but in contrast to the large separations occurring from the 7 m medians onwards. The higher 40% range subsumes all the separations for dimensions of less than 4 m as "small", in contrast to the large separation values for the 9, 15 and 24 m medians.

The spatial pattern in the settlement should, therefore, be divided into two sections which relate to the accuracy of perception required to deal with them. When the coarse grain of accuracy is used, only distinctly large separations can be recognized for dimensions in excess of 7 or 8 metres. But there is another, more precise perceptual accuracy which relates to the distinction between smaller and larger separations for dimensions ranging from 40 cm to 7 metres.

2. Relevance of the divide

In practical terms this divide coincides with the overall radial dimensions of the residence units (28) (29). These occur primarily in the 4.50 m and 7 m clusters. It is only from 9 m upwards that the trend of large separations is once more, clearly restored.[14] **Lengths** in excess of 6 and 8 m, whether unobstructed distances or dimensions with no visible subdivisions, will normally be perceived only outside the residence unit. Such visual ranges, without any nearer visual reference point, cannot occur within the confines of a courtyard. Even ignoring features such as ovens, fireplaces and mortars, the huts jut so far into a courtyard that there can rarely be more than **4-5 m** between a hut

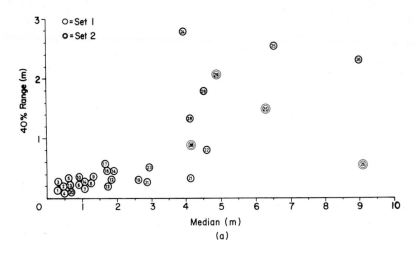

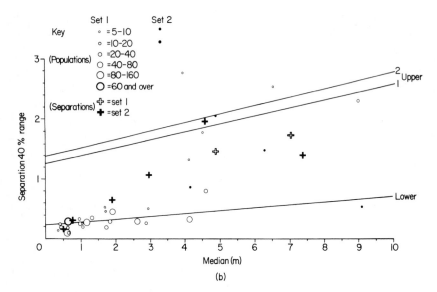

FIG. 20. 40% ranges, Konkomba settlement (also a 40% range of 7 m at 39 m (32). Correlation at $P = 0.05$.

and a major structural boundary. When the smaller features are included, the greatest distance from a visual reference point is about 2.80 metres. Courtyards are either small with no central features, or are large and possess a central fireplace. The location of entities in an open area must, therefore, be considered both as a functional requirement for particular tasks and as a visual reference to aid human beings in their movements through the area.

The two different levels of variation can, in consequence, be seen as complementary to the two major classes of open space into which the settlement is divided by the continuous wall of each residence unit. Courtyards and the open space outside the residence units differ substantially in the frequency of personal interaction and the density of object occurrence for any given area. It is also interesting to note that social activities which occur both within residence units and in the open areas, are located in similar visual frames. People sitting to shell groundnuts, or just resting and talking outside the residence unit, are always located where the maximum distance from visual reference points such as trees, fireplaces and platforms, is around 4.50 m (Fig. 21).[15]

Pragmatically, greater precision of observation is needed within a courtyard than in the open areas. Anyone colliding with his wife's cooking pot would not receive a kind welcome, but tripping over the woodpile outside the house just classes him as a fool.

D. RELATIONSHIP BETWEEN CLUSTERS (Fig. 22a, b)

The picture of spatial arrangements in the settlement can be clarified further by assessing the relationship between the clusters of medians. The pattern can either be described in terms of the separations between individual medians; or the large separations can be used to define clusters of values whose relationship can be stated as the connection between the general description of each cluster. One such description would be the average of all the medians in a cluster. This would specify each cluster in terms of the value around which the medians in it appear to concentrate (Fig. 15).

Defining the clusters is difficult only for the previously mentioned medians around 1.10 metres. The separations on either side of the aberrant values are not very different, but, in the median description, the smaller separation is between them and the 1.10 m values. When allocated in this way the aberrants raise the average of the cluster from 1.03 to 1.13 metres. Though aberrant when seen in terms of separations, these medians, (9) (19), have little significant effect as members of the nearest cluster. The purpose or effect of the shift is impossible to explain at present.

The use of these average descriptions provides a clear illustration of

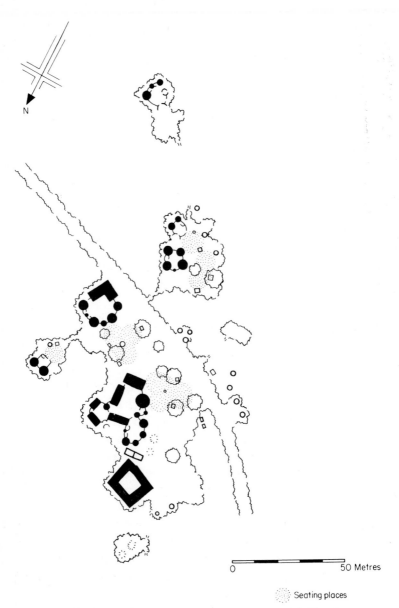

N

0   50 Metres

Seating places

FIG. 21. Seating areas. Konkomba settlement (cf. Fig. 2).

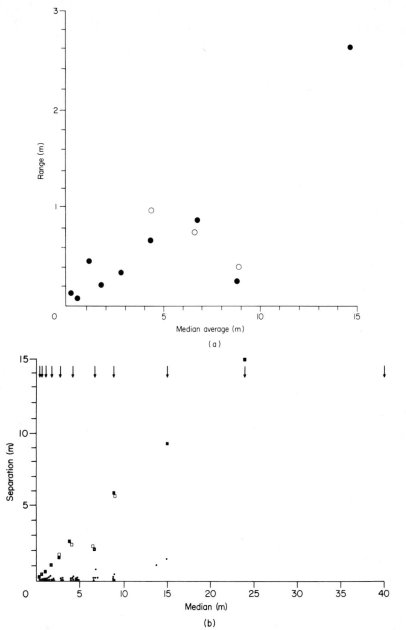

FIG. 22. Description of median clusters. (a) Ranges for median clusters. For trend of ranges including and excluding the 8.80 m value; correlation at $P = 0.05$ (apparent anomaly at 8.80 m). ● = set 1, o = set 2. (b) Large and small median separations. Cluster description. For trend of large separations; correlation at $P = 0.05$.
■ = set 1 averages for cluster, □ = set 2 averages for clusters. ● = separations within clusters.

CARL A. RUDISILL LIBRARY
LENOIR RHYNE COLLEGE

the separations trend but it must be recognized that this represents a tidying of the picture (**Fig. 22**). The regression for the trend, either including or excluding the anomalous 7 m value, resembles the slope for a Fibonnacci series.[16] The two initial values of a Fibonnacci series are always the same (**Fig. 17d**). If the series describes the increase in the size of the separations, then the "step" in the separations at 6 m can be seen as the start of a new series within the general trend. The 4.40 m cluster would be the first point in the series with a separation to the 6-7 cm cluster which in turn is equally distant from the 8.80 m group.

There is no equivalent "step" at the beginning of the lower series but it could be provided by adding an ideal cluster around 20-25 cm which would apparently be submerged in the 40% range, but is actually the basic structural dimension of the settlement, the width of a wall.

E. THE SPATIAL MODEL (Table 2)

In this Konkomba settlement, there appears to be a two part model of the horizontal dimension of space (**Fig. 23**). Each part apparently commences with a primary structural dimension. The first part of the model describes space within the residence unit, commencing with the thickness of a wall, 20-25 cm, and including all dimensions up to and around 7 metres. The second part starts from about 4 m, the basic radius of a residence unit, and includes all dimensions at least up to values around 40 metres. It describes the open spaces around the residence units.

These two portions of the model relate to two functionally distinct types of area in the settlement and are connected to two distinct degrees of perceptual accuracy. Within the residence unit, considerable precision is needed in locational behaviour, while for general activity

TABLE 2. Description of the model (see Fig. 23)

	Separations	Variation
0-7	$S = 0.53 M + 0.06$[b]	$V = 0.05 M + 0.22$
4-40 m	$S = 0.67 M - 0.93$[a]	$V = 0.14 M + 1.23$
0-40 m	$S = 0.62 M - 0.22$[a]	$V = 0.18 M + 0.19$

Units: metres. M = median.

[a]The separation regressions are derived from the median averages for the clusters.
[b]The Set 1, 2 values are used for the maximum information available on the relevant trend of variation.

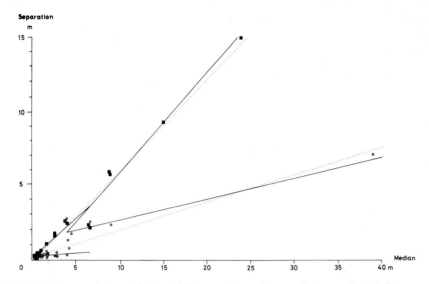

FIG. 23. The spatial model. For all illustrated trends; correlation at $P = 0.05$. • = 40% values; ■ = cluster averages; ———— = regressions for two part model; ....
= regression for combined model.

in the open areas around the residence units a very much lower degree of locational accuracy is required. Fewer objects and people are encountered outside the residence units, compared to the densities occurring in courtyards and rooms. The formal order in the horizontal dimension of space is complementary to the pragmatic, functional necessities of daily life.

The two portions of the locational model can also be subsumed in a description of the general increase in the separations between dimensions which are classed as distinctly different by the community. This can be combined with an overall description of the increase in variation as the distance estimated increases.

Relevance of the anomalies   Four spacing categories could not be included in this study because of the polymodal character of their distributions (Appendix C). One of them, the lengths of firescreen walls (15), contains only five examples, each of which could be members of the four clusters from 60 cm to 2.80 metres. The size of each firescreen is most obviously connected to the number of women who use or once used it. Only with a much larger population of firescreens could any formal significance be ascribed to their lengths.

The remaining three categories have more relevance. For convenience they can be divided into two; the lengths of benches (20), and the lengths of walls between huts, whether link walls (16) or the end walls of baths (11). The walls provide dimensions which combine with the radii and lengths of huts to produce the overall radial dimensions of the residence unit. This category could therefore satisfy the need for an entity to absorb any strain set up by packing a number of dimensions together to produce a further dimension consistently related to them.

The lengths of the benches are part of an areal entity that occupies an area of courtyard or floor space. Just as the link walls might take the strain in linear order, so one could imagine the areal entities as adjusters between the spatial needs of people and the areas produced by a formal order of linear dimensions.

For future formal studies of settlement structure, the anomalies in the linear pattern suggest that a description based on area characteristics may be more inclusive. Alternatively a complex analysis could be attempted, treating each category of spacings as a strain adjustment to all the others. Compared to these, a description based on linear dimensions would seem to be an economical approach to the problem, but the linear order is only one of many possible descriptions and it cannot include certain features. Recognizing this basis, it is possible then to ask whether the description says anything further about human locational behaviour.

4. Serial order and functional factors

The Fibonacci series acts as a description of the relationship between clusters of medians but does not describe the connection between each of the median values for the individual categories of spacings. As was mentioned before, the Fibonacci series has been proposed several times as a description of structural order but has referred either to a few categories of dimensions or to the overall arrangement of areas. Such partial regularities might be expected as a result of a pattern of clusters analogous to the Konkomba example. Depending on the position of each central tendency in its cluster, a Fibonacci series could appear to be present or absent. The nearer the values are to the average for each cluster the more like a Fibonacci series they would seem. Whether or not such a series for clusters of central tendencies would produce areas that could be described by Badawy's method is difficult to assess. The character of the enclosed area depends on the use of the members of the series to create its boundary dimensions.

Seeking regularity between individual central tendencies would, according to the Konkomba case be an unjustified and spurious claim for precision. The individual central tendencies are related within their clusters. Visually, the community accepts them as similar. But when the values being compared are members of different clusters, then the regularity is perceived in terms of the overall characteristics of each cluster. There is therefore a hierarchy to the arrangement of dimensions in the settlement. Any attempt to explain the pattern must avoid confusing the different parts of the hierarchy.

The contradictions between formal and functional interpretations now become more meaningful. Each example of a spacing can be understood as a functional response to circumstances. When comparing all the spacings in a settlement, it is the total visual effect which displays regularity, but this includes degrees of variation which can cover differences produced by material, functional requirements. Conversely, the functional controls are not so stringent that an entity can have only one possible form.

As can be seen from Table 1, dimensions of entities with no direct functional connection, built of different materials and located in different parts of the settlement, can occur in the same cluster of central tendencies. Most obvious is the similarity between doorwidths (4) and the circle post spacings (5) in granaries. Gaps to enter the granary baskets are provided between the circle posts. These fourteen examples have widths very similar to the widths of timber and mud built doors, but there are many other possible gaps which could have been used. The need for doors to enter the granary is not therefore the determinant of the circle post spacings. Substantially larger gaps could have predominated, with the doorwidths arranged between the few narrow ones.

The spacing cluster around 1.70 m is utilized in the location of wooden posts; for the spacings between swish and mud brick pillars (17) and for the radii of the round huts (13). None of these types of entity are functionally linked to the other. Large boughs are used in platforms, smaller branches to roof round huts. Furthermore lintels in verandahs are carpentered and do not support the same load or direction of thrust as the beams in granary platforms.

The distributions for uprights in platforms (8) (9) (12) (14) indicate the constraints set by timber length on the spacings of the uprights

(Fig. 9). There is a considerable spread within which a relatively restricted range of lengths are more frequently used. Many of the timbers are about 1.70 m long but can be supported either by a post at each end or with an additional upright supporting the middle portion of the branch. The timber is not usually worked along its length but most of the branches have been chopped at one end or both. They project beyond the uprights by considerably varying distances and the community tolerates variation in the location of the posts which support them.

It is unnecessary to argue therefore that the supply of timber stringently restricts the options of the community. The people are capable of cutting timber to selected lengths, altering the natural dimensions of the raw material they use. A considerable tolerance appears to be accepted since the post spacings for similar parts of the platform can vary considerably. The activities of subsistence economy communities frequently involve a satisficer policy (Gould, 1963; Clarke, 1968). The structures they use need be no exception. Although a satisficer solution may, in overall terms, be the most effective in the context, its value derives from the interaction of many factors. No simple determinism is applicable.

Most of the round huts in the settlement are of similar size within the constraints set by wall strength and the length of branches for roofing. But these constraints have not prevented the creation of the exceptional Zoh (entry hut) of residence unit II. When necessary, walls can be built thicker and assisted by wooden posts to support a roof. Plainly, the external environment exercises no direct, deterministic control on the dimensions of rooms and buildings in the settlement. Factors of man power availability linked to social ranking are also regulating the form of the structures.[17]

Since the external environment exercises no narrow restriction on structural forms latitude is available within which the community may operate as if it is making consistent locational choices. Because order in settlement form is not rigidly defined by order from the natural world, a consistent and limited environment must be produced by the activities of the community if it is to maintain coherence in its behaviour. Whether or not that order is produced consciously is incidental to the issue.

It would now appear that the spatial arrangements within settlements have seemed confusing because they are due to mediation between formal and functional conditions both of which will tolerate some latitude in adjusting to each other. But this adjustment conforms to two precise conditions of uncertainty: functional latitude in the stability of any given structure; and the degree of variation coherent with the dimensions in the formal pattern. If these conditions do not coincide, the pattern will fall apart. If for instance the variation in the formal pattern was restricted, the range of structural choices available to the community would be very limited. The natural environment sets the primary rules of success and failure. The baffling variety of responses that can occur should become less confusing when the role of variation in the formal order of structural dimensions is understood.

The serial order and its specific character also has a functional role in the activities of the community. As pointed out earlier, the search and estimation procedure, in particular, would be aided by this arrangement. Human response to entities depends on decisions about their size and the distance from any other entity. If a human being is uncertain about these dimensions, the task of making a decision is simplified if particular spacings are more likely to occur than others. Instead of exactly judging the distance, the eye/brain can assume that the distance will be within the expected variation around one of the several, possible standard spacings. A rapid estimation will indicate the magnitude of the distance involved, restricting the probable value to a small number of the standard spacings. The expected variation for a given standard distance could be used to predict the distance that would in most cases ensure that a person could avoid the edge of an entity. Within this general context, the eye/brain could then concentrate on precise estimation at close range to decide whether or not the entity is significantly divergent from the predictions. When searching for the limits of an entity or the position of one entity in reference to another, the eye/brain could simply check each spacing concentration distance in turn without having to scan deliberately across the entire range of possible distances. If the limits of an entity are not separated by about 4.50 m then the next most likely separation will be near 7 m and so on up the scale of distances.

There is also the possibility that the particular form of the series is connected to the requirements of locational activities in a small settlement. In computer programming, the Fibonacci series has useful applications for data sorting, information retrieval and indicating the limiting values for complicated functions with unknown derivations (Gardner, 1969). These are analogous tasks to those the human brain must carry out when locating itself in a structural context, where it must anticipate possible dimensions and predict relationships between incompletely observed lengths. Many claims have been made in botanical studies for Fibonacci sequences in organic growth and the ordering of parts of plants (Briggs and Walters, 1969). One accepted example is the packing of seeds in spirals in the head of some sunflowers (Gardner, 1969). As a particular solution to the problem of high density packing the series might also be applicable to dimensions in residence units where the location of entities must satisfy a large number of functional and visual conditions within a restricted area.

5. Conclusion

The occupants of the settlement behave as if they use a model of the horizontal dimension of space to locate entities in the settlement. It seems unlikely that they are unique in this respect since all communities appear to have their own coherent locational preferences in proxemic behaviour. Human beings are plainly capable of consistent estimation of distances within certain limits of accuracy.

The drop-off rate,[18] which applies independent of population size and materials used, suggests that the one factor common to all locational acts, the degree of inaccuracy in human activity and distance estimation, is a major determinant of order in settlement form.

It should not be presumed that the order of every settlement will be identical, except at the very general level that a series/variation description should be applicable in most cases. The range of settlement form and the many different proxemic systems used by human communities at the present time suggests variety rather than conformity in human locational behaviour (Hall, 1966).[19]

Part III. Archaeological Example

1. Introduction

All the data used in the analysis were derived from the structures of a settlement (Bingham, 1930; Bruyère, 1939). No verbal information is required from the community and the method of analysis should be applicable to any settlement where the basic date can be obtained. Contemporary occupied settlements provide the information on ideals and variability at any one time and may ultimately enable us to link locational behaviour to other aspects of the social and economic life of a community. Settlements which are no longer occupied and have long development histories can be used to study the manner and rate of change in locational organization. They also provide the essential information on other possible locational patterns, for structural types and environmental contexts which no longer occur.

The study of locational organization in settlements depends on data from both past and present (David, 1971; Ucko *et al.,* 1972). Long-term trends cannot be studied in currently occupied settlements and details of spatial organization at any one instant cannot be obtained in archaeological contexts (except for abnormal circumstances). If exactly what is happening to the pattern is known, exactly what form it has at one instant in time cannot be known.

Because I know that time is always time
And place is always and only place
And what is actual is actual only for one time
and only for one place (T. S. Eliot, *Ash Wednesday,* 1930).

A model of adaptive behaviour must be derived from data on the mechanisms that apparently regulate change and stability in a community. The predicted consequences of the model must then be tested in the archaeological record.

For this to be possible it must first be shown that the presence *or absence* of the locational organization identified in contemporary settlements can be demonstrated in an archaeological site. Unless a method of testing whether *or not* the pattern occurs in the past can be produced, the procedure is useless because there will be no way to prove the pattern incorrect. Our knowledge of spatial distributions in the present cannot be used to arrange or repair the "damaged" information from the past because there is no independent basis against which to check our reconstruction. No derived data can be used in testing an evolutionary model because the procedure would be circular. Any prediction must be specified in terms of data which can be obtained directly from the relevant context.

ROLE OF LOCATIONAL DATA

The data used in this study satisfy the conditions outlined above. Classification of similar, linked entities exists independent of the categories recognized by the occupants of the settlement. Consequently, the spacing distributions can be obtained directly from the plans of any settlement. It is then possible to test whether or not order occurs by following the procedure used for an occupied settlement. But, however many times the series model is confirmed, every settlement must always be tested. Interest will ultimately centre on behaviour in those settlements which are exceptions to the pattern, just as it centres in the Konkomba settlement on the aberrant polymodal distributions.

Spatial organization provides a basis for using contemporary and past settlements to analyse settlement dynamics without using one to reconstruct the other. Potentially, studies in either context should suggest predictions to be tested in the other context. Further study of occupied settlements will, without doubt, require a reassessment of the current model but these new proposals will also have to provide predictions testable in the archaeological record. Conversely, studies of the rate and manner of change in locational organization will demand a reappraisal of the role and relative status of the mechanisms indicated by observation of human behaviour.

The data on locational organization from occupied and deserted settlements are, in each context, associated with different categories of information. The connection to social behaviour, for example, can only be studied in occupied settlements. This is a problem in its own right, not a piece of "action archaeology" to help reconstruct the past (Freeman, 1968; Andersen, 1969; Trigger, 1970), even if such studies begin under that title.

The overall aim of archaeological research in settlements seems to be the creation of equivalence between the data on human activities, past and present (Trigger, 1970; Hawkes, 1968; Neustupný, 1971; Isaac, 1971; Watson, 1972; Clarke, 1972, 1973; Leach, 1973; Stanislawski, 1973). In theory, the equivalence of past and present could be specified by the characteristics of either source of data, the present is used as a standard because of the belief that the past is damaged badly, if not hopelessly in some cases. Archaeologists act as if the present is an intact version of the past but, as has been pointed out by several archaeologists, the past provides data on human activities which cannot be obtained at the present time (Hole, 1973). The quality of the data depends on the questions that are asked of it, not on a comparison with any other category of data. It is, therefore, legitimate to use spatial data as a basis for describing past and present in equivalent terms without devaluing the past.

2. The Hopi pueblo and Franciscan mission at Awatovi. 17th Century A.D.

A. INTRODUCTION

The site of Awatovi in Arizona (Montgomery *et al.*, 1949; Figs 24 and 25) has been selected as an illustration of the complementary value of archaeological data and to assess the possible use of available archaeological evidence. The particular value of the site depends on the 70-80 year building sequence it contains and the presence of structures erected by two different communities with coincident periods of occupation. These characteristics make it possible to enquire about changes in spatial arrangements over time and to compare two different responses to the same environment.

Historical evidence leaves no doubt that both the indigenous Hopi indians and immigrant Franciscan monks lived at Awatovi at the same time. For a brief period they were even contemporary neighbours occupying the structures discussed in this paper. Two primary difficulties in studying the response of different communities to the same environment are therefore overcome. The two communities were not in adjacent areas sufficiently far apart for differences to be ascribed to microenvironmental factors. Nor in any long term sense were they successive occupants of the site, with the later occupants having to use the resources of a natural environment transformed by their predecessors.

When the monks initially built their mission, at some time in the 1620's and 1630's, the mesa top was already occupied by the Hopi (Montgomery *et al.*, 1949). The monks had part of the pueblo demolished so that they could build their mission (Montgomery *et al.*, 1949). By the time the mission had reached its greatest extent around 1670, the Hopi pueblo surrounded the remaining sides of a large plaza on the north side of the mission. After the initial destruction of the mission in 1680, the Hopi took it over and altered the rooms to their preference, creating structures like the rest of the pueblo and resembling the earlier Hopi structures on the mesa (Montgomery *et al.*, 1949; Smith, 1971a).

The remainder of the pueblo has not been completely excavated but the available plans indicate that the southern wing of the whole settlement can be treated as one major section of the pueblo as could the structures on the other side of the plaza. When Mindeleff made his plan in 1882-3, the church of the pre-rebellion mission was completely

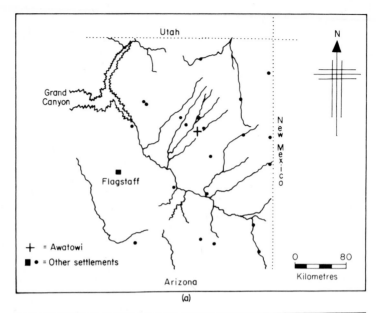

(a)

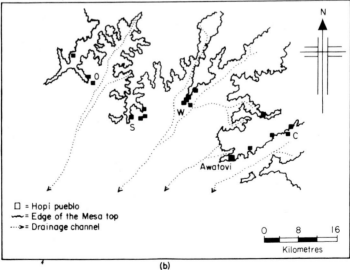

(b)

FIG. 24. Location of Awatovi. O = Oraibi pueblo; W = Walpi pueblo; S = Shungopari pueblo; C = Chakpahu pueblo.

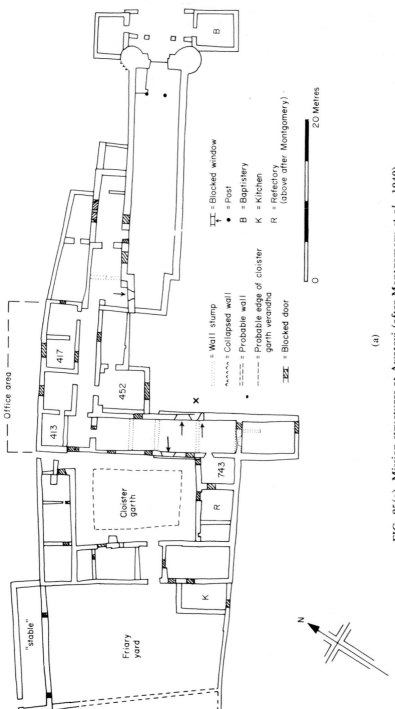

(a)

FIG. 25(a). Mission structures at Awatovi (after Montgomery *et al.*, 1949).

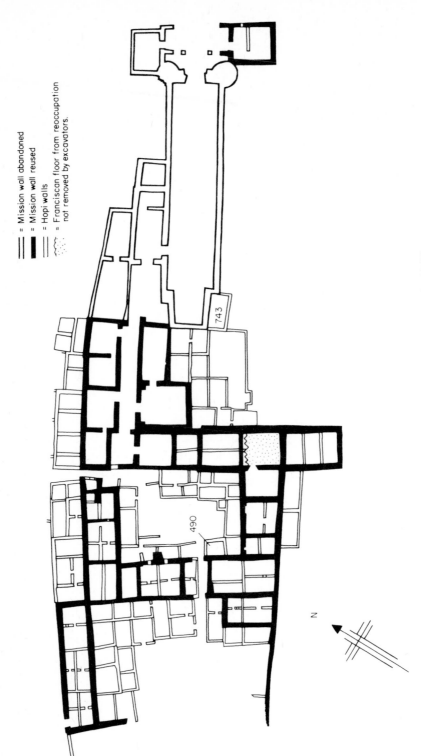

= Mission wall abandoned
= Mission wall reused
= Hopi walls
= Franciscan floor from reoccupation not removed by excavators.

743

490

N

FIG. 25(b). Pueblo structures (Montgomery *et al.*, 1949).

concealed by the walls of animal corrals (Mindeleff, 1891; Fig. 26). Judging from the excavation report most of them should postdate the abandonment of the pueblo, because the church was used as a Hopi burial ground (Montgomery *et al.*, 1949) and the rooms must have been clear to allow the Franciscans access to the office area in 1700. The date of the corral walls south of the church is unclear and no measurements are available for them (Montgomery *et al.*, 1949; Fewkes. 1898).

For a brief period the Friars returned to Awatovi, reorganized part of the mission to live in and occupied it while the Hopi continued adding their structures on either side. In the cold of late 1700 or early 1701, vengeful Hopis from the adjacent mesas sacked Awatovi (Montgomery *et al.*, 1949; Mindeleff, 1891). Once again the people of Awatovi had allowed Christianity and the Spanish Crown a foothold on Hopi land. The community was savagely wiped out; the men slaughtered, some probably hacked to pieces in a nearby valley; the

———— = Wall line
– – – – = Probable wall
▬▬▬ = Thick, standing walls in 1882–1883
········· = Buried walls of church Ⅱ

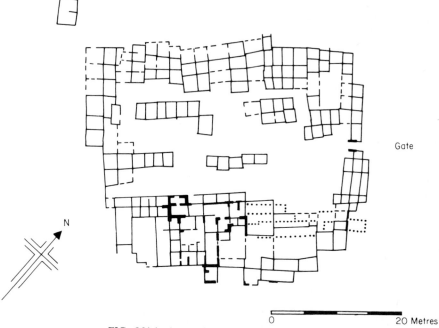

FIG. 26(a). Awatovi pueblo, after Mindeleff.

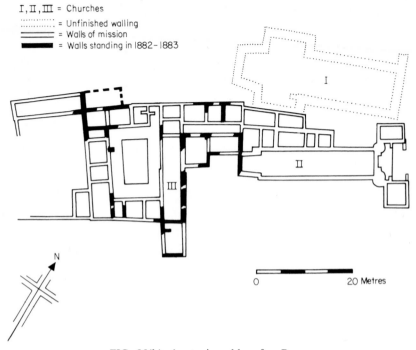

I, II, III = Churches
.... = Unfinished walling
========== = Walls of mission
▬▬▬▬ = Walls standing in 1882–1883

0   20 Metres

FIG. 26(b). Awatovi pueblo, after Brew.

women and children either taken away, or burned to death trapped in
their rooms. Awatovi was left to its broken ruins and to the sheep
corralled among them in the passing years (Mindeleff, 1891).

B. DEVELOPMENT OF THE STRUCTURES

1. Structural zones

The development of the mission and the pueblo buildings erected in
and around it cannot be described in terms of room by room
additions. From the wall junctions of the mission, it is plain that the
expansion consisted of additions of groups of rooms. Though the
pueblo may have built up by single room aggregation, one cannot say
with any precision what the sequence of individual additions might
have been. There were at least nine exterior wall frontages against
which simultaneous additions could have been made. In the pueblo,
each new structure did not directly predefine the possible location of
the next addition.

Both the mission and pueblo building sequence must, in consequence, be described in terms of groups of rooms most likely to have been contemporaneous. When Brew analysed the development of the sacristies, he defined five phases of successive arrangements of contemporary rooms (Montgomery *et al.*, 1949). As he pointed out, it should not be supposed that the Friars saw the development as five successive rebuildings with long static periods in between. The phases are a convenience, enabling Brew to describe and the reader to comprehend the overall growth of the sacristy area.

Exactly how long each Brew phase lasted cannot be known as yet and is incidental to the purpose of this study. It is likely that structural rearrangements requiring new rooms, the blockage of old doors and the rearrangement of the church would have been used for a few years at least. They would overlap with alterations in other parts of the mission in intervening building seasons. The whole development of the mission can therefore be divided into successive groups of structures which can be reasonably regarded as contemporary. For clarity and to keep continuity in the study of Awatovi I have linked the successive possible descriptions to the Brew phases. The sacristies are a valuable basis because they do refer to the manpower changes occurring in the mission.

Each group of structures will be referred to as a structural zone. The zones are not necessarily representations of long persisting situations which abruptly altered to create the pattern of the next zone. Nor do they mark equal time spans in the growth of structures. In buildings made of timber and adobe, continuous additions and alterations are required. Convenience also requires that single new features be added. The "stable" that abuts the N.W. corner of the friary was clearly one such addition. The zones are therefore like single frames of a moving picture and provide a rough illustration of the sequence of spatial changes.

From the identification of the zones, the amount of change can be assessed if any occurred in the general trend of development. Any overall trend can be described and its relevance to human use of the environment can then be considered. The task is somewhat easier with the mission than with the pueblo. The growth of the mission was effectively a linear succession of additions from east to west though minor changes were continually occurring at the east end of the site (Fig. 27). There is also documentary information on the names and the activities of some of the Franciscans at Awatovi, to which the structural changes can in part be correlated (Montgomery *et al.*, 1949). In contrast, the pueblo developed from several points but with an overall trend to the east. The documentary information provides only indirect illumination of Hopi activities, so the zones used to describe the Hopi constructions are less clearly defined.

2. Structural zones at Awatovi (Fig. 27)

(a) *The mission*

The reasons for selecting the zones can be readily presented, though more detailed and particular examples reinforce the choices made. Our basic guide to the growth of the mission is its expansion from a church and sacristy with a priest either visiting or temporarily resident in the pueblo (Montgomery *et al.*, 1949), to a complete mission with a friary, office area and church even if it was a little short on resident Friars (Montgomery *et al.*, 1949). From the plan, the abutting walls in the building can be seen. Brew's phases describe a growth from one room to a large sacristy, followed by a reduction to the area used shortly before the massacre in 1680 (Montgomery *et al.*, 1949). The zones proposed commence from a sacristy and a church to which various additions were made (zones 1 and 2) (Montgomery *et al.*, 1949). When a guardian was assigned, it is probable that a cell, office and verandah were added along with the expansion of the sacristies (Montgomery *et al.*, 1949) (zone 3). The great extension of the sacristies in Brew phase 4, and the use of the baptistry, form a convenient structural zone with the great expansion of the residential part of the mission (zone 4) (Montgomery *et al.*, 1949). Into this zone I have also placed structures which may slightly postdate the initial construction of the friary. The "stable" and the kitchen are certainly later than the friary proper and the S.E. extension may also have been a later addition.[20]

A final zone (zone 5; Fig. 28) can be proposed containing all the features that indicate a recession in the occupation and use of the mission. These are features coincident with a declining, less secure community. The outer sacristies are abandoned and, according to Montgomery *et al.* (1949), the refectory was reduced in size. The altered north entry and the addition of the south west unit (452) suggests that the Friars had begun to restrict access to the mission.

There is one other zone which must be mentioned which covers the brief reoccupation before the destruction of Awatovi in 1700-1701

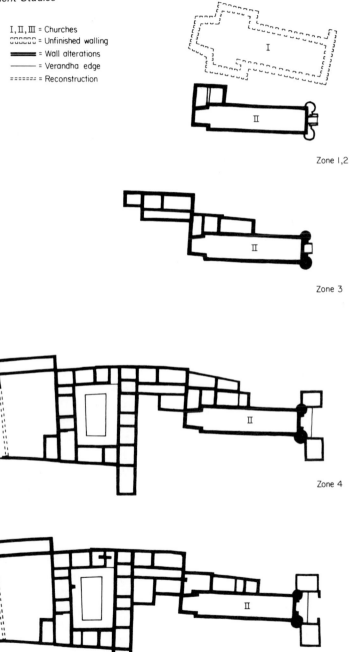

I, II, III = Churches
ᴜᴜᴜᴜᴜᴜ = Unfinished walling
▬▬▬ = Wall alterations
——— = Verandha edge
======= = Reconstruction

I

II

Zone I,2

II

Zone 3

II

Zone 4

II

Zone 5

FIG. 27. Development of the Mission.

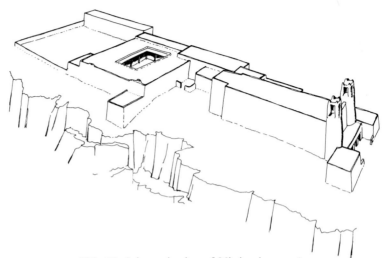

FIG. 28. Schematic view of Mission in zone 5.

(Figs 29 and 30). Debris was cleared from the office area (Montgomery *et al.*, 1949); room 452 which had apparently been an open court used as a corral was also cleared and roofed over. In the east wing of the friary, both the Hopi and Franciscan dividing walls were demolished to create a new church (church III) (Montgomery *et al.*, 1949). Hopi and Franciscan residence for a very brief and uncertain period was juxtaposed at this time. Some Hopi rooms abut the reinforced walls of church III,[21] and it is therefore unlikely that the Friars had either the power, confidence or need to persuade the Hopi occupants of the rest of the mission to depart. Rooms of the reoccupation were clearly identified by the absence of Hopi occupation debris on the highest floor levels. When found they were full of blown sand unlike the abandoned areas such as church II and the friary yard, where a layer of animal dung illustrates their use by the Hopi from 1680 onwards (Montgomery *et al.*, 1949). Church II was also used as a graveyard (Montgomery *et al.*, 1949). No evidence for any Franciscan occupation after 1680 occurs either west of church III and its sacristy in room 734, or east of the steps to the passage way in the office area.

The study of the dimensions used in the mission begins with zone 3. There are insufficient values available in zones 1 and 2.

(b) The pueblo

The three zones used to describe the pueblo growth are based on an

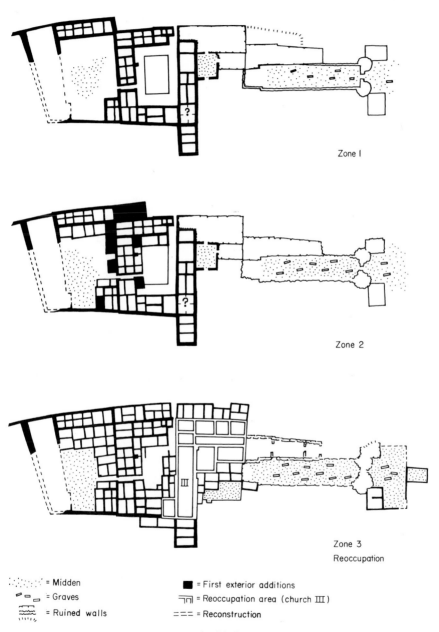

Zone I

Zone 2

Zone 3
Reoccupation

:·:·:·: = Midden   ■ = First exterior additions

⌐□ = Graves   ⌐⊓⌐ = Reoccupation area (church Ⅲ)

≈≈ = Ruined walls   ≡≡≡ = Reconstruction

FIG. 29. Development of Hopi pueblo.

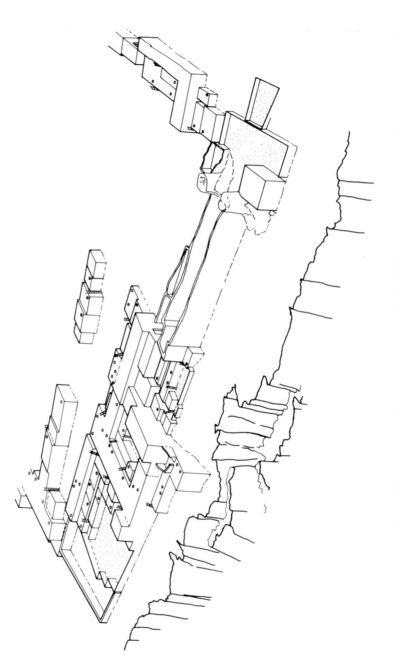

FIG. 30. Schematic view of the pueblo in zone 3, including the mission reoccupation.

eastward trend of occupation around the walls of the mission (Fig. 29).

Functional convenience would suggest that the Hopi sub-divided the interior of the friary before beginning to add rooms abutted on the outer faces of the structure. The primary evidence for an initial occupation of the interior of the friary are the numerous points at which the first exterior elements were added, usually in corners of the abandoned building. There is no evidence for a continuous trend of external aggregation from west to east, but expansion of the pueblo in the western portion certainly predated the Hopi additions in the east. The extreme eastern parts of the mission were never apparently occupied but were used as graveyard, midden and animal pen. There was no clear evidence of Hopi structures in the office area unlike the situation in the east wing of the friary.[22] The Franciscans may therefore have reoccupied the offices precisely because there was only domestic rubbish to clear out.[23] They would have been able to persuade the Hopi to leave the east wing because the alterations there were very recent and the Hopi had not completely settled in.[24] The Hopi rooms abutting the reinforced walls of church III must postdate a return to Awatovi by the Franciscans.[25]

The friary rooms were divided up into pairs of rooms, by the addition of longitudinal central walls and by putting in more cross walls (zone 1). The initial exterior additions can be envisaged as rooms for the growing families of the people occupying the subdivided Franciscan rooms. Since the Hopi rooms around church III and north of the offices area cannot have been occupied for very long, there should therefore have been a time when the pueblo consisted only of the interior rooms and the first "layer" of Hopi exterior additions in the west (zone 2).

This pattern requires the block of rooms abutting the east end of the "stable" as a necessary Hopi addition providing access between the roof of the "stable" and the friary (Montgomery *et al.*, 1949). The anomalous character of this block can then be explained as a Hopi adjustment to the problem of the high Franciscan walls. Most of the Hopi rooms would only have been about half the height of the mission walls (Montgomery *et al.*, 1949). Much thicker Hopi walls were needed if they were to support a structure with its roof near the level of the friary roof.

The same explanation would then apply to the external addition, east of the north entry, which also has abnormally thick walls for a Hopi building (Montgomery *et al.*, 1949). In this case, the limiting factor would have been restricted access over the roof of the old mission office area. During their brief re-occupation, the Franciscans would not have wanted Hopis walking on the roof (Montgomery *et al.,* 1949). Structural instability may also be involved. Even if the additions were put up before the Friars returned to stay in 1700, there would have been a period when the offices were scavenged for materials and were structurally neglected. The roofs would rapidly deteriorate so that any access to additions along that north facade would soon depend upon the roof of room 413. This is the smallest room in the area and has relatively thick walls. Its structural stability would also be of concern to the Hopi because it provided the eastern side of the north entry which they continued to use.

Zone 3 includes all the Hopi rooms now extant in the site and would be a description of this block of the whole pueblo immediately before the destruction in 1700-1701 (Fig. 30). The rooms on the south and east sides of the old friary cloister are part of this zone because of their relationship to the reinforced wall of church III and the complete corner of room 490 against which they abut. Between church III and the rear of church II is another late block of rooms. Some like 743 could be much earlier than their neighbours but must for consistency of procedure be allocated to zone 3. It would be attractive to imagine that all these rooms and the two exterior rooms on the south facade of the friary could be alternative residences for Hopis who moved out of the east wing when church III was built.

3. A Hopi upper storey

The possibility exists that the Hopi also added rooms on the roof of the friary (Montgomery *et al.,* 1949). If they did almost all must have been narrow rows of rooms with a terrace for access in front. There is no way to be sure where such additions might have been, but several alternative descriptions of the zones are presented in the analysis to show the range of possible spatial patterns that might result. Evidence for an upper storey over the east end of the "stable" is difficult to interpret (Montgomery *et al.,* 1949), and such a construction would have blocked all lateral access to the rest of the roof of the "stable". Only one upper floor set of dimensions is included in the schematic description of the pueblo. Over the kitchen there could have been a complete duplicate of the lower rooms without blocking access along the adjacent roof. These values are included in zone 3.

3. Analysis and results

A. METHOD

All the measurements used are taken from the available plan. This limits the accuracy that is possible, in particular the class interval which has been set at 25 cm instead of 20 cm. Because of the small scale of the plan it is impossible to obtain every category of spacing.

No direct proof of the series regularities can therefore be obtained using the available data. This will probably be a feature of much published settlement data because detailed measurements are rarely provided for all the required spacing categories. This analysis discusses only the general features of the spatial patterning, and the changes which occurred through time.

A few walls could not be measured because they are absent from the plan (Montgomery *et al.*, 1949). There is no indication of the Hopi room arrangements at the south end of the east wing of the friary. An estimate could be obtained for the northern portion. Some Hopi rooms adjacent to the known structure might possibly exist outside the limits of the excavation but the Mindeleff plan suggests that there are no significant omissions.

As mentioned there are several alternative descriptions of possible upper storey rooms in the pueblo. It was found that the overall spatial pattern resulting from the various alternative descriptions can be conveniently illustrated by the schematic sequence of zones discussed in the previous section. Some ground floor dimensions could not be clearly allocated to a zone but the interpretation used depends on sufficiently general characteristics for this uncertainty to be tolerable. Doorwidths in the mission, for instance, are somewhat ambiguously related to room additions because several alternative routes are possible for any one extension. In practice, however, the options have little effect on the shape of the distributions. The basic characteristics of zone 3 and zones 4 and 5 persist through the alternatives.

The possible alternative associations of dimensions create uncertainty about the formal order in the structure of the mission. As with the pueblo, alternatives are presented and the overall pattern is described using the schematic zones.

In the assessment of regularity, a mean and standard deviation description has been used for convenience and consistency. The distributions cannot be assumed to be "normal" and the description is therefore only a general statement of the order involved.

B. RESULTS

1. Coherence in spatial arrangements

The mission is a remarkable illustration of stability in spatial organization (Figs 31 and 32; Table 3). As it was extended the dimensions used
were kept substantially the same. There is almost no increase in

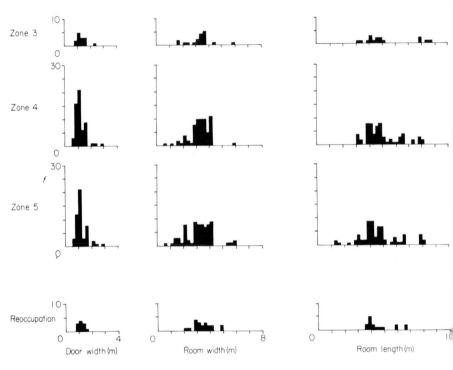

FIG. 31. Distributions of dimensions, Franciscan mission (see Table 3).

variation with increasing length and throughout the development of
the mission this pattern also does not alter. The Friars must have
retained a rigorous control over building operations otherwise the
necessary use of Hopi labour would surely have produced more
irregularity than is in fact observed (Montgomery *et al.*, 1949). Not
only do the dimensions and the variation remain constant but the
distributions are also very similar in shape. The main distributions for
room dimensions have a plateau shape rather than the ideal bell

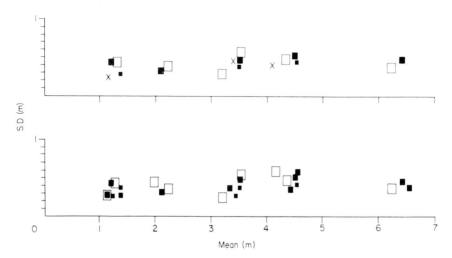

FIG. 32. Development of dimensions, Franciscan mission. ■ = zone 3; ■ = zone 4; □ = zone 5; × = reoccupation (zone values only).

shaped curve. In Franciscan zone 3 the same pattern applies to doorwidths, though for zones 4 and 5 more of a peak appears. With their reoccupation of the early buildings of the mission and the alterations they carried out at that time, the Franciscans returned to the approximate plateau distribution for doorwidths.

The pueblo dimensions (Figs 33 and 34; Table 4) by contrast, show how change occurs in a coherent pattern. Initially, the Hopi room dimensions were seriously affected by the frame they had taken over. Hopi building developments show a trend away from the Franciscan dimensions and towards a new, coherent pattern of their own. From zones 1-3 the lengths of Hopi rooms shift around and away from the Franciscan pattern (Figs 35 and 36). The process begins with two main groups of lengths around 2 and 4 m. In zone 2, a 3 m distribution appears at the same time as the 4 m peak begins to aggregate lengths somewhat above its initial peak. Zone 3 shows the 3 m peak further developed and the shift in the 4 m values continuing. This trend can be understood as a move from the constraint of the numerous lengths around 4 m available in the empty mission, toward a pattern including 3 m and 4 m dimensions that were more tolerable to the Hopi.

TABLE 3. Dimensions for Franciscan zones

	Zone 3			Zone 4			Zone 5			Reoccupation		
	N	M	S.D	N	M	S.D	N	M	S.D	N	M	S.D
Doorwidths	14(15)	1.41	0.29	58	1.21	0.41	50	1.23	0.43	11	1.17	0.25
Room widths	13(18)	3.47	0.36	10(67)	2.10	0.32	12(73)	2.20	0.31	16(20)	3.40	0.39
				54(67)	3.50	0.43	49(73)	3.51	0.44			
Room lengths	10(18)	4.51	0.42	40(63)	4.48	0.47	10(64)	3.18	0.24	12(16)	4.06	0.39
				10(63)	6.42	0.46	35(64)	4.36	0.43			
							10(64)	6.22	0.37			

N = Population used. M = Mean. S.D = Standard deviation. ( ) = Population total.
For the zone descriptions some values are excluded. The lengths for the corridor in the office area, churches II and III, and the "stable" are excluded from the population totals.

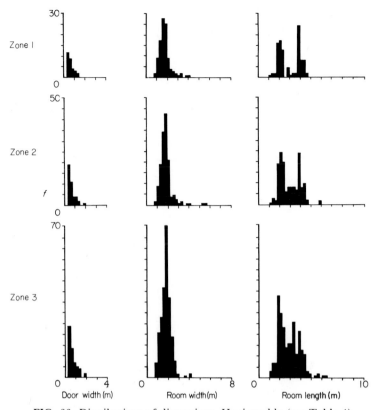

FIG. 33. Distributions of dimensions, Hopi pueblo (see Table 4).

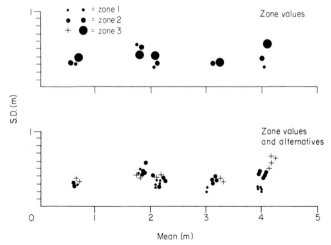

FIG. 34. Development of dimensions, Hopi pueblo.

TABLE 4. Dimension for Hopi zones

	Zone 1			Zone 2			Zone 3		
	N	M	S.D	N	M	S.D	N	M	S.D
Doorwidths	28	0.66	0.32	39	0.63	0.36	54	0.69	0.39
Room widths	102	1.78	0.55	148	1.85	0.51	242	1.82	0.48
Room lengths	53(104)	2.05	0.29	75(152)	2.12	0.32	128(248)	2.10	0.41
	45(104)	4.02	0.26	24(152)	3.16	0.31	57(248)	3.23	0.32
				51(152)	4.02	0.40	63(248)	4.16	0.58

N = Population used. M = Mean. S.D = Standard deviation. ( ) = Population total.
For the zone descriptions some values are excluded.

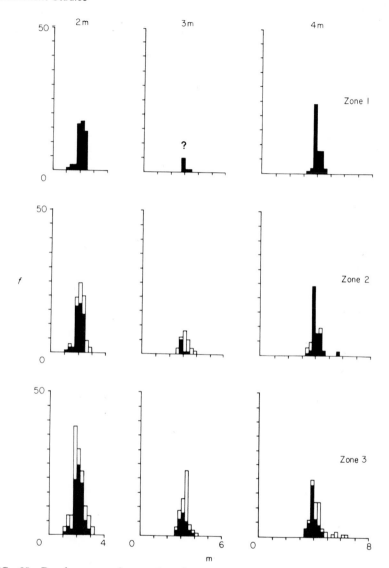

FIG. 35. Development of room lengths, Hopi pueblo (see Table 3). Shaded is dimensions present and unshaded denotes those added.

Note that the 4-5 m lengths are not simply determined by their Franciscan predecessors. Kivas excavated at Awatovi that were used in the period 1600-1630 (Fig. 37; Smith, 1971b) often have widths of 4-5 m so these dimensions were part of the Hopi repertoire even before the friars arrived. The Hopis' continued use of these dimensions is shown

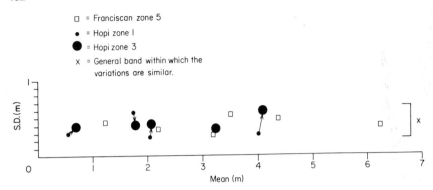

FIG. 36. Comparison of Franciscan and Hopi dimensions.

by their occurrence in the outermost "skin" of Hopi additions on the north facade of the friary; in the cloister on the south facade and in one room abutting the north east corner of the office area. None of these cases are regulated by Franciscan structural constraints and they are all part of apparently late additions. The interesting feature of the Hopi 4 m lengths is the shift in the central tendency of the distribution to make "room" for the 3 m values. The destruction of Awatovi prevents us from knowing whether the shift would have continued any further.

However, the most notable feature is the development of a consistent trend of variation. In zone 1, the trend appears to decline with increasing length.[24] The successive additions produced a steady trend to larger variation for the large dimensions and a "recentering" for the variation of lengths around 2 m (Fig. 34). Both these shifts apply even in the broad description using several alternative sets of dimensions for each zone.

The shapes of the Hopi distributions are all similar and illustrate how two different communities could extract different proportions of dimensions from the same environment. Though the distributions differ in shape, the standard deviations for the Hopi and Franciscan assemblages are quite similar. More elaborate statistical description will ultimately be required if further progress is to be made in the study of settlement dimensions.

2. Alternative use of the same environment

As to be expected, if each human community uses its own spatial model, the two different communities at Awatovi had different

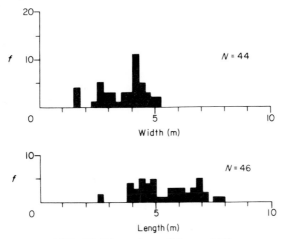

FIG. 37. Dimensions of Awatovi Kivas.

methods of arranging space. They utilized different elements of the environment and different characteristics of the same materials.

There is no dispute that the alternative patterns are integrally connected to the different social practices and intentions of the two communities, but the study of the Konkomba settlement shows that the community's conception of space can itself be regarded as a factor in social behaviour. The order in structures is not merely a derivative of material and social functional requirements but is a variable with its own functional relevance. It is the relationship between this variable and the ecological conditions in which it exists that I shall be assessing. The purpose of the analysis is to link the characteristics of spatial order to the manner in which the attributes of a community become adjusted to their total context.

As is apparent, the Franciscan mission is an extreme example of coherence in formal order. I do not intend to argue that it is typical of the behaviour of human communities. With the variations possible for different settlements, any description of "typical" behaviour would involve a sliding scale of manner of response against degree of variation. But, because of its extreme character, the mission does clearly illustrate locational mechanisms whose less obvious effects in other settlements can then be comprehended.

(*a*) *Facades* (Fig. 38)

The most obvious visual difference between the mission and the pueblo is the dimensions of wall lengths forming the facades of the two

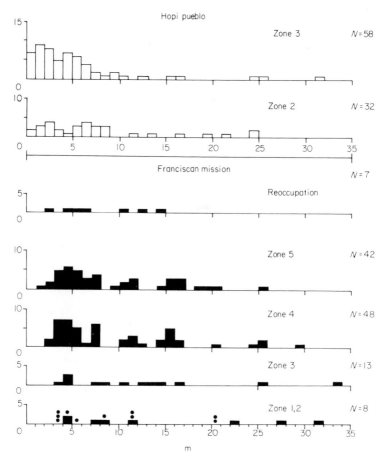

FIG. 38. Facade dimensions. • = church I.

structures. The contrast sharply illustrates the different perceptual tolerances of the Hopi and Franciscans. For the friars, the facade walls displayed several distinct dimensions, but the Hopi pattern contracts the image to a blurred range of dimensions from about 1-10 m in length combined with a few exceptionally long frontages. At most, the pueblo facade was clearly displaying only two dominant dimensions around 1 m or between 5 and 6 m in length. The two distributions markedly overlap. The function of facade dimensions in relation to the onlookers has yet to be clearly understood.

(b) Interior areas (Fig. 39)

Taking the general description of interior spaces, the ratios for the sides of Hopi and Franciscan rooms and open spaces have different and distinct patterns. The majority of the Franciscan enclosed spaces have an almost constant width but with a trend to a slight increase that cumulates against length, reaching its largest expression in the cloister garth and church II. Above the trend is the ratio for the sides of the friary yard and below it the dimensions for the two smallest rooms in the mission.

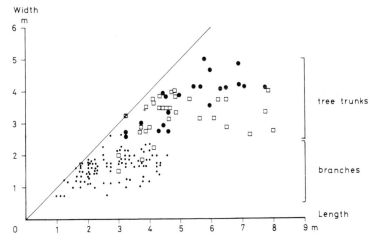

FIG. 39. Ratios of room dimensions. • = Hopi rooms; ● = Awatovi Kivas; □ = Franciscan rooms.

This is contrasted by the trend for the pueblo structures. To identify the trend it has been necessary to include the data on the known kivas of pueblo IV (1300-1630). Combined with the room ratios for the Hopi rearrangement of the mission they form a trend of steadily increasing width as length increases. As room area increases, the ratio of width to length lies in a band just below the line of 1.1 values.

Once again the variation occurring in spatial order is apparent. For both structural patterns, the ratios form a regular band, not a narrowly defined set of values.

(*c*) *Doorwidths* (Figs 31 and 33)

Hopi and Franciscan doors are very different both in shape and width. Moreover, the Hopi made frequent use of roof entries which were rare or completely absent in the mission. Doorways in the pueblo are very narrow, possibly some of the narrowest occurring in any ordinary housing context. A Franciscan wearing his habit would have suffered some inconvenience getting in and out of a Hopi room. The wide doors in the mission are surely complementary to a friar's mode of dress, but there can be no single functional factor determining doorwidths. Many of the Hopi examples are much narrower than any human used doors I ever saw in Ghana, but everyday clothing, especially in the savanna areas of the north, does not have significantly more bulk than known styles of Hopi clothing. Other factors also intrude, like temperature requirements in rooms (see below).

That doorwidths are complementary to a range of functional factors cannot be disputed. One of these factors is the community's need for a coherent visual context. To argue that the material, functional factors determine the dimensions not only ignores the formal evidence, it is also an incomplete functional explanation.

(d) Room dimensions (Figs 31, 33 and 35)

Similar dimensions are used for rooms in the pueblo and the mission, but for different structural purposes and in dissimilar structural systems, using a variety of combinations of adobe and masonry. Most Hopi rooms are about 2 m wide while this width is only rarely used by the Franciscans. Although both use 3 m values in room shape, this is the length for a pueblo room and the width for Franciscan ones. Both have rooms 4 m in length but, as pointed out earlier, the Hopi pattern is not regulated by the frame they took over. One might argue that the 4 m lengths represent control by the natural materials used. This would be immediately acceptable if the wall thicknesses and materials were the same in each case. But the Franciscans built adobe and masonry walls that must have seemed exceptionally thick to the Hopi. The length of a room is specified by no direct structural factor except that extremely long walls will ultimately buckle if there are no buttresses. Since the Hopi and Franciscan walls are of differing construction, can functional studies show that the stable linear dimension for a wall will be constant for both cases?

On width, however, more stringent functional restrictions would be expected, yet most mission rooms are as wide as a pueblo room can be long. The dominant width for a pueblo room is shorter by a metre or more. An extreme formal view could contend that the environment has no controlling effect on building form. This is clearly not the case, however, when we consider the widths of the kivas. Many have widths between 4 and 5 m very like the Franciscan rooms. There is evidence on Hopi building method from a kiva which was buried intact below the altar of church II (Smith, 1971b; Montgomery *et al.,* 1949). From this example it would appear that the 4 m widths were spanned using tree trunks. Then the smaller gaps between these beams and the walls were spanned using branches. The generally available maximum size of timber from tree trunks in the mesa area does therefore restrict the width of normal rooms whether built by Hopis or Franciscans.

Yet even this did not delimit what human beings could do. The Franciscans must have gone to extraordinary efforts in obtaining the roof timbers for church II. They may even have been prepared to go outside the immediate area to get them (Montgomery *et al.,* 1949; Mindeleff, 1891). What the natural resources specify is how much effort must be expended to gain a particular end. The consequences of energy expenditure are defined by the energy relationships for obtaining and utilizing natural resources but, as the Franciscan behaviour illustrates, these conditions do not predefine the specific actions of a community. If the stories are true, the Franciscans demanded too much energy expenditure from the Hopi in order to obtain large roofing timbers. The excess energy output was redressed by the Hopi. They resented the compulsory labour and massacred the Spaniards in part to relieve themselves of the burden. The large timbers were then reused in the pueblos and some may still be supporting roofs that would otherwise have demanded further re- duction in the local timber resources.

3. Visual coherence and environmental conditions

How, therefore, can the overall regulating effect of the environment be integrated with the internal need for visual coherence in settlement form? In the pueblo, ordinary rooms can be both 2 m wide and 2 m long. Some kivas are 4 m wide but others are 4 m long. These repeat occurrences of the same dimensions with no direct functional con- nection are consistent with the idea of a formal order in the structures. But each of these dimensions is also connected to the sizes of available timber, of sufficient strength to hold up a roof. At any one time, the two factors are complementary but cannot be integrated. They are both plainly involved in producing the pattern of dimensions, but without adding in a time factor the juxtaposition must simply be accepted as a description of the situation.

Consider the ecological effects in the external environment, of the two alternative building policies. To build a Franciscan structure it was necessary to cut down entire trees. Only on the relatively infrequent occasions when a large kiva was built did the Hopi have to do the same. In the long term the Hopi style of construction was better adapted to its context since it depended primarily on branches, leaving the partially stripped trees to regenerate the timber supply. This was not so if the Franciscan policy were pursued for long enough. The environment around the mesa (Hack, 1942) therefore contained sufficient alternatives for a potentially maladaptive building policy to start. Neither the size of available timber nor the specific features of any other element of the environment determined the form of the mission, since alternatives were always available. The existence, within the community, of a mechanism making choices from the available options has to be presumed. As the mission shows, however, there can be no assumption that the mechanism always makes the choices in accord with the ecological balance of the environment. If this is so, the mechanism will not lead to a successful utilization of the environment by every community. For ecological reasons, time must be involved in the integration of formal and environmental requirements but cannot be presumed sufficient.

Can, however, a mechanism making choices independent of ecological demand be reconciled with the Hopis' adaptation to their environment? The pueblo indicates that, looking in an area some considerable time after a number of communities have settled in it, settlements will be found whose behavioural patterns are in accord with the ecological conditions (Higgs and Jarman, 1972; Higgs and Vita-Finzi, 1972; Higgs, 1968). It does not specify that any one community, given long enough, will ever become adapted to its environment. Nor is it necessary to claim this in any functional study where the primary concern is those economic policies which, by whatever definition, are successful in an area.

If the mechanism is making independent choices there is either no order in its chosen options or there is an internal criterion of consistency. The coherence of the spatial model used by a community is an obvious candidate. Montgomery points out that the Franciscans must have frozen in their huge rooms during the winter, while all around them the Hopis were warm behind the narrow doors of their houses. The friars had to conform to a rule book which defined the form of the buildings and matched them to rules of social life (Montgomery *et al.*, 1949). It has already been seen that they tolerated very little variation in the dimensions of their structures. The

Franciscan spatial arrangements made it impossible for them to adopt components of the Hopi pattern. Yet they had lived in the area, and probably even at Awatovi, in rooms of the pueblo, for about twenty years before the mission was built (Montgomery *et al.*, 1949). Nor did they apparently adopt the use of coal and persisted in what must have been a wasteful and inadequate burning of timber (Montgomery *et al.*, 1949).[26] It was not the environment but their own criteria which prevented an initial effective adaptation.

For the Hopi, obvious personal experience of building effort and winter conditions were coincident with the need for coherence in their spatial context (Montgomery *et al.*, 1949).[27] But personal experience in itself is an insufficient explanation of their actions at any one time. It cannot equally explain the Franciscans' behaviour, nor can it be considered in isolation from the preceding activities of the Hopi community. The requirement of internal coherence will, however, cover both the Franciscan and Hopi responses since neither adopted any structural feature of consequence from the other.

The Awatovi examples have provided the case of negative choice, where the coherence of spatial order restricted the options, particularly in the Franciscan community. Theoretically, perfect coherence would prevent any choices since no other coherent elements could be added, but the spatial pattern, even for the Franciscans, always includes some variation. Choices that are actually made by a community should, therefore, relate to the variation as a consistent part of the spatial order. It must now be considered whether this mechanism could produce adaptation by operating over long periods of time.

C. CONSEQUENCES

The environment has no immediate determining effect on the building technology or social aims of a community. But in the long term, success or failure will depend upon the coincidence between functional conditions and formal intentions. What a community actually does at any one time is specified by its need for formal regularity. The issue is not what defines the success or failure of the pattern, nor what decides the spatial responses of the community at any one time. Our problem is to decide by what consistent procedure adaptation to the environment can come about, given the two limiting conditions.

Adaptation involves two factors; the capacity to adjust, and the specific policies pursued to obtain resources from the environment.

Contemporary interest in archaeology concentrates on the latter, probably because the process of adjustment has usually been ascribed to sensible and intelligent recognition of necessity. Without such a belief, the choices made by communities would appear to be arbitrary and idiosyncratic, but it is not simply some universal criterion of "least effort" which defines human activity (Zipf, 1965; Berry, 1961; Chorley and Haggett, 1968). The formal and functional regularities within communities have also to be considered. Many of these, as Leach (1973) and Douglas (1972) point out, are inaccessible to the archaeologist because their recognition depends on verbal evidence or direct observation of human behaviour. There is one category of data, the spatial, structural context of human communities, on which there is abundant information in the archaeological record. The use of space is obviously crucial to man's use of the environment; and it has already been shown that spatial arrangements have an internal coherence.

From a description of formal order in settlements and its connection to the use of space between settlements, a consistent procedure should therefore be devised whereby communities adjust or fail to adjust to their spatial environment. The mechanism proposed will depend on two factors; the coherence of the absolute dimensions in the settlement, and the consistent variation for those dimensions.

4. Adaptation and spatial order

The pattern of spatial arrangement discussed in this chapter can be fitted in to a possible adaptive model (Higgs, 1968; Trigger, 1970; Young, 1971; Hamilton, 1967) for the human use of space.

The genetic specification of the nature of reality for man would seem to be a range of signals that the sense organs can receive; some standard way of converting these signals for the brain, and an instruction in the brain that an internally consistent pattern can be produced from the data. The overall adaptive ability of human groups would, therefore, correlate to this model making characteristic, which enables each group to pattern its own consistent responses to the environment. The species as a whole is not limited to any particular environment by a conception of reality appropriate only to a limited range of stimuli (Lettvin *et al.*, 1959; Eibl-Eibesfeld, 1970).

A community's conception of spatial order must be an incomplete reflection of reality. In consequence, the group's behaviour should in part be incompletely correlated with the nature of its environment.

This makes incomplete adaptation a possibility, providing a means for natural selection to act against a group. Yet it also gives latitude for more effective adaptation if the community can tolerate change. The use of models provides advantage in itself, in that a creature or community can respond selectively to those features which are relevant to it. Conversely, the model never guarantees a successful response and may produce behaviour that is potentially maladaptive (Douglas, 1966).[28] Because the description of reality will always be incomplete, many alternative responses to a given reality will be possible, some of which may be more effective than others, as has been seen at Awatovi. In no case will a community ever approach complete adaptation to its context since, to achieve this, it would need to completely perceive reality.

A. VARIABILITY AND ADOPTION OF IDEAS

In consequence, the survival potential of a group must depend on the model's capacity to alter so that it might attain the nearest possible coincidence with circumstances that the group's life style requires. Also, the survival of the group depends upon its capacity to change the model as the situation itself changes. The capacity to change will be regulated by the number of new notions and behavioural patterns a group produces or is offered, but *primarily* by the degree to which a group is willing to adopt new features.

The willingness to adopt is regulated by the nature of the model in use. It can be presumed that a group's model possesses some internal logical coherence (Ashby, 1959) because human groups do not accept all apparently reasonable propositions made to them. A community, therefore, has some internally coherent criteria by which it accepts or rejects options. It cannot be presumed, however, that there is some absolute criterion of sense and efficiency that defines how human groups make choices. If every community views the world in a slightly different way, there can be no standard of response to reality, except in the most basic cases of species and individual survival in stress situations. Furthermore, many communities can make choices which prove to be maladaptive.

If the concepts of each community form a logically coherent set, then adoption of a new feature should depend on logical coincidence between it and the established pattern. The more variability a group will tolerate in its concepts, the more likely it is that a new idea will be acceptable to the group because its chances of being logically coincident or closely related to the established values are much higher. The more options are accepted the more probable it becomes that, by chance or intent, a change of adaptive value will occur. Therefore, toleration of high variability in a group's behaviour should be a factor of high adaptive value (Piggott, 1965; Popper, 1945).

It should be noted that a high survival capacity would correlate to the variability tolerated by the community, not to the variation *produced* by the group. Since behavioural variance can develop in a community and be rejected by it, the degree of variation tolerated by the community must be presumed to have some logical correlation to the concepts in use, otherwise the notion of acceptable variation could not exist independent of the variation actually produced.

B. SOURCES OF VARIATION

One idiosyncratic source of variants in design and behaviour, much beloved by the archaeologist, is of course the observation of attributes used by another human group.

There are also many internal mechanisms which produce variation. For instance, inheritance systems can be seen as creators of variation because they transform the design assemblage of a household after each death (see Deetz, 1967). They alter the context in which children of successive generations grow up by introducing or removing entities. Since structures are also transmitted through successive generations the different procedures used in each society or community should produce differing degrees of change in visual context. Among the Lodagaba, the dual descent system moves the residence unit through the agnatic line and the moveable estate such as cattle and equipment in the uterine line (Goody, 1962). The visual effects of this procedure will be different to a pattern which transmits a structure and its contents together. Frequency of rebuilding will also affect the variability in a settlement since each replication introduces new factors. Demolition of a dead person's hut, for instance, is an editing procedure (Schwerdtfeger, 1971). Addition of the sons' courts onto the father's restricts the choices available to the younger man. The social system of a human group is, therefore, closely connected to the variability which occurs in the structures used by a community.

The model of reality is replicated by transmission to successive generations but in the process it will inevitably be altered by errors in the copying process. If a child learns by indirect example, it will inevitably recognize spurious correlations. Any training that occurs simply by observation of preferred design, such as pot shapes and house forms, must result in a slight alteration in the transmitted model of reality. It is unlikely that parents would be able to create their ideal, especially in house form, due to economic limitations. Children, on the other hand, gaining their conception of space at a very early period from the form of the structures in which they live, would accept the specifics of the house form as normal. The idiosyncrasies of each household will affect the young occupants, so that any individual's notions about reality should differ somewhat from those of contemporaries who grew up in other houses. The children will attain a different concensus of opinion to that held by their parents' generation. Although practical training in youth may reduce the variation between peers and between youth and the older people of the community, it is unlikely to eliminate the effects of early locational experience.

The degree of interaction possible between the units of the group will also regulate the degree to which variability can occur and persist. Dispersed and adjacent house locations should affect the frequency of interaction between persons and so influence the degree to which the behaviour of any household is subject to control by the community.[29]

Individual idiosyncrasies will also be an important factor. Individuals are patently capable of producing designs or behaviour that are totally unacceptable to their community. An individual's acts need not therefore be a direct product of the preferences of the community, and will provide new options that the group may either adopt or reject. The free will of human beings is therefore an adaptive characteristic in the response of communities to their environments.

Discussion

A range of processes can be identified which could produce variations in behaviour and design in a community. These provide a source of potential adaptations to the environment; it should be emphasized that communities will adopt new attributes not necessarily because they correctly discern their adaptive value, but because the new behaviour has consistency with the group's formal and functional patterns and only produces a slight shift in their form. It would be expected that many existing communities are well adapted to their environment since they are the products of long periods of selection (McGregor, 1965), but from this it cannot be concluded that the community is well adapted because of a series of conscious, sensibly made, efficiency based decisions. Any explanations of human adaptive behaviour must also explain human maladaptive responses. It is unnecessary to argue that maladaptive communities are less "intelligent" than successful ones.

Furthermore, many communities cannot explain why they carry out certain acts other than to say "because our ancestors did it like that", or to offer a magical or scientific explanation whose validity has been questioned by concepts more coincident with reality. There can be no assumption that a full understanding of reality was involved in the adoption even if it was in the individual's invention of the pattern that was adopted.

C. VARIATION AND ECONOMIC ACTIVITY

The study of the distributions for the eight settlements in Ghana shows that human communities differ in the amount of variation they produce or tolerate. Communities which operate on a rapidly increasing drop-off rate will tolerate a variation for short distances that is applicable to very much greater dimensions in a community utilizing low variability and a minimal drop-off rate. The low variation community will be imposing group judgement and demanding consistency in dimensions for which other communities will accept considerable variation. Within the limits of a settlement the degree of variation may only have a limited, direct adaptive significance but outside the settlement, adaptation depends on adjustment to the particular characteristics of the environment. A low variation community will be expending effort imposing conformity, while a high variation system can accept individual adjustments and their economic gains without the inevitable variation doing violence to community coherence.

Compared to the domestic scale, the major economic context of human activity involves very large distances. There must be a limit to a community's ability to judge distance with any meaningful accuracy in reference to a tolerated variation. A community might, therefore, believe that the large visible dimensions such as field limits and distances to the next hill do conform to its ideals because it is unable to perceive that they do not. Cross checking to walk rate or other criteria introduces ambiguities and personal variation which would not aid agreement on precision of estimation. It is not surprising, therefore, that most of man's use of his environment in the areas outside settlements can be understood using the thesis of "economic man" (Jarman, 1972; Chisholm, 1962; Baumhoff, 1963). Intense social control within settlement limits is not irreconcilable with economical, effective adjustment to the outside environment.

D. INDETERMINACY, VARIATION AND SOCIAL COHERENCE

The indeterminacy in human locational behaviour is obviously important as a source of changes but it also has a paradoxical role in maintaining stability. One of the sources of indeterminacy are the immediately adjacent yet alternative limits to the edge of an entity such as a doorway. Very large distances also introduce indeterminacy because of the limitations of human distance estimation.

The association of absolute limits, great precision and immense size should therefore have an extraordinary visual effect. An implication of exactness would be combined with the impossibility of ever being sure about the dimensions by visual estimation alone. In itself the effort which has produced accuracy on such a scale is staggering, but it is not the effort alone which affects us. Using precision in very large structures sets up a visual paradox. The human brain cannot judge such distances accurately, yet the limits of the dimensions signal that absolute certainty is available. Structures such as the Valley Temple of Chephren at Giza, the Mausoleum of Lenin in Moscow, and the Zeppelinweise at Nuremburg effectively claim for themselves and their creators that there is a precision and order beyond the judgement of mere mortals. Great monuments act as symbols of community action or concrete expressions of political systems and also display a paradoxical order in which the visual ideals of diverse communities could be subsumed.

E. CONCLUSION

The presence of a model of reality ensures stability for the behaviour of a human group. It maintains the homeostasis of the group and its component individuals, a situation which would not exist if human groups were continuously subject to immediate and direct adjustment to the demands of their environments. It is the variation inherent in the model which specifies the community's potential capacity to adjust to its circumstances. The degree and rate of increase of the variation should define the number of new options a community can adopt. It also introduces an indeterminacy for very large distances which may reduce any deleterious effect that a group's concepts might have on the collection of resources.

Current human adaptation appears to be based more on the community model than on changes in the genetic specification for brain response to spatial data. This would be expected because the concept model, being independent of the biological reproduction rate, can change more rapidly and is more immediately related to the tempo of circumstances.

All these characteristics should contribute to the survival capacity of man, but this hypothesis about human adaptive behaviour does not allow man the freedom he has liked to imagine that his intelligence gives him. Consequently, many human groups must be expected to be unable to adopt new spatial arrangements simply because these are irreconcilable with a community's internally coherent spatial model. The individual is free to adopt anything but may lose the protection of his community if he does so, while any community that tolerates high variation could lose behavioural consistency and become incapable of maintaining itself as a coherent group.[30]

5. Spatial models, adaptation and anthropology: general conclusion

A study of locational organization in small-scale settlements has suggested that human communities use models of space in order to cope with their environment. A partial description of their locational behaviour can be derived from the position and size of entities in the settlement. The procedure used makes it possible to organize large amounts of data and facilitates comparison of widely differing settlement types. An adaptive model of human locational behaviour can be produced into which the characteristics of each community's model could be integrated. Variation acceptable to human groups, the processes which cause the variation, and the associated indeterminacy of judgement appear as a crucial element of adaptive behaviour.

The adaptive model indicates that data from both archaeological sites and occupied settlements are essential to an understanding of settlement dynamics. The archaeology, ethnography and social anthropology of settlements should, therefore, be complimentary, rather than archaeology depending on social studies for methods of reconstructing the past. From the current research, the main issue which arises is the relationship between variation and adaptation in settlement structure. The processes whereby social behaviour produces and regulates variation must be studied in an inhabited settlement. However, it is in archaeological contexts that the relationship between variation and rates of change in locational behaviour can be assessed.

The initial analysis provides some indication of the spatial factors involved and the problems associated with them. The archaeologist should not attempt to seek extreme precision in the locational behaviour of human beings; the description of regularity will always include a statement of indeterminacy. Larger distances are less accurately recognized by an observer than short ones, so criteria of similarity change with the increase in dimensions. Human perception of space is not clear cut, and blurs away with distance.

Standard units of length, though they are essential to construction work in some societies are only a small part of the overall visual regularity produced. Planning as it is known, in the context of large scale technology, can be seen as a specialized and deliberate version of a general characteristic in human locational behaviour.

To understand the shapes created by man, a knowledge of the human eye and brain will surely be essential. It is a surprising paradox that human perceptual inaccuracy at large distances should ultimately appear as an adaptive quality. Because of this paradox, studies of space within and between settlements are complementary. On a short time scale, regularities of structural form within settlements relate to social requirements of formal and functional coherence. The persistence of the community's visual frame through time, depends in the long term on the effectiveness of the community's response to its circumstances.

The degreee of variation tolerable to a community is the link between short term coherence and long term effectiveness. Tolerance of variation regulates adjustment to the environment by defining the number of new options a community can accept while maintaining the coherence of its spatial frame.

Appendix

A. DEFINITIONS AND USAGE

1. Anthropology   The study of man: subsumes archaeology, ethnography and social anthropology.

Archaeology   The study of the material traces left by past human activity.

Ethnography   The study of material forms and their effects in occupied settlements.

Social anthropology   The study of social and conceptual forms currently in use in human communities. (In particular in small-scale settlements.)

N.B. these divisions are made for convenience in this study of small-scale settlements. When dealing with recent material data, there is obviously an overlap of the archaeological and ethnographic fields as defined here. Any association to social anthropology is considered in the text.

2. Evolution and development   The term evolution is to be avoided because of its frequent misuse in anthropology as a synonym for "progress". Development simply refers to successive interrelated changes in the form of residence units and settlements and in the social patterning of their occupants.

   Adaptation   A two part process involving the capacity to adjust to circumstances, and the specific policies used to obtain resources effectively in a given situation.

3. Reality   Reference to the existence of the environment, independent of any mechanism perceiving that environment.

4. Residence unit and household   Distinguish the occupants of a group of closely associated rooms and courtyards from the structures which they occupy.

   Residence unit   A component of a settlement, consisting of rooms and courtyards which are more closely interconnected with each other than with any other equivalent entities.

   Household   The occupants of a residence unit.

5. Settlement and community   Distinguish the occupants of associated residence units from the structures which the people occupy.

   Settlement   The structures occupied by a community.

   Community   The people who occupy a group of structures and identify themselves as a group in reference to those structures.

6. Types of settlement

   Agglomerate settlement   Residence units are contiguous.

   Settlement of adjacent residence units   Gaps between residence units but settlement as a whole is a distinct entity.

   Dispersed settlement   Residence units widely separated. Limit of settlement defined by statement from the members of the community.

B. DATA COLLECTION

1. Field method

The aim of a survey of this nature should be to collect all the relevant data in as short a time as possible, in order to limit any confusion caused by changes in community behaviour over time.

2. Area survey

The survey of the settlement area was carried out by triangulation using a military ranging compass and a steel tape. In this way, all the small structural features, such as timber stands and dumps in the open areas, were related spatially to the main entrances and the limits of each residence unit (Fig. 2). The positions of all the trees within the settlement were also surveyed as well as the boundaries of thick bush and trees which delimit the area frequently used by the community.

The survey within each residence unit was done by eye and the positions of all the objects within the rooms and courts were drawn in (Fig. 3).

3. Measurements

In the Konkomba settlement it was possible to measure every spacing example in each category of available spacings between man-made, similar, linked and structural entities (Fig. 6). Spacings which were specifically not available or un-useable within the terms of the study are mentioned below.

All the measurements are taken in the relevant horizontal plane. For spacings of small entities, this is the separation at ground level. In some cases, such as the interior dimensions of rooms where pots and boxes are piled against the walls, this is impracticable. But in general the measurements need not be more than 50-60 cm above floor level, though in some rooms the pottery may be stacked almost to the ceiling. Collecting interior measurements is a labour intensive, dusty and difficult activity. The separation of some large entities, such as granaries and whole buildings, is defined by roof level points such as the peak of a conical thatch roof. Technically the dimensions should be measured at that level but in practice the point can be projected to ground level and the value can then be measured from a survey plan.

Wherever possible the measurements should either follow a concrete entity such as a wall threshold, or should be the shortest distance between the limits of the space as defined above. The latter condition is set by the judgement of minimal separation that the eye would make in tracing the limits of the distance between two entities.

These characteristics also aid stringent data collection by closely defining the measuring procedure. From the surveys and the detailed measurements, plans of the residence units can be produced and checked against photographs and drawings. Further measurements can then be obtained from the completed survey of the settlement. Some distances such as the dimensions of courtyards and the separation of the residence units are very difficult to collect in the site by direct measurement. The accuracies obtained would not justify the staggering effort. These dimensions were therefore obtained from the survey. Information about the development of the settlement, the kinship link between the members of the community and the use and ownership of the parts of the residence units was also collected to provide a general picture of the human group whose locational behaviour was being studied.

4. Limitations of data collection

The measuring of any distance, whether directly or from a surveyed plan, involves inherent error which must be recognized in the presentation of the data. The class interval used is increased by stages from 20 cm at 4-5 m to 2 m for lengths of 35 m or more. A constant interval has been used in any one category of spacings presentation in Fig. 9.

C. DATA PRESENTATION AND ITS CONSEQUENCES

1. Defining the distributions

The measurements collected are presented as distributions for each set of spacings. Definition of the sets of spacings for similar, linked entities has to be considered with the associated problem of the class interval used to present the distribution. Since human beings behave as if they prefer particular distances for specific purposes, each discrete category of spacing should be characterized by a preponderance of a limited range of distance values producing a predominantly unimodal distribution.

A method must therefore be proposed which can define categories of spacings characterized by unimodal distributions. The simplest procedure is to divide the spacings into gross categories, such as doorwidths and post spacings, and then use one class interval to present each distribution. Any polymodal distributions can be checked for connections between distinguishable modes and any discreet type of spacing within the general category. For instance, the sides of rooms and stands are distinguishable as long and short. This procedure enables us to obtain categories of spacings which are of the same visual status in the settlement since each can be arranged around a predominant length.

There are, however, several categories of spacing which produce a wide scatter of values in a polymodal distribution, but provide no clear basis for separation and cannot be subdivided by reference to any distinguishable feature of the entities concerned. The spacings in the following categories could not, therefore, be used or included in the present form of the study. One exception in the situation is that the class of arc benches can be defined out of the distribution for the lengths of benches.

    End walls of baths (11)   Link walls (16)
    Firescreen walls (15)   Lengths of benches (20)

    Four other categories with small populations of spacings could also not be used but, in these cases, circumstances made it impossible to obtain the necessary measurements.

Not measured, due to difficulty	Reason
Chicken coops in zone II	Occupied
P/S of temporary fencing in baths of II, VII	In ruins, then removed
Graves	Respect
Interior, rectangular building V	Access blocked, then used as yam store

It was found that a 20 cm class interval produced dominantly unimodal distributions each of which corresponds to one category of spacings. Not every population of spacings, however, could be presented in this way. The 20 cm interval is applicable up to and including dimensions in the 4-5 m range but, at this limit, it overlaps with distributions of values derived from survey work. For dimensions up to 5 m this description refers on the whole to behaviour depending on a grain of detail concerned with differences of more than 20 cm between spacings. The character of the distributions for dimensions around 4 m or more, which do not display regularity at the 20 cm interval, is discussed in detail in the analysis of the measurements (see p. 156). Even when a larger class interval is used it can be seen that the spacings for the categories of large dimensions are very scattered and the distributions must be defined in terms of the maximum separations between groups of values.

2. Statistical description and interpretation

The use of statistics has been kept to a minimum in this study to avoid complicating an already unfamiliar case, and to indicate that the methods required for this type of study need not initially be elaborate.

Any study of a small scale settlement is dominated by two stringent conditions. The population sizes needed for statistical manipulation limit the number of examples that can be used, but the logical need for a description that incorporates as many examples as possible must also be satisfied. The more examples that are excluded by statistical criteria of quality, the lower the overall relevance of the description becomes. These two conditions are in part irreconcilable in this case, but the problem is caused by the characteristics of small scale settlements. Even in settlements of 20 residence units or more, numerous distributions occur with populations of less than 10 examples.

A description must be found which can deal with this difficulty. The policy chosen works from an initial assessment using a standard statistical description to decide whether or not order occurs. A further assessment is made using criteria which can include the largest possible number of available examples. The resulting description will then satisfy the two conditions as nearly as possible.

The analysis involves the description of central tendency and variation, but the smallest populations useable in each case are different. An average length can be derived from two values although a useful index of variation cannot. The description of variation that will include the largest number of examples is therefore the determinant of the description of central tendency that should be used.

It is also necessary, when considering the central tendencies alone, to include as many examples as possible. Although the conditions for a description of variation set the type of central tendency that is used, the analysis of the central tendencies cannot be restricted to those examples for which variation statements can be provided. Consistency in procedure and the need for an inclusive description demand that the number of values used in the two analyses will differ.

When describing both the central tendency and the variation for a given distribution, there is no way of knowing the connection to any specific, spatial ideal in the brains of the builders. The study merely has to identify order occurring in any possible statistical description as a partial reflection of whatever order created the structural dimensions. Initially, therefore, the frequently used mean and standard deviation description was used even though the distributions were not "normal". Its value is, however, rather limited by this and by the minimum useable population, which has been set at the low level of 8 or more examples because of the small size of the settlement.

The above description in fact suggested the occurrence of order and a search was then carried out for the statistical description that might best handle the data. This proved to be extremely simple; the median and the central range within which 40% of the values in a distribution would occur.

The median central tendencies are used in this paper because they can be associated with descriptions, like the interquartile range that can be obtained very simply by scrutiny of the values in the distributions. Such a description is also useful for dealing with the large positive skew occurring for the distributions of large dimensions in this settlement. The description reduces the effect of the extreme terminal values. As is shown in the analysis (p. 96), the 40% range proved to be the most applicable. The range values for this percentage occurrence can just be obtained from very small populations of five or more examples. In consequence, some of the median values used in the study of the central tendency separations cannot be used in the correlation of variation with central tendency, because the populations have less than five examples.

Using medians and the 40% range provides a simple basis for analysis which could be carried out during fieldwork, apart from the visual aid provided by the regressions for the various trends, which are most easily obtained using a calculating machine.

Notes

1. The fascination of the books by Hall and Fast is that people have to be told about the spacings and signals they use.
2. As Whorf stated for the terminology of Hopi architecture: "the language [of the Hopi] has no architectural terminology that classifies buildings into types — in spite of the fact that it does have a considerable architectural terminology serving another

purpose . . ." "it is rather queer that there should be no term for such distinctly different shapes of building as, for example, the one-storey building, the two-storey set back building and the kiva; this fact has to be recorded as a peculiar datum of the language not explainable either from other patterns in the language or from anything in the architecture or anything else in the culture." "Many people know that our word kiva is taken from Hopi, but they think that it is the Hopi word for kiva, which it is not."

Whorf's belief in the predominance of language as a definer of thought processes is now generally regarded as an insufficient explanation of cultural variation. Though his linguistics were very good for its time, his correlations to cultural patterns are generally not now accepted. The Hopi problem is of interest because it appears to have defeated Whorf's aim of connecting language and culture.

3. The cattle originally belonged to the first headman who built and occupied residence unit 1. When he died, his brother, who is the present headman, inherited the cattle.

4. In my rapid estimation of the population, I regarded all people beyond puberty as adult. The number exercising direct control over economic resources is, obviously, rather less than the estimate. There were also about 30 visibly young children in the settlement.

5. The spacings used from the settlements in Ghana, with the exception of the Konkomba case, were all directly measured by hand in the settlement. The dimensions of some larger structural units could be obtained because the stands and some residence huts have a primary structure composed of timber uprights with easily measurable spacings between them, especially in the Ewe settlement.

No sampling procedure was used to select the categories of spacings. I measured all the available types of spacings that it was practical for me to collect during my fieldwork. There was a general tendency therefore, for bench dimensions, doorwidths and post spacings to be measured.

6. If in general, the trend of variation becomes steeper as settlement size increases then a state should ultimately be reached where the settlement structure lacks visual coherence. Communities might be expected to limit their settlement size by population dispersal or else by attempting to restrict the variation. If part of a community shifts to a new site, when the variation becomes intolerable, the visual frame of the settlement would be acting as a social mechanism regulating population density in a given area. To retain high population density, communities might either tolerate high variation or internally subdivide their settlements to produce local "quarters" each with its own visual coherence.

Human population dispersal; the possibilities of overexploitation; and the development of new economies might therefore be connected to the variation tolerated by communities. The topic cannot be pursued further in this paper. See in context of: V. C. Wynne-Edwards, 1962, *Animal Dispersion in Relation to Social Behaviour*.

7. There is a high standard deviation of 1.41 m at 8.46 m for the exterior lengths of rectangular buildings. But an alternative splitting of the values can produce a low standard deviation of 0.52 at 8.99 metres.

8. Medians are used because they can be derived from very small populations of examples *and* can be connected to a simple description of variation like the interquartile range.

For some of the distributions around the 4 m and 7 m lengths there are two possible medians depending on a "lumping" (set 1) or a splitting (set 2) treatment of the dimensions (see also note 11 on 40% range). The dimensions can either be treated as one population or be divided using the largest differences between adjacent values as the splitting points.

The set 1 and 2 values for the dimensions of residence units (28) (29) result from the alternative descriptions of residence unit VI. Because the courtyard area is coincident with the straight wall limits of the residence unit, either a radial or direct linear description could be used. The radial values for all the residence units other than I are defined as set 1. In the set 2 description, the linear values for VI are substituted. Coherent classification is treated as the equivalent of "lumping"; divergent classification as the equivalent of "splitting".

In both the sets 1 and 2 descriptions, the only possible values for residence unit 1 are the exterior linear dimensions. No other procedure can be justified, even though the radial values would be near the 7-8 m lengths occurring in other residence units. (Note: in Fig. 9 (28) (29) the set 1 values are used.)

9. When the range between the maximum and minimum medians in each cluster is correlated with the median average for each cluster, correlation coefficients in excess of 0.185 are obtained for all descriptions. (See Relationship between Clusters.) Note anomaly for the 8.80 m median cluster (Fig. 22a).

10. The principle used is as follows: if the smaller separations are correlated to the central tendencies then the more descriptions of this relationship that are available the better the correlations should be, given the increase in degrees of freedom as population size of examples increases. The declining significance for the correlation is contrary therefore to expectation. This would suggest a very poor correlation between these separations and the values for the central tendencies.

11. 40% range.

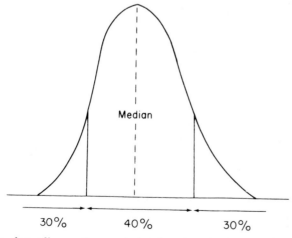

| 30% | 40% | 30% |

In some cases, depending on the population size, the value used to describe the range in which 40% of the population occurs must be an average of two possible nearest descriptions. "Lumping" and "splitting" of the blocks of values around 4 and 7 m produces two alternative descriptions of variation which are connected to the two sets of medians mentioned above.

12. The upper trend of variation is not an artifact of data collection procedure. The exterior widths of rectangular buildings (23) and the distances between centres of round huts (22) had to be obtained by survey but have 40% range values in the lower trend. All the other upper trend values are from surveyed dimensions, but the exterior lengths of rectangular buildings (26) produce two alternative values from "lumping" (set 1) and splitting (set 2) which are respectively in the upper and lower trends.

13. As can be seen from Fig. 20a, the set 1,2 values for exterior length of rectangular buildings (26) and radial widths of residence units (28), can in each case be allocated to the upper and lower trends of variation. This circumstance defines the use of the set values in describing the spatial model. The above mentioned set 2 values combined with the other lower trend values provide a maximum population for describing the lower trend of variation. Set 2 medians must therefore be used in any comparison between separations and variation in relation to the lower trend alone. Conversely the set 1 medians must be used in relation to the upper trend of variation. In the combined description the set 1 values are used because the set 2 variation for (26) is an extreme anomaly in terms of an overall trend.

14. The radial values around 9 m refer to the headman's court (see Fig. 3) and to residence unit VII. The length and width values around 14 m are the linear distances for the limits of residence unit I.

15. Because I lived in the settlement, I was able to make continuous note of seating places though no statistical comparison of frequency at each site is possible. In addition two hour sessions were spent in the middle of the day and on most evenings making detailed observations of route activity in and around the residence units.

16. Description of a Fibonacci series.

Where F_n = any series number.

$$F_{n+1} = F_n + F_{n-1}$$

For instance:

$F_1, F_2, F_3, F_4, F_5, F_6, F_7, \ldots$
1, 1, 2, 3, 5, 8, 13, ...

17. The construction of a residence unit depends upon co-operation between kin, and the provision of food and drink by the owner for those who come to help.

18. Though human perceptual accuracy declines with increasing distance to be estimated there can be substantial personal variation.

The military sniper for instance is trained to, or possesses, visual precision for great distances. To what degree the visual acuity needed in hunting might produce a spatial order different to the pattern described will be an interesting topic to pursue.

19. "Arabs . . . . are, however, apt to take offense when Americans use what to them are ambiguous distances, such as the four- to seven-foot social consultative distance."

20. There is no way at present of assessing the time lag between these construction periods. Whether it was a week or a year, the break is still a chronological divide if one is needed.

21. R. G. Montgomery, p. 227 and general discussion of wall X. There seems little doubt that church III was built in 1700. If so then the Hopi additions must represent a brief flurry of building that was abruptly ended by the final massacre.

22. The test excavation carried out in the office area revealed no Hopi walling. Also, the east wall of 417 was partially reconstructed, probably post-rebellion. This would suggest that there was no Hopi occupation of this area and that it had in part fallen into ruins by 1700.

23. There is an indication that the people of Awatovi may have repaired the offices before the Franciscans came back into residence. This would leave more time for the building of church III in the brief re-occupation. Note the complication that Awatovi submitted to Crown authority in 1692. The church was reconsecrated.

24. The east wing of the friary might not have been part of the initial occupation by the Hopi if they did begin at the west end of the mission. But for consistency in procedure the east wing alterations must be put in zone 1. In part they account for the anomalous decline in the variation with increasing length.

25. Note that from 1680 to 1692 there was an undisturbed period for the Hopi at Awatovi. Even after the Spanish temporary return in 1692 there were another eight years of life left to the community.

26. See Montgomery *et al.*, 1949; p. 76. Wood ash in Franciscan fireplaces; p. 52. Coal seam at foot of mesa; p. 88. Coal fragments in adobe bricks; p. 166. Charcoal for cooking. Montgomery is not sure whether coal was used. But see p. 76 and above for transportation of firewood.

27. See Montgomery *et al.*, 1949; pp. 22, 48. Cold as the criterion; pp. 79, 80. Hopi notions of privacy and comfort as further criteria.

28. Note the dangerous consequences of some illusions causing miscalculation of height or distance.

And M. Douglas, 1966; p. 179: "Not only was her menstruation certain to wreck any enterprise in the forest that she might undertake, but it was thought to produce unfavourable conditions for men. Hunting would be difficult for a long time after, and rituals based on forest plants would have no efficacy (they believed: my comment). Women found these rules extremely irksome, specially as they were regularly short handed and late in their planting, weeding, harvesting and fishing". Note: the rituals may have prevented over-exploitation of resources and may persist for that reason. What the examples do show is that formal rules could cause labour shortages deleterious to the community. It is clear that the women do *not* obey the rituals because they perceive any adaptive value in them!

29. If the personnel of a dispersed settlement are to obtain the same frequency of interaction between members of different households as the people who occupy a settlement of adjacent residence units, they will have to expend relatively more effort.

30. For instance, a Vagala settlement in Ghana consists of flat roofed residence units, which are aggregated so that large residential sections are formed. It is possible to walk across the roof of each section. These huge areas are used as routes, for immediate access and as resting places.

Because of their structural form, they cannot incorporate zinc-roofed buildings without drastically altering the use of space and the location of personnel. Individuals could, of course, leave and build their own residence units in the nearby town. Many members of the community could therefore survive a radical alteration of that particular structural, social and political pattern even if the settlement and its community as a whole does not thrive.

Bibliography

Abrahams, R. G. (1967). *The Political Organization of the Unyamwezi.* Cambridge University Press, Cambridge.

Andersen, K. M. (1969). Ethnographic analogy and archaeological interpretation. *Science,* 163, 133-138. New York.

Ardener, E. (1971). The new anthropology and its critics. *Man* (New Series), 6, no. 3, 449-467.

Ashby, W. R. (1959). *Design for a Brain* (2nd edn). Chapman Hall, London.

Badawy, A. (1965). *Ancient Egyptian Architectural Design: A Study of the Harmonic System.* Near Eastern Studies, 4, Berkeley, University of California Publ., 1965.

Baddeley, A. D. (1971). Human memory. In *New Horizons in Psychology,* 2, (P. C. Dodwell, Ed.). Harmondsworth, Penguin Books.

Bateson, G. (1973). *Steps to an Ecology of Mind.* Paladin edn, 1973.

Baumhoff, M. A. (1963). Ecological determinants of Aboriginal California populations. *Publs in American Archaeology and Ethnology,* 49, No. 2, Berkeley, University of California, 1963.

Berry, B. J. L. (1961). City size distribution and economic development. *Economic and Cultural Change,* 9, 573-587.

Bingham, H. (1930). *Machu Picchu: A Citadel of the Incas.* Yale University Press, New Haven.

Bloch, M. (1971). *Placing the Dead; Tombs, Ancestral Villages and Kinship Organization in Madagascar.* Studies in Anthropology. Academic Press, London and New York.

Bondi, H. (1967). *Assumption and Myth in Physical Theory.* Cambridge University Press, Cambridge.

Boudon, . (1968). *The Uses of Structuralism.* Heinemann Educ. Books, London.

Briggs, D. and Walters, S. M. (1969). *Plant Variation and Evolution.* World University Library, Weidenfeld and Nicolson, London.

Bruyère, B. (1939). Rapport sur les Fouilles de Deir el Médineh (1934-35) Troisième partie. *Fouille de l'Institut Française du Caire,* XVI.

Casson, S. (1939). *The Discovery of Man.* Hamish Hamilton, London.

Chisholm, M. (1962). *Rural Settlement and Land Use: An Essay in Location.* Hutchinson, London.

Chorley, R. J. and Haggett, P. (1967). *Socio-Economic Models in Geography.* Methuen, London.

Clarke, D. L. (1968). *Analytical Archaeology.* Methuen, London.

Clarke, D. L. (1972). A provisional model of an Iron Age society and its settlement. In *Models in Archaeology* (D. L. Clarke, Ed.), pp. 801-869. Methuen, London.

Clarke, D. L. (1973). Archaeology; the loss of innocence. *Antiquity,* XLVII, 6-18.

Cunningham, C. E. (1964). Order in the Atoni house. *Bijdragen Tot de Taal- land-en Volkenkunde, Deel 120,* S'Gravenhage.

David, N. (1971). The Fulani compound and the archaeologist. *World Archaeology,* 3, No. 2.

Deetz, J. (1967). *Invitation to Archaeology.* Natural History Press, Double Day, New York.

Dickson, K. B. (1969). *A Historical Geography of Ghana.* Cambridge University Press, Cambridge.

Douglas, M. (1957). Animals in Lele religious symbolism. *Africa,* **XXVII,** 46-57.

Douglas, M. (1963). *The Lele of Kasai.* Oxford University Press, London.

Douglas, M. (1966). *Purity and Danger.* Routledge and Kegan Paul, London.

Douglas, M. (1972). Symbolic orders in the use of domestic space. In *Man, Settlement and Urbanism* (P. Ucko, R. Tringham and G. W. Dimbleby, Eds). Duckworth, London.

Douglas, M. (1973). *Rules and Meanings: The Anthropology of Everyday Knowledge; Selected Readings.* Penguin Modern Sociology Readings, Penguin Books, Harmondsworth.

Edwards, I. E. S. (1967). *The Pyramids of Egypt.* Pelican, London.

Eibl-Eibesfeld, I. (1970). *Ethology; The Biology of Behavior.* Holt Rinehart and Winston, New York.

Eliade, M. (1954). *The Myth of the Eternal Return.* Routledge and Kegan Paul, London.

Eliot, T. S. (1930). Ash Wednesday. In *Collected Poems 1909-1962.* Faber and Faber, London and Harcourt Brace Jovanovich, New York.

Fast, J. (1970). *Body Language.* Pan Books, London.

Fewkes, J. W. (1898). Archaeological expedition to Arizona in 1895. *17th Annual Report of the Bureau of American Ethnology,* Part II, Washington, D.C.

Forde, D. (1934). *Habitat, Economy and Society.* Methuen, London.

Forde, D. (1970). Ecology and social structure. *Proceedings of the Royal Anthropological Institute, London, 1970.*

Forge, A. (1970). Learning to see in New Guinea. In *Socialization: The Approach from Social Anthropology* (P. Mayer, Ed.), A.S.A. Monograph 8. Tavistock, London.

Fortes, M. (1945). *The Dynamics of Clanship among the Tallensi: Being the First Part of an Analysis of the Social Structure of a Trans-Volta Tribe.* Oxford University Press, London.

Fortes, M. (1949). *The Web of Kinship among the Tallensi: Being the Second Part of an Analysis of the Social Structure of a Trans-Volta Tribe.* Oxford University Press, London.

Fraser. D. (1968). *Village Planning in the Primitive World.* Planning and Cities Series, Braziller, New York.

Freeman, L. G. (1968). A theoretical framework for interpreting archaeological material. In *Man the Hunter* (R. B. Lee and I. de Vore, Eds). Aldine, Chicago.

Gardner, M. (1969). Mathematical Games. *Scientific American,* **236,** 121-126.

Gil, B., Aryee, A. F. and Ghansh, D. K. (1964). 1960 Population Census of Ghana; Special Report: Tribes of Ghana. (Accra, 1964).

Gluckman, M. (1963). Gossip and scandal. *Current Anthropology,* **4,** 307-316.

Goffman, E. (1969). *Behavior in Public Places: Notes on the Social Organization of Gatherings.* Free Press, New York.

Goffman, E. (1972). *Interaction Ritual.* Allen Lane, London.

Goody, E. N. (1973). *Contexts of Kinship: An Essay in the Family Sociology of the Gonja of Northern Ghana.* Cambridge Studies in Social Anthropology, Cambridge University Press, Cambridge.

Goody, J. R. (1956). _The Social Organization of the Lowilli._ Colonial Research Studies, 19. H.M.S.O., London.

Goody, J. R. (1962). _Death, Property and the Ancestors: A Study of the Mortuary Customs of the Lodagaa of West Africa._ Stanford University Press,

Gould, P. R. (1963). Man against his environment: a game theoretic framework. _Annals of the Association of American Geographers,_ **53,** 290-297.

Graham, J. W. (1960). The Minoan unit of length and Minoan palace planning. _American Journal of Archaeology,_ **64,** Baltimore.

Graham, J. W. (1962). _The Palaces of Crete._ Princeton University Press, Princeton.

Graham, J. W. (1968). The Cretan palace: Sixty-seven years of exploration. In _A Land Called Crete_ (N. S. Hoyt, Ed.). Smith College Studies in History, XLV, Northampton, Mass.

Gregory, R. L. (1966). _Eye and Brain._ (World University Library), Weidenfeld and Nicolson, London.

Griaule, M. (1965). _Conversations with Ogotemmêli: An Introduction to Dogon Religious Ideas._ Oxford University Press, London.

Hack, J. T. (1942). The changing physical environment of the Hopi Indians of Arizona. _Papers of the Peabody Museum,_ **XXXV,** No. 1, Cambridge, Mass.

Hall, E. T. (1966). _The Hidden Dimension: Man's Use of Space in Public and Private._ Bodley Head, London.

Hamilton, T. H. (1967). _Process and Patterns in Evolution._ Concepts of Current Biology Series, Collier Macmillan, London.

Harris, M. (1969). _The Rise of Anthropological Theory; A History of Theories of Culture._ Routledge and Kegan Paul, London.

Harvey, D. (1969). _Explanation in Geography._ Edward Arnold, London.

Hawkes, J. (1968). The proper study of mankind. _Antiquity,_ **XLII,** 255-262.

Higgs, E. S. (1968). Archaeology, where now? _Mankind,_ **6,** 12, 617-620.

Higgs, E. S. and Jarman, M. R. (1972). The origins of animal and plant husbandry. In _Papers in Economic Prehistory_ (E. S. Higgs, Ed.). Cambridge University Press, Cambridge.

Higgs, E. S. and Vita-Finzi, C. (1972). Prehistoric economies: a territorial approach. In _Papers in Economic Prehistory_ (E. S. Higgs, Ed.). Cambridge University Press, Cambridge.

Hole, F. (1973). Questions of theory in the explanation of culture change in prehistory. In _The Explanation of Culture Change: Models in Prehistory_ (C. Renfrew, Ed.). Duckworth, London.

Isaac, G. L. (1971). Whither archaeology? _Antiquity,_ **XLV,** 123-129.

Jarman, M. R. (1972). A Territorial Model for Archaeology: a behavioural and geographical approach. In _Models in Archaeology_ (D. L. Clarke, Ed.). Methuen, London.

Kinzel, A. F. (1959). Towards an understanding of violence. _Attitude,_ **1,** no. 1.

Klein, R. G. (1969). _Man and Culture in the Late Pleistocene._ Chandler Publs in Anthropology and Sociology, Chandler, San Francisco.

Leach, E. R. (1966). Anthropological aspects of language: animal categories and verbal abuse. In _New Directions in the Study of Language_ (E. J. Lennenberg, Ed.). M.I.T. Press, London.

Leach, E. R. (1967). *The Structural Study of Myth and Totemism.* A.S.A. Monograph 5, Tavistock, London.

Leach, E. R. (1973). Concluding address. In *The Explanation of Culture Change: Models in Prehistory* (C. Renfrew, Ed.). Duckworth, London.

Lebeuf, J. P. (1962). *L'habitation des Fali.* Hachette, Paris.

Le Corbusier (1959). *The Modulor.* London.

Lettvin, J. Y., Maturana, M. R., McCulloch, W. S. and Pitts, W. M. (1959). What the frog's eye tells the frog's brain. *Proceedings of the Institute of Radio Engineers,* **47,** 1940-1951.

Lévi Strauss, C. (1963a). *Structural Anthropology.* Penguin Books, Harmondsworth.

Lévi Strauss, C. (1963b). *Totemism.* Beacon Press, Boston.

Lévi Strauss, C. (1966). *The Savage Mind* (Nature of Human Societies Series). Weidenfeld and Nicolson, London.

McGregor, J. C. (1965). *Southwestern Archaeology.* University of Illinois Press, Urbana.

Mindeleff, V. (1891). A study of Pueblo architecture: Tusayan and Cibola. *8th Annual Report of the Bureau of American Ethnology,* 1886-87, Washington, D.C.

Moholy-Nagy, S. (1968). *Matrix of Man: Illustrated History of Urban Development.* Pall Mall Press, London.

Montgomery, R. G., Smith, W. and Brew, J. O. (1949). Franciscan Awatovi. *Papers of the Peabody Museum,* **XXXVI,** Cambridge, Mass.

Neustupný, E. (1971). Whither archaeology? *Antiquity,* **XLV,** 34-39.

Piaget, J. (1971). *Structuralism.* Routledge and Kegan Paul, London.

Piggott, S. (1965). *Ancient Europe: From the Beginnings of Agriculture to Classical Antiquity.* Edinburgh University Press, Edinburgh.

Pochan, A. (1933). Metrologie des anciens Egyptiens. *Bulletin de l'Institut d'Egypte, XV Session,* Le Caire, 1932-33.

Popper, K. (1945). *The Open Society and its Enemies.* Routledge, Kegan Paul, London.

Previosi, D. A. (1967). Minoan palace planning and its origins. *Summary in American Journal of Archaeology,* **71.**

Previosi, D. A. (1970). Project on architectural and settlement analysis. *Labrys,* **1,** no. 1.

Prussin, L. (1969). *Architecture in Ghana: A Study of Forms and Functions.* University of California Press, London.

Rapoport, A. (1969). *House Form and Culture.* Prentice Hall, Hemel Hempstead.

Schmidt, R. R. (1930). *Jungsteinzeit-Seidlungen in Federseemoor.* Dr. Benno Filser Verlag, Augsburg.

Schwerdtfeger, F. W. (1971). Housing in Zaria. In *Shelter in Africa* (P. Oliver, Ed.). Barrie and Jenkins, London.

Smith, W. (1971a). Painted ceramics of the Western Mound of Awatovi. *Papers of the Peabody Museum,* **XXXVIII,** Cambridge, Mass.

Smith, W. (1971b). Prehistoric kivas of Antelope Mesa. *Papers of the Peabody Museum,* **XXXIX,** no. 1. Cambridge, Mass.

Sommer, R. (1969). *Personal Space: Behavioural Basis of Design.* Spectrum Books, Prentice Hall, Hemel Hempstead.

Srejović, D. (1972). *Europe's First Monumental Sculpture: New Discoveries at Lepenski Vir.* New Aspects of Antiquity Series, Thames and Hudson, London.

Stanislavski, M. B. (1973). Review of W. A. Longacre: Archaeology as anthropology: a case study. *American Antiquity,* **38,** no. 1, 117-122.

Stauder, J. (1971). *The Majangir; Ecology and Society of a South west Ethiopian People.* Studies in Social Anthropology, Cambridge University Press, Cambridge.

Tait, D. (1961). *The Konkomba of Northern Ghana.* International African Institute Series, Oxford University Press, London.

Tambiah, S. J. (1969). Animals are good to think and good to prohibit. *Ethnology,* **8,** pt 4.

Thom, A. (1967). *Megalithic Sites in Britain.* Clarendon Press, Oxford.

Trigger, B. G. (1970). Aims in prehistoric archaeology. *Antiquity,* **XLIV,** 26-37.

Ucko, P., Tringham, R. and Dimbleby, G. W. (1972) (Eds). *Man, Settlement and Urbanism.* Duckworth, London.

Vernon, M. D. (1962). *The Psychology of Perception.* University of London Press, London.

Watson, O. M. (1969). Symbolic and expressive use of space: an introduction to proxemic behaviour. *Current Topics in Anthropology,* **4.**

Watson, R. A. (1972). The "new archaeology" of the 1960's. *Antiquity,* **XLVI,** 210-215.

Whorf, B. L. (1953). Linguistic factors in the terminology of Hopi architecture. In *Language, Thought and Reality; Selected Writings of Benjamin Lee Whorf* (J. E. Carrol, Ed.). Wiley Interscience, New York.

Wooldridge, D. E. (1963). *The Machinery of the Brain.* McGraw Hill, Maidenhead.

Wynne-Edwards, V. C. (1962). *Animal Dispersion in Relation to Social Behavior.* Hafner, New York.

Young, J. Z. (1964). *A Model of the Brain.* Oxford University Press, London.

Young, J. Z. (1971). *An Introduction to the Study of the Brain.* Clarendon Press, Oxford.

Zipf, G. K. (1965). *Human Behaviour and the Principle of Least Effort.* Hafner, N.Y.

Acknowledgements

My especial thanks go to Merride Posnansky and the staff of the Archaeology Department, University of Ghana. To Munyimba and his people, I am grateful for the tolerance and kindness that made this study possible. My thanks go to Augustine for his help. Shiona Archibald gave me more help than I had really the right to receive. I am indebted to Mrs. P. M. E. Altham of the Statistical Laboratory in Cambridge for advice on statistical issues. I have received much help and advice; whatever this study lacks is my responsibility.

4

Space and Energy: A Method for Analysing Habitat Value and Utilization in Relation to Archaeological Sites

ROBERT FOLEY

National Museum,
Nairobi, Kenya

1. Introduction

The development of site catchment analysis by Vita-Finzi and Higgs (1970) and the various applications by archaeologists interested in the economic aspects of prehistory (see Higgs, 1972, 1975 for various papers) have strongly influenced the analysis of archaeological sites in relation to their spatial environments. Using a small number of ethnographic and theoretical studies as a base (Lee, 1968; Chisholm, 1962), the suggestion was made that resource usage was distance dependent, and consequently it was postulated that for any site the resources that were utilized habitually, as the main part of the subsistence activities, lay within a set distance of the settlement— 10 km for hunter-gatherers and 5 km for agriculturalists. These distances equate with optimal two hour and one hour walking radii from the site. Essentially the site catchment is circular, although variations in terrain will produce distortion. Within this circular area habitat types, the location of water resources, topographic, geomorphic and land-form features are noted, and from this estimation potential economies of the site are assessed; given certain assumptions of stability.

On a more technical level, the analysis is usually carried out in terms of four radii from the site, to either the one hour or two hour circumference. During any such analysis it is necessary to assess the probable changes that have occurred in terms of ecology and land-use during the period since the site was occupied. For precise details of the methodology Higgs (1975: Appendix A) is the most succinct description, suggesting a generally applicable procedure to enhance comparative studies. Site catchment analysis is not the first attempt by prehistorians to assess the ecological context of a site, and its locational determinants; most archaeologists have given at least sketchy and qualitative environmental descriptions, and others have used relatively detailed descriptions in relation to the organic remains found on the site and the proposed land and resource use (Byers, 1967). However catchment analysis represents the most explicit formulation of such an approach as a generally applicable system, essential to all archaeological work. The stimulus that it has given to British archaeologists to examine more closely the environmental aspects of the site has resulted in a more realistic assessment of the life of prehistoric man. As a technique, though, it has many drawbacks that may lead to a misunderstanding and misinterpretation of human palaeoecology.

The most crucial criticism that can be made is that despite its technical sounding terminology it is not really an analysis of the value of an area for human use, any more than some of the earlier descriptions. All that occurs is a qualitative description of arbitrary habitat *types* that are available around the site. These habitats are then correlated with particular economic forms. This is by no means the same as measuring the *extractive value* of the habitats, even less so the extractive value in relation to the site or a particular technological system. When dealing with any form of energy expenditure and utilization, we are concerned with primary and secondary production in relation to the extractive efficiency of the exploiting organism or population at whatever trophic level it may occur. For catchment analysis this is not attempted beyond the assumption of, on the one hand the one/two hour distance thresholds, and on the other the correlation between major soil and vegetation types with gross economic forms. Thus site catchment analysis does not make use of the concept of an energy balance that is fundamental to any analysis of energy exchange systems.

As an initial formulation, the system that needs to be analysed may be defined as: $E = e_1 - e_2$, where E equals the energy balance that is the measure of whether a system is working efficiently; e_1 equals the total energy extracted from the environment and e_2 equals the amount of energy expended in the process. In point of fact, this formulation is likely to be of only limited use, and more informative mathematical formulations need to be made. Lawton (1973) has made some attempt to assess this value through the formulation:

$$\frac{\text{Food energy gathered or consumed}}{\text{Energy expended during its collection}}.$$

On the assumption that 50% of what is gathered or consumed is actually absorbed by the body either as energy or body tissue then the value of this index in an efficient system must be greater than or equal to two. Lawton has computed this value for a series of animals — hummingbirds, a finch, a bumblebee, a freshwater damsfly and a freshwater bass. The range of these are shown in Fig. 1, plus the extractive efficiency of a human group on a coral atoll. As can be seen all the values are greater than two, with the exception of the lower range of the bumblebee. It would seem to be important to determine

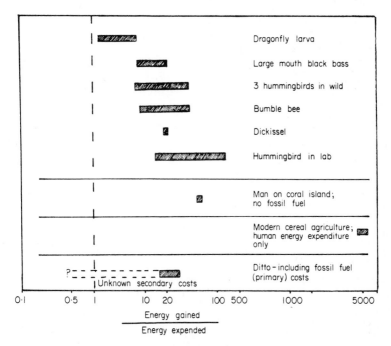

FIG. 1. Energy gained in relation to energy expended in food gathering for various species including man. (Note: scale is logarithmic.) (After Lawton 1973.)

whether there is some value greater than two, beyond which efficient systems dare not fall. The point of this discussion is to show the sort of ecological information we wish to derive from archaeological data to elucidate human palaeoecology. Attempts at analysing the environmental context of archaeological sites represent an attempt to discover the spatial configuration of a human group's method of coping with the energy balance. The aim of this paper is to set up a methodology whereby it will be possible to model and describe the spatial nature and levels of human resource usage in prehistory.

Prior to outlining the methodology, it will be useful to follow up the discussion on the relationship between energy consumed and expended, by looking at some other energy relationships of potential interest. Very little work has been put into the question of energy ratios in human subsistence systems, especially in an archaeological context (except Clarke, 1976).

Human palaeoecology is concerned with the use of energy by human groups. In particular, a major aspect of the work should concern the relationship between energy utilization and the total energetics of an area. In crude terms, it is possible to use a small number of formulations to define the important variables.

1. The total amount of energy in the system (AE); in practical terms, the amount of primary production.
2. The breakdown of this total energy into its various components as they affect human units, e.g. edibility/non-edibility; animal/plant; species composition ($c_1, c_2 \ldots \ldots c_n$).
3. The amount of energy that may be extracted without damage to the source populations; this is a quantity defined in relation to the structure and population dynamics of the components (SE).
4. The amount of energy that is necessary for supporting an individual or population, usually human. Sometimes it may be necessary to define this for animal populations (E). This value will be a function of metabolic rate.
5. The amount of energy that it is physiologically or technologically possible to expend in a unit of time. This quantity will help define the potential of a system (EU).
6. The amount of energy extracted from the environment in a unit of time (EE).
7. The amount of energy expended in extracting the energy (EX).

All the quantities outlined and defined above refer to quantities of energy; it is important to remember that these relate to populations of various species, and a knowledge of some of the populations' attributes is essential. A subset variable that ought perhaps be considered is the absolute minimum of energy required to physiologically support a human population, in contrast to the amount necessary to maintain a fully functioning society. This might produce some interesting insights into the type of situation described by Turnbull (1973) for the *Ik*, as opposed to more stable situations.

The inter-relationships of these variables are of ecological interest. We are concerned with the values they attain in situations of ecological stability, to understand how human systems use energy. It is tentatively possible to hypothesize some of these values for stability.

$\dfrac{AE}{EE} > 1$: what percentage of the available energy is utilized? In all working situations this must be considerably greater than 1, as EE is always likely to be negligible in relation to AE. Phillipson (1973) has produced a model for two natural systems that suggest the order of this ratio for various trophic levels.

$\dfrac{SE}{EE} > 1$: how stable is the situation? This index should show if the system is likely to work in the long term.

$\dfrac{EE}{E} > 1$: this is a crucial test of ecological success. In a situation where EE is vastly greater than E, then a surplus will occur, with various concomitants.

$\dfrac{EE}{EU} > 1$: if this value drops below one then the system will not have the capacity to expand without changing technology or physiology, or discovering new resources.

$\dfrac{EE}{EX} > 1$: this is the efficiency index described by Lawton (1973).

$AE > SE$: this is the index of the potential for maximum stable exploitation, and productivity may be measured by how close SE may be brought to AE.

$AE > E$: AE will always be considerably greater than E, but it is interesting to speculate on how much. The same is true for AE and EU.

$\dfrac{EX}{AE}$: this should represent an index of energy exchange efficiency.

$\dfrac{SE}{E} > 1$: this is an alternative to the measure $\dfrac{EE}{EX}$ in terms of availability rather than actual extraction.

$\dfrac{E}{EU} > 1$: this will hold true probably by a large margin until the system is at capacity.

$\dfrac{EX}{E} > 1$: should be a coefficient of extractive efficiency.

$\dfrac{EU}{EX}$: this is a measure of the technological pressure on the system.

These are examples of possible relationships that concern palaeo-ecologists. Such indices of energetics are of the type sought by ecologists concerned with optimal population levels. Plant and animal ecologists have suggested that there are fairly consistent levels of populations in relation to resources (Rosenzweig, 1968; Phillipson, 1976; Coe *et al.*, 1976). It is now a valid question for archaeologists to ask about human populations, and to look at various measures of productivity in the spatial context of prehistoric resource usage. With human populations, we are dealing with a higher level of the trophic pyramid for at least some of man's activities, and thus we cannot expect a one-to-one correlation with human population levels. We need to look also at the components of the production and the structure of habitats. Furthermore, with archaeology the most accessible dimension for analysing this type of problem is the spatial one — i.e. how habitats, biomass and productivity are related to sites. It is to measure this that the techniques and methods described below have been developed.

2. Prehistoric resources

The objective is to measure the various components of production in an ecosystem, analyse them in the context of exploitation by human groups in the past, and thus describe the various spatial configurations produced by relating availability to costs of exploitation. In other words, the distribution of resources acts as a determinant in economic strategies, and the quantification of these in a spatial context will provide a useful technique for analysing human palaeoecology. There are thus two major strands of information that we are seeking. The first is the overall levels of resource usage by human groups, looking for some formulation of the relationship between populations and resources. The second is the more particular problem of using a knowledge of prehistoric resource availability and site location to delimit home ranges, and thus particular strategies of exploitation.

Because the technique is essentially for archaeologists, it is necessary to assess the effects of time on the ecosystems in question. However, this specifically palaeoenvironmental question should be considered independently and should not determine the selection of the ecological variables.

The techniques suggested here are derived from ecology. This will contrast with the procedure developed by Higgs *et al.* which was primarily concerned with economics, and in particular agricultural economics and land use. Higgs and Jarman (1975) dismiss ecology, and the "ecological approach", as being ecosystem orientated — i.e. concerned with all the organic complexities of an area, rather than allowing man to form the pivot of the study. However, ecologists would distinguish between *synecology* and *autecology,* the former being concerned with all the interactions within an ecosystem, the latter being concerned with a single species and the factors that control its lives (Colinvaux, 1973, p. 3). Archaeology's primarily human interest clearly puts it in the class of autecology. In this context there are many ecological procedures, including some derived from synecology, that are applicable. The techniques outlined here are drawn from the range of studies concerned with the productivity of an area, whether it be primary or secondary production, and the distribution of the productivity. Principally this is a description of the densities of various organisms.

The approach may be outlined in the following way. The analysis is initially not centred on the site, but is based on the concept that precipitation and primary productivity act as major ecological determinants. The region of interest should first be defined in terms of the appropriate ecosystem. This will not be completely closed, and human systems are probably more open than most. However, for the purposes of subsistence activities, it should be possible to delimit some physiological limits to the system. These are probably of the order of a lake basin or a valley. The habitat analysis should then be carried out independently of the site locations. Returning to the equation given above we are concerned with the "e_1" part of the equation, and to include any aspects of the "e_2" side would destroy the independence of the analysis. Figure 2 shows a model ecosystem — in this case a lake basin — to show the nature of the methods.

1. The area should be gridded out to provide a series of quadrats

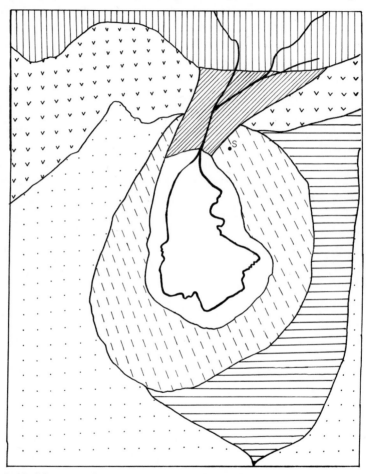

FIG. 2. Model area to show nature of the method proposed. The scale of the area is not relevant (see text). S = the location of the site used in the construction of the resource usage method.

		P:A%	
Key:	1. Lake and swamp	60	40
	2. Flood plain	50	50
	3. Gallery woodland	55	45
	4. Upland forest	70	30
	5. Light woodland	45	55
	6. Open grassland	40	60

For explanation of symbols see p. 183.

that will form the main unit of analysis. The size of these quadrats will be dependent upon the size of the area and the scale of the analysis. It may be that some areas require a detailed analysis not necessary in more uniform regions. Additionally, it may be necessary to utilize some sampling techniques. The important thing is to be able to assign to all quadrats the relevant figures for energy production, either through direct analysis or extrapolation. In practice it is expected that the quadrat size will seldom be smaller than 1 km^2 and seldom larger than 5-10 km^2 (Figs 3, 4).

2. Primary production: the first measurement is the energy produced at the plant trophic level — the net annual actual primary productivity. While being a function of the efficiency of photosynthesis by plants, it is also dependent upon such factors as rainfall, temperature, soil, etc. This may be a direct measurement through analysis of the vegetation, procedures for which are well developed in plant geography and plant ecology. For these techniques see Kershaw (1964) or Mueller-Dombois and Ellenberg (1974). The principle function of these techniques should be to measure the variance in productivity caused by local and seasonal factors, and may be as simple as variation in vegetation cover, or deal with the complexities of plant associations (Fig. 5).

3. Secondary production: onto this measure of energy should be added the animal biomass. This should include the total animal community from insects to elephants, but for the purposes of human ecology it is likely that the larger animals are of greater interest. This is a matter for archaeological debate. General techniques for the census of animals and the measurement of biomass are available, and the results would then form one of the components of the "e_1" value (Fig. 6).

4. It is immediately obvious that such a gross energy figure is liable to be so vast as to be beyond any or much relevance for human behaviour. It is this fact that makes any direct correlation of primary productivity and human densities tenuous. Consequently, the next step is to break down this overall quantity into more manageable quantities. Taking the plant level first we may distinguish between the following.

(a) Plants edible to man/plants not edible.
(b) Plants edible to any domestic stock (or various animals in general).
(c) Plants serving any other than a directly nutritional function (e.g. for house building, artefacts, medicines).

(d) A hierarchy of the calorific value of various plants and their other nutritional qualities.

(e) A hierarchy of abundance.

Exactly the same procedure would apply to the animal part of the ecosystem. It should be stressed that we are still dealing with the

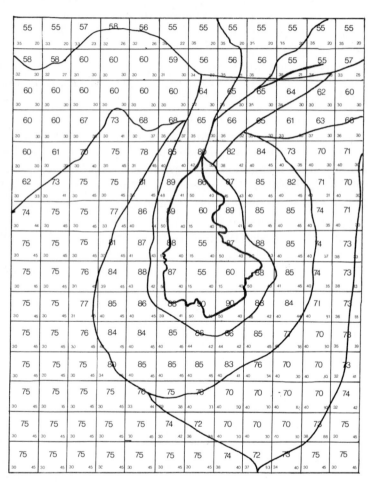

FIG. 3. Model area with grid, showing productivity for each quadrat. The large central figure is the total productivity value. The left hand corner value represents plant productivity, the right hand animal productivity. The values are simply ordinal numerals on a percent scale to show relative productivities of different habitats. Practical applications would normally be in units of g/m^2 dry wt per unit of time, or else kg/km^2 live wt per unit of time. Figures used here are simply illustrative of a method.

production side of the equation and that this is entirely a measure of availability.

5. Another aspect of availability, that must be subsumed within the analysis, is the degree of variance caused by seasonal and even annual fluctuations in the level and nature of productivity. These fluctuations have been of great interest to archaeologists, and the measurement of them in terms of energy may lead to a more accurate assessment of the importance of seasonality. Figure 3 shows total productivity values for the model area.

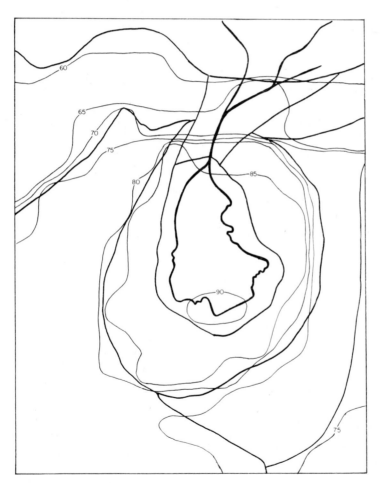

FIG. 4. Productivity contours (total productivity) of the model ecosystem. The values are absolute and do not take account of energy costs.
Contour interval = 5.

It has been stated that the measurement of all these quantities is derived from some level of on-the-ground analysis of the present day ecosystem. In some cases it may be that ecological work has already been carried out, and that empirical data for some of the variables are directly available. In other situations it will be necessary to incorporate such a study into the archaeological fieldwork. A further complication is that many areas have been so drastically altered by man that figures of productivity, especially for the secondary level, will be almost inaccessible; it is here that it may be necessary to use some models of energy levels and exchange rates as a lever into the past. Such approaches are often viewed with scepticism by the more empirically

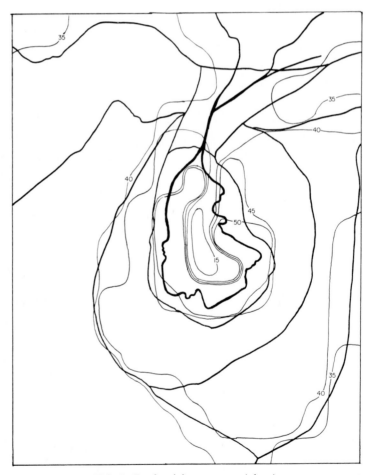

FIG. 5. Productivity contours (plant).

minded. This is an understandable position, but one not in keeping with the inherent inaccuracy of most archaeological surmises and inferences. In virtually all levels of archaeological work, especially the ecological aspects, some level of modelling occurs. The position taken here is that for this particular procedure there are sufficiently accurate models of production to be used in archaeology. The first of these theoretical short cuts is that formulated by Rosenzweig (1968) for the relationship between above ground primary production and available moisture as known from the level of evapotranspiration. This formula will allow an estimation of the amount of energy locked up in the vegetation if the net balance of precipitation and evaporation is

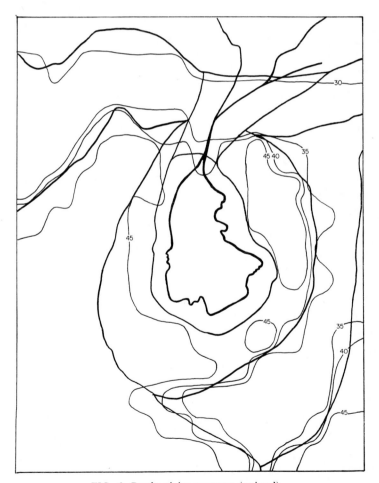

FIG. 6. Productivity contours (animal).

known. This may then be related to the actual nature of the flora. Palaeo-productivity is accessible if some knowledge of precipitation is known or hypothesized.

When dealing with the secondary production there is no equivalent relationship that has been demonstrated. What determines the level of animal populations is unclear. This methodology has been developed with a view to application in the savanna areas of Africa. With this in mind there is a much better scope for assessing the actual range of and the optimal level of secondary production. This may take the form of using empirical data in the same regions, or environmentally similar regions to those of archaeological interest. The wide range of faunal information and quantitative data now available from various parts of East Africa may be used to model prehistoric levels of secondary production. More recently, though, there has been some development towards a theoretical approach; i.e. is there any consistency in the levels of herbivore density in relation to other environmental factors. Such a pattern has indeed recently been suggested, both for large African herbivores in general and for elephant populations in particular (Coe *et al.*, 1976). In the Amboseli, an area where water acts as one of the main determinants of secondary production, Western has looked at the distribution of the ungulates in the context of water availability (Western, 1973, 1975), and at densities as a function of distance from surface water rather than overall water content.

Thus, for the African situation at least there is good reason to believe that accurate predictions of secondary production may be made and extrapolated to a prehistoric situation. For areas such as Europe, where so much of the natural fauna has been exterminated or greatly reduced in range, the process of extrapolation may be more difficult (Clarke, 1976). Europe as a high latitude continent is also less likely to be controlled to the same extent by the level of available moisture. Perhaps the greatest scope for this type of study in Europe lies in using the abundant data for agricultural productivity.

For the sake of completeness, it is necessary to mention tertiary levels of production — i.e. the amount of energy being transferred through the herbivores to the carnivores. For this there are few data, but some models of the rates of energy exchange exist (Phillipson, 1973). This level is in many ways the most interesting because human groups derive a lot of energy at this level, and the factors controlling the level of predator populations may well be analogous to those affecting human populations. Work in East Africa on lions and hyaenas in particular (Schaller, 1972; Bertram, 1975; Rudnai, 1974) especially the patterns of home range and territoriality, will be extremely useful as a spatial model for human habitat utilization.

This section has suggested that the key to the measurement of prehistoric resources lies in determining levels of energy productivity for the primary and secondary trophic levels, through both empirical evidence and the use of energetic models that predict these. Although derived from contemporary situations, their extrapolation to a pre-historic context is possible. It is now necessary to consider the other part of the energy balance, bringing in the question of human energy expenditure.

3. Human energy expenditure

So far only the "e_1" part has been considered. Energy expenditure (e_2) is a much more elusive quantity, there being few elements of it that can be assessed accurately without recourse to the detailed parameters of the population in question. This is archaeologically difficult, and attracts much of the criticism that is directed towards ecological or demographic archaeology. The difficulty is that while it is possible to know the extent of resources available, the use of them is a function of human population size and cultural selection, and is a less accessible form of data. This may, and does, lead to a deterministic approach (Higgs, 1968), a stance that excites even more criticism from cultural archaeologists. Therefore, a key factor in the success of any technique of palaeoecology is whether it can solve the problem of assessing "demand" in prehistory. By actually measuring what is on the site, the analysis of floral and faunal remains is generally accepted by archaeologists, whereas off-site techniques are not.

The approach suggested here cannot accomplish this essential measurement of requirements. What it can do is provide the necessary quantitative material of availability of resources to make modelling of alternative systems and levels of extraction possible. By constructing and quantifying potential strategies of spatial exploitation, a general comparison of their attributes and consequent elimination may be possible. In other words, in mapping component resources we will have an estimate of energy available from different parts of the ecosystem. For the purposes of exploitation these absolute values may be adjusted to reflect their real availability from the site—i.e. the energy balance between availability and cost. The spatial construction of this balance for the various different resources is a tool for the comparison of strategies.

Thus we are now interested in the variables of energy expenditure. It is not the aim of this paper to discuss the possible values that may be ascribed to these variables, but simply to attempt some definition of them.

One of the measures that must at some point be incorporated into the modelling is the amount of energy required to support an individual or population. Earlier this was abbreviated to E, and a relationship with productivity variables suggested. As this is a direct function of the population size, this is one of the values that we most want to determine, but is also one of the least accessible. The ratio of energy consumed to energy available is the ultimate ecological question.

While total consumed energy is the value sought, the value that is of more direct interest in delimiting resource usage is that of the amount actually used in extracting and utilizing the resources. This is the ratio that Lawton has attempted to delimit with respect to a number of species (1973). It is this value that truly constitutes e_2. We are thus dealing with technological and physiological efficiency of energy exchange, for which there are two main aspects. The first is ascribing energy costs that relate to the exploitation of each resource. Principally this is likely to be, for animals at least, a function of the size of the animal, its habitat, and anti-predative behaviour. Variations in density, i.e. availability, are always likely to affect the amount of energy used. Thus there would be a greater amount of input, and obviously output; hunting buffalo rather than an impala. This leads into the second aspect, which is the distance involved in acquiring the resource. Again taking animals, species that occur in a habitat close to the site will have a lower energy cost than those found in distant habitats. It is these two factors together that provide the value for e_2 and thus convert the absolute resource values into their actual value for the site concerned. The technology of the human group involved will be another determinant of the energy output, and some method of quantification of this is essential.

We have now defined the parameters and methods by which both e_1 and e_2 may be assigned values. Through discovering E we can determine the value of a resource for a particular site. In crude terms we may suggest that if the availability/cost ratio is positive, then it can profitably fall within a home range. Equally if the balance is negative then profitable exploitation is impossible. In order to reduce the crudity of this system, we are interested in suggesting what the lower limits of profitability are in a functioning system. However, whatever the levels of accuracy, the index should provide a method for delimiting the probable configuration of resource usage, both for complete economic systems and particular resources. The actual method of drawing these would be a contouring procedure (Figs 7, 8, 9, and 10).

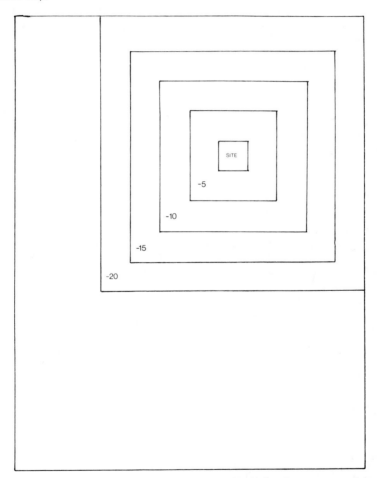

FIG. 7. Isocals: for assessment of productivity levels in the context of human utilization, expenditure rates need to be taken into account, to provide relative values for a particular site. Fig. 7 shows the rate of diminishing returns according to distance used here. In this illustration only a simple fall-off with distance has been used; in reality the fall off will be habitat, topographic, resource and technology dependent.

It should be emphasized that this form of analysis is crude, the real determining factor being how the distance and technology values are tailored; it is here that experimentation with alternative models will be necessary. In the actual equation used above only the simplest mathematical formulation has been used, simply to show the type of relationship we are trying to define. A formulation that expresses better the behavioural characteristics of human resource usage is likely to be much more complex. At this initial stage, it is necessary to experiment with alternative expressions, starting with the simplest. One of the main aims of this type of ecological work is to produce

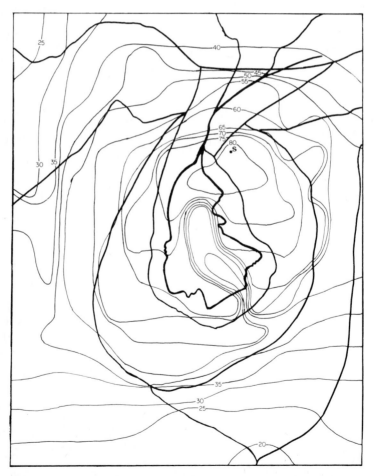

FIG. 8. General isocals for a particular site (S). Contour interval = 5.

equations which express human population size and spatial dispersion as a function of resources, so that variations caused by time, technology and culture may be measured.

4. Home range

The technique very briefly described here has been developed in order to analyse the spatial configurations of human subsistence activities. Site catchment analysis was a response to this, involving a hypothesis that made the distance factor a determinant in economic systems. The problem with site catchment analysis is that the technique imposed is

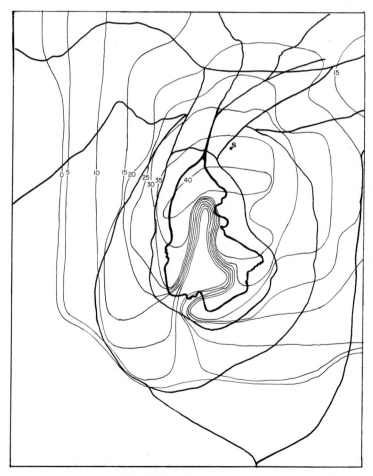

FIG. 9. Plant isocals.

the direct product of a hypothesis about resource utilization, rather than a tool to *test* it. It is to avoid this problem that the new method has been developed.

The term *home range* for the area where the extraction of resources shows a positive energy balance, or a series of these areas that grade the energy balance, is preferred to that of *territory* or *catchment area*. In animal behavioural studies, the term territory has connotations of a defensive response, and there is not a direct correlation between this and resource usage. The term home range refers to the area habitually

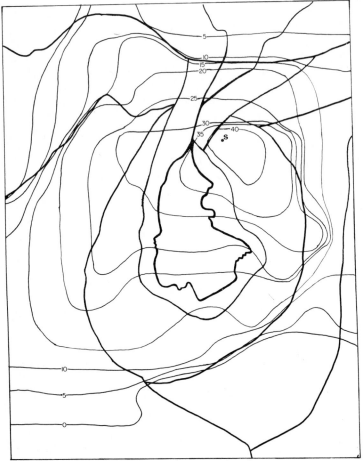

FIG. 10. Animal isocals. Note very different configurations and fall off rates for animal and plant resources.

Productivity			Environment	Key
total	plant	animal		
55	35	20	Upland forest	
60	30	30	Woodland	
70	40	30	Bush	
65	30	30	Riverine forest	
85	40	45	Floodplain	
75	30	45	Grassland	
55	15	40	Lake and lake edge	
90	40	40		

exploited, and as this is exactly what we are trying to define, the term catchment area becomes redundant.

This method does not automatically predict or assume the size of the home range. This leaves the analyst free to construct the home range in relation to the habitats and geography involved, and the nature of the site(s) being studied. Home ranges need not necessarily be independent of the culture or society that is being dealt with.

The system of contouring the range in accordance with the values of the energy balance is as follows (see Figs 7, 8, 9, and 10). The lines are drawn along what may be called *isocals*, i.e. areas with the same extractive value for a particular site. Within which isocal the actual home range falls would be dependent upon, among other things, the levels of demand, the balance of animal and food plants, seasonal availability and the level of technological efficiency. Different strategies would produce different isocals. The emphasis throughout is on experimentation and consideration of alternative models.

While resource values for sites are an important product of the technique, the absolute resource values will also be valuable for looking at the question of site distribution on a larger spatial scale.

5. Discussion

Increasing interest in aspects of prehistory other than the delimitation of cultural entities has meant that archaeologists have had to develop new techniques to cope with their very specialized needs. In general, studies dependent upon the physical sciences have made great advances, and there is now a multiplicity of methods available for archaeologists interested in chronology, technology, material composition and site analysis. In contrast to this, despite an interest in human palaeoecology, there has been little advance in the methods of analysing the way a site is related to its spatial environment. Techniques for describing actual palaeo-environments are greatly improved, but not so, human usage of them. Site catchment analysis was one of the few important developments in this direction. However, this method suffers from lack of quantitative attributes and assumption of many of the variables that are of interest. A numerical resource analysis such as the one described here should help bring the study of human palaeoecology more in line with the other "scientific" aspects of spatial archaeology.

The main advantage of this system is that it draws its information from an aspect of ecology, productivity, that is not only quantifiable but beginning to be understood in terms of inter-related variables. In this way, when dealing with the past, it should be possible to use any one of the variables to help predict others. Despite this, a large number of problems remain.

1. It is extremely dangerous to make any assumption of ecological constancy through time, regardless of the time period involved. There is increasing consensus among ecologists that the concept of a "natural" environment is not applicable. It is, therefore, necessary to take into account all the possibilities of change induced by climate, man and ecological successions or cycles. This will involve full use of available methods of describing palaeoenvironments. In particular some knowledge of the evapotranspiration will be highly desirable, i.e. palaeo-temperatures and precipitation.

2. While productivity is a much used concept it should be used only within the limits of its own accuracy. Application of it has generally been to contemporary situations, and it is likely to lose resolution when applied to prehistoric contexts.

3. Empirical ecological data will form the backbone of many spatial analyses; in some cases theoretical models will be sufficient to delimit to some extent resource availability. The main implication of this is that the success of application will probably be higher in an area where detailed ecological work has been done. In particular, well developed areas may be problematic. The method outlined here is best suited to low latitude contexts.

4. The technique does not claim to avoid all the usual problems of hypothesis testing that archaeologists have to deal with. It is extremely difficult to articulate off-site and on-site data. It is unlikely that high correlation will regularly be found, only that elimination of some hypotheses should be possible. Recovery and analysis of the organic remains of a site will form an important part of the total approach, and may suggest which of various potential strategies is of interest.

5. Emphasis throughout has been on the organic realm of human behaviour; it is this that home range refers to. Less easy to accommodate within the spatial system will be inorganic resources that are not evenly distributed and cannot be measured in terms of calorific value. These non-continuous resources may require special consideration.

6. Conclusion

The analysis of resource usage in relation to resource availability and the spatial consequences of this forms an essential part of any study of human behaviour. Home range and other units of distribution may not be assumed. Instead it is important to have a method of measuring the relevant variables of energy availability and expenditure that may be related to locational, economic and cultural evidence derived from archaeological sites. The measurement of ecological variables of productivity should be the starting point for analysing the exploitive strategies of prehistoric man.

Acknowledgements

A draft of this paper was presented to the Old Stone Age Seminar Group, Cambridge, organized by Dr Glyn Isaac. I would like to thank him and others at the seminar for their helpful comments. The ideas discussed here are the result of many discussions with Vicki Morse, and my concern with the question of ecological productivity owes much to Dr Malcolm Coe and other members of the Animal Ecology Research Group, Oxford. I would like to thank them all for their help and criticism.

Bibliography

Bertram, B. C. R. (1975). The social systems of lions. *Scientific American*, **232** (5), 54-65.

Byers, D. S. (Ed.) (1967). *The Prehistory of the Tehuacan Valley: Environment and Subsistence*, Vol. 1. University of Texas Press, Texas.

Chisholm, M. (1962). *Rural Settlement and Land Use*. Hutchinson University Library, London.

Clarke, D. L. (1976). Mesolithic Europe, the economic basis? In *Festschrift to Professor J. G. D. Clark* (I. Longworth and E. Sieveking, Eds). Duckworth Press, London.

Coe, M. D., Cummings, D. H. and Phillipson, J. (1976). Biomass and production of large African herbivores in relation to rainfall and primary production. *Oecologia*, **22**, 341-354.

Colinvaux, P. A. (1973). *Introduction to Ecology*. Wiley Interscience, New York.

Higgs, E. S. (1968). Archaeology, where now? *Mankind*, **6** (12), 617-620.

Higgs, E. S. (Ed.) (1972). *Papers in Economic Prehistory*. Cambridge University Press, Cambridge.

Higgs, E. S. (Ed.) (1975). *Palaeoeconomy*. Cambridge University Press, Cambridge.

Higgs, E. S. and Jarman, M. (1975). Palaeoeconomy. In *Palaeoeconomy* (E. S. Higgs, Ed.). Cambridge University Press, Cambridge.

Kershaw, K. A. (1964). *Quantitative and dynamic plant ecology.* Arnold, London.

Lawton, J. H. (1973). The energy cost of food-gathering. In *Resources and Populations* (B. Benjamin, P. R. Cox and J. Peel, Eds). Academic Press, London and New York.

Lee, R. R. (1968). What hunters do for a living. In *Man the Hunter* (R. R. Lee and I. de Vore, Eds). Aldine, Chicago.

Mueller-Dombois, D. and Ellenberg, H. (1974). *Aims and Methods of Vegetation Ecology.* Wiley Interscience, New York.

Phillipson, J. (1973). The biological efficiency of protein production by grazing and other land based systems. In *The Biological Efficiency of Protein Production* (J. G. W. Jones, Ed.), pp. 217-235. Cambridge University Press, Cambridge.

Phillipson, J. (1976). Rainfall, primary production, and "carrying capacity" of Tsavo National Park (east), Kenya. *East African Wildlife Journal,* 13, 171-201.

Rosenzweig, M. L. (1968). Net Primary Productivity of terrestial communities: prediction from climatological data. *American Naturalist,* 102, 74-76.

Rudnai, J. (1974). The pattern of lion predation in Nairobi National Park. *East African Wildlife Journal,* 12, 213-225.

Schaller, G. (1972). *The Serengeti Lion.* Aldine, Chicago.

Turnbull, C. (1973). *The Mountain People.*

Vita-Finzi, C. and Higgs, E. S. (1970). Prehistoric economy in the Mount Carmel area of Palestine: site catchment analysis. *Proceedings of the Prehistoric Society,* 36, 1-37.

Western, D. (1973). *The Structure, Dynamics and Changes of the Amboseli Ecosystem.* Nairobi University, Ph.D Thesis.

Western, D. (1975). Water availability and its influence on the structure and dynamics of a savanna large mammal ecosystem. *East African Wildlife Journal,* 13, 265-286.

5

The Analysis of the Urban Structure of Pompeii: A Sociological Examination of Land Use (Semi-micro)

R. A. RAPER
31, Ayresome Ave.,
Leeds

1. Introduction

The aim of this project is to apply relevant modern urban geographical techniques of analysis to the study of an ancient town. Pompeii lends itself to such an investigation because of its unusually fine state of preservation caused by the eruption of Vesuvius in A.D. 79 and subsequent burial beneath a layer of lava and ashes.

By the means of scientific excavations students of archaeology have been able to penetrate into the intimacy of a whole urban society. All the aspects of ancient public and private life have been considered by the study of the structures, the decoration, the furniture, and the graffiti. However, the present literature concerning Pompeii remains to be dominated by an appreciation of the features of daily life, not their function.

This functional viewpoint as an interpretation of the life of Pompeii is a useful generalization as it indicates the mode of adaptation of the inhabitants to their urban environment. Urban geographers are concerned with the search for generalizations — generalizations about cities and their interiors (Everson and Fitzgerald, 1972). However, the function that most interests the author and that appears to be as relevant in antiquity as it is to modern cities, is the actual sociological thought behind the city structure. As Emrys Jones maintains: "The urban geographer should assess the part played by society in giving character to cities and parts of them" (Jones, 1960).

Pompeii, by virtue of its contemporaneity in the first century A.D., produces the most intact ground plan of any Roman provincial city. Thus the urban structure can be readily perceived from classifications of the use of its urban space. It is the actual treatment of the urban structure that is instrumental in revealing the thought behind the town plan. This chapter shall attempt to employ a sociological study of land use which relies initially on an ecological approach that arose from the work of a group of ecologists at the University of Chicago, including R. E. Park (1952), E. W. Burgess (1925) and R. D. McKenzie (1925). The specific ecological approach chosen is a modification of this work containing cultural data, available from the interpretation of diagnostic archaeological evidence from Pompeii, which shall be examined by a social action scheme (after Willhelm, 1962).

The project is purely concerned with the internal structure of a city and the interrelations of its inhabitants. This is not to say that external factors contributing to the urban structural development are ignored but rather that they are recognized as inputs to an urban system in keeping with the urban geographer's attitude towards generalizations. Certainly, it has been a feature in recent archaeological considerations of settlement patterning that cities have been studied in relation to other cities, particularly in the Roman period (Hodder, 1972), yet because Pompeii presents such a complete ground plan suitable for scientific examination, internal analyses are possible.

2. The adaptability of Pompeii in A.D. 79 for social analysis

The fact that Pompeii grew up through various historical phases, from Greek to Samnite to Etruscan periods, before it was conquered by Sulla in B.C. 80 and became a Roman colony, is attested by both the irregular outline of the walls and the haphazard arrangement of the streets in the area of the initial building phase around the forum. This would seem to suggest that Pompeii was not built according to a set plan as was the feature of most towns under Roman auspices, but grew and altered over centuries. Nevertheless, because the city experienced a vast expansion in commercial importance in the Roman Republican period and the population increased accordingly it was realised that the best use of land required an orderly use, hence the grid plan in the final period. Therefore, Pompeii is to an extent unusual when compared with other Roman and Etruscan cities, as it shows various expressions of land use.

The Roman city strikes one at first as so little a product of the artless processes of nature and growth. The ground plan, for example, is a grid plan. The unit of distance is the insula. The *Decumani* and the *Cardo maximus* are readily apparent. This geometrical form suggests that the city is a purely artificial construction.

The fact is, however, that the city is rooted in the habits and customs of the people who inhabit it. It is the structure of the city which first impresses us by its visible vastness and complexity, but this structure has its basis, nevertheless, in human nature.

The city plan establishes metes and bounds — as provided by the mere presence of the walls, it fixes in a general way the location and character of the city's constructions — the centrally located *templa* or the *thermae,* and it imposes an orderly arrangement, within the city area, upon the buildings which are erected by private as well as by public authority. Aristotle was aware of this methodical planning of cities. He likened it to the natural organism as a perfect paradigm of the relation of form to function. Within the limitations prescribed, however, the inevitable processes of human nature proceed to give these regions and these buildings a character which is less easy to control. The Roman Censors, whose concern it was to allocate the planning of the urban land use, could not fix land values and, for the most part, the task of determining the location of the city's residential and industrial districts was left to private enterprise. Perhaps it may seem surprising that archaeology can give an indication of land values but it is obvious that, for example, shop fronts locating along the main traffic arteries such as the Via dell'Abbondanza (*Decumanus*) or the Via de Stabia (*Cardo maximus*) would occupy higher value land than those locating in more residential areas. Furthermore, the expression of human nature in personal tastes and convenience, vocational and economic interests, infallibly tends to segregate and thus to classify the population of Roman cities. In this way, the city acquires an organization and distribution of population which is only designed and controlled to a small extent.

Pompeii is seen to present a dichotomy in the analysis of the urban structure. It certainly would be possible to study the actual physical remains and their functional interrelations, yet this would ignore the underlying social processes. It seems equally important therefore, to understand the social structure as a persisting pattern of relationships among units, where the units are preferably recognized as socially significant areas of differential land use. The social structure can then be perceived in various areas, for example the examination of the consequences of social structure for the characteristics of residential areas. The residential areas of Pompeii show marked similarity in the large sizes of *atria,* proliferation of murals and frescoes, increased occurrence of private baths and hypocausts and many other variables of wealth value. Given these characteristics we can examine the influence of location or space upon social behaviour, structure, and finally culture.

Social analysis of urban structure will also take into account any anomalies that may occur in the unit interrelationships. This is important in that Pompeii was affected by a growing process of "democratization" following the commercial expansion under Roman provincial rule. Such a feature of social positioning was not an easy task to indicate but was obviously well evolved by A.D. 79. The port of Pompeii was largely instrumental in operating a thriving trade between northern Italy, Greece and the countries of the East. As a feature of this growth, Pompeii became the commercial centre of the Campanian plain. The prosperity of its industries raised men of lower-middle class to the status of eminent citizens. The actual buying power of the commercial classes increased, allowing them to purchase larger establishments which, because of the high density building in the forum area, forced them to move into the peripheral residential regions. Simultaneously came the decline of the aristocracy as they did not enter into trade or business.

The overall effect of this social change on the urban structure was dramatic. Initially, the upper classes were able to rent the entrances of their houses as shop fronts, which were seen to be sensible allocations of land use. However, as the commercial prosperity continued the tenants were able to buy out the whole ground floor and eventually the upper classes were beginning to move out to nearby villae (excavated examples of which seem to show no other function than that of suburban houses; the recently discovered site at Oplontis — as yet unpublished — serves as a case in point), or to towns like Herculaneum where the urban space was almost entirely given over to residential purposes. By A.D. 79, the composite character of the city with its elegant neighbourhoods and business streets was not particularly distinct but intermingled. The archaeology serves to illustrate this social phenomenon. There were great contrasts between the aristo-cratic elegance of certain dwellings and the vulgarity of the trades or businesses established in them. For example The Casa dei Vetti (VI 15, 1) perhaps one of the most beautifully decorated of all Roman townhouses, was filled with a kitchen range and large bronze vessels. The House of the Tragic Poet (VI 8, 5) is perhaps the most typical habitation of the enriched middle-classes. The *tabernae* on either side of the door, communicating with the vestibule, show that the master of this elegant abode did not disdain to exercise his business.

The "democratization" process in Pompeii also caused the ownership patterns to change. Following the disaster of the earthquake in A.D. 62, the process was given impetus as there was a need for rebuilding and re-planning large areas. Industries and workshops originally centrally located around the forum were de-centralized and nuclei sprang up at intersections of major roads as secondary market places. Many of the larger urban "villae" were split up into flats, as their owners saw both the necessity of housing the homeless and finding new incomes. The House of the Centenary (IX 8, 3) serves as an example; it represents one of the largest and most complex houses in Pompeii, yet it had at least three independent habitations thrown into one. Similarly the House of the Ephebe (I 7, 10-12) once had as many as three different entrances and it too is formed by several houses thrown into one or communicating with each other.

"Democratization" was at the centre of disturbing any planned organization Pompeii had, as the population virtually had the necessary wealth to choose their location. The eruption of Vesuvius in A.D. 79 halted progress, yet offers enough contemporary evidence to illustrate the direction of the social forces and their effect on urban structure. It also allows a valuable insight into contemporary day-to-day life. Consequently, the socio-cultural traits of the population can be studied and their effect on the land use is not difficult to isolate.

3. The ecological approach to land use

In Section 2, it was proposed that the city be viewed as a social organism. R. E. Park, one of the most prominent human ecologists concerned with the planning of Chicago in the 1920s, summarizes this point well.

The city is a state of mind, a body of customs and traditions and of organised attitudes . . . . . The city is not, in other words, merely a physical mechanism and an artificial construction. It is involved in the vital processes of the people who compose it; it is a product of nature and particularly human nature (Park, 1952).

Thus it was necessary to adopt an approach which accentuated the aspect of human nature.

Ecology offers such an insight. There are forces at work within the limitation of any natural area of human habitation which tend to bring about an orderly and typical grouping of its population and institutions. Thus ecology "searches for the logic in the use of space" (Anderson and Ishwaron, 1965). By definition, ecology is

the science which seeks to isolate these forces and to describe the typical constellations of persons and institutions. That which the cooperation of these forces produces, is what we call human, as distinguished from plant and animal, ecology (Park, 1952).

Criticism has been levelled at human ecologists, as they are indeed trying to adopt the concepts of a science which relates mainly to plant and animal life. However, in both situations, there is a stress on the essential characteristics of a community. These include, in both human and plant and animal spheres, a population territorially organized that is more or less rooted in the soil it occupies. Its individual units live together in a relationship of mutual interdependence that is symbiotic rather than societal. Here the term "symbiotic" is used in a sense where it applies to human beings in that there is a biotic balance that preserves the community, with a mechanism for regulating numbers and preserving the balance between the competing species of which the community is composed. The balance of nature relates to a question of numbers — when the pressure of population upon natural sources of the habitat reaches a certain degree of density something usually happens. This can be seen in Pompeii where habitats of the residential area are "invaded" by the lower-middle commercial classes. If man cannot eliminate competitors he must find ways of sharing the situation with them. Hence, when work on a small scale has to be in a small space, if more spacious rooms are needed, they will become located far from the urban centre where space rent is cheaper.

Human ecologists make use of specific ecological terms as they affect functional or natural areas of an urban community. These include dominance — obviously the more successful form of land use is the use of space which can afford the highest land values and rents; the dominant force will be that most successful land use. Succession is the expansion of the dominant land use leading to invasion of the lower land value areas further out from the urban centre. Both dominance and succession are functions of, and dependent upon, competition as the primary shaper in human as well as animal communities. Naturally, every user of space tends to locate where the greatest economic advantage can be gained. Competition expresses this feeling. In Pompeii, however, the land use patterning would seem to suggest that the competitors have realised that extremes of contest can be damaging to all, therefore cooperation seems to come about. Many examples of land use in the *insulae* show that clustering of competitors can be more profitable than isolation. There was also an important feature of this clustering, for in a society with limited communication, when the retail land use was clustered, the foreign buyers knew where to find types of shops.

When studying ecology as applied to urban residence, there seems to be a number of kinds of determinants that affect the choices of urban space in Pompeii. Initially, there are the impersonal and economic forces, essentially materialistic in outlook, where man locates in respect to land use for work. This is expressed in the market nuclei concentrations of retailing and service land use at the intersections of the *Cardo maximus* (Via di Stabia) with the two *Decumani* (Via di Nola and Via dell'Abbondanza). There are also determinants that express social values, such as the natural wish to be removed from the bustle of the forum region, and the noise level of the heavy wheeled transport that was, by Roman law, only allowed into the city at night. Further social values are indicated in Pompeii by the proliferation of "atria" townhouses that were a mark of the wealth of the gentry. These were desirable residences, generally on flat land with pleasant vistas, in the peripheral regions. However, human ecology, because it searches for logic in the use of space, tends to expose many examples that are far from logical. As a case in point, sometimes the economic influences which normally were to distribute space users ecologically are interfered with by official action. This was the case when Sulla ordered the building of the House of the Faun VI 12, 2-5) after the Roman colonization, which occupied a complete *insula*.

A further important outcome of the ecology of human communities has been the implication of models for the analysis of the urban ecological pattern by human ecologists who have wanted to find a theoretical basis for urban research. E. W. Burgess in his *Concentric Zone Theory* (Burgess, 1925) saw that "in the absence of counteraction factors, the American city should take the form of five concentric zones". Here I am alluding to somewhat dangerous analogies of the Roman colonial town with planned American cities. However I feel the parallel to be justified, not only because the forum area can be seen to equate with the central business district, or the fact that shops of Pompeii locate along the main traffic arteries (as Berry noted in his article concerning urban business types locating in ribbons along modern major arterial roads, Berry, 1959), but mainly because, as Brogan put it,

> Regularity of plan was a feature of all towns constructed under Roman auspices; and in this the Romans and the modern Americans have a good deal in common. The foundations of large numbers of new towns had to be carried out by both within a comparatively short time, and it is natural that a standard type should be used. This is the chessboard pattern early developed for the layout of Roman colonies (Brogan, 1953).

Furthermore the five features of Burgess's theory have certain parallels in Pompeii.

The first zone comprises the central business district. Here was the focus of the city's commercial, social and civil life. The Roman forum (Fig. 5b) acted in a similar way, yet it was also the religious centre. Shop fronts, *cauponae* (bars), *thermopolia* (hot-drink bars) and *tabernae* (inns) are all found in increasing abundance to meet the service requirements of the forum area. Zone two, in Burgess's model, was a zone in transition where residential patterns were deteriorating, and business and manufacturing users of space began to encroach. Zone three was essentially one of independent workingmen's houses. Pompeii does show analogies here as it was a feature that the forum tended to take on increasing importance as a place of business transaction, tariff collections and general administrative activities. The building of Eumachia originally had religious functions, but later housed the corporation of fullers, the most important group of workers in Pompeii. The *Comitium* housed the principal magistrates of the city and the electoral polling office, and the *Basilica* contained the law courts. Also the forum was enclosed with boundaries preventing the entry of vehicles, which presented difficulties for the retail and manufacturing interchange. In this way, the location of shops and the various *officina* (workshops) such as fullers, bakeries, oil merchants, potters and smithies moved into the neighbouring zones (equating with Burgess's second and third zones). Since the *atrium* townhouse had developed for some four hundred years, in the Etruscan phase this zone represented the periphery and residential area. Consequently Burgess's ecological forces of competition for land values, entailing dominance and subsequent invasion of land use, took place. The result was that much of the parts of Regio VII around the forum were as much commercial as residential in character. Burgess's fourth zone was one of better residences of middle-class citizens. Certainly much of Regio I, III, IV and V show largely residential land use, removed from the economic growth centre of the forum (sadly much of this area remains unexcavated, yet the very regular grid plan has been established by trial-trenching, and predictions seem feasible). The fifth zone was a commutor zone, with a ring of small cities or dormitory towns. This, perhaps, is the most difficult to substantiate, but one cannot help but look to the suburban villae, as residences connected to the city, as there is scant evidence of the immediate sites operating on purely agricultural levels.

Certainly each city is unique in combination of detail in the urban land market, yet there does seem to be a general degree of order underlying land use. This is also the case in Pompeii. Burgess, by interpretation of his zoning, shows that accessability is assumed to decrease uniformly in all directions from the city centre, and by implication the rent that an activity is prepared to pay for the site decreases from the central point. The residential areas of Pompeii would be affected by problems of accessability to an even greater degree as they are hindered by the proximity of the walls, and particularly, variations in distance from the eight gates of Pompeii. The fact that land values decrease from the city centre is indicated by the desire of the commercial classes to locate in areas where the actual space is greater and can meet their increasing demands as the process of democratization increased.

Burgess attempted to study natural areas, that is, the identification of districts of distinctive social significance. These areas included expressions of monitary values, such as rent values in modern times. Similarly it could be possible to study diagnostic wealth variables of antiquity as a feature of monitary value, such as house types, wall paintings, mosaics, sizes of rooms and the like. The division of natural areas was a purely ecological approach because it isolated the reasons for the grouping of population.

Other models or theoretical explanations of city structure have been promoted in opposition to Burgess's theory as it was argued whether only this type of zoning occurred in a city. Homer Hoyt advanced a

"Sector Theory" (Hoyt, 1964) where "residential land uses tend to be arranged in wedges or sectors radiating from the centre of the city along the lines of communication." This is only true partially in Pompeii, and is in fact more probably due to later Roman planning. The east ends of the Strada di Nola and Via dell'Abbondanza may conceivably attract wedges of residential land use. However, Hoyt's model does not take into account land use other than residential, and certainly in Pompeii the high rent value street frontage is given over to retail use, while the gate areas (which in effect distort the model, as do the walls) are predominantly service areas orientated towards the traveller.

Harriss and Ullman (Harriss and Ullman, 1945) prefer a "multiple nuclei concept," where the nucleus is "any attracting element around which growth, residential, business, industrial or otherwise, takes place." This is certainly a feature of later Pompeii as the industries became de-centralized, yet the theory goes on to state the existence of several discrete nuclei not the existence of a single centre, and this is not the case for Pompeii.

I have tried to indicate the various general explanations of land use patterns. All have some relevance to the patterns in Pompeii, and can partially explain the urban structure. Limitations do arise in that rentable values cannot be seen from precise monitary values but only from the wealth connotations of various archaeological, architectural, and artistic forms. Nevertheless, ecology presents a useful insight into the interrelationships of the living community of the city. To this extent urban archaeology fuses with urban geography; both are concerned with the relations among the individuals, direct and indirect, one upon the other. It allows the city to be seen as a functional unit where, in the natural aspects of human ecology, man adapts to the lie of the land. Moreover, the seeming chaos of an urban community vanishes, once the ecological pattern of space or land use is visualized.

4. Materialistic ecology versus voluntaristic ecology

Before continuing the theme of explaining the ecology of a city in social terms, it is hoped that there was noted a deliberate discrepancy in the discussion concerning the ecological approach to land use of Section 3. The reason for this action was that initially the writings of Park, Burgess and McKenzie, the instigators of human ecology, explained ecological conditions in "nonsocial" terms. They implicitly or specifically denied the relevance of social values or culture and relied instead upon biotic premises. However, in Section 3, human nature was constantly put forward as an underlying condition of man's social activities. Certainly ecology, as the instigators defined it, was far more based on competitive forces. Park defines these competitive forces as part of a science that tends to bring "an orderly and typical grouping" (Park, 1952), while McKenzie saw that competition accounts for the "function of order" (McKenzie, 1925). This discrepancy was necessary in that, although ecology was originally materialistic in outlook there had to be an explanation of all its features before modifications could be made to insert the aspect of social choice. Since materialism, as it was expressed in ancient Pompeii, was naturally not as developed as the economic force we now know it to be, social choice plays a far greater role in the analysis of the urban structure — as does social behaviour and particularly culture.

There are in fact various approaches to the study of human ecology. Basically, however, the field is narrowed by an acceptance of either materialistic or voluntaristic concerns.

The materialistic approach itself is separated into "traditional materialism" stemming from the aforementioned founders of ecology, where ecology is interpreted as the investigation of the impersonal competition that determines man's symbiotic adaptation to space, and "neo-classical materialism" where ecology is viewed simply as the study of impersonal functional relationships that supposedly exist between social activities connected with man's sustenance efforts within a physical habitat. The former, traditional materialism, maintains that there is an ecological order resulting from biotic processes that affect man's cultural life. In this way, it is the competitive framework upon which the social order is woven. The latter, neo-classical materialism, is defined by Amos Hawley as the study of man's adaptation to physical space through the "morphology of collective life" (Hawley, 1950). Ecology is here dealt with as a field concerned primarily with sustenance and social organization. Both views are only partially correct, in my opinion, when applied to Pompeii.

The main failing is that both traditional and neo-classical materialists rely upon nonsocial conditions in offering ecological theories. Man locates on a materialistic basis only, complying with either impersonal biological and/or physical conditions. These theories seem regardless of man's culture and desires, and particularly his social activities.

Volition, as a cause for spatial location in a city is never mentioned; this appears often in the various classifications of land use in Pompeii. For example, in the recent excavations by the University of Maryland in the large insular 5, Regio II, there was discovered a large and valuable piece of land within the city walls, used purely as a vineyard. This vineyard occupied not only most of the insula itself but also abutted onto the Via dell'Abbondanza, one of the three major arterial roads of the city. The excavator naturally saw this feature of land use as of special significance as it was surprising that the area was not given over to commercial or residential purposes. Furthermore, it was odd that such a large area should actually be within the city walls, for it opposed what had already been written regarding the "increase in population and shortage of land . . . . in Italian cities in the early Empire" (Carrington, 1936). The discovery of the huge insula led the excavator, Wilhemina Jashemski, to look for, and subsequently locate, other large open areas which had been planted and not given over to commercial or other purposes. The significance of these excavations to the study of ancient land use and city planning was left open to speculation, yet I cannot help but conclude that it was a purely voluntaristic choice on behalf of a community not nearly so concerned with competition and materialism as was previously supposed. The mere fact that land of such rentable value was used for agriculture indicates something of the underlying modes of thought behind the planning of Pompeii. Questions of dominance, succession and invasion seemed somewhat insignificant.

Materialistic ecology, therefore, is not concerned with values, attitudes or other variables of a psychological nature. The traditional materialists omit the influence of culture but separate this essential component from consideration. Both studies prefer to perceive man's spatial distribution as an inevitable consequence of cooperation, either economically, or collectively, which overlies the social order. This I feel is inadequate, particularly as Roman social order was the strongest in the West until the mediaeval period. Consequently, volition cannot be ignored in seeking ecological explanations; it is imperative that an investigator acknowledges the significance of culture and the role of social values as well as materialistic approaches. Therefore, a voluntaristic approach is offered as an alternative ecological framework for the analysis or urban structure.

The recognition of social values as an essential component of ecological thought characterizes the voluntaristic approach to human ecology. Competition is by no means completely impersonal, rather social forces within a society regulate and prescribe the conditions under which competition operates. Pompeii offers an excellent study of this approach in its process of democratization. The high position of the lower-middle classes in A.D. 79 as eminent citizens in the social order tended to determine their competitive powers. Thus competition was not determinative of social conditions, but one of the institutional arrangements characterizing a society. Therefore it can be stated that the mixed nature of the distribution of Pompeii's land use in A.D. 79 was a feature of competition between cultural usages and values; social forces within a society, contrary to the materialist's position, which regulated and prescribed the conditions under which competition operated.

To integrate the variety of insights and propositions advanced by various voluntaristic ecologists, a cultural approach shall be adopted here (after Willhelm, 1962) where "man adapts to space through the social activities he seeks to perform." If it can be shown that the people of Pompeii adapt to space because of their social position and economic position as a feature subservient to this, then such characteristics become ecologically relevant. The cultural approach to human ecology does not study the individual in psychological terms, but in the shared systems of symbolic ideas. The ideas of the inhabitants of Pompeii can be seen from the social connotations of its archaeology, the study of the socially different areas of land use and from an investigation of the Roman way of life itself — its moral code, laws, religious precepts and the social standing of its people. All these features will be brought together as cultural data in the application of a model in the following section.

5. Application of the social action scheme

In the analysis of the land use for Pompeii, the contention is that the distribution of man over space is not haphazard but that man locates by the social activities he creates and sustains through culture. The raw data for Pompeiian culture mainly comes from the analysis of the land use plan (see Section 6) and the diagnostic interpretations of the archaeology. There empirical data are then analysed by a specific social action scheme (after Willhelm, 1962), the hypothesis of which states the following.

1. End   An anticipated state of affairs to be realised through the Pompeiians' own efforts.

2. Norm   A standard of expectation for social conduct to be actualized in performance.

3. Normative system   A set or arrangement of interrelated norms for accomplishing a given end.

4. Means   The presence of alternative norms open to the Pompeiians as they selected ways in which they located.

5. Social condition   A norm for accomplishing an end that excludes the presence of alternative conditions within a situation.

6. Value   A concept specifying what aspects of an urban situation are desirable.

7. Value system   A set of interrelated values that individuals utilize to decide what is to be desired.

8. Cognitive data   Conceptualized criteria defining social and physical objects and their properties.

The application of the social action theory specifies the interrelationships between the concepts given above, and examines the Pompeiian data in the following manner. In locating over space, individuals seek to attain a certain end. The end for Pompeii demonstrates the fact that there was a situation in A.D. 79 where the commercial classes sought to locate residentially yet continue in their place of work simultaneously. The archaeology regularly reveals this situation, as shops and *officina* often had backstairs to flats above, or *atria* houses were themselves split up into retail or manufacturing establishments on the ground floor and residential housing elsewhere in the building. Other features of Pompeii's given end included the desirability to obtain space where rent values were low and floor space was great, necessitating the movement away from the urban centre. Accessibility needed to be high, and the peripheral insulae, with their orderly gridded layout provided this. The actual function of the land changed from being purely residential to that of adding some purpose to enhancing the economic base activities of the city. To accomplish this goal, a specific norm must be selected from the means in accordance with social conditions that prescribe the course social action is to take. In Pompeii, the norm is the movement away from the forum area into the residential insulae to allow more viable commerce in an indiscriminate expression of land use. The various means possible included features such as competition for occupation of land, dominance of certain more powerful commercial land uses and succession of those uses. Pompeii did not follow these biotic progressions which were described by modern-day traditional materialists, rather the norm of necessary rapid expansion because of the prevailing social conditions in A.D. 79 was adhered to. Democratization as a rising feature in the Roman Republican period offered the social conditions, and the social action was the physical interpretation of this as the ability for the lower-middle classes to purchase increasingly more space occurred. Because the goal, means, normative conditions and cognitive data must be given specificity to arise at concrete decisions and conclusions, the Pompeiian people had to develop and employ valuative standards, i.e. value systems.

As previously stated "value" refers to a concept specifying what aspects of the urban situation were desirable. By implication of the social value systems, Pompeiians had to select a norm from the several possible alternatives that constitute the means for achieving an objective. Initially location in urban space was to be ordered solely by the work of the Roman planners and particularly the censors. This would have given Pompeii an urban structure that was zoned with the forum area as the commercial, business and administrative place, and the peripheral regii as purely residential. However, this was not the case because of the overlying social conditions and, consequently, Pompeiians had various possible social value sets that oriented them towards locations. Willhelm indicated three types of value set, the economic-protective, the individual-collective and the present-future time value. The last is difficult to substantiate from the evidence at Pompeii, for the anticipated land use can only be supposed from studying parallel cities with similar functions. In the economic values, land would be dominated by the prevailing market situations, while in the protective values the residential utility of space would be chosen. In the individual collective formula life would become either an aggregate phenomenon where the city had a commercial function, or an individualistic expression, where personal wealth dominated. The most applicable value set for the Pompeiians is probably a development of the economic protective values where the economic viewpoint dominates the land use, yet protective arguments are acknowledged. This is particularly illustrated by the fact that the residential land use was increasingly taken over for commercial purposes. However, within this framework, there were varying expressions of collective welfare for in a few cases commercial concerns located in close proximity so as to benefit from shared products, with distance from raw materials minimized. Similarly individualism was a traceable feature as some of the more wealthy commercialists saw it desirable to maximize their own personal worth. An instance of this can be seen from the house of Vedius Siricus, where in the entrance there is an inscription on the pavement stating "Salve Lucrum". Siricus and his partner Nummianus directed an important commercial enterprise, and this would seem to be an address solely to profit; a welcome into his home of people of his own class, or it could be an invitation to money itself. Nevertheless, in general it can be said that the economic protective value set best interprets the Pompeiians' desire to locate.

Finally, the cognitive data available to the inhabitants as shared objectified knowledge recognized certain features. These included position of the land in question, the size of the building, the topography of the area, the proximity to secondary commercial interests and various other economic concerns.

The social action scheme as applied to Pompeii indicates that individuals did in fact perceive space as the location necessary for the performance of social activities. That is, persons interpreted space in terms of utility. No longer was residential land use dominant, but houses were increasingly used as commercial places. *Tabernae* (taverns) occupied the street frontages, as did shops, and houses were actually broken down after the earthquake of A.D. 62 for utility, not grandeur. Also, it can be observed that Pompeii's land use structure was competitive rather than characterized by conflict or pure co-operation, because of the social value sets chosen.

To indicate the way in which the residential regions were indeed characterized by intermingled commercial and residential land use in the final period more specifically, it seems worthwhile to take a region and investigate it more precisely. In this way the archaeology offers the data for the social processes mentioned. Regio VI has been chosen for various reasons — it was planned in the Roman Republican period, it was peripheral and therefore initially supposed to be residential, it was made up of many large *atria* and also it shows the most regular grid pattern of any region excavated in Pompeii. However, that the land use was varied cannot be denied, thus it indicates the effect of democratization as a dominant and determinant social process.

REGIO VI

VI 1, 14-18, 20-21, were both dwellings and places of business.

Shops, *cauponae* (bars), stairways and mezzanine floors were characteristic.

VI 2, 9-10, entirely residential; two families lived here. The first floor making up one residence and the second floor an additional one or two flats.

VI 4, 5-10, although there were several habitations in this dwelling, it was primarily commercial in function. This was undoubtedly because of its central location near the forum baths, at the corner of the Strada di Nola and the Via Consolare. It consisted of a row of four shops and their rear store rooms.

VI 6, 6-7, constitutes an apartment house. The lower floor was the first apartment, the upper the second.

VI 6, 10-11, duplex apartment block.

VI 7, 8-14, whilst the ground floor is partially devoted to shops, it contains at least two residences and additional apartments above.

VI 8, 9-13, commercially important land use as it faces the Strada di Nola to the north and the Strada di Mercurio to the east, and is therefore one of the busiest corners in the town. The forum baths are also directly across the street. Because of these attractive features, shop building was inevitable with *thermopolia* and foodstores.

Vl 11, 6 and 13, because these buildings are situated in a quieter section of town they were more exclusively residential. Nevertheless, there is an *officina* as well as a private house. Graffiti revealed the *officina* to be concerned with the manufacture of sailors' clothing. Also, workmen slept in the west wing of the house.

VI 9, 14, an entirely residential building with an *atrium* (central hall), *alae* (adjoining wings) and *cubicula* (bedrooms).

VI 14, 23-26, buildings that open onto the Via di Stabis, the most important north-south street of the city. The facade is, therefore, devoted to lucrative shops. The building was repaired with brick, and has partitions of walls with unfaced concrete constituting signs of the post-earthquake period.

VI 15, 22, a house of long corridors serving various rooms.

VI 16, 8-9, relatively humble tenant housing with an extremely simple ground floor containing two rooms separated by a stairway. The entire structure was post A.D. 62, shown by the presence of walls of unfaced concrete. The repair works after the earthquake serve to illustrate the process of democratization as buildings took on a utility function, housing larger numbers of people, or becoming commercial establishments.

VI 16, 11, a single shop occupies the east facade of the first house, and the upper floor duplicates the plan of the ground floor.

Regio VI is not unique as many other regions combine living quarters with shops and workshops, but it serves to demonstrate how the use of the *atrium* house, as a principal abode of one man and his family, later became a fully developed "utilitarian" architectural type of town house, characterized by a fusion of shop-tenement land use.

The cultural approach, although seeking the determinant elements of ideas by a social action scheme, still belongs to the voluntaristic perspective. The essential ingredient of choice remains: individuals may choose from the means to bring about a development which without their efforts, would not have happened, as the planning precision of Roman provincial cities would have prevailed. Furthermore, volition is most evident in the sense that the inhabitants could attain a certain end in the face of social conditions designed to restrict social action or change, such as the Roman social organization, and the once overriding position of the gentry as pre-eminent citizens. Culture encompasses the entire system of meanings by which man orients to a geographical surrounding. Within this comes a demarcation of distinguishable ideas. Because of the divergent content that ideas contain, the introduction of a social action theory is palpably justified, since it relies upon values, social conditions, goals, cognitive data and means to analyse cultural data. Thus the explanation of man's adaptation to space, the resultant physical features and the ideas behind them can be illustrated.

6. Interpretation of the land use plan

The importance of the land use plan as the basic data to the geographer and evidence to the archaeologist cannot be overstressed. As Murphy noticed

> a knowledge of the arrangement of land uses in the city and of the relative proportions of land devoted to the several uses is basic to geographical research and to planning. The traditional way of gaining this knowledge is through the preparation of a general land use plan (Murphy, 1966).

The "style of life" of a person, his income and his prejudices are all reflected in his choice of dwelling. It is an interesting feature that in Pompeii the dwellings of all classes were remarkably similar, revealing the desire of the commercial classes to own similar, indeed the same, establishments as the gentry.

The social ideas behind the distribution of the inhabitants in space will be seen in the pattern of relations among the units. The fact that there was no homogeneity suggests that the aggregate social structure of the city had undergone a breakdown. Works and shops were established where possible as opposed to essentially competitive locations, for space was at a premium in this city whose walls prevented her from expanding in proportion to the growing need caused by the social war.

Pompeii offers cartographic information that is readily perceived in the form of an almost total sample, which in archaeology is elsewhere so difficult to obtain. Much of this information has been preserved by the scientific nature of the excavations. Since the 1860s and the work of Guiseppe Fiorelli, the directors of excavations have had to cope with the problem of a vigorous social revolution in Pompeii. This initially meant that the archaeology faced a dilemma of whether to leave the aristocratic houses taken over by trades and businesses in the state in which the eruption found them, or should they rather be restored to their original condition of before the democratization. The procedure chosen has been to respect entirely the state of things at the moment of the eruption and everything has been left in place, handsome statues juxtaposed with dye vats.

Fiorelli also began the division of the houses and quarters of Pompeii. In effect, this has meant that for the time of A.D. 79 every building in Pompeii can be immediately located and identified. The city is divided into various quarters by its three main thoroughfares (Via di Nola, Via dell'Abbondanza and Via di Stabia). By following the lines of the *decumani* (Via di Nola and Via dell'Abbondanza), a division may be made into North, South and Central quarters: if the line of the *cardo maximus* is followed the East and the West quarters can be seen. Fiorelli took these arteries and produced a basis for the division of the city into nine regions; each region was further divided into insulae. In this way every building in Pompeii has three numbers; those of the region, the insula and its entrance. On this basis, a classification of land use has subsequently been inferred.

From the information concerning the function of each building given by Hans Eschebach as an appendix to his town plan of Pompeii (Eschebach, 1970), the land use has been classified into twelve categories.

1. Common shops, including foodstores.
2. Workshops (*officina*), smithies, granaries, bakeries, foundries, fullers and potters.

3. Inns, post houses, taverns and brothels.

4. Houses of trade and business houses.

5. Storerooms, adjacent rooms and stables.

6. Private houses, flats and *domii*.

7. Larger houses, manors and urban villae.

8. Places of entertainment, theatres, baths and public gardens.

9. Places of education, schools and business schools.

10. Public and administrative buildings (particularly around the Fora).

11. Religious places, temples, sanctuaries and shrines.

Eschebach's town plan was also reproduced (see example sector in Fig. 5) (see also Table 2), yet for reasons of size it was more practical to reduce the plan to A4 size. Every part of the urban space was classified and by consulting the index map (Fig. 3) the information on each sheet could be related to the base map (Fig. 1). Superimposed upon Fig. 5 is a sheet overlay of a one hundred metre grid in order to obtain percentile land use data; this in turn can be related to the base grid map (Fig. 4).

From the table of percentage land use (Table 1), the amount for each one-hundred metre square can be calculated. Only 39 squares are representative of the city as the excavated sample had to exceed 70% to qualify for analysis. Initially, from the twelve categories of land use, each theme in turn can be isolated, and its distribution and relationships studied. Certain interesting features resulted. For instance, in the commercial sector of the land use, the ratio of *officina* to taverns (categories two and three respectively) was often similar for each 100 m square. This may possibly suggest that the commercialists realised the importance of balance in retail activities, yet there is little suggestion of spatial zoning as these businesses were separated. The distribution of common shops (category one) was mainly on an optimizing basis, particularly along the main street frontages and in areas of high density building around important urban features (such as the Fora, the three bath establishments and the *compita* or major road intersections). However, the fact that many shops were also distributed in markedly residential areas does indicate that values other than economic were considered.

In the residential sector of the land use, figures were high for most of the squares, yet rarely were they dominant. The commercial structures tended to be constant in their association with the private houses and mansions suggesting a continuum of indiscreet usage of space. The

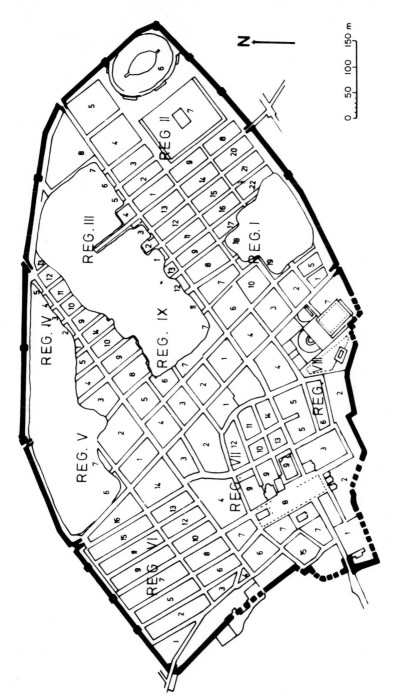

FIG. 1. Pompeii: base map.

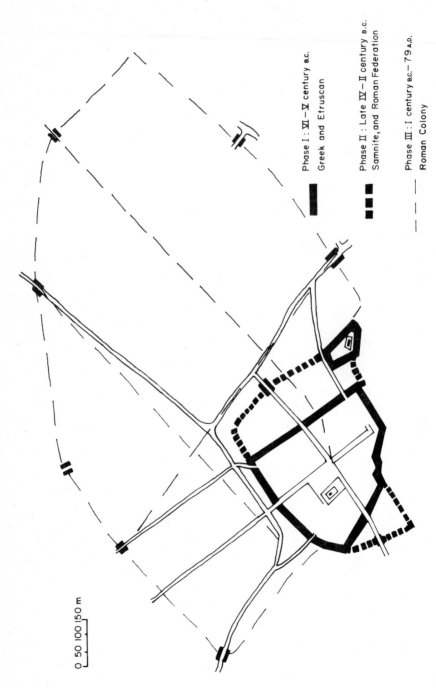

Phase I : VI – V century B.C.
Greek and Etruscan

Phase II : Late IV – II century B.C.
Samnite, and Roman Federation

Phase III : I century B.C. – 79 A.D.
Roman Colony

0 50 100 150 m

FIG. 2. Pompeii: phases of expansion.

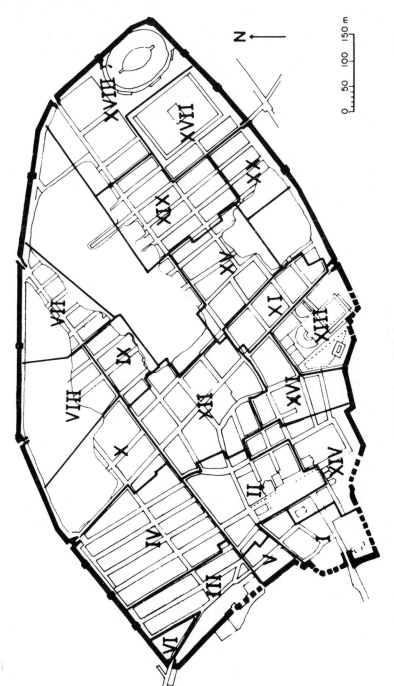

FIG. 3. Pompeii: index map.

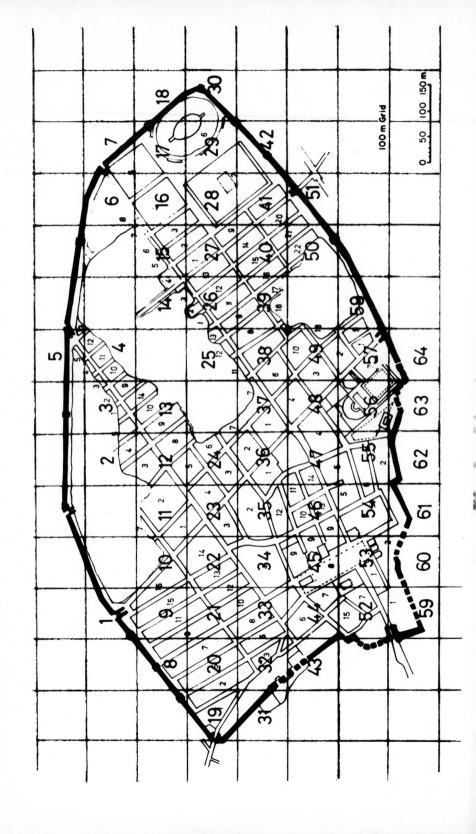

100 m Grid

0   50   100   150 m

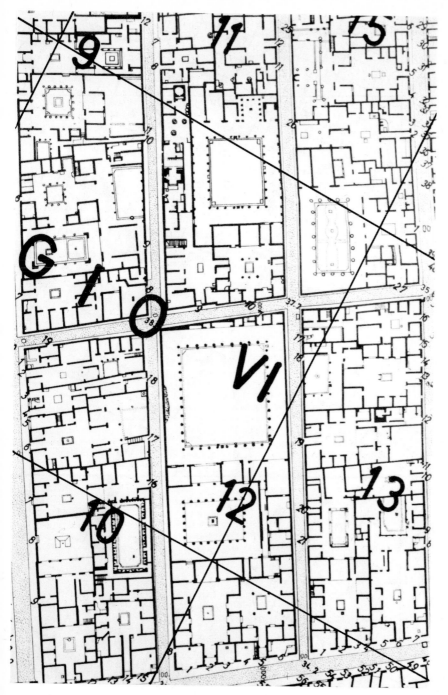

FIG. 5(a). Section of Eschebach's plan of Pompeii whose buildings were classified by 12 landuse categories in Table 2 (Eschebach, 1970).

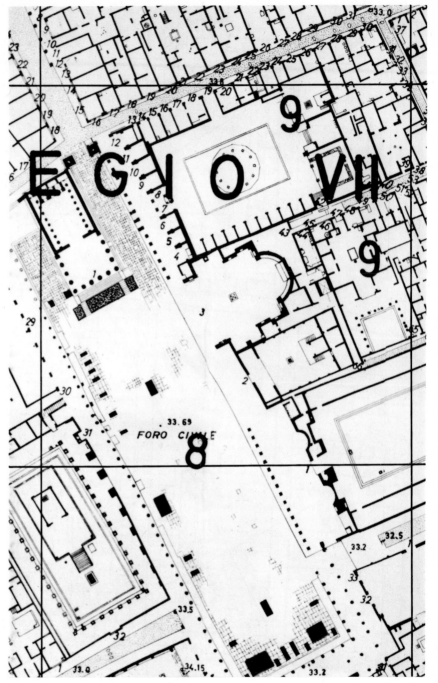

FIG. 5(b). Section of Eschebach's plan of Pompeii whose buildings were classified by the 12 landuse categories in Table 2 (Eschebach, 1970).

TABLE 1. % land use of the 100m grid

	6	9	10	11	12	16	17	19	20	21	22	23	24	26	27	28	29	32	33	34	35	36	37	38	39	40	41	44	45	46	47	48	49	52	53	54	55	56	57
1		4	9	4	8			19	1	3	8	19	5	7	3	1		8	6	19	11	12	8	6	3	2	1	8	6	15	19	11	5	4		5	1		
2	3	13	8		10	2		7	2	3	8	6	3	13	3	1		7	10	6	13	7	5	9	6	8	2	4	5	7	7	6	6	2					8
Commercial 3	13		6	5	7	2		5		4	9	7	9	5	8			7	7	4	6	8	4	7	6	11	5	10	3	7	5	5	5	5	2	2	1		10
4																												10		2									14
5	1	1	1	1	1			2	1	1		2	1	1	1	2		5 10		1	1	3	3	1	1	2	5	5	3	2	2	3	2	5					2
Total	4	30	24	10	26	4	0	33	3	11	25	36	18	26	15	2	0	27	23	30	31	30	20	23	16	23	13	27	14	33	33	25	18	11	2	7	2	3	36
6	44	32	32	41	45	12		33	81	38	53	27	45	45	48	6		42	36	33	58	40	44	57	57	59	31	49	9	39	33	36	47	63	15	73	39	3	21
Residential 7	11	23							36		22				4	74	73	11 36	36	22			7 36								13 11							
9											1										2		1															
Total	55	32	64	45	45	12	0	33	81	74	53	50	53	45	52	6	0	53	36	55	60	40	52	36	59	59	31	49	9	39	33	49	58	63	15	73	39	3	21
8	55					60	74	15				11		13			73	17	17	1		11	17			1 36		6 48		15						21	68		15
Public 10																				1									24 14			2			37	16 25		
11																																4						
12	20	15	10	19	19	24	26	19	16	15	20	14	16	13	20	18	27	12	18	14	9	19	10	18	13	17	20	13	5	14	19	20	17	8	21	17	1		19
Total	75	15	10	19	84	100	34	34	16	15	20	27	13	33	33	92	100	12	35	15	9	30	10	35	18	56	25	25	77	28	34	26	17	83	20	59	97		34
% Unexcavated	20	0	29	16	10	0	0	0	0	0	0	0	0	0	0	0	0	8	6	0	0	0	0	6	14	0	0	0	0	0	0	0	7	0	0	0	0	0	9
Av. mean	C	O	M	M	E	R	C	I	A	L		18%		R	E	S	I	D	E	N	T	I	A	L	41%			P	U	B	L	I	C	37%					

(Unexcavated 4%)

TABLE 2. Classification of land use categories

1. Common shops
2. Workshops
3. Taverns, inns, post houses, brothels
4. Houses of trade and business
5. Storerooms, adjoining rooms, stables
6. Private houses and appartments
7. Larger houses and manors
8. Places of entertainment
9. Places of education
10. Public and administration buildings
11. Religious buildings
12. Streets

educational category (category nine) was added to the residential sector as it was contested by epigraphy and by the documentation provided by the writings of various scholars and poets associated with Pompeii, that the sons of the gentry were the only ones who received teaching.

As one would expect the public sector has a varied percentage land use. The administrative, religious and entertainment centres were very large and took a traditionally integral part in city life. Consequently, the percentages are high for certain areas where the forum, the baths and the theatres are located, but very low elsewhere.

The average mean of the three sectors is generally consistent with little deviation by the single squares from it. Certainly traditional areas, such as the amphitheatre and its surrounding public gardens show a marked homogeneity in their land use. For example, square 17, covering the main part of the amphitheatre in region two, provides 74% in the entertainment category, and 26% of roads and open space. *In toto,* however, the land use is indeed intermingled. Even in the peripheral areas, where the percentage of residential space is high, the commercial land use seems to be encroaching.

In conclusion, with the exception of the large traditional high density public centres which naturally attract services of every nature, and perhaps the gate areas which offer food and rest for the traveller, the urban land use is consistent in its diversification. The residential sector, for instance, does predominate numerically, yet the proportional ratio of the commercial land use, occupying smaller establishments, is high. In very few examples is there a purely residential square. Thus the conception of patterning over the whole urban space is not evident. This would be the expected result if the democratization process was indeed an overlying social value, as has been suggested in the preceding discussion of other sections. Economic competition is not the primary cause for location — the idea of "man the optimist" is the economist's dream not reality.

7. Conclusions

The urban structure of Pompeii in A.D. 79 was in a rapid transition from an expression of status characterized by a non-competitive social structure of an imperial society to an active process of competition. Status was not an active process, as it was simply a rule of conservation, a makeshift to avoid the consequences of continual readjustment. This was the overlying social value present before the democratization of the social war occurred.

It was, therefore, an investigation of the effects of democratization upon the urban structure that was made to explain the land use regularities, or irregularities. This feature was central to the pattern of urban space in A.D. 79. All possible means of social forces have been suggested to analyse the reasons behind Pompeiian location in space, from the traditional materialist point of view to the voluntaristic perspective.

The major point that I have tried to bring out is that competition should not be readily accepted as the primary shaper of urban structure, rather there should be awareness of other value sets open to the Pompeiian. These value sets were not consciously chosen, as people are often unaware of judgements taken in daily life, yet in retrospect certain value sets are applicable. It is an assessment of all causative factors that produce a sociological examination. In fact, there seems to be a very narrow line between social values, such as volition, status and culture, and pure economic forces. All these features were present in the social war, and it would be wrong to isolate any one particular value.

Nevertheless, as R. E. Park and E. W. Burgess (Park and Burgess, 1921) have pointed out, "throughout history there has been a struggle between the principles of status and competition regarding the part each should play in the social system." The democratization process, effecting Pompeii in the Roman Republican period, begins to show the general increase of this conflict. The economic competition, however, is by no means one of pure economic drive, characteristic of modern cities, but a tentative movement towards it. Thus other social values remain very much in evidence.

The actual physical effect of these values upon the urban structure is seen in the varied nature of the land use. Because Pompeii was in a definite period of change in power, taken from the exalted position of the gentry to the rapid rise of the commercial middle-classes, the structure is largely of an irregular nature in A.D. 79. The major buildings of the administrative, entertainment, and religious sectors of the structure necessarily remained as urban foci with related service areas, as the basic Roman way of life continued. Thus the overall picture was one of traditional centres with little patterning elsewhere, except perhaps along the major lines of communication, where retail services proliferated.

In making this dissertation study, I have been led to consider further lines of investigation with a view to future research in the urban social structure of ancient towns. Initially, the conception of some kind of classification strategy for residential insulae seemed possible. This could entail a classification strategy indicating degrees of similarity between areas in terms of various characteristics, such as accessability to services, gates and major streets, measures of residential density; degree of infiltration by industry, and various measures of wealth shown by the furniture of each building or the artefacts therein. The emphasis of the classification will be affected by the proportion of variables selected to express any one aspect of the residential areas. Therefore, some method of selecting attributes of classification will be necessary. Naturally, the variables would preferably be those having the greatest variation between areas, to aid in the identification of dissimilar areas. The archaeology of Pompeii offers numerous attributes which vary on a social status level; for example very few *atria* had private baths, and only few had gardens or stables. A similarity measure would be required to indicate the closeness of the relationship between every pair of residential insulae, in terms of the chosen attributes. Also a grouping strategy would be needed that would produce the most efficient and significant grouping of similar residential areas. In this way spatial distribution of similar and dissimilar insulae, on the basis of their taxonomic relationships, could be studied and the urban social area analysis revealed.

The distribution of single land use categories might also be studied in greater detail. For instance the "tavern" category (category three) increases in density around the fora, the theatres, places of high building density and particularly the gates, as a service to travellers. The importance of the "shop" category (category one) in indicating the major road system and resultant high land values, has already been discussed. Ideally, distribution maps of each category could be prepared and then correlated with each of the other categories to see what relationships prevailed and whether any patterning was evident.

The relevance of this type of study of urban structure and land use for Pompeii is mainly the fact that so little analytical work has been advanced before. This becomes even more pronounced when one attempts to consider the social structure. Yet, in keeping with the view of a city as a natural, functioning organism, social interpretations of the evidence are necessary. Beyond the scope of the Roman provincial cities of the Campanian plain, there is no reason why certain regular aspects of the Roman system should not be applied to Roman cities elsewhere, so long as enough of the town plan is available for interpretation. In Britain, parts of Verulamium (St. Albans) and Calleva (Silchester) might be suitable subjects for this kind of analysis. Also, urban geographical techniques would provide a valuable perspective into any period of urban development, particularly in the study of economic base analysis, zonation of various features, land values and ownership patterns. Archaeology can produce the data, particularly in the form of the land use plan, so long as the evidence is present.

Acknowledgements

I should like to thank Professor A. C. Renfrew of the Department of Archaeology, University of Southampton, for his help and advice during the course of writing this dissertation. I am also indebted to the late Dr. D. L. Clarke, Fellow of Peterhouse College, Cambridge, for his encouraging conversations; and to Dr. J. B. Ward-Perkins, late Director of the British School in Rome, for allowing me to study in the British School library at will.

Bibliography

Alonso, W. (1964). The historic and structural theories of urban form. *Land Economics*, **40**, 227-231.
Anderson, N. and Ishwaron, K. (1965). *Urban Sociology*. Asia Publishing House, London.
Balsdon, J. P. V. D. (1969). *Life and Leisure in Ancient Rome*. Bodley Head, London.

Berry, B. J. L. and Horton, F. E. (1970). *Geographic Perspectives on Urban Systems.* Prentice-Hall, New Jersey.

Berry, B. J. L. (1959). Ribbon developments in the urban business patterns. *Annals of the American Association of Geographers,* **49,** 145-155.

Beshers, J. M. (1962). *Urban Social Structure.* The Free Press of Glencoe, New York.

Bourne, L. S. (Ed.) (1971). *The Internal Structure of the City: Readings on Space and Environment.* Oxford University Press, London.

Boyle, B. M. (1969). The ancient townhouse reconsidered. *American Journal of Archaeology,* **73,** 231-232.

Brion, M. (1960). *Pompeii and Herculaneum.* Elek Books, London.

Brogan, O. (1953). *Roman Gaul.* G. Bell and Sons, London.

Burgess, E. W. (1925). Can neighbourhood work have a scientific basis. In *The City* (R. E. Park, E. W. Burgess and R. D. McKenzie, Eds). University of Chicago Press, Chicago.

Burgess, E. N. (1925). The growth of the city: an introduction to a research project. In *The City* (R. E. Park, E. N. Burgess and R. D. McKenzie, Eds). University of Chicago Press, Chicago.

Carrington, R. C. (1933). The ancient Italian townhouse. *Antiquity,* **7,** 133-152.

Carrington, R. C. (1936). *Pompeii.* Clarendon Press, Oxford.

Chorley, R. J. and Haggett, P. (1970). *Socio-economic Models in Geography.* Methuen University Paperbacks, London.

Clark, B. D. and Gleave, M. D. (1973). *Social Patterns in Cities.* I.B.G. Special Publication No. 5, Alden and Mowbray, Oxford.

Della Corte, M. (1965). *Case ed Abitanti di Pompeii.* Soprano, Napoli.

Department of Geography, University College London (1971). *The Multivariate Classification of Local Labour Market Areas.* Housing and Labour Mobility Study, Working Paper No. 2.

Dilke, O. A. N. (1971). *The Roman Land Surveyors.* David and Charles, Newton Abbot.

Eschebach, H. (1970). Die Stadtebauliche Entwicklung des Antiken Pompeji, mit einem plan 1:1000. In *Mitteilungen des Deutschen Archaeologischen Instituts Roemishe Abteilung, Erganzungsheft,* **17.**

Everson, J. A. and Fitzgerald, B. P. (1972). *Inside the City.* Concepts in Geography, No. 3, Longman Group, London.

Gittus, E. (1964). The structure of urban areas: a new approach. *Town Planning Review,* **35,** 5-20.

Grant, M. (1971). *Cities of Vesuvius: Pompeii and Herculaneaum.* Weidenfield and Nicholson, London.

Grigg, D. (1965). The logic of regional systems. *Annals of the American Association of Geographers,* **55,** 465-492.

Guido, M. (1972). *Southern Italy: An Archaeological Guide.* Faber and Faber, London.

Haggett, P. (1965). *Locational Analysis in Human Geography.* Edward Arnold, London.

Hammond, N. (1972). The planning of a Maya ceremonial centre. *Scientific American,* **226,** 82-92.

Harriss, C. D. and Ullman, E. L. (1945). The nature of cities. *Annals of the American Academy of Political and Social Science,* **CCXLII,** 7-17.

Hartman, G. W. (1950). The central business district: a study in urban geography. *Economic Geography,* **25,** 237-244.

Hawley, A. (1950). *Human Ecology.* Ronald Press, New York.

Hesbert, D. T. (1970). Principal component analysis and urban social structure: a study of Cardiff and Swansea. In *Urban Essays: Studies in the Geography of Wales* (M. Carter and W. K. D. Davies, Eds). Longman, London.

Herbert, D. T. (1967a). Social area analysis: a British study. *Urban Studies,* **4,** 41-60.

Herbert, D. T. (1967). The use of diagnostic variables in the analysis of urban structures. *Tijdschrift voor Economische en Sociale Geografie,* **58,** 5-10.

Hodder, I. R. (1972). Locational models and the study of Romano-British settlement. In *Models in Archaeology* (D. L. Clarke, Ed.), Chap. 23. Methuen, London.

Hoyt, H. (1964). Recent distortions of the classical models of urban structure. *Land Economics,* **40,** 99-212.

Jashemski, W. F. (1972). The discovery of a large vineyard at Pompeii; University of Maryland excavations, 1970. *American Journal of Archaeology,* **77** (Jan. 1973), 27-43.

Jones, E. (1960). *A Social Geography of Belfast.* Oxford University Press, London.

Maiuri, A. (1960). *Pompeii.* Instituto Geografico de Agostini, Novara.

Maiuri, A. (1970). *Pompeii.* Guide books to the museum and monuments of Italy, Instituto Poligrafico dello Stato, Roma.

Martin, L. and March, L. (1972). *Urban Space and Structures.* Alden and Mowbray, Oxford for Cambridge University Press.

McKenzie, R. D. (1925). The ecological approach to the study of the human community. In *The City* (R. E. Park, E. W. Burgess and R. D. McKenzie, Eds). University of Chicago Press, Chicago.

Moser, C. A. and Scott, N. (1961). *British Towns: A Statistical Study of their Social and Economic Differences.* Oliver and Boyd, Edinburgh and London.

Murphy, R. E. (1966). *The American City: An Urban Geography.* McGraw-Hill, New York.

Park, R. E. (1952). *Human Communities: The City and Human Ecology.* The Free Press of Glencoe, New York.

Park, R. E. and Burgess, E. N. (Eds) (1921). Personal competition, social selection, and status. In *Introduction to the Science of Sociology,* pp. 708-714. University of Chicago Press, Chicago.

Packer, J. E. (1971). The Insulae of Imperial Ostia. *Memoirs of the American Academy in Rome,* XXXI.

Reid, J. S. (1913). *The Municipalities of the Roman Empire.* Cambridge University Press, London.

Smith, R. E. (1965). Method and purpose in functional town classification. *Annals of the American Association of Geographers,* **55,** 339-348.

Timms, D. N. (1971). *The Urban Mosaic,* Alden and Mowbray, Oxford for Cambridge University Press.

Willhelm, S. M. (1962). *Urban Zoning and Land Use Theory.* The Free Press of Glencoe, New York.

Wilson, F. H. (1953). Studies in the Social and economic history of Ostia. *Annual of the British School in Rome,* **13,** 41-68.

6

Some New Directions in the Spatial Analysis of Archaeological Data at the Regional Scale (Macro)

IAN HODDER
*Department of Archaeology,
University of Leeds*

1. Introduction

There has always been a very strong spatial component in archaeological work. The distribution map lies behind some of the most central themes in archaeology, such as trade, diffusion and the most important concept of culture, as developed in the writings of, for example, Childe, Fox and Hawkes. The analysis of such patterns has, however, been limited to visual and subjective inspection. As a result, early hypotheses concerning spatial behaviour as seen in archaeological material have not been subject to any detailed and systematic analysis, and have shown little development.

The study presented here, is an attempt to apply quantitative and statistical techniques to archaeological distribution patterns, so that they, and the concepts based on them, may be examined with greater objectivity and rigour. A further aim is the formulation of explicit models, in a mathematical form, concerning human spatial behaviour. This approach allows the behaviour to be described clearly and clarifies the fitting of models to data. Explicit models are beginning to be used widely in archaeology but, unless their "fit" to the data is testable, their appropriateness often remains difficult to demonstrate (Hodson, 1973). If various aspects of behaviour can be modelled in this way, it may be possible to examine systematically the interplay between different parts of the total field of human behaviour (Doran,

1969). In addition, it is hoped that the models which are examined in
this study are of interest to other social sciences. It is often the case that
the greater time depth of archaeological material allows concepts and
models in, for example, geography and anthropology to be broadened.
The formulation of these models in a quantified form allows them to
be used and tested in other branches of the social sciences with greater
facility.

A concept to be found in the following sections should be explained
at the outset. Non-random spatial patterns (e.g. Fig. 1) are expected
because individual behaviour is not random but is constrained and
determined by, for example, kinship factors in the exchange of goods
and economic and physical factors in the location of sites. However, it
will be found that this non-random behaviour is often not apparent in
the spatial patterns. Many of the observed archaeological patterns
have a form which is similar to patterns produced by a random
process. If the form of the pattern is similar to the end result of a
random process, this does not necessarily mean that the process which
produced the observed pattern was random. It is possible, however,
that, given a "satellite view", aggregate human behaviour is often best
simulated by a random process, or by very simple models incorporating
a strong random element. This view has been put forward by Curry
(1964, 1967) and developed, for example, by Cliff and Ord (1973,
1974). According to Curry,

> every decision may be optimal from a particular point of view and yet the resulting
> actions as a whole may appear as random. Lack of information, social ties, and so
> on will change an economic optimizing solution but not the randomness formulation
> (Curry, 1964, p. 138).

It is possible to consider behaviour as rational when all the constraints
of a decision are known, and this is the level at which social
anthropologists are able to work in studying human interaction (e.g.
Barnes, 1972). However, especially in a dynamic framework, there is
such a large number of decisions being taken, rarely coincident in time
and being separately motivated under differing circumstances and
degrees of information, that comprehension of rationality on a wide
scale is impossible. Thus, "men, motivated by various ideas, act so that
from the point of view of the locational structure as a whole their
actions appear as random" (Curry, 1964, pp. 145-6).

It is perhaps helpful to compare this notion of random aggregate
behaviour with that of entropy in information theory. In a system in
which the items can behave in an unconstrained fashion there can be

said to be much entropy. In this situation, there is a wide variety of choice available for any action so that the aggregate pattern of actions shows little order and provides little information about the actions. This is comparable to the notion of randomness discussed above.

> The results of an unrestrained random process can be defined as showing zero order. Order is achieved by placing constraints on the freedom of choice of action. This variety of available choice may be called entropy and is the complement of the degree of ordering (Curry, 1964, p. 144).

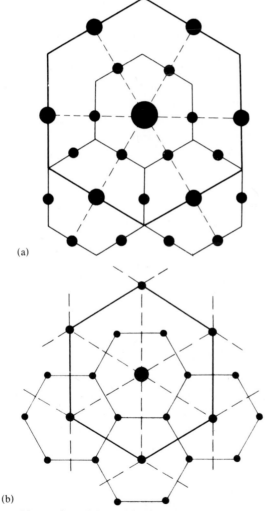

(a)

(b)

FIG. 1. Two problems of spatial organization according to Christaller. Larger and smaller service centres and their service areas are shown.

An obviously important point for most archaeological distributions is that much of the patterning which they exhibit results from spatial variation in the intensity of research, motorway construction, site survival, etc. Many archaeological distribution maps can be shown to be so disturbed in these respects that there is little value in applying methods of spatial analysis in an attempt to understand the past spatial processes which underlie the maps. In such cases, research effort may be more profitably employed in the collection of further primary data and in historical studies of the pattern of destruction, erosion and fieldwork which has affected the distributions. Even when apparently reliable distribution maps can be constructed, it is wise to assume that any structured patterning that can be detected in the distributions may be the result of survival and recovery factors. It is only when the play of these factors can be accounted for and understood that interpretation in terms of past spatial processes (such as trade and exchange mechanisms, and hierarchical relationships between settlements of different types and sizes) may be confidently entertained. The effects of survival and recovery factors and ways of assessing these effects are discussed in detail by Hodder and Orton (1976). The importance of survival and recovery effects will be frequently mentioned below. However, the main aim of this chapter is to provide some examples of the techniques that can be applied to well-documented and thoroughly studied archaeological distributions, i.e. those for which some attempts have been made to understand the play of survival and recovery factors. It is only as further detailed fieldwork of high standard is carried out that the methods to be discussed here can become of wide use and importance.

2. Point patterns and probability distributions

This section is concerned mainly with settlement distribution patterns although artefact patterns can also be included. Many of the models discussed are also relevant to artefact distributions within a site. The general approach is to examine the nature of the point distributions by fitting probability distributions.

A. THE SIMPLE POISSON PROBABILITY DISTRIBUTION

Take an area divided up into quadrats and allocate points to the area at random, in the sense that every quadrat has an equal and independent chance of receiving a point and every point in turn has an equal chance of occurring in any one quadrat. What is the probability that a chosen quadrat will contain exactly x points? It can be shown that this probability is given by a Poisson function (King, 1969, p. 42).

This Poisson law has been widely applied to locational patterns as a useful norm against which empirical patterns may be compared. There are difficulties, however, in inferring the nature of a process from the form or end result of that process since many processes may produce the same end pattern (Harvey, 1968; King, 1962). Although the form of many locational patterns can be shown to be comparable to a Poisson distribution, most location theory does not suggest that settlements are located as a random and independent process.

> On the contrary, it is known that the probability of a store locating in any area is conditional upon a number of factors, not the least important of which is the relative location of other stores. Therefore, a simple model such as the Poisson law hardly is suggested by theory, and while it may serve as a convenient first approximation of the location pattern, it reduces to simplicity a situation which already has been acknowledged as a complex one. Besides, it is almost certain that other probability models could be found which would fit the observed facts equally as well, and unless there is theory to guide us in our choice, one model may appear no better than the others (King, 1969, p. 43).

It shall be seen below, however, that a theory for a process of settlement which appears as random can be developed.

Tests for randomness are based on quadrat methods and distance methods. In the case of the quadrat methods, the area is usually divided into contiguous quadrats and the number of observations in each quadrat recorded. The resulting observed distribution of quadrat counts may then be compared with the Poisson distribution (Greig-Smith, 1964, p. 61; Whallon, 1973). There are a number of problems associated with the use of the quadrat count method. For example, the results are seriously affected by quadrat size (Greig-Smith, 1964, pp. 56-7). The effect of the shape of the quadrats is less marked (Ord, 1972). An important assumption of the model is that the counts for different quadrats are independent of each other. This problem is discussed by Cliff and Ord (1973) and Pielou (1969). In view of these considerations, methods based on distance measures have been widely used in studying spatial point patterns. These methods vary according to whether distances are measured from each site to its first, second, . . nth nearest neighbour, or from random points to nearest individual. Methods based on random pairs (Cottam and Curtis, 1949) and a wandering quarter (Catana, 1963) have also been developed. The tests for randomness which use such measures depend on whether the density (λ) is known, as in the case with the Clark and Evans (1954) test which has been applied to archaeological data by, for example, Hodder (1972), Newcomb (1970) and Peebles (1973). This test indicates departure from randomness towards clustering or uniform spacing. When λ is estimated, Pielou's (1959; Mountford, 1961) statistic may be used, and when λ is unknown the tests of Hopkins and Skellam (1952) and Holgate (1965) are most appropriate. Perhaps the most serious difficulties connected with the use of distance methods are the effect of the size of area included in the analysis (Getis, 1964), and the effect of the imposition of a boundary onto the point pattern (Hodder, 1971). The boundary effects are of considerable importance and have been discussed by, for example, Hsu and Tiedmann (1968) and Kariel (1970).

Patterns of prehistoric settlement have repeatedly been found to have the form of random distributions in respect to one type of site in the British Isles. Tests on Iron Age hillfort distributions in a limited area in Wales (Pierson-Jones, 1973) and in Cornwall (Hodder, 1971; Newcomb, 1970) found no significant difference from random. A further study is presented here of hillforts in the Wiltshire area. Detailed maps of the hillforts were constructed (Figs 2 and 3), and the internal acreage measured from detailed O.S. maps. The forts were classified according to whether they are univallate or multivallate. To avoid edge-effects (Hodder, 1971), an area was chosen for the analysis so that measurements could be made to forts outside the area and so that the nearest neighbour distance from any fort was less than or equal to the distance from that fort to the coast, and straight line distances to nearest neighbours measured. The results of the application of Clark and Evans' (1954) test to all the hillforts in the study area are given in Table 1. This shows that the overall pattern is not significantly different from a pattern produced by a random process.

It seems that two factors may be involved in forming this apparently random pattern. The first is that the aggregate pattern of hillfort locations at any time may have been random. A wide range of variables had to be taken into account in locating a site, such as the distance to water, the type of soil and vegetation cover, the location of other sites, defence, the distance to suitable building materials and the proximity of routes or roads and markets. Differing reactions to this variety of constraints may have resulted in an aggregate random pattern. However this is certainly not true of all types of hillfort (p. 236).

TABLE 1. Nearest neighbour analysis of southwestern hillforts

	A	N	P	rE	rA	R
All hillforts	266	148	0.556	0.672	0.683	1.017
All hillforts $\geqslant$ 13 acres	266	49	0.180	1.177	1.140	0.968
All univallate forts	266	97	0.361	0.832	0.751	0.903
Univallate $\geqslant$ 12 acres	266	31	0.113	1.488	1.329	0.893
Univallate $\geqslant$ 8 acres	266	48	0.177	1.189	1.248	1.050
All multivallate forts	266	51	0.188	1.153	1.341	1.162[a]
Multivallate $\geqslant$ 12 acres	266	24	0.086	1.7	2.138	1.257[a]

For explanation of symbols see Hodder (1972).
[a]significant at 0.05.

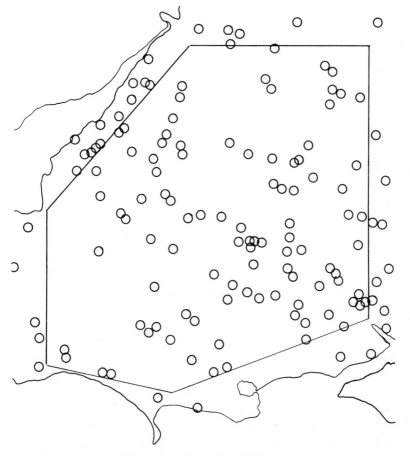

FIG. 2. The Univallate hillforts.

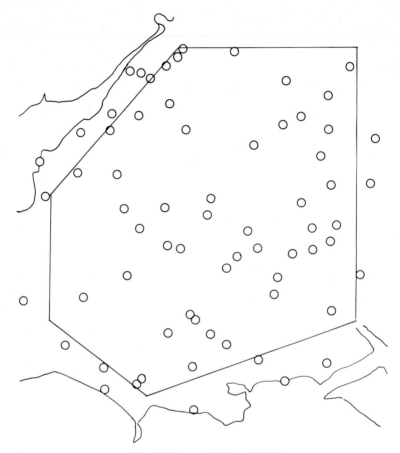

FIG. 3. The multivallate hillforts.

The second main factor which has affected the distribution is the pattern of site survival and fieldwork. Again, there are a large number of variables to be considered. Perhaps most important in the case of the hillforts is that the modern distribution represents a palimpsest of distributions of different dates. Also it is possible that all the sites classified as hillforts do not represent one category of site. Some may have been more stock enclosures than settlements. Regional variation in site survival must also be considered, with upland, massively constructed forts, surviving better than small lowland examples (Taylor, 1971). Some areas of Britain have been subject to much more detailed study, and this is a general problem in the analysis of archaeological distributions.

It is possible, in certain cases, to gauge the impact of fieldwork on site retrieval. The detailed distributional studies by Kruk (1973) and Laux (1971) include maps of fieldwork intensity (Figs 4-7). In Laux's study of part of the Tumulus grave bronze age in North Germany, the patterns of finds made at different time periods between 1820 and 1964 by museums and private collectors are shown. He concludes (ibid., p. 29) that each part of his study area was at some time well studied so that there are no gaps in the pattern of research. It is, therefore, possible to conclude that if an artefact type is not found in an area it was not used there. It does not mean that the type just has not been found there.

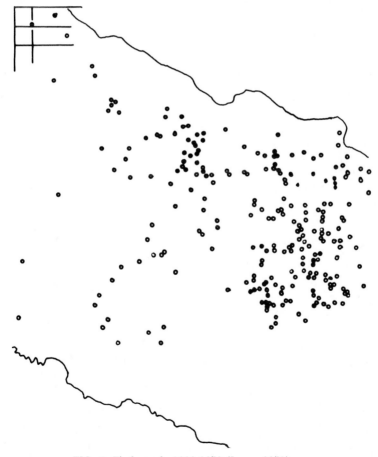

FIG. 4. Finds made 1820-1879 (Laux, 1971).

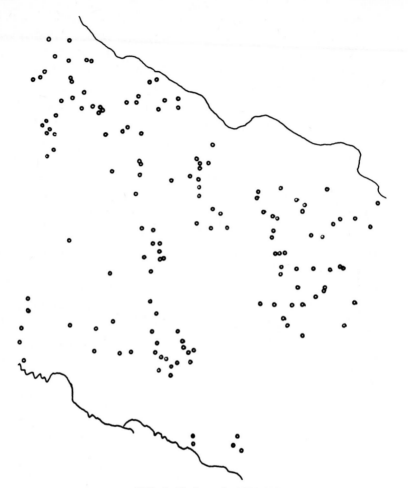

FIG. 5. Finds made 1921-1964.

The factors influencing the recovery of artefacts at different periods in Laux's study vary considerably. It is of interest to see whether the varying influence of these different factors has a great impact on the overall pattern of artefact retrieval. This was tested by using the V coefficient of spatial association (Pielou, 1969). It can be asked whether the patterns of finds at different phases vary significantly in the area between the Elbe and Aller rivers (Figs 4 and 5). If the pattern of finds made in the period from 1820 to 1879 is compared with that in the period from 1921 to 1964, significant association between the two patterns at $p = 0.01$ is found.

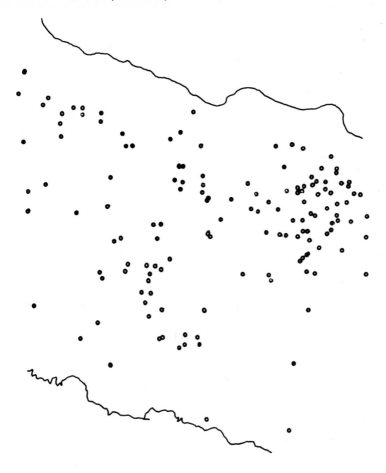

FIG. 6. Finds made 1876-1920.

This association was considered at the scale of the squares in Fig. 4. If, however, all adjacent four squares are joined to produce a larger quadrat, the V coefficient of association is increased.

There is thus greater similarity between the two distributions at a less detailed scale. With greater detail, variation is noticeable. For example, there are more late finds to the northwest and south, and more early finds to the northeast. It is of great importance that, in general, the effect of differential survival and fieldwork depends to a considerable extent on the scale at which the pattern is studied.

If two more recent periods (1876-1920 and 1921-1964) are compared, an even higher degree of association at the smaller scale is found.

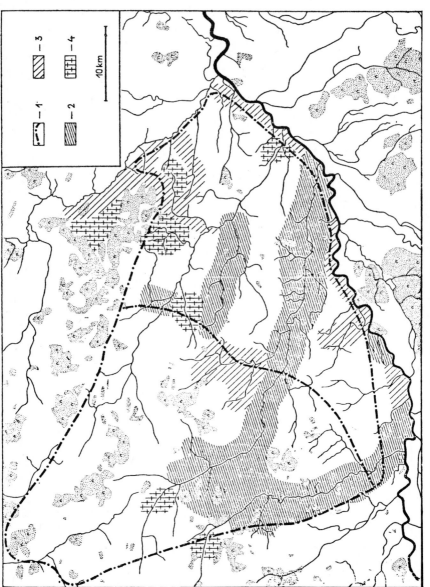

FIG. 7. The areas of study in S. Poland. 1. Limits of region; 2. Surveyed area; 3. Surface research; 4. Area not closely searched. (Kruk 1973.)

TABLE 2

		1820-1879		
		Present	Absent	
1921-1964	Present	56	52	108
	Absent	57	175	232
		113	227	340

$V = 0.28$. Significant at $p = 0.01$.

There is less difference between the two later periods than between the earliest and latest.

On the whole, it seems that, although the factors influencing the recovery of the artefacts change through time, the overall pattern of finds does not in this case vary significantly. Major fieldwork effects which have been made apparent in other areas, e.g. gravel digging, air photography and motorway construction, can usually be taken into account when considering archaeological patterns. These major effects are likely to produce a structured pattern whose structure can be interpreted accordingly. In other cases, there is clearly a great variety of factors influencing site survival and recovery as we have seen above. It is possible that the overall effect of these factors may help to produce a random pattern of sites. Dacey and Tung (1962) have shown that as the "random disturbance" of a pattern of points increases, so any trace of that pattern may be lost (King, 1969, pp. 103-107).

Skellam (1952) has pointed out that if random elimination of individuals occurs in a randomly distributed population, the distribution remains random, and, more important, if individuals are eliminated randomly from a non-randomly distributed population, a random distribution will eventually be produced when the density is sufficiently reduced (Greig-Smith, 1964, p. 217).

TABLE 3

		1820-1879		
		Present	Absent	
1921-1964	Present	40	12	52
	Absent	12	19	31
		52	31	83

$V = 0.39$. Significant at $p = 0.01$.

TABLE 4

		1921-1964		
		Present	Absent	
1876-	Present	42	9	51
1920	Absent	9	21	30
		51	30	81

$V = 0.52$. Significant at $p = 0.01$.

It is possible, therefore, that, in the case of the hillforts, the varied disturbances of the distribution may have helped to produce a random pattern. By more detailed analysis, however, it is often possible to identify some of the factors which go to make up the aggregate pattern of sites. For the hillforts in the Wiltshire area, the sites were grouped into various sizes of univallate and multivallate forts. As with the total pattern, these various types of hillfort are randomly spaced, except in the case of the multivallate forts (Table 1). These show a significant departure from randomness in the direction of uniformity of spacing. This movement towards uniformity is greater when only the multi-vallate forts of more than twelve acres internal acreage are considered. Cunliffe (1971) has given a visual impression of the regular spacing of major hillforts at one period in Wiltshire. By considering one class of site, and so removing some of the disturbance to the pattern, it appears that some degree of ordering, in this case competition between sites, is recognizable in the aggregate random pattern. The identification of this non-random pattern indicates that the degree of contemporaneity and competitive relationship between these sites would be worth examining in greater detail.

The distribution of Mayan ceremonial sites (data provided by N. Hammond) was also analysed in detail. Surveys of varying intensity have been carried out in three parts of the area covered by the sites. These three subsets of the total distribution have been used for the following analysis (Hodder and Orton, 1974). The boundary around the sites was assessed by drawing perpendiculars at the mid-points between peripheral sites in each subset, and the nearest site outside the subset. Connecting these perpendiculars gave an area enclosing the sites in each subset.

In all three cases, using Clark and Evans' test (1954), the pattern was not significantly different from a random pattern of the same density.

However, c, the standard variate of the normal curve, showed a movement towards a significant departure from random (in the direction of uniform spacing) as the density of sites increased. Thus subset 3 had the lowest density (0.0012/sq. km) and the least significant departure from random ($c = 0.495$), while subset 1 had the highest density (0.0030/sq. km) and the most significant departure from random in the direction of a uniform distribution ($c = 0.92$). This covariation between increasing density and increasingly significant departures from random could easily be due to chance. However, it was thought worthwhile to examine further whether in the higher densities of Mayan ceremonial sites any uniformity or competition in the pattern could be detected.

In many populations of, for example, plants or sites there may be competition, as seen in a uniformity of distribution, in the areas of highest density, even though the overall pattern appears random or aggregated when methods such as that of Clark and Evans are applied. But localized uniformity can be detected if only the short distances between sites are compared with the short distances between sites which would be expected in a random distribution. The closer two sites are to each other, the more intensely will they compete with each other, so that there may be a lower limit to the distances between sites.

To detect competition in higher densities a method similar to that used by Pielou (1962) was used. The distances from each site to its nearest neighbour were calculated but those greater than 14 km were ignored as only close neighbours were being studied. Thus a truncated frequency distribution of nearest neighbour distances was obtained.

It is necessary to fit a curve of form

$$f(\omega | 0 \leqslant \omega < c) = \frac{\lambda e^{-\lambda\omega}}{1 - e^{-\lambda c}} \tag{1}$$

to the truncated sample, where $\omega = r^2$ (r = nearest neighbour distance), $c = 196$ (c = the chosen upper limit of ω) and λ is to be estimated. In this case, λ was estimated from the site density (untruncated observations), using the formula

$$\lambda = \frac{n\,\pi}{A}, \tag{2}$$

which for all areas together gave $\lambda = 0.00636$, $\lambda c = 1.236$ and $1 - e^{-\lambda c} = 0.7095$. The nearest neighbour distances between 0 and 14 were divided into equal classes or cells and the number of sites

TABLE 5. Basic data

	subset 1	subset 2	subset 3	others	all
Area (km²)	4680	5002	10608	3616	23906
n (all)	16	9	14	9	48
n' ($\leqslant 14$ km)	15	6	6	9	36

falling in each class was compared with the number that would be expected to fall in that class if the distribution was random. The distances for all the Mayan sites were divided into seven equal classes, the boundary values being found by

$$\omega_r = \frac{-1}{\lambda} \log(1 - \frac{r}{i} (1 - e^{-\lambda c})) \qquad (3)$$

when $0 < r < i$. The observed and expected number of sites in each class are shown in Table 6.

TABLE 6. Mayan ceremonial sites

Cell	1	2	3	4	5	6	7
Boundaries	0-4.0	4.5-5.5	6.0-7.5	8.0-9.0	9.5-10.5	11-12	12.5-14.0
No. of observations	0	4	4	5	11	9	3
Expected no.	5 1/7	5 1/7	5 1/7	5 1/7	5 1/7	5 1/7	5 1/7

Interest is centred on whether competition occurred at higher densities, and an exact binomial test (preferable to Pielou's approximate normal test) gives the probability of having no observations in the first cell, given a random distribution of sites, of about 0.4%. There is thus significant evidence for competition.

If the same method is applied to the three subsets in turn the results shown in Tables 7, 8 and 9 are obtained.

TABLE 7. Subset 1

Cell	1	2	3	4	Total
Boundaries	0-4.5	5.0-7.0	7.5-10.0	10.5-14.0	0-14
No of observations	0	2	5	8	15
Expected no.	3 3/4	3 3/4	3 3/4	3 3/4	15

Probability of 0 in first cell = 1.3%.

TABLE 8. Subset 2

Cell	1	2	3	Total
Boundaries	0-6.5	7.0-10.5	11.0-15.0	0-15.0
No. of observations	0	4	3	7
Expected no.	2 1/3	2 1/3	2 1/3	7

Probability of 0 in first cell = 5.9%.

There is thus evidence of competition at high density (subset 1) and medium density (subset 2), but not at low density (subset 3). The pattern of sites using Clark and Evans' test proved to be random. It does seem, however, that localized competition does occur so that the closer together sites are located, the more intensely do they compete, resulting in a lower limit to the distances between sites.

In contrast to the hillfort data and the Mayan ceremonial sites, the overall pattern of Romano-British walled towns is significantly non-random with a marked tendency towards uniform spacing (Hodder and Hassall, 1971; Hodder, 1972). The factors producing this pattern can be considered in the same two groups as for the hillforts. In the first place, it is likely, in the context of Roman Britain, that there were considerable constraints on the choice of location of the walled towns. Although market forces (Hodder and Hassall, 1971) must have been important, so were administrative and military considerations (Webster, 1966). This restriction on choice resulted in a non-random pattern. The second main factor is that there has been considerably less distortion of the pattern than in the case of the Iron Age hillforts. The Romano-British sites are all contemporary and it is likely that most of the walled towns which existed have been found. With this much better sample the original ordered pattern can still be detected.

TABLE 9. Subset 3

Cell	1	2	3	Total
Boundaries	0-7.5	8.0-11.0	11.5-14.0	0-14.0
No. of observations	4	2	0	6
Expected no.	2	2	2	6

Deviations from the expected pattern are not significant, but, as in subset 2, the sample is very small.

Any non-randomness that has been found in the above examples has been in the direction of uniform spacing. A clustered pattern can also be detected with the same tests. An example of a study which has detected clustering is that by Peebles (1973) of mound sites in Alabama. Hill (1966) has looked at the pattern of objects within a site.

> Non-random distributions of ceramic design elements, pottery types, firepit types, storage pits, "chopper" types and animal bone indicated discrete *localizations* within the pueblo (which could not be explained in terms of functionally specific areas) (ibid., p. 17).

It was considered of interest that only the female items showed spatial clustering while the spacing of male items appeared random. Within-site patterns have also been examined by Dacey (1973) and Whallon (1973).

But spatial clustering of sites and artefacts will often be the result of local variation in the intensity of research or the pattern of site survival. The problem of differentiating between different types of clustered pattern will be examined in the following section.

B. GENERALIZED AND COMPOUND POISSON PROBABILITY DISTRIBUTIONS

The use of a simple Poisson probability distribution assumes a random allocation of points so that any quadrat has an equal and independent chance of receiving a point (Harvey, 1968). There is frequently a tendency in locational patterns towards clustering. In order to analyse such a pattern by comparing its observed quadrat count frequency distribution with a theoretical distribution derived from some hypothetical spatial process, use must be made of probability distributions rather different from the simple Poisson.

First of all, let us consider one sort of spatial process which would lead to clusters of settlement. Hudson (1969) has suggested a theory for the spread of settlement. An initial stage is that of colonization of an area by individual settlements or small groups of settlements. The spacing of these colonizers may appear random. A second stage of spread from these initial centres then occurs as population increases. There is a tendency to move short distances outwards from the initial colonies. Such a process may be aided by movement into the area from elsewhere, but the resulting pattern is one of clusters of settlement, which may be placed at random. A final stage in the development of the settlement pattern is a movement towards regularity of spacing due to increased overall density and pressure on the environment, a stage for which Hudson (ibid.) was able to give empirical support.

Wood (1971) has suggested that, for prehistoric settlement processes, this model of the generation of clusters by a contagious process of spread could be examined by fitting probability distributions to frequency information based on quadrat counts. Indeed plant ecologists and geographers have made use of a number of "contagious" models in which each occurrence (of a settlement for example) increases the probability of further occurrences nearby (King, 1969, p. 45). These models include the Neyman type A and the negative binomial. The hypothetical spatial process which lies behind the negative binomial and which may be termed *true contagion* or generalized Poisson (Cliff and Ord, 1973) has the following form. The clusters of points in the study area are defined as having a Poisson distribution, with each cluster containing one or more points. The number of points in each cluster follows a generalized distribution. If the generalizing distribution is logarithmic, the generalized distribution is written as Poisson $\vee$ logarithmic, which is equivalent to the negative binomial, while Poisson $\vee$ Poisson yields the Neyman type A (Cliff and Ord, 1973). According to Harvey (1968), the spatial law governing the distribution of offspring around a centre in the negative binomial case appears to be circular normal in form. "Insofar as the existence of a cluster means that an object is 'more likely' to have other similar objects nearby, we say that these processes represent 'true contagion' " (Cliff and Ord, 1973). A strict assumption is that the clusters are "sufficiently well spaced from one another for it to be impossible for a quadrat of the size selected to include more than one cluster" (Harvey, 1968; see also Skellam, 1958). Thus the size of quadrat used must be about the same as the size of the clusters.

This model for the generation of clusters of settlement has also been discussed by Anscombe (1950, p. 360).

> If colonies or groups of individuals are distributed randomly over an area . . . so that the number of colonies observed in samples of fixed area . . . has a Poisson distribution, we obtain a negative binomial distribution for the total count if the numbers of individuals in the colonies are distributed independently in a logarithmic distribution.

Harvey (1968) has suggested that the spatial diffusion of information is basically of the same form.

However, the negative binomial distribution will also give a good fit to clusters which have been arrived at by a different spatial process.

Clusters of settlement can be derived when the allocation of settlements is a random process (simple Poisson), but the mean density of that process varies from place to place according to some specified law. If the mean density (λ) itself is assumed to be a random variable, then if λ follows a γ distribution, the compound distribution is Poisson $\wedge$ γ, which is the negative binomial. Likewise, Poisson $\wedge$ Poisson yields the Neyman type A (Cliff and Ord, 1973). This compound Poisson or *apparent contagion* process simply implies random inhomogeneity in the density of the population. Harvey (1968) has also discussed this model in relation to the diffusion of innovations. In this case, with the compound model, inferences are being made about regional variation in the susceptibility of a population to accepting information. This might result, for example, from varying density of the population through which information is being diffused, or from spatial inhomogeneity in the cultural characteristics of the population accepting the information.

It is important to note that the very different spatial processes of true and apparent contagion can both yield the same negative binomial or Neyman type A distribution and this difficulty has been widely discussed (Harvey, 1968; Wood, 1971). However, an approximate procedure for the negative binomial which can be used to distinguish between the real and apparent contagion models, and which is based on the variation of the parameters of the model with changes in quadrat size, has been developed by Cliff and Ord (1973; see also Dacey, 1968).

Suppose that a study area has been partitioned into quadrats and a "good fit" of the negative binomial to the frequency arrays of items in the quadrats has been found by using for example a X^2 test. The negative binomial density, and the probability of getting r, when r is the number of items in a quadrat, can be written as

$$f_r = \text{prob}(R = r) = \binom{k + r - 1}{r} p^k (1 - p)^r, \qquad (4)$$

with parameters p and k. Consider a Poisson distribution with parameter λ, and a logarithmic distribution with parameter a. Then the Poisson $\vee$ logarithmic model (the "true contagion" negative binomial) has parameters

$$k = -\frac{\lambda}{\ln(1-a)},\tag{5}$$

and

$$p = a .\tag{6}$$

If s of the original quadrats are combined so that the Poisson parameter becomes $s\lambda$, it follows that k becomes

$$k = -\frac{s\lambda}{\ln(1-a)},\tag{7}$$

but p remains

$$p = a .\tag{8}$$

For the Poisson $\wedge$ γ model (the "apparent contagion" negative binomial), with γ density,

$$g(\lambda) = \frac{\lambda^{b-1}\,a^b\,e^{-a\lambda}}{\Gamma(b)},\tag{9}$$

the negative binomial has parameters

$$k = b\tag{10}$$

and

$$p = \frac{a}{a+1}.\tag{11}$$

In this case, if s of the original quadrats are combined, the parameters are

$$k = b,\tag{12}$$

as before, while p becomes

$$p = \frac{a}{a+s}.\tag{13}$$

Thus by calculating estimates for p and k for different sized lattices, we can see which of the models appears to be nearer the truth. This is only an approximate method of analysis because we cannot be certain that the quadrats combined to form larger quadrats have the same value of λ initially in the compound Poisson model. However, the procedure would seem to provide a reasonable check (Cliff and Ord, 1973).

Cliff and Ord have used this method to analyse a modern settlement pattern in Japan which had been suggested to be one of nucleated villages. The apparent contagion (compound Poisson) version of the negative binomial model was found to give a better fit to these data than the generalized model.

> This would seem to argue for a pattern of colonization essentially random (Poissonian), but with varying propensities to settle in different parts of the region (because of different land quality, for example) (ibid.).

This method for distinguishing between the apparent and true contagion versions of the negative binomial model has obvious importrance in archaeology. Settlement and artefact distributions (whether over a wide area or within one site) frequently exhibit some degree of clustering. It is usually difficult to understand the process which produced these clusters since regional variations in site occurrence, survival and retrieval result from a wide range of inter-related variables. As an initial example of the application of the method to archaeological data, distribution maps were studied of the early neolithic in a small area of the south Polish loess zone (Kruk, 1973). This is an area of intense archaeological activity and the pattern of survey and excavation is shown in Fig. 7. The earliest neolithic occupation of the area was by Bandkeramik settlements. Although the sites are mainly on "brown soils" formed on the loess, it is clear from Fig. 8 that there is no close relationship with any one soil type. The sites do, however, tend to occur on the lower part of valley slopes immediately above river silts of various rotation. In spite of this geographical constraint on the location of sites, "the occurrence of habitation traces in small isolated concentrations shows a striking regularity" (ibid., p. 247). The groupings suggested by Kruk are shown in Fig. 9.

> The Danubian 1 sites [Bandkeramik], which formed small and compact groups, fell into two distinct categories, the one comprising large and probably stable villages often situated in topographically exposed spots, and the other including small camps or offshoot settlements associated with places of permanent settlement. The concentration of habitation traces, their density, the differentiation of sites and finally the spacious wastes dividing particular concentrations—all this seems to point that we deal here with small isolated organisms which formed settlement microregions (ibid., p. 250).

The larger of the following Lengyel sites occur in similar positions, but smaller and perhaps seasonally occupied sites are found rather more on the interfluves. The groupings of sites are as in the Bandkeramik but usually "they consist of a larger number of settlements and occupy a distinctly larger space" (ibid., p. 250).

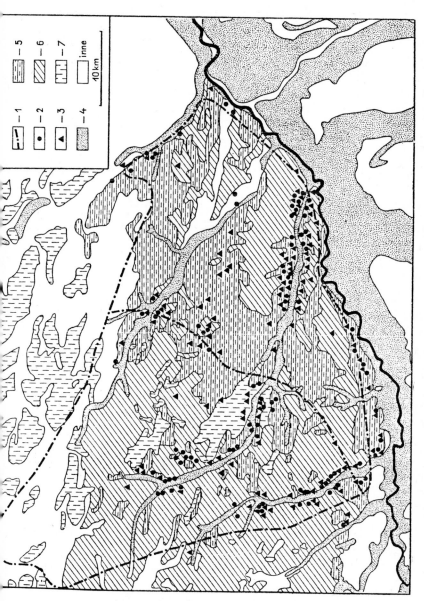

FIG. 8. Banderamik sites. 3. Lengyel sites; 5. "Black soil" on loess; 6. Deep "Brown soil" on loess; 7. Miscellaneous fertile soils (Kruk, 1973).

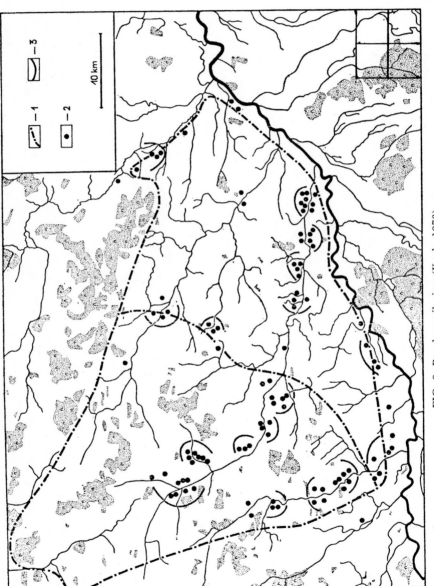

FIG. 9. Banderamik sites (Kruk, 1973).

The third stage of settlement in the area is that of the TRB culture (Fig. 11). "The appearance of the TRB culture marks a new period in the history of neolithic settlement in the area" (ibid., p. 247). There is a greater use of the "black earth" soils and a tendency to occupy the higher land of the interfluves. A mobile economy is envisaged with an emphasis on agricultural burning techniques in contrast to the earlier more stable settlements with their intensive agriculture economy. The following Corded Ware sites occupy much the same area as the TRB settlements.

In order to fit the negative binomial, the map of Bandkeramik sites was partitioned by a grid of the size shown in Figs 9-11. So that changes in the parameters of the model could be examined as the quadrat size increased, adjacent cells of the base lattice were combined in various combinations to produce new quadrats. The value of s in Tables 11-17 indicates the number of adjacent quadrats which were combined to form one quadrat in the new lattice. The negative binomial was then fitted by maximum likelihood to the observed frequency distribution of settlements in the quadrats for each lattice. (I should like to thank A. D. Cliff for making the computer programme available to me. It was written by A. F. Bussell, I.C.I. Fibres, Pontypool, Ltd.) The goodness-of-fit between the observed and expected frequency arrays (the expected values were obtained by reference to Williamson and Bretherton, 1963) was evaluated using X^2 wherever sufficient data existed. The results are given in Table 10 and indicate that the negative binomial is a good fit to the data. The maximum likelihood estimates of the parameters k and p for all the lattices are shown in Table 11 together with the values "expected" for lattices 2-9 from equations (7)-(13) given the results for the base lattice (1). Finally, the percentage differences between the estimated and "expected" values of the parameters are presented. Percentage difference is defined in this case as

$$100 \times \frac{\text{estimated parameter value} - \text{"expected" parameter value}}{\text{estimated parameter value}}.$$

With regard to the Bandkeramik data, it is clear that the generalized model of true contagion fits better than the compound model for all lattices and in respect to both parameters. It seems that the pattern of settlement may, therefore, be compared with a true contagious process. This may be due to clustering around the initial colonizers as in the model suggested by Hudson (1969). This is also clear if the

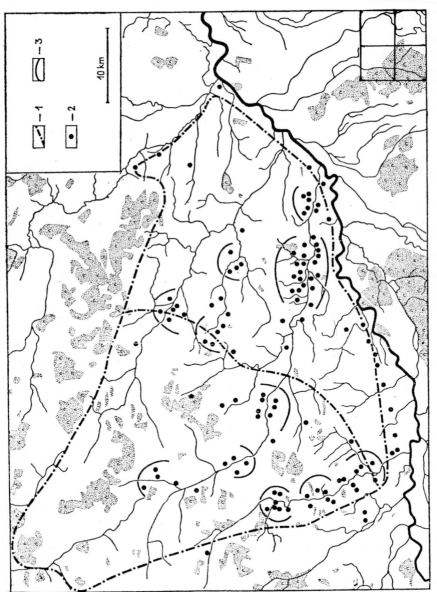

FIG. 10. Lengyel sites. 3. Some hypothetical boundaries of settlement micro-regions as suggested by Kruk (1973).

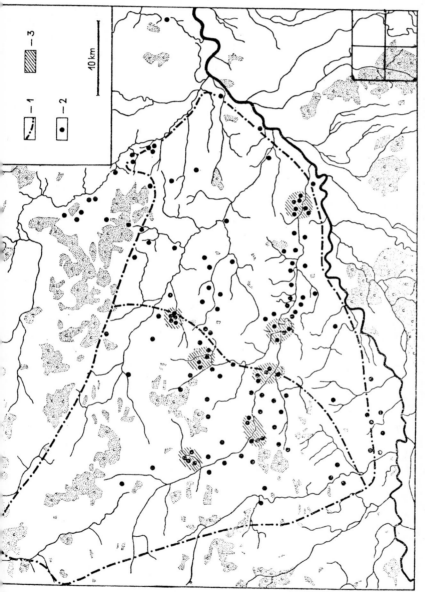

FIG. 11. TRB sites (Kruk, 1973). 3. Some regions of dense settlement suggested by Kruk.

TABLE 10. Fitting the negative binomial to Polish Bandkeramik sites

| | Lattice number | | | | | | | | | | | | | | | | |
| | 1 | | 2 | | 3 | | 4 | | 5 | | 6 | | 7 | | 8 | | 9 | |
Class value	O	E	O	E	O	E	O	E	O	E	O	E	O	E	O	E	O	E
0	66	69.6	23	21.4	25	23.0	11	9.3	2	1.9	4	4.1	7	6.1	7	6.1	1	0.64
1	11	11.1	5	8.5	6	7.6	5	5.3	2	1.8	5	4.0	2	4.0	2	3.5	1	0.86
2	4	5.2	5	5.1	4	4.5	2	3.6	2	1.6	2	3.4	3	2.9	2	2.5	1	0.94
3	4	3.2	3	3.4	2	3.0	2	2.7	0	1.4	2	2.8	1	2.2	2	1.9	1	0.95
4	3	2.0	4	2.4	2	2.1	4	2.1	2	1.2	3	2.2	3	1.7	1	1.5	0	0.91
5	3	1.3	1	1.7	0	1.6	2	1.6	1	1.0	0	1.7	1	1.4	2	1.2	1	0.86
6	2	0.86	3	1.2	4	1.2	1	1.2	0	0.88	1	1.3	0	1.1	0	0.9	0	0.79
7	2	0.67	3	0.91	2	0.91	1	0.99	1	0.75	2	1.0	2	0.8	0	0.77	2	0.72
8	0	0.48	0	0.67	0	0.72	1	0.77	1	0.64	0	0.79	0	0.7	0	0.62	0	0.65
9	1	0.38	1	0.53	3	0.58	1	0.62	1	0.54	3	0.60	3	0.5	2	0.51	1	0.59
10											2	0.46	0	0.4	1	0.39	0	0.51
11													0	0.4			1	0.45
12													2	0.3			0	
13									1								1	
16															1		0	
17																	1	
19																	1	
21									1									
X²	5.68		4.8		4.9		2.7											
Significant difference between O and E at $p = 0.05$	No		No		No		No											

O = observed. E = expected.
] = cells combined for purposes of X^2 test.

TABLE 11. Maximum likelihood estimates and "expected" values of parameters k and p for the derived lattices from the Polish Bandkeramik sites

Parameter	Lattice 1	2	3	4	5	6	7	8	9
Estimated values									
k	0.235	0.518	0.381	0.659	1.087	1.340	0.807	0.701	1.57
p	0.195	0.211	0.164	0.190	0.153	0.255	0.172	0.160	0.167
s	2	2	2	3	6	4	4	4	8
"Expected" values—generalized Poisson model									
k		0.470	0.470	0.705	1.410	0.940	0.940	0.940	1.880
p		0.195	0.195	0.195	0.195	0.195	0.195	0.195	0.195
"Expected" values—compound Poisson model									
k		0.235	0.235	0.235	0.235	0.235	0.235	0.235	0.235
p		0.107	0.107	0.074	0.038	0.057	0.057	0.057	0.029
Percentage differences—generalized Poisson model									
k		+9.2	-22.8	-6.9	-29.7	+29.8	-15.2	-34.1	-19.2
k		+7.6	-18.8	-2.6	-27.4	+23.5	-13.4	-21.9	-17.4
Percentage differences—compound Poisson model									
k		+54.6	+38.3	+64.7	+78.4	+82.5	+70.9	+66.5	+85.6
p		+49.3	+34.8	+61.1	+75.1	+76.8	+66.8	+64.4	+82.6

TABLE 12. Fitting the negative binomial to the Polish Lengyel data

| | Lattice number | | | | | | | | | | | | |
| | 1 | | 2 | | 3 | | 4 | | 5 | 6 | 7 | 8 | 9 |
Class value	O	E	O	E	O	E	O	E	O	O	O	O	O
0	56	55.9	17	17.6	15	14.4	6	6.6	3	4	4	1	0
1	17	16.5	11	9.4	12	10.1	9	5.5	5	4	2	1	2
2	7	8.5	6	6.0	2	7.0	3	4.4	3	2	3	3	1
3	5	5.1	3	4.1	8	4.9	2	3.5	2	2	2	0	0
4	4	3.2	2	2.9	5	3.4	2	2.7	1	2	4	2	0
5	3	2.1	2	2.1	0	2.4	2	2.1	0	1	1	0	1
6	1	1.3	3	1.5	1	1.7	4	1.6	4	3	0	2	0
7	1	0.86	1	1.1	2	1.2	1	1.2	2	1	2	2	1
8	1	0.57	1	0.77	1	0.82	0	0.96	1	0	2	0	1
9	0	0.38	0	0.57	0	0.58	0	0.73	0	0	2	0	1
10	1	0.29	1	0.43	2	0.38	1	0.57	1	3	0	0	2
11										1		0	1
12											1	2	1
13											1	0	
14			1				2					2	
15									1			1	
16									1				
21													1
X^2	0.83		1.26		6.8		3.68						
Significant difference between O and E at $p = 0.05$	No		No		No		No						

TABLE 13. Maximum likelihood estimates and "expected" values of parameters k and p for the derived lattices from the Polish Lengyel data

Parameter	Lattice 1	2	3	4	5	6	7	8	9
Estimated values									
k	0.414	0.719	0.968	1.062	1.282	1.355	1.541	1.955	2.495
p	0.269	0.244	0.301	0.239	0.222	0.251	0.255	0.225	0.236
s		2	2	3	4	4	4	6	8
"Expected" values—generalized Poisson model									
k		0.828	0.828	1.242	1.656	1.656	1.656	2.484	3.312
p		0.268	0.269	0.269	0.269	0.269	0.269	0.269	0.269
"Expected" values—compound Poisson model									
k		0.414	0.414	0.414	0.414	0.414	0.414	0.414	0.414
p		0.156	0.156	0.109	0.085	0.085	0.085	0.058	0.044
Percentage differences—generalized Poisson model									
k		−15.3	+14.4	−16.9	−29.0	−22.2	−7.4	−27.8	−32.8
p		−10.3	+10.6	−12.6	−21.1	−7.2	−5.5	−19.6	−13.9
Percentage differences—compound Poisson model									
k		+42.4	+57.2	+61.0	+67.7	+69.1	+73.1	+78.8	+84.9
p		+36.1	+48.1	+54.4	+61.7	+66.1	+66.6	+74.3	+81.4

development of the settlement groupings into the Lengyel phase is compared. Most groups show a marked tendency towards expansion outwards. The formation of groupings is, however, also the result of the functional inter-relationship of sites noticed by Kruk. In view of the lack of any strong relationship between the settlement distribution and environmental factors, it seems that the main determinants of the pattern could be a process of contagious spread and a functional interdependence of settlements.

The same procedure was also applied to the distribution of Lengyel and TRB sites. For the Lengyel distribution, the generalized model again fits better than the compound model for all lattices. The true contagious process suggested in this way is also apparent in the growth of the clusters, as discussed above. The TRB results are rather different however. As the lattice size increases, the compound model of apparent contagion becomes a better fit than does the generalized model. The estimated values of k and p for lattices 4 and 5 are closer to the expected compound model parameter values than to the expected generalized model parameter values. It is not clear which model gives the better fit, but there is a tendency, for the first time, towards the compound model. Although groupings still occur, as suggested by Kruk in Fig. 11, the pattern is becoming more like one in which sites are located by a random process (Poisson) with density variation according to, for example, the position of rivers and the pattern of site retrieval.

C. THE RANK-SIZE RULE

An important empirical finding, which should be included in a discussion of settlement patterns, is the rank-size rule. If the settlements in an area are ranked in decreasing size from 1 to n, then the rank-size rule states that

$$Sn = S_1(n)^{-1}, \tag{14}$$

where Sn is the size of the nth ranked settlement (Haggett, 1965, p. 101). Haggett (1972) has suggested that the Romano-British walled town rank-size relationship (Pounds, 1969) fits this rule. If the relationship is written as

$$\log Sn = \log S_1 - b\log n, \tag{15}$$

the parameters of the model may be obtained by the "least squares method" (Blalock, 1960). A group of Welsh hillforts (Pierson-Jones,

TABLE 14. Fitting the negative binomial to the Polish TRB data

	Lattice number									
	1		2		3		4		5	6
Class value	O	E	O	E	O	E	O	E	O	O
0	44	42.0	11	11.0	2	1.6	0	0.54	0	0
1	21	22.7	11	10.2	2	2.5	2	1.0	0	0
2	11	12.9	8	7.9	5	2.9	2	1.3	3	0
3	12	7.5	6	5.7	0	2.9	1	1.4	0	0
4	3⎤	4.4	3⎤	3.9	2	2.6	0	1.5	0	1
5	0⎟	2.6	0⎟	2.7	3	2.3	0	1.4	0	1
6	2⎟	1.5	3⎦	1.8	2	1.9	2	1.3	1	0
7	3⎦	0.86	3⎤	1.2	1	1.6	1	1.2	1	0
8	0	0.48	1⎟	0.80	4	1.2	1	1.0	0	2
9			0⎟	0.51	0	1.0	2	0.89	0	2
10			1⎦	0.33	1	0.77			1	1
11									1	1
12					1		1			0
13							1		1	1
14					1		2			
15										1
16										2
17							1			
18									1	
20									2	
X^2	3.56		2.49							
Significant difference between *O* and *E* at $p = 0.05$	No		No							

1973) for which the acreages are known may be analysed in this way, with the result that

$$Sn = 17.54(n)^{-0.8421}. \tag{16}$$

Comparative studies may be able to determine the reasons for variation of the parameter b (-1 in eq. 14). The relationship between the rank and size of the hillforts is shown in Fig. 12. It is clear that, although the model (eq. 16) gives a good fit to most of the data, this is not the case for the smaller range of forts. A similar lack of fit for small settlements has been found in other studies (Haggett, 1965, p. 107).

Berry (1961) has made a wide-ranging study of the relationship between rank and size in modern societies. He found two major types

TABLE 15. Maximum likelihood estimates and "expected" values of parameters K and p for the derived lattices from the Polish TRB data (see p. 254)

Parameter	Lattice 1	2	3	4	5	6
	Estimated values					
k	0.893	1.462	2.424	2.598	2.538	22.315
p	0.409	0.376	0.323	0.251	0.197	0.683
s		2	4	6	8	8
	"Expected" values — generalized Poisson model					
k		1.786	3.572	5.358	7.144	7.144
p		0.409	0.409	0.409	0.409	0.409
	"Expected" values — compound Poisson model					
k		0.893	0.893	0.893	0.893	0.893
p		0.256	0.147	0.105	0.079	0.079
	Percentage differences — generalized Poisson model					
k		−22.2	−47.3	−106.2	−181.5	+68.0
p		−8.8	−26.6	−62.1	−107.6	+40.1
	Percentage differences — compound Poisson model					
k		+38.9	+63.1	+65.6	+64.8	+95.9
p		+31.9	+54.5	+58.2	+59.9	+88.5

of relationship, the one corresponding to the rank-size rule and the other being a "primate" relationship in which there are deficiencies of intermediate sizes so that one or two very large settlements dominate the distribution. Simon (1955) has suggested that the rank-size rule represents a condition of entropy in which the forces affecting the distribution are many and act randomly. The relationship is found in more complex societies, or in a settlement pattern of some age in which, over time, many forces have had effect. In the case of the "primate" relationship, fewer forces have produced inhomogeneities in the system. Berry suggested that this form of rank-size relationship is found more often when the country is small, has had a shorter period of settlement development, has a simpler economic and political life, or a lower degree of economic development.

Cliff *et al.* (1974; summarized in Cliff and Ord, 1974) have obtained a model from Whitworth's (1934) work. Whitworth took a line of unit length cut at $(n-1)$ points located at random along it. That is, a line of unit length was broken at random into n segments. Whitworth gave the relationship between the size shares. A threshold minimum share size (Cohen, 1966) may also be introduced into the model. Cliff *et al.*

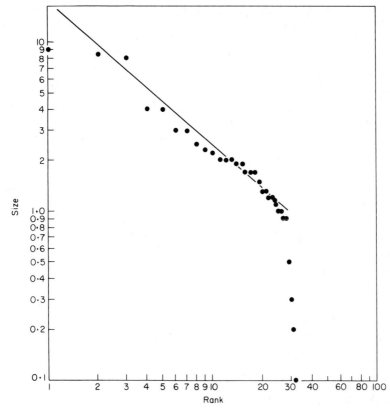

FIG. 12. Welsh hillforts: rank-size rule.

(1974) have tested the goodness-of-fit of the rank-size rule and this model to some real data. In most cases the random splitting process with a minimum share size gave the best fit to the data.

Curry (1964) argues that

> the rank-size rule can be regarded as the outcome of constrained, spatially random processes which allocate people to cities with attention concentrated on the "contagiousness" of numbers of people attracting further people (Cliff and Ord, 1974).

This is clearly an area in which it would be worthwhile to examine the fit of a model to archaeological data. Variation in the rank-size relationship in different regions, with different types of site, and over the great time span offered by archaeological material, may be noticeable and of interest. As was found in the study by Berry (1961), this variation might relate to differences between the social organization of societies.

3. The simulation of the spread of settlement

In Section 2.B there was some consideration of the process of settlement expansion. Detailed archaeological studies are beginning to appear of small areas in which precise chronological phases of settlement have been obtained. In these cases, it is perhaps possible to understand the process of expansion in greater detail, and a fruitful approach would seem to be by simulation.

A. SIMULATION

The possibility of computer simulation to examine archaeological hypotheses has been discussed by Doran (1969). In the following account, simulation will be used with the meaning: if there are n phases of settlement then begin with the pattern of sites in phase 1 and simulate through phases 2, 3, 4, . . . to phase n according to some hypotheses about the process of settlement spread. Different hypotheses can be experimented with until the simulated phase n pattern is similar to the observed pattern. Simulation is, therefore, a method of experimenting with and examining hypotheses. The process of spread in this study will be considered as stochastic.

> Many ingredients of individual human behaviour are causally so complex that their aggregate spatial expression is usually randomly determined within *certain constraints* (stochastically determined), even though the decisions behind this behaviour are not randomly motivated (Pred, 1967, p. 307).

It might be objected, however (ibid.), that, if we start with the observed pattern and simulate the spread of settlement according to probabilistic rules which are derived from the observed process of spread, it is hardly surprising that the simulated pattern at phase n is somewhat similar to the observed pattern at phase n. Indeed, in reference to Morrill's (1962, 1963, 1965) work on simulation, Pred (1967, p. 319) suggests that "we gain absolutely no additional comprehension of the processes involved". It will be shown, however, that simulation is a useful way of examining hypotheses if, as with Hägerstrand's work, it is coupled with detailed empirical work. A further problem is that different processes may yield the same result, and this is a difficulty which must continually be borne in mind and examined with different simulations. Other difficulties are discussed by Brown and Moore (1969).

Perhaps the major problem connected with simulating archaeological material is that the relative length of phases of settlement is often unknown. In certain cases, such as the development of settlement in the Aegean Bronze Age, some idea of the length of periods can be gained (Renfrew, 1972). However, in most cases in prehistoric Europe the phases of settlement are based on pottery typology, and carbon 14 dating does not usually provide a sufficiently accurate time scale for these typological changes. Thus, for example, similar processes of settlement spread in two archaeological phases may appear as different processes if the phases are of greatly differing length. This is clearly a serious difficulty in using simulation to examine such evidence, although it may be minimized by applying it to very detailed studies in which all the phases can be assumed to be comparatively short. In general, it is to be hoped that, in the future, sophisticated simulation procedures may be able to examine the impact of incomplete and imprecise data on the generation of hypotheses about settlement.

B. THE SPREAD OF SETTLEMENT

The most important types of diffusion which have been noticed in other social sciences are *relocation* and *expansion* diffusion (Gould, 1969; Haggett, 1972). In relocation diffusion, the area of settlement or acceptance of an idea moves completely at different time periods. This type of diffusion is seen in the pattern of site movement in the phases of La Tène in the Marne area in France (Bretz-Mahler, 1971). In the following study, examination will be made of expansion diffusion in which the settlement or acceptance area remains the same but expands at the periphery and intensifies at the centre.

Expansion diffusion can be subdivided into contagious diffusion in which the process of spread depends on direct neighbourhood contact, and hierarchic diffusion in which innovations spread first to the largest centres and then move down the hierarchy to smaller centres. Empirically the diffusion of innovations often seems to be a mixture of contagious and hierarchic diffusion (Abler *et al.*, 1971; Hägerstrand, 1967; cf. Jope, 1972).

Important developments in the simulation of innovation diffusion have been made by Hägerstrand (1953), and the methods employed are relevant to the diffusion of settlement. Hägerstrand (ibid.) noticed that in a number of studies of human interaction, interaction (I) with a centre decreased with distance (D) in a negative exponential manner (Hodder, 1974a):

$$I = aD^{-b}. \tag{17}$$

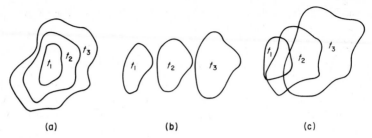

(a)   (b)   (c)

FIG. 13. Distinction between the main types of spatial diffusion. (a) Expansion diffusion. (b) Relocation diffusion. (c) Combined expansion and relocation process. (Haggett, 1972.)

If there is a point at which an innovation has been accepted in an area of non-adopters, then interaction with that point will decrease with distance according to the exponential model. Hägerstrand suggested that a non-adopter accepts an innovation as soon as he is contacted by an existing adopter (this assumption was modified in later, more complex, simulations). Thus, if the probability of contact decreases with distance according to the model (eq. 17) so does the likelihood of adoption of the innovation. Therefore, for any point of acceptance, it is possible to predict the probability of acceptance in the surrounding area as a result of contact with that initial point. With this model it is possible, therefore, to simulate the spread of the innovation as a stochastic process. Hägerstrand (ibid.) examined a number of different hypotheses in this way, and the result of a simple two dimensional process is shown in Fig. 14, in which at each iteration of the model, each adopter tells one other person, adopter or non-adopter. The main characteristics of the pattern are that over time the area of acceptance becomes quite irregular in shape, although a certain *central stability* is maintained. "High acceptance frequencies tend to emerge where the diffusion originally began" (ibid., p. 256). It was also found, however, that long distance leaps which occur by chance early on, tend to develop into peripheral groupings of high acceptance.

> The scatter of informed persons at the very beginning of the process proves to be the decisive factor in the later location of those areas where we find high percentages of acceptances (ibid., p. 256).

Bylund (1960) has discussed the diffusion of settlement in Sweden. The recent settlement pattern does show a preference for good soils and favourable climate for example, and these areas were exploited before inferior areas (cf. Sherratt, 1973). This does not account for the whole

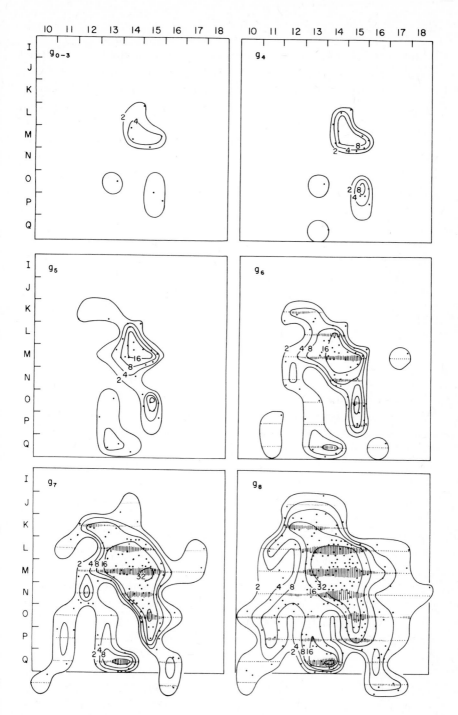

FIG. 14. Hägerstrand's (1953) diffusion simulation.

pattern of settlement spread since some areas have good soils and are not exploited or settled, while some inferior land is sometimes cultivated surprisingly early. Bylund therefore suggested a "clone-colonization" model in which settlements send off two offshoot settlements at each stage of the process. There is a strong tendency to remain near other settlements although competition for land has also to be considered. Certain areas, for example those near roads, are more attractive to new settlements however. A simulated pattern of spread of this form was compared with the actual pattern in Lapland (Sweden).

Recent developments in the study of diffusion in the social sciences have been reviewed by Brown and Moore (1969), and the problems met with discussed. Attempts at modelling diffusion processes have been mainly modifications of the basic Hägerstrand model (Cliff and Ord, 1974), and it is a model of this general form that will be used in the simulation of some archaeological data.

C. THE SPREAD OF BANDKERAMIK SETTLEMENT

Ammerman and Cavalli-Sforza (1971, 1973a, 1973b) have applied simulation techniques to the spread of neolithic farming across Europe. Their preliminary results are of great interest, but it might be objected that the scale at which the process is considered is too broad. The spread of the Bandkeramik is treated as a uniform phenomenon when regional variation seems probable (Newall, 1970). An alternative approach is to examine the pattern of spread of Bandkeramik settlements at a detailed scale, since in this way it is more likely that the process of expansion can be understood.

Detailed study is made possible by a number of recent publications. Meier-Arendt (1966) was able to identify five phases of Bandkeramik settlement, based on changes in pottery styles, in the Untermaingebiet. These changes are related to changes in pottery styles found widely in the Bandkeramik, and have little stratigraphical support. They can only be considered, therefore, as preliminary schemes. Four phases of Bandkeramik settlement in southern Oberrhein and in middle Neckarland are published by Sielman (1971, 1972).

Meier-Arendt (1966) and Bohmers *et al.* (1959) have noted the relationship between Bandkeramik sites, favourable land and river terraces (see also, for example, Kruk, 1973). Sielman (1972) has conducted a detailed analysis of the relationship of Bandkeramik sites to soils and to other environmental factors such as precipitation. In the earliest phase of settlement, sites are not found off the loess in the three areas mentioned above, and they are restricted to particular precipitation zones. It is only as population increases that spread off the loess and into different precipitation zones occurs (see also Sherratt, 1973). Any detailed simulation of the pattern of spread should take into account environmental factors. However, it seems possible that the main part of the process can be simulated successfully with simple models which do not incorporate such factors, and this is the preliminary approach which will be followed here.

The hypothetical process of settlement spread has two main ingredients: the growth of population and the distances moved by sites. Renfrew (1972) has used an exponential model for the increase in the population, as seen in the increasing number of sites, in the Aegean Bronze Age. This model appears to give a good fit to some of the Aegean data sets. The exponential model for population increase has the general form (Haggett, 1972)

$$N_t = N_O e^{bt}, \tag{18}$$

where N_t = the number of sites at time t, N_O = the number of sites at time O, b = the rate of increase. Growth of this form is unchecked. If we wish to introduce an upper limit (u) to the increase, which may be termed the carrying capacity or saturation level of an area at a particular stage of technological, economic and social development (Sherratt, 1972), the logistic growth curve is more appropriate.

$$N_t = \frac{u}{1 + e^{(a - bt)}} \tag{19}$$

where a is the value of N when t is zero.

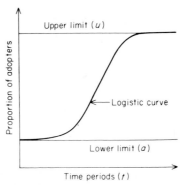

FIG. 15. The logistic growth curve (Haggett, 1972).

It is not clear what happens to human populations as the carrying capacity is reached (Haggett, 1972). Little is known of the rate of increase stopping abruptly, declining towards the ceiling or over-shooting before reaching an equilibrium, in different circumstances. Overshooting is common in animal populations but "because accurate census data for human populations became available only in the late eighteenth century, it is difficult to determine which, if any, of these simple models are appropriate" to human population growth (ibid., p. 164; see also Meadows *et al.,* 1972). This is an area in which archaeological evidence may be of considerable value and the irregular pattern of increase in some of Renfrew's Aegean Bronze Age data and in the increase of sites in the Untermaingebiet, perhaps suggests the model of overshooting. It is clear, however, that a number of different patterns of increase may occur, and future work may be able to identify with what factors variation is found.

If the model for logistic growth (eq. 19) is rewritten as

$$\ln\left(\frac{u-N}{N}\right) = \ln a - bt \qquad (20)$$

it is possible to obtain the parameters a and b by the "least squares" method (Blalock, 1960). This equation has been used to model the increase in Bandkeramik sites in the Untermaingebiet. This can, however, only be an approximate procedure since there are few data points (phases) and since there is only slight theoretical basis for the use of the logistic growth model. Ammerman and Cavalli-Sforza (1973b) used a logistic growth model in their simulation of Bandkeramik settlement because the exponential model yielded unacceptable results.

The relevance of the model can only be adequately tested in cases such as these by the collection of further data. As data becomes available for a greater number of short-lived phases within an area then the use of the logistic growth curve in this instance may well be shown to be inappropriate.

For the moment, this growth model has been used for the Untermaingebiet data, phases I-IV (Figs 17-20). Each site at phase t produced one further site at $t + 1$. Certain sites produced 2 offshoot sites at $t + 1$ to make up the necessary number of sites at $t + 1$ predicted by the logistic growth model. The sites which were to produce 2 new sites were chosen by numbering the sites at t and then picking from these by looking through a table of random numbers. Cunliffe (1972) has shown some of the variety of processes possible in the formation of new settlements and Soudsky (1962, 1968) and Modderman (1970) have discussed different types of Bandkeramik settlement move. Different processes of settlement splitting and formation will have to be simulated before the spread of Bandkeramik settlement can be said to have been adequately examined. For the moment, however, the

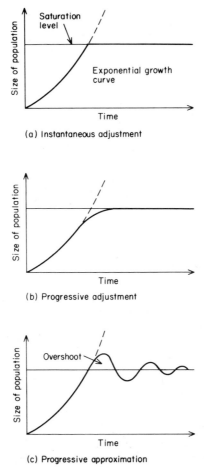

(a) Instantaneous adjustment

(b) Progressive adjustment

(c) Progressive approximation

FIG. 16. The three hypothetical relations between population growth and a limited carrying capacity (Haggett, 1972).

simple model of increase already outlined has been used in an initial run of the Bandkeramik Untermaingebiet data. That this is to some extent realistic is indicated by Meier-Arendt's observation (1966, p. 68) that a very large number of the sites have finds of one phase only.

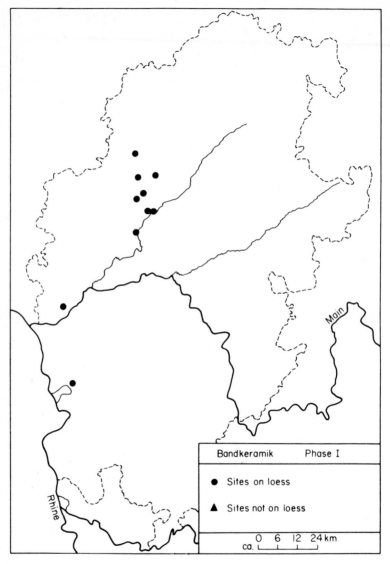

FIG. 17. Untermaingebiet sites (Sielman, 1972).

If material is found on a site from earlier or later phases it is usually so small in amount as to carry little weight. Of 24 sites in phase 2, only five have phase 1 material.

The second main component of the simulation procedure is the distance moved by sites. Sielman (1972, p. 45) has discussed the factors

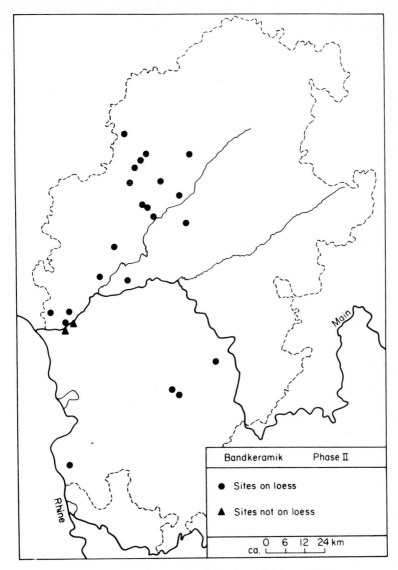

FIG. 18. Untermaingebiet sites (Sielman, 1972).

involved in the spread of Bandkeramik settlement. He suggests there is a "conservative tendency" which encourages short distance moves. He lays stress on the need to stay within the same environmental conditions as the mother settlements, and also on political, social and transport factors which have the aggregate result that offshoot settlements tend

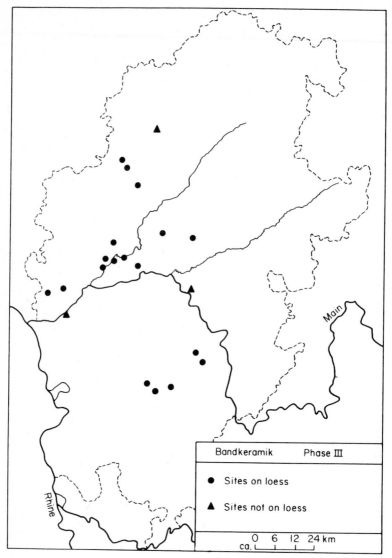

FIG. 19. Untermaingebiet sites (Sielman, 1972).

to move short distances. Similar factors have been discussed by
Ammerman and Cavalli-Sforza (1973b). The suggested model of
settlement diffusion is, therefore, one of gradual contagious spread
outwards and, before the simulation procedure can be applied, it is
necessary to see whether this model is appropriate for the Bandkeramik
data.

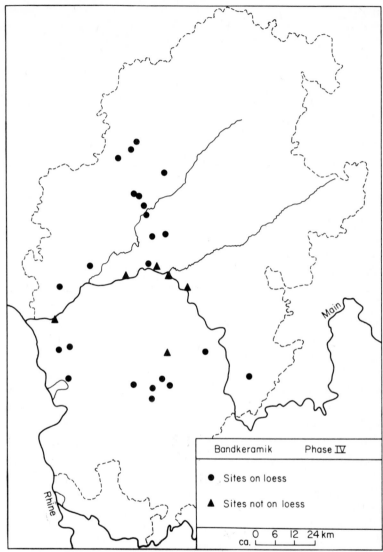

FIG. 20. Untermaingebiet sites (**Sielman, 1972**).

The relevance of the model can be tested with Barnard and Pearson's (1947) "2 × 2 comparative time trial" (Cliff, 1968). The data analysed are a pair of populations, in this case (a) sites at phase $t+1$ which were not occupied in phase t, and (b) locations which became sites at $t+2$ . . . . . . n. The time trial is used to examine whether sites at $t+1$ are nearer t sites than are sites occupied at $t+2$ . . . . n. A 2 × 2 contingency table can be set up of the form in Table 16.

TABLE 16

| | | Sites at t + n which were not occupied at t | | |
		$t + 1$ sites	$t + 2 \ldots n$ sites	Total
Whether neighbours include t sites	t sites included	c	a	m
	No t sites included	d	b	n
	Total	s	r	N

The variate

$$u = \frac{(cb - da)}{N} \bigg/ \sqrt{\left(\frac{mnrs}{N^2(N-1)}\right)} \tag{21}$$

is approximately normally distributed with unit variance (Cliff, 1968). If it exceeds the established significance levels, it is possible to accept the hypothesis that $t + 1$ sites are nearer t sites than are $t + 2 \ldots . n$ sites. Cliff (ibid.) used this test for first, first and second, first to third and first to fourth nearest neighbours. In an examination of the Untermaingebiet settlement spread, first and second nearest neighbours were considered. The relationship between sites of phase 1 and 2 shows that sites newly occupied in phase 2 are significantly nearer phase 1 sites than are new later sites (Table 17). In later phases, however, this process of contagious spread cannot be identified in the total distributions. After the initial stages of expansion, in which the greatest increase in the number of sites occurs, the sites cease to show a significant outward expansion and they locate to new points within much the same area so that sites of different phases appear randomly intermingled.

To examine the distances moved by sites for the simulation procedure, the distances between sites newly occupied at phase $t + 1$ and the nearest site occupied at phase t were measured (for an example see Fig. 21). It is clearly the case that there is a gradual decrease in the distances moved, but that, in addition, sites are not often located very close to earlier sites. In the Untermaingebiet pattern, there is a limit of between 2-3 km between sites. As a result of an inspection of the distribution of Bandkeramik sites in the Aldenhover and other areas, Ammerman and Cavalli-Sforza (1973b) suggest an average distance between contemporary sites of between 3 km and 0.5 km.

The form of the frequency distributions for the distances between $t+1$ and nearest t Bandkeramik sites suggested that the negative binomial distribution might provide an adequate fit to the data. In the cases where the X^2 test could be made (middle Neckarland data) this did prove to be the case (see Fig. 21). It should be emphasized that this

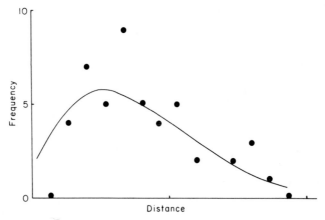

FIG. 21. The negative binomial curve fitted to the distance between sites. Middle Neckarland data, phases 1-2.

is an empirical finding which has no theoretical support. An alternative approach would be to consider the case of the relationship between two populations (a and b) located in the same area at random. The distances from each b point to its nearest a point, squared and multiplied by $2\pi\lambda$, can be shown to be distributed like X_2^2 (chi-squared with two degrees of freedom; I should like to thank I. Robertson for providing me with the proof of this which, in the one dimensional case, is given by Pielou, 1969). Since an important assumption of this model is that the two distributions are randomly distributed, it is not surprising that X_2^2 does not give a good fit to the data (the distribution was fitted to the middle Neckarland phases 1 and 2 sites).

The negative binomial distribution has been used to give the probability that new sites will move a given distance in the simulation of the Untermaingebiet pattern. As has already been said, there is no theoretical basis for the use of this model, and its applicability to the distances moved by sites must await their empirical support. For its tentative use here, the parameters of the model are derived from the distances between $t+1$ and nearest t sites. Thus, in effect, around

TABLE 17. Untermaingebiet: phases 1-2

| | | Sites newly occupied after phase 1 | | |
		Occupied in phase 2	Occupied after phase 2	Total
Whether later sites include sites at phase 1 amongst their two nearest neighbours	Phase 1 sites included	9	6	15
	Phase 1 sites not included	10	29	39
	Total	19	35	54

$u = 4.6$ (significant at $p = 0.01$).

every site at phase t a circular probability surface can be placed and the probability of moving a given distance at $t + 1$ indicated. There are, of course, considerable problems associated with this approach. In the first place, the negative binomial model is derived from distances to the nearest earlier site. This assumes that every site at $t + 1$ has been occupied from the nearest t site. This is clearly unrealistic and a very different pattern of moves may have produced the observed end result. The second main problem is that, by placing a probability surface around each site at a time, it is possible to locate new sites very near other sites. The resulting frequency distribution of distances between $t + 1$ and t sites may therefore be rather different from the observed pattern. To avoid this difficulty computerized simulations could check that new sites were not locating too close to existing sites.

A long programme of simulations is needed to examine these problems, but as a simple illustration of the method an initial procedure was followed using the negative binomial distribution for the distances

TABLE 18. Untermaingebiet: phases 2-3

| | | Sites newly occupied after phase 2 | | |
		Occupied in phase 3	Occupied after phase 3	Total
Whether later sites include sites at phase 2 amongst their two nearest neighbours	Phase 2 sites included	12	6	18
	Phase 2 sites not included	7	8	15
	Total	19	14	33

$u = 1.18$ (not significant at $p = 0.05$).

TABLE 19. Untermaingebiet sites. The probability of moving given distances according to the fitted negative binomial model

Phases 1-2

Distances (mm)	2	4	6	8	10	12	14	16	18	20	−30	−60
No. of sites	5.4	2.7	2.2	1.9	1.4	1.2	0.9	0.7	0.6	0.5	1.0	1.0
Number shares for random numbers	1-54	55-81	82-103	104-122	123-136	137-148	149-157	158-164	165-170	171-175	176-185	186-200

Phases 2-3

Distances	2	4	6	8	10	12	14	16	18	20	22	23-
No. of sites	2.9	4.6	5.2	4.5	3.2	2.2	1.3	0.8	0.6	0.5	0.3	2.9
Number shares	1-29	30-75	76-127	128-172	173-204	205-226	227-239	240-247	248-253	254-258	259-261	262-290

Phases 3-4

Distances	2	4	6	8	10	12	14	16	18	20	22	23-
No. of sites	2.7	4.9	5.8	5.2	3.2	2.7	1.6	0.8	0.6	0.4	0.3	2.8
Number shares	1-27	28.76	77-134	135-186	187-218	219-245	246-261	262-269	270-275	276-279	280-282	283-310

2 mm = approximately 1 1/2 km.

moved. The parameters of the model for every two phases were calculated using maximum likelihood (see above, Section 2.B). The percentages of new sites (the number of new sites was as predicted by the logistic growth curve) expected to move a given distance were then derived from this model. Each distance was allotted a share of numbers according to the expected percentage of sites to be moved that distance (Table 19). For each site movement, therefore, the next number was found in a table of random numbers and the distance indicated moved. As already mentioned, this amounts to placing a circular probability surface around each site to be moved, and this surface for phases 1 — 2 is shown in Fig. 22.

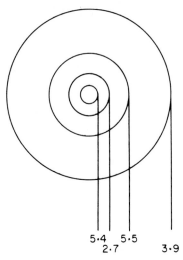

FIG. 22. Banderamik simulation. The number of sites to be moved within given distance bands.

The direction of the move was obtained by finding random numbers between 1 and 360, which provided the angle of move in relation to a fixed axis.

The result of the simulation procedure is that in phase 2 the simulated and observed patterns are closely similar. Hägerstrand (1953) discussed the difficulties in assessing the similarity between simulated and observed patterns, and Cliff and Ord (1973, 1974) have suggested some appropriate tests. For the moment, however, a visual impression will be made.

By phase 4 the similarity between the simulated and observed patterns is not close, but it is this lack of similarity which is of interest because it indicates to what extent the hypotheses incorporated in the simulation model are inadequate. In the first place there is a movement towards the main river valley in phases 3 and 4 which is identified in Fig. 25. This attraction to rivers has been noticed in relation to other studies of the Bandkeramik (see Kruk, 1973, for example). In future simulations some weighting would have to be given to riverside locations.

A second difference between the observed and simulated patterns is that in the simulated pattern there is insufficient growth south of the river. Although the one site in this area in phase 1 does lead to a small grouping by phase 4 (cf. Hägerstrand's comments (above p.) on the development of peripheral groupings from early offshoots), this does not reach the observed size. On the other hand, there are "too many" simulated sites in phase 4 north of the river around the initial phase 1 cluster. This main cluster has simply spread out slowly in the simulated phases, maintaining a strong "central stability" (Hägerstrand, 1953).

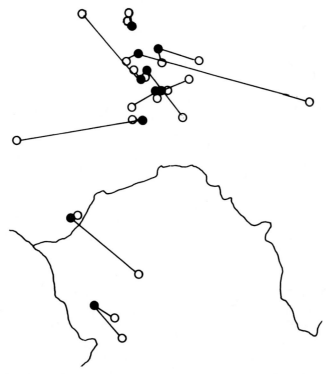

FIG. 23. The simulation of phases 1-2. Filled circles = phase 1; open circles = phase 2.

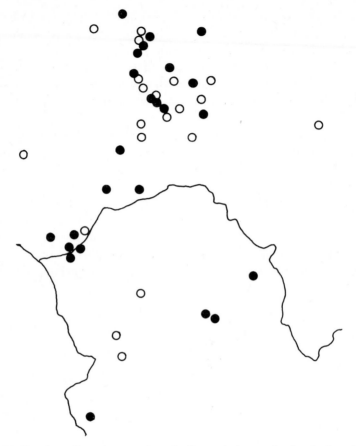

FIG. 24. Banderamik settlement phase 2. Open circles = simulated phase 2; filled circles = observed phase 2.

To adjust for this, future simulations would have to either allow relatively faster growth in the less dense peripheral areas, or direct some additional movement from the area north of the river to the south, perhaps because of soil preferences.

It is clear, therefore, that by simulating the spread of settlement we can begin to experiment with some simple hypotheses. In the future, more complicated simulations will be able to take into account the relationship of sites to soils and the numerous problems encountered above. In the initial procedure discussed here, the observed sites have been considered as representing a total settlement pattern. A major development in this field would be to examine the effect on the process

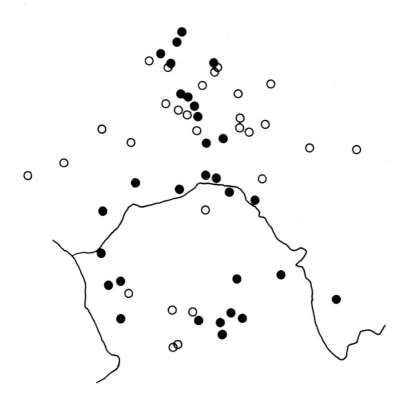

FIG. 25. Banderamik settlement phase 4. Open circles = simulated phase 4; filled circles = observed phase 4.

of spread of losing a number of sites (through destruction and lack of discovery). Simulation allows the possible effects of a wide range of variables to be examined.

4. Areas of interaction: the structure of single artefact distributions

The aim of this section is to discuss some methods for the examination of the spatial pattern and structure of distributions of single artefact types. One possible approach would seem to be by means of regression analysis.

A. THE FRICTION EFFECT OF DISTANCE

If a central node is considered with people going to and from the surrounding area, *interaction* with that centre can be defined as, for example, the frequency of visits or the amount of products or services obtained from it. The fall-off in interaction (I) or contact with distance (D) away from the centre has been examined (Hodder, 1974a) by fitting the following model to the observed patterns:

$$\log I = a - bD^a + e. \tag{22}$$

a and b are constants, a being the amount of interaction irrespective of distance and b being the rate of decrease in interaction with distance from the origin. This relationship appears as a straight line of negative slope when interaction (vertical axis) is plotted against distance (horizontal axis) on arithmetic graph paper (Blalock, 1960). e is an error term expressing the deviation of each point from the regression line. The variation of the exponent of distance (a) allows us to identify and compare the friction effect of distance on the movement of different artefact types. A number of distributions of archaeological material from known sources have been examined by reference to this model (Hodder, 1974a) and the best-fit a values of these data sets have been shown to form two groups which correspond in character to two types of interaction identified by geographers. For the archaeological data, the first group has low a values and includes comparatively small-scale local concerns producing the commoner and coarser products such as roofing tiles and coarse pattery. For the distribution of such products distance seems to have had an important friction effect. The group of data sets with higher a values consists of very large scale concerns associated with fine products. There is less friction caused by distance and the overall pattern of contact appears in all cases to have been complex, and to be comparable to the movement of objects from a point source by a random walk procedure (i.e. the direction taken at each step of fixed length is chosen at random). In the examined cases, then, it is the type or value of the artefact which relates to variation in the friction effect of distance and in the overall pattern of fall-off in frequency of the artefact away from its source. Other factors, such as changes in the technology of transport and production, might also be expected over time to affect patterns of fall-off.

Only the fall-off in objects made at a known source has so far been mentioned (see also Hodder, 1974a). It is also possible to examine the fall-off in similarity between objects with increasing distance. This can be illustrated by work on the middle Bronze Age palstaves of England studied by Rowlands (1970). (I should like to thank M. Rowlands for allowing me to use these data. The results of the analysis are to be published by us in greater detail.) A detailed study of these palstaves by Rowlands suggested a pattern of "repetitive production accompanied by a limited regional distribution for the metal types produced (i.e. localized demand)" (ibid., p. 229). Metalworking was a "dispersed occupation possibly associated with small settlement units" (ibid.). Various types or classes of palstave could be distinguished, mainly on the basis of the decoration of the blade face. Different types were found more commonly in different areas, the main distinct regions being the Cambridgeshire Fens area, the middle and lower Thames, the Sussex coast, the Isle of Wight and S.W. Hampshire and the Somerset area. A further group was found in the extreme southwest. The groups identified corresponded to the areas of highest density of middle Bronze Age metal finds.

The aim of the following study is to examine the nature of these regional groupings, and the pattern of fall-off in similarity with distance from them. This may be accomplished by taking from each regional group a palstave considered by Rowlands as representative of that group, and calculating the similarity of all other palstaves with that one example. The similarities between 542 palstaves drawn and measured by Rowlands or published in *Inventaria Archaeologica* were computed, based on size, shape and decorative criteria. A coefficient of similarity based on Gower's (1971; see also McNeil, 1972) general coefficient was used. (I should like to thank I. Robertson, Department of Mathematical Statistics, University of Cambridge, for discussing this coefficient with me, and for writing the computer programme.) Unfortunately there is little variation in the palstaves as a whole, except in the limited range of decorative features. There are few similarities less than 0.60, and any one palstave has a very large number of palstaves similar to it above the 0.85 level. This general lack of variation must be borne in mind in the following discussion.

As an initial step, classic examples of the regions defined by Rowlands were taken, and the similarity with these examples plotted in Figs 26-28 (see Table 20). Contours can be drawn at decreasing levels of similarity. The pattern of fall-off in similarity with distance away from a palstave in the Werrar, Isle of Wight, hoard is shown in Fig. 29. It is clear from the three maps that there are many localized

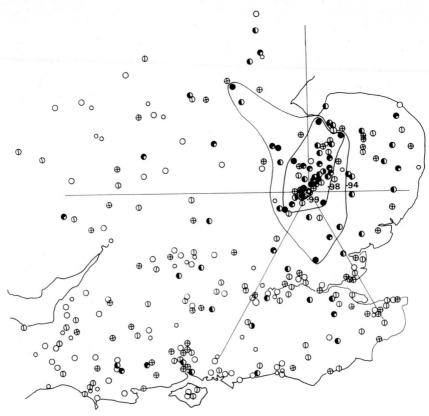

FIG. 26. Similarities with a palstave in easter England.

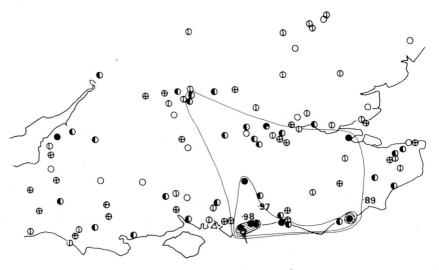

FIG. 27. Similarities with a Sussex palstave.

FIG. 28. Similarities with a palstave in the Isle of Wight.

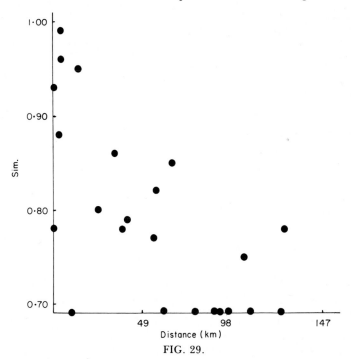

FIG. 29.

TABLE 20. Key to Figs. 26-28

⬤	Similarity greater than 0·95
◗	Similarity greater than 0·90
◖	Similarity greater than 0·80
⊕	Similarity greater than 0·70
⊕	Similarity greater than 0·60
○	Similarity greater than 0·50
○	Similarity greater than 0·30

Areas of highest similarity shaded.
Arrows indicate position of reference palstave.
Contours enclose areas in which palstaves at particular levels of similarity are found.

areas of palstaves which have very close similarities with the reference palstave, with a gradual fall-off until an area of fairly widespread similarity is reached. The small areas of close similarity appear to correspond well with Rowlands' suggestion that production was a dispersed occupation (see also below).

In the case of the reference palstave in the Cambridgeshire group (from Bottisham), the average similarities with this object in zones away from Bottisham were calculated. Concentric circles were drawn around this point and the average similarity in each band assessed by summing all the individual similarities and dividing by the number of palstaves in that band. The same procedure was carried out for each of the transects shown in **Fig. 26**. The best fit regression line for the relationship between similarity and distance was then obtained as for the trade distributions (Hodder, 1974a). In all cases, a pattern of gently decreasing similarity was apparent without marked and abrupt deviations from the fitted curves. This highlights the problem faced by Rowlands in his initial sorting of the material. Because it was necessary to produce groupings of his material in the manner followed by archaeologists, he had to choose, in effect, a boundary at some point along the gradual fall-off shown, for example, in Fig. 30.

It seems that two factors are involved in this pattern of gradual decrease in similarity. The first is that the number of objects made at one point were traded to a distance-dependent area (Rowlands, 1970). Only a few of these objects would have been widely dispersed. The second factor is that, as distance increased, there was decreasing contact with an area with a distinct tradition. This decreasing amount of contact is reflected in the decreasing similarity of locally made products. A pattern of local copying is suggested if the distances between extremely similar objects are considered.

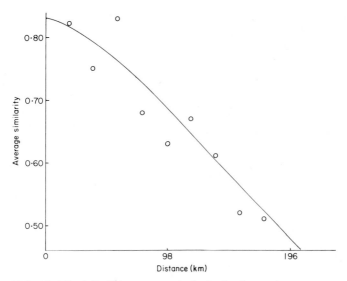

FIG. 30. The fall off in average similarity in the southern transect.

The distances between objects of 0.99 and 1.00 similarity are shown in Fig. 32, and the frequency of occurrence of each distance is shown in Fig. 33. Most of the close similarities are in the same hoard, at the same location, or in the immediately surrounding area. This again supports Rowlands' claim for dispersed localized production. It might be suggested that the pattern of close similarity links in Fig. 32 picks out the main metalworking traditions in the Cambridgeshire region and along the axis of the Thames. The separate traditions in Sussex and the Isle of Wight can perhaps just be detected.

The metalworking traditions and areas of contact are also visible in middle Bronze Age ornament distributions. For example, the zone of contact from the Isle of Wight across Dorset to S. Somerset (Fig. 28) is followed by the distributions of spiral twisted torcs and lozenge sectioned penannular armrings (Rowlands, 1970). Differences in metal content between the main areas have also been identified (ibid.).

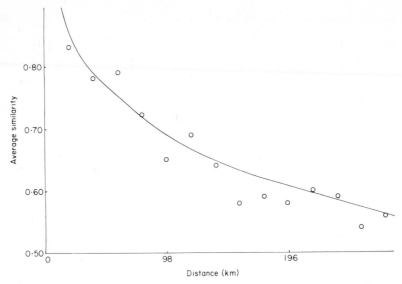

FIG. 31. The overall fall-off in average similarity with the Bottisham palstave.

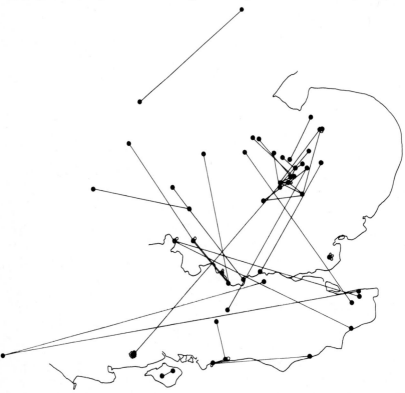

Fig. 32. Links between very similar palstaves. Close similarity between palstaves at the same location is shown by a loop.

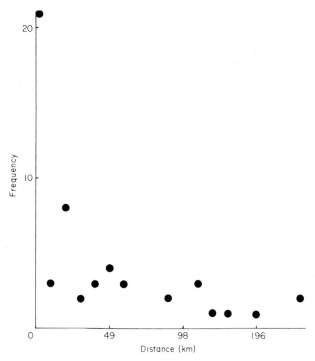

FIG. 33. The frequency of distances between very similar palstaves.

The structure of the overall pattern (in particular the smooth and gradual fall-off in similarity) can be compared with that found by Rowlett and Pollnac (1971) in their study of the similarity between Marnian Iron Age sites. Spatial groupings of sites were identified which show preferences for particular artefact types. With distance away from these groups, there is gradually less similarity in the artefact content of site assemblages. In the case of the palstaves, there are spatial groups of artefacts with particular typological traits. With distance away from these groups or traditions, there is a smooth and gradual decrease in the similarity of the artefacts.

Binford (1963) has suggested a possible model for gradual spatial (and temporal) change in styles which may be appropriate for the palstave data. A settlement or social unit may maintain a type but with considerable variation around this norm (see White and Thomas, 1972). Neighbours or offshoot settlements wishing to copy a type may be seen as taking a sample from this variation around the norm.

Binford sees this sampling as being comparable to random sampling subject to error. As a result of this sampling error the norm in the offshoot settlement may be rather different from the original one. The aggregate pattern would be one of gradual spatial change. Binford examined the typology of Pomranky points in a number of graves of the "Red Ochre" type in the late Archaic period in the Michigan area.

> Study of the patterns of variation between the several sites and their recognised variants shows that demonstrably different variants occurring at a single site are more alike than variants manufactured of the same material or other materials occurring at different sites. In addition, it is suggested that for any given attribute there is a rough correlation between the degree of similarity and the spatial proximity of the samples, suggesting that the Pomranky points were locally manufactured and not widely traded. . . . Examination of the concept of cultural drift leads to the postulate that such a configuration of regional variation would be expected if the variation arose from discrepancies in the generational continuity between social units within the region. This lack of continuity would result in the appearance of real differences between populations, stemming from sampling error in the manifestations, between generations, of the range of individual variability in the execution of norms (Binford, 1963, p. 106).

More recently, however, Binford has preferred a simpler and more generalized concept. "No communication system is perfectly efficient. There will inevitably be some inefficiency; some lack of perfect replication in behaviour which is learned via communication between individuals is to be expected" (Binford, 1972, p. 193).

It seems then that both traded or exchanged items and local styles may have a structure of gradual fall-off with distance. But it should be recognized that both the trading of objects and the diffusion of ideas or styles may underlie a distribution patterns. For example, the Romano-British tankards made in the Severn Valley area were traded to a limited distance (although some examples occur on Hadrian's Wall) and copied in local fabrics outside this area (Fig. 34; Webster, 1972). The processes which result in an apparently simple spatial structure may thus be extremely complex.

The friction effect of distance is only one of the factors determining the structure of single artefacts distributions. Important additional constraints on areas of interaction, whether artefact movement or artefact similarity is being considered, can now be discussed briefly.

B. OTHER FACTORS AFFECTING INTERACTION

The effects of geographical factors on archaeological artefact distributions are well known and of considerable importance. The friction effect of distance is, for example, relatively less along lines of easier movement. In the context of Roman Britain, the presence of a link by water to the Oxfordshire kilns has been shown to correspond to a relative increase in the amount of pottery obtained from there (Fulford and Hodder, 1974). The impact of relatively more difficult terrain on

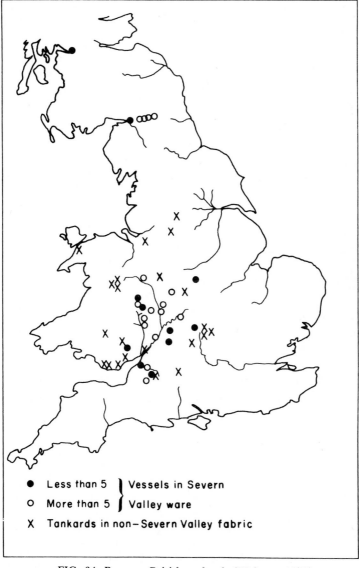

FIG. 34. Romano-British tankards (Webster, 1972).

the distribution of artefacts is evidenced by the pattern of Grand-Pressigny flint products (Jacob-Friesen, 1959). These show a gentle fall-off from the production area, but with areas of relatively less dense finds in mountainous zones.

Another factor affecting artefact distribution patterns is the "range" of the artefact related to its social and economic value. In a market economy, the range of a good, or the size of the area to which it is supplied, varies with local purchasing power, and the type or value of the good. A centre providing goods which are costly, or for which there is little demand, needs a wider area to obtain sufficient purchasing power than does a centre providing commoner goods. Certain goods are, therefore, only provided by centres located farther apart from each other than smaller, more closely spaced centres. In an area with n types of good, the goods can be ranked from 1 to n according to the size of area around a centre, or the amount of purchasing power, needed for the good to be supplied from that centre. The centre supplying all n goods will require the largest market area (in terms of the amount of purchasing power).

In Roman Britain, there was a low and dispersed demand for the expensive service of installing a mosaic. As a result, the centres providing this service were widely spaced, and served a wide area (Hodder, 1972). Roofing tiles, on the other hand, were in high demand and were supplied to small areas by local, closely spaced centres. The ranges of the two goods differed considerably. The fine ware products of the late Romano-British Oxfordshire, Nene valley and New Forest kilns cover much wider areas than the coarse ware products made at a large number of local kilns (Hodder, 1974d).

It seems that this same general model may be of importance in the analysis of prehistoric distributions. Objects of high value and/or low local demand might be expected to cover a wider area than objects which were of lesser value or which were used frequently.

The idea that, in both monetary and non-monetary economies, different commodities will move with unequal ease depending on their desirability, implies that long distance trade will tend to be limited to luxury durables that will retain a consistently high value (Rowlands, 1973, p. 595).

Thus in many non-monetary economies, subsistence goods and particularly food-stuffs, that are widely available and do not travel well, tend to have a lower exchange value and a much narrower circuit of exchange (both in distance travelled and in their trade with other commodities) than durable, prestige or luxury items (ibid., p. 594).

However,

> although goods can have an intrinsic value that may be expressed in a set of mutually accepted exchange rates with other goods in a network, desirability is not necessarily an absolute quality but can change in relation to factors like distance, mode of transport, freedom of exchange and accessibility to other exchange networks as alternative sources of goods (ibid.).

The value of the artefact was seen to be the main factor causing variation in the distance transformations of a wide range of fall-off curves (Hodder, 1974a). In addition, during the neolithic in Britain, the very coarse picrite hammer-axes have a much more localized distribution than the very fine axes of much harder rock from the Great Langdale source (ibid.). Similarly, the neolithic Hembury "f" ware made in Cornwall has a distribution source in an area adjacent to that of the neolithic group I axes. The main difference in their distributions is that the bulky, fragile pottery is found much less widely than the axes. Rowlands' (1970) study of middle Bronze Age metalwork in England, which has already been discussed, found that the spearheads and rapiers in this period have a distribution markedly different from the ornaments and palstaves. Localized groupings of the weapon types are not found, and the typological differences which can be identified do not relate to spatial differences. Each typological variation is found widely across southern England. Similarly, in the study by Bergmann (1970) of the early Bronze Age in north Germany, which is to be considered in detail below (p. 297), axe types, for example, are found over much wider areas than are a wide range of ornament types such as pins and fibulae. A problem here is that the specificity of definition is less with simpler classes of artefact. This difficulty will be discussed below (p. 292).

The location of competing centres also affects patterns of movement. The idea that interaction is more likely with the nearest centre than with any other similar centre, has recently been made explicit in a number of archaeological examples by the drawing of Thiessen polygons around hillforts (Cunliffe, 1971), Romano-British walled towns (Hodder, 1972), neolithic long barrows (Renfrew, 1973a), Mayan ceremonial centres (Hammond, 1972) and Maltese temples (Renfrew, 1973b). These Thiessen polygons simply enclose areas nearer to the site in question than to any other similar contemporary site.

A similar idea has been discussed fully by Bradley (1971a) in relation to prehistoric artifact distributions. Artefacts, such as pots, made in one centre, might be expected to be found over an area nearer to that centre than to another centre. A good example of this pattern which is given by Bradley is the distribution of Iron Age pottery made in the Mendips. Even when a centre of production is not relevant to the argument, similar objects and even similar typological traits will often tend to find different areas of use or demand. For example Scott (1969, p. 212) has discussed the distribution of Passage Graves around the periphery of the area covered by the Clyde cairns. The absence of Passage Graves

> from the heartland of the region must surely indicate the vigour and persistence there of the Clyde culture. Conversely their foothold in Galloway may mark a temporary weakening there of the Clyde culture, understandable because Galloway, on the southern fringe of the region, must have been especially subject to alien influences entering by the way of Luce Bay, in Wigtownshire

in the middle or late neolithic periods. It is also of interest that the Clyde region has one cairn which can be classed as a Severn-Clyde cairn, inasmuch as its affinities are rather with Cotswold-Severn than with Clyde cairns. This is the cairn at Cuff Hill, near Beith, in Ayrshire. "Its peripheral position, east of the Clyde region and north of Galloway, in an area in which the Clyde culture seems never to have taken root, may be significant" (ibid.). In these cases there appears to be a pattern of repulsion of like traits to the periphery of an area with a strong tradition. It should be pointed out that the processes which produced these patterns and which are not being discussed here may be extremely complex.

In many other cases, however, artefacts from one centre spread through different cultural regions without restriction and without apparent regard to the location of other similar and contemporary centres. Good examples of this are the distributions of neolithic axes. Clark (1965, p. 5) has remarked the great overlap in the distributions of these axes in Britain. Similarly, in the course of its movement from a source area in central France, "Grand Pressigny flint traversed cultural boundaries and was used indifferently by the makers of late Chassey, Seine-Oise-Marne, Corded Ware and Bell Beaker pottery" (ibid., p. 11). Clark has compared the pattern of axe trade in prehistoric Europe with that in Australia, Melanesia and New Zealand, where most axe movement was by reciprocal gift exchange and often between rival groups. The random walk pattern found for the neolithic group VI axes (Hodder, 1974a) might be suggested as being an appropriate model for this form of exchange.

Larger centres tend to attract interaction from larger areas than smaller centres, a situation for which the gravity model is appropriate (for a fuller discussion see Hodder, 1974a; see also Atkinson, 1972). This model can be used to predict the relative amount of interaction around contemporary centres of known size. When some measure of the size of settlement clusters, such as the area covered or the density of sites, can be obtained, it is also possible to use the gravity model to predict the pattern of contact between clusters. The number of sites in settlement clusters, and the area covered, depend to a considerable degree on the relative intensity of fieldwork. In well studied areas this difficulty can perhaps be minimized. The density of male and female graves in the early Bronze Age, period 2, in north Germany, as mapped by Bergmann (1970), is shown in Fig. 35. These density groupings, obtained from a square grid placed over the distribution, correspond to Bergmann's typological divisions of the material (ibid., map 2). The number of sites in each group can be used as an approximate measure of the relative importance or size (S) of that group. The amount of interaction (I) between each pair of groups (i and j) is inversely proportional to the distance between their centres (Dij) and directly proportional to their size, such that

$$Iij = \frac{Si\ Sj}{Dij^2}. \tag{23}$$

The pattern of contact predicted in this way (Fig. 35) will be found to relate closely to much of the apparent "distortion" and unevenness of the artefact distributions in the area (see below, p. 300).

Another factor affecting artefact distributions is the pattern of settlement in the area in which interaction takes place. It has been shown that interaction decreases with distance. As a development of this theme, sites close together have greater opportunity for interaction than those sparsely or widely spaced. Areas with a high density of settlement, therefore, might be expected to have some expression of this closer contact. In spite of the difficulties of recognizing groupings of settlements as opposed to areas of fieldwork in the archaeological record, there is much evidence for this pattern (see Chapter 5). For example, in Kossack's (1959) maps of the Hallstatt period (Hallstatt C and D), all sites of the period known to him (ibid., p. 285) are indicated. Several types of artefact are confined to the distinct regions of dense settlement which can be identified.

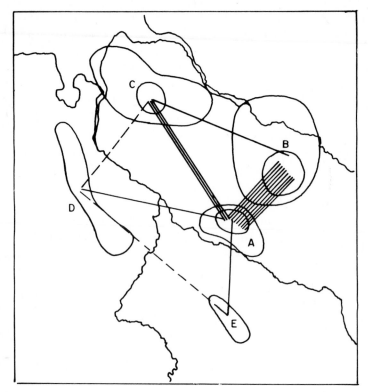

FIG. 35. The predicted pattern of interaction between N. German early Bronze Age sites. The contours indicate the density clusters. The predicted amount of relative interaction between these clusters is shown by the number of connecting lines.

C. DISCUSSION

In the preceding sections, the main factors which determine the more immediately apparent structure of single artefact distributions have been mentioned. But, in discussing the similarities between locally-made items, the spatial structure of the similarities between objects is closely related to the way the artefact types are defined. Stjernquist (1966, pp. 18-21) has given a good example of this difficulty. She compared the map by Sprockhoff (1930) of bronze vessels with cruciform handle fittings with that by von Merhart (1952) of the same objects. Sprockhoff's map shows no differentiation between the various examples. On von Merhart's map, localized groups of vessels are distinguished which have a chronological significance. As Stjernquist stated (1966, p. 18), "the interpretation of the chronologically differentiated map as regards the place of manufacture and the lines of communication will be totally different depending on whether von Merhart's map or Sprockhoff's is followed." It is also the case that simple types such as some pin types are less able to be closely defined than more complex types. This is an area which clearly needs considerable study, and the problem must continually be borne in mind (see also Hodson, 1962, p. 154).

In spite of this difficulty, it does seem that a simple basic model for many artefact distributions can be seen, in which interaction decreases gradually and smoothly with distance and in which the precise form and structure of the decrease is determined by the range of constraints identified in Section 4.B. Although this general model appears to give a good fit to a wide range of artefact distributions, it may be towards the cases which do not fit the model that most attention should be directed. As an example of this approach, we can consider whether "cultural" factors affect artefact distributions. The discussion in this chapter has made little mention of any notion of social or cultural effects on the distributions, since it seems quite possible to understand and model artefact distributions without reference to cultural restrictions and boundaries. In a discussion of animal and human territoriality, Soja (1971) suggests that territorial behaviour produces discontinuities and "plateaus" in normally expected patterns of spatial interaction (Fig. 36). "Territoriality is associated with a concentration of activities and communication within localized areas, inserting boundaries as it were into normal distance-decay relationships" (ibid., p. 34). If this point of view were to be accepted, it would be towards patterns which do not fit the model which has been discussed in this chapter that attention would have to be directed in order to identify "cultural" or territorial behaviour. It seems however that artifact distributions do not often exhibit the discontinuities that Soja suggests indicate territorial behaviour, and none were found by Hodder (1974a). As regards the distribution of neolithic obsidian, Renfrew (1969) has claimed that the flattening of the fall-off curves near the sources relates to the distribution of archaeological cultures, with a sharp fall-off occurring only outside the cultures which contain the obsidian sources. This flattening of the curve near the origin is, however, characteristic of the random walk type of fall-off curve. It is likely that objects of different demand or value but from the same source area would have more localized or more widespread distributions. The presence and width of the apparent "plateau" may often depend on the value of, and the level of demand for, the artefact, rather than on the location of archaeological cultural boundaries.

Soja (1971) has also suggested that at the boundary between the areas around adjacent centres there might be a recognizable difference between territorial (Fig. 37b) and non-territorial (Fig. 37a) behaviour. This can be examined for archaeological data by plotting the distributions of late Iron Age Dobunnic coins around Bagendon and Cunobeline coins around Verulamium. These distributions have long been assumed (Allen, 1944; Radford, 1954; Rivet, 1964) to be clear archaeological examples of tribal or cultural groupings. However, if we take a broad transect from Bagendon to Verulamium and assess the density of coins in sections along this transect, the pattern of fall-off from the two centres clearly does not suggest "territorial" behaviour. In both cases (Fig. 38), there is a gradual decrease in density, with the Dobunnic coin distance-decay relationship being a good example of the random walk type (see Hodder, 1974a). Hogg (1971) has found a similar pattern of gradual fall-off in discussing the relationship between the Dobunnic and Durotrigian areas. It is possible, however, that any sharp boundaries which did exist in the distributions have been disturbed due to the lack of detailed archaeological information. Changing boundaries at different dates may have produced a blurred aggregate pattern. This is a problem which can only await further study and more detailed chronologies.

5. Areas of interaction: the association between distributions

A. INTRODUCTION

Childe (1951, p. 40) defined the archaeological culture "as an assemblage of associated traits that recur repeatedly". Hodson (1962, p. 153) has used a similar definition. "A classification into archaeological groups or 'cultures' must start from an objective material basis, and in fact must simply recognise groups of types that are regularly associated together". Clarke (1968) retains a similar emphasis on the recurring association of artefacts. "An archaeological culture is a polythetic set of specific and comprehensive artifact-types which consistently recur together in assemblages within a limited geographical area" (ibid., p. 285). Areas which have a degree of overlap of artefact distributions, termed here *association groups,* seem, therefore, to be the essence of archaeological cultures. In the sense in which it is used

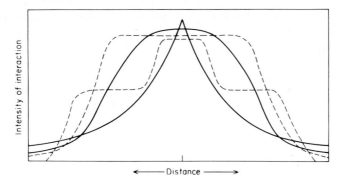

FIG. 36. Territorial and non-territorial activity patterns (Soja, 1971).

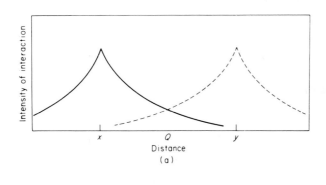

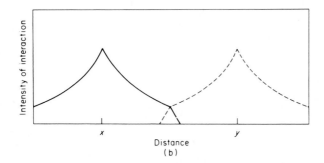

FIG. 37. Territorial and non-territorial patterns of activity around central places.

by Hodson (1964), only two or three generalized artefact types need to overlap in distribution for a culture to be claimed. It has been noticed that the "boundaries of the several fields of culture do not necessarily coincide" (Childe, 1951, p. 47). Different artefacts have different distributions, while Childe also noted from anthropological and

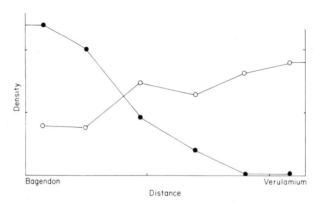

FIG. 38. The decrease in the density of Dobunnic coins (filled circles) with distance from Bagendon, and of Cunobeline coins (open circles) from Verulamium.

historical examples that there is often a discrepancy between material culture and language or political allegiance. In terms of distributions of artefacts, Clarke (1968) has, therefore, preferred a polythetic definition.

> The available evidence suggests that the individual distributions of the specific artifact-types from one culture extend in irregular lobes in various differing directions, many types also occurring as components in other cultural assemblages in neighbouring areas, and vice versa (ibid., p. 248).

These are all very broad definitions and there seems to be little clear idea of the structure of archaeological cultures. Indeed, for some time there has been considerable disillusion with the term. "Are there really things called *cultures?*" (Hawkes, 1973, p. 177). It is not at all clear, in any case, what archaeological cultures represent.

> Perhaps we might call its members a people, but we should have no right to assume that this people as a whole spoke a single language or acted as a political unit, still less that all its members were related physiologically or belonged to one zoological race (Childe, 1951, p. 49).

There seems to have been little development in the archaeological concept of culture since Childe's definition, and for the moment the concept is too vague to be of value in interpreting archaeological material. There is clearly a need for the structure of archaeological cultures to be examined and defined. Hawkes (1973, p. 177), referring to the use of the term by English archaeologists, suggests that "its popularity in English, owed largely to Gordon Childe, deserves a stricter analysis than it commonly seems to get".

An important step in such an examination might be to identify the precise structure of the archaeological association groups called cultures. One advance in this direction would be to consider the nature and degree of the association between the various distributions which make up the association group. This involves a more detailed break-down of the structure of the cultures. In order to achieve this for most archaeological material, it is extremely important to be able to assess the association between the distributions of artefact types which do not occur together on sites, but which occur as single finds. A large number of archaeological distributions (neolithic axes, Bronze Age palstaves and Iron Age coins for example) are in this category. Techniques which enable us to examine the association between distributions, including those of the latter type, have been developed in plant ecology (Pielou, 1969) and social anthropology (Driver, 1961). The application of these techniques to archaeological material is to be discussed by Hodder and Orton (1976) and will not be examined in detail here. Most of the measures of association between two distri-butions are based on the degree of co-occurrence of members of the two distributions in the cells of an imposed lattice grid. Other measures are based on nearest neighbour links. The modal centres of the distributions (i.e. the high points on the smoothed density surfaces) can also be compared (Warntz and Neft, 1960).

B. SOME PATTERNS OF ASSOCIATION

In this section a number of data sets will be examined which provide a large number of overlapping contemporary distributions in a limited area.

Figures 40-45 (pp. 300-305) show the distribution of some early Bronze-Age metal types studied by Bergmann (1970). For his second period in this area, Bergmann has plotted 112 very specific types which occur more than three times. The objects appear in a range of contexts such as graves and hoards and as single finds. He found that the types were restricted to certain sub-regions which can be identified with the density groupings shown in Fig. 35. The grouping have been given a "tribal" definition by Bergmann (1968, p. 236; 1970, p. 57).

A grid of the size shown in Fig. 41 was constructed so that it could be imposed on each distribution map, and the occurrence of each type in the lattice noted. A computer programme was then used to compute the V coefficient of spatial association (Pielou, 1969) between every pair of the 112 distributions. In order to group similar distributions, it was then possible to carry out a single link cluster analysis based on the V coefficients of association. Hodson (1969) has discussed the inadequacies of this clustering method. One of these problems is apparent in this example. As the level of similarity is lowered, large numbers of distributions are added to the main group, producing a "chaining effect" (Hodson, 1969, p. 305). In Fig. 39, therefore, only those distributions which are grouped at a high level of similarity are shown. The clusters indicated in Fig. 39 relate to the density groups in Fig. 35 and to the spatial groupings suggested by Bergmann. Some closer definition, however, is given, since the association groupings, B1 and B2, identify a division within Bergmann's groups (Fig. 40). It is of interest that these localized groupings are distributions of small ornaments such as pins, pendants, finger- and arm-rings. Distributions of a similar range of jewellery identify the B group as a whole, and the A group. An example of the distinction between the A and B groups is shown in Fig. 41. Moving up a hierarchy of groupings, it is found that further types, such as the dagger in Fig. 42, cover both the A and B groups. The C group is identified very distinctly in the cluster analysis (Fig. 39) and its distribution is shown by the sword types in Figs 43 and 44. Other types have a concentration in the same C area but are spread much wider, for example the axe type shown in Fig. 45. It is of interest that in the central area of this axe distribution, finds occur in hoards and graves (filled circles), while outside the core area they occur as single finds (open circles). This is a pattern that recurs and signifies a difference in burial tradition. The C association group is distinctive in that it does not contain a wide range of ornament types. Only a fibula type is centred in this group, and this is a rare type of ornament in this period. This difference may support Bergmann's hypothesis of a cultural distinction between the groups.

There seems, then, to be a hierarchy of association groups, with small localized groupings incorporated into larger clusters, until finally the A, B (1 and 2) and C groups are covered by the distributions of more widespread types. It is of interest that the pattern of group

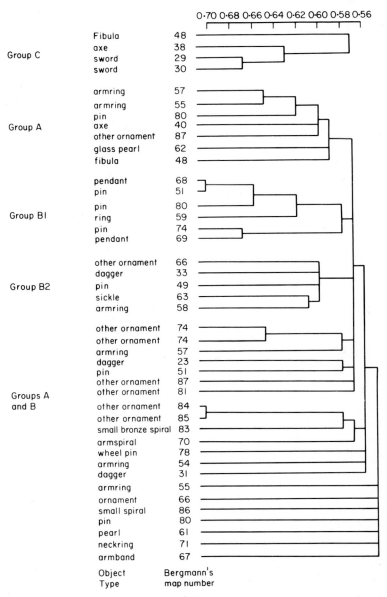

FIG. 39. Clustering Bergmann's distributions according to the *V* coefficient.

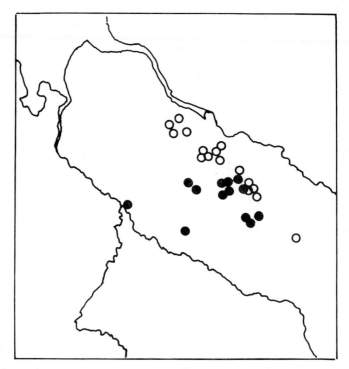

FIG. 40. Association groups B1 (filled circles; types 69, 74 and 59) and B2 (open circles; types 58, 63 and 49).

formation is as predicted by the gravity model (Fig. 35). The strong link predicted between the A and B density groups is evident in that a large number of distributions are common to both groups. Similarly the strongest predicted ties from C are to the southeast, and this is indicated by a number of distributions such as in Figs 42 and 45 which run along this axis. This method of analysis was unable to identify association groups at D and E.

It is also clear that the different classes of artefact define different levels of association. Nearly all the localized types clustered in Fig. 39 are ornaments. In Fig. 45 (p. 305), an axe type has a much wider distribution although being centred on one of the smaller groupings. Indeed the pattern of axe distribution is different from that of other artefact types. This is clarified in the matrix (Fig. 46, p. 306). In this matrix some indication of the V coefficient value for each pair of distributions is given. The distributions are ordered along the margins according to the class of object. Of the axes, only two show any close

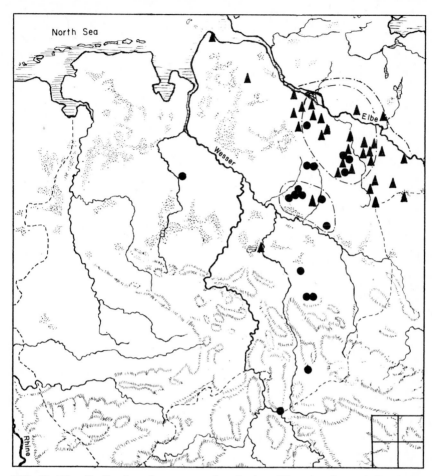

FIG. 41. The distribution of two types of neck ring. The triangles and the circles indicate the two types. The A and B density clusters (from Fig. 35) are shown by dot-dashed lines (Bergmann, 1970, map 67).

association with the range of ornaments. This is because the axes have concentrations of their distributions in areas (C group and at a number of other points) different from the ornaments and because they are much more widely spread. The spearheads and swords are also not closely associated with types of ornament, while the ceramic traits have diffuse and scanty distributions. What is perhaps misleading, is that a number of pin types do not appear to be closely associated with the other ornaments. These are small samples of 3 or 4 examples, sometimes

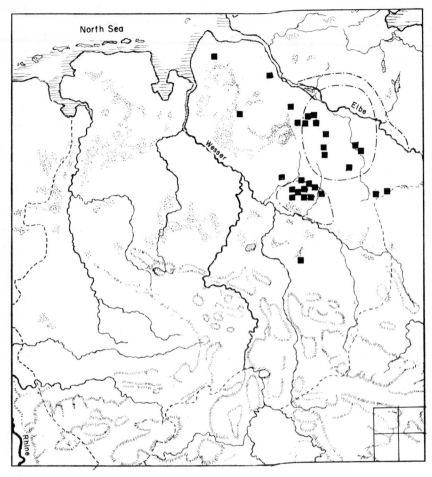

FIG. 42. The distribution of a dagger type. Each **find is indicated by a square. The A** and B density clusters (from Fig. 35) are shown by dot-dashed lines (Bergmann, 1970, map 31).

spread widely. Other pin types have very localized distributions, and these are closely associated with the wide range of ornament types found mainly in the A and B regions.

The concept of range and value (Section 4.B) is, therefore, of considerable importance in the study of patterns of interaction in this area in the early Bronze Age. The size and shape of the association groups which can be identified depend very much on the type of artefact considered. However, the problems connected with the level of

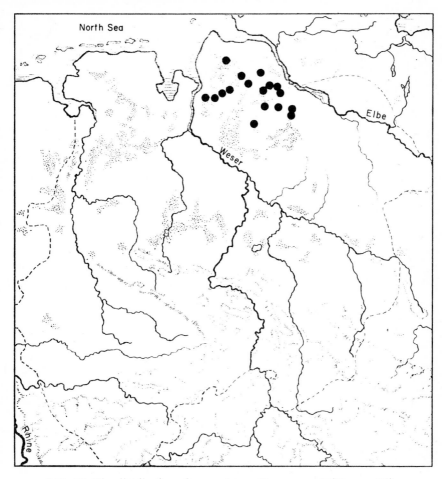

FIG. 43. The distribution of a sword type (Bergmann, 1970, map 29).

specificity of definition of the types (p. 292) should be borne in mind. The complexity of the artefact types and the degree of detail possible in their definition must play a large part in the spatial patterning that is obtained.

Another study is based on some middle Bronze-Age distributions in the Carpathian Basin (Hänsel, 1968). To examine the pattern of association between the distributions in phase MDI their modal centres were obtained. Any tendency for these centres to cluster in particular areas can then be identified. The centres are shown on the base lattice in

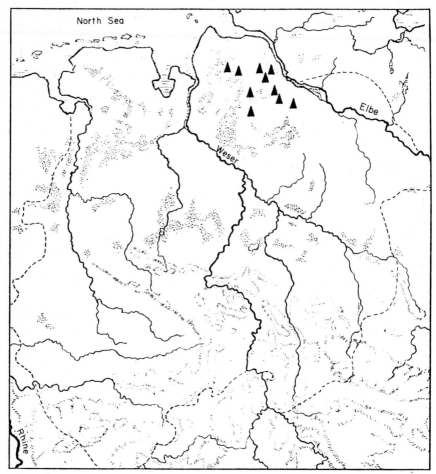

FIG. 44. The distribution of a sword type (Bergmann, 1970, map 30).

Fig. 47b. They cluster in the two areas of highest density of finds indicated in Fig. 47a. Since these are the areas of highest densities of finds it is, perhaps, hardly surprising that most modal centres occur in them. However, it is clear in the patterns in Fig. 47 c, d and e that types are often restricted to one or other of the density groups. Other types are found more widely but with marked concentrations in one of the groups, as opposed to having marked concentrations in both. If axe types are considered, on the other hand, wider distributions are found (e.g. Fig. 47 f).

The pattern, therefore, seems to be one of association groups of ornament types occurring in areas of higher densities of finds, and

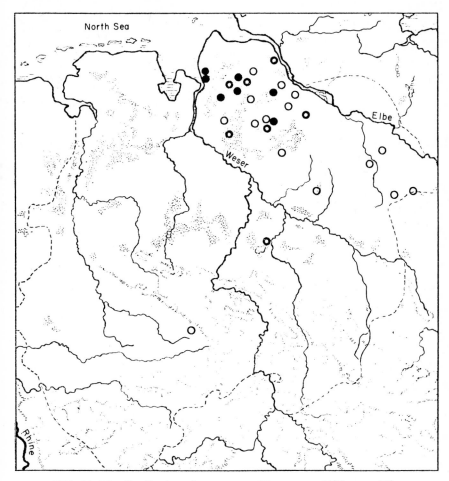

FIG. 45. The distribution of an axe type (Bergmann, 1970, map 38).

perhaps of settlement. Outside its core area, a type is found with decreasing frequency as distance increases. The maximum distance at which a type is found depends to some extent on the type of object. Thus, types such as the axes and swords probably had a comparatively low level of local demand and, whether they were manufactured in one centre or not, these types are more widely spread than the ornaments. They could relate, for example, to interaction at a high level in the social hierarchy (Dalton, 1969).

A further study is based on Cunliffe's (1966) work on Iron Age pottery in southern Britain. His second phase (the "saucepan pot

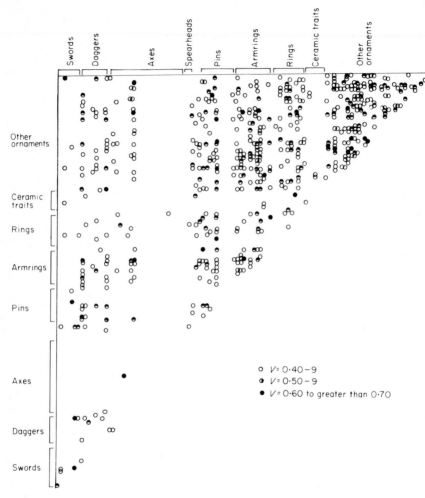

FIG. 46. The matrix of V coefficients for Bergmann's data.

continuum") will be used. In examination of a large amount of pottery in southern Britain enabled Cunliffe to identify a number of regional groups or styles termed "style zones".

> The term "style zone" can be defined as a group of assemblages occupying a definite geographical area, sharing a series of common cultural traits and being restricted to a certain period of time (ibid.).

Thus the groupings are based mainly on the recurring association at different sites of a number of pottery shapes and forms of decoration. Individual traits or pot types may thus be spread over a wider area

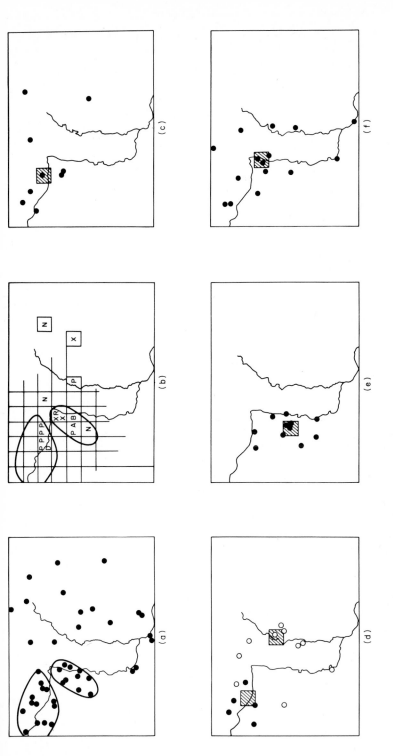

FIG. 47. (a) Find spots with two or more objects of Hänsel's period 1. The two areas of highest density are indicated. (b) Location of modal centres: P = pin, D = dagger, N = pendant, X = pendant, A = axe, R = armring, A = arm spiral, B = beltpiece. (c) The distribution of pin type 67; modal centre shaded. (d) The distribution of pin types 71 (open circles) and 76 (filled circles). (e) The distribution of the pendant type 128. (f) The distribution of the axe type 58.

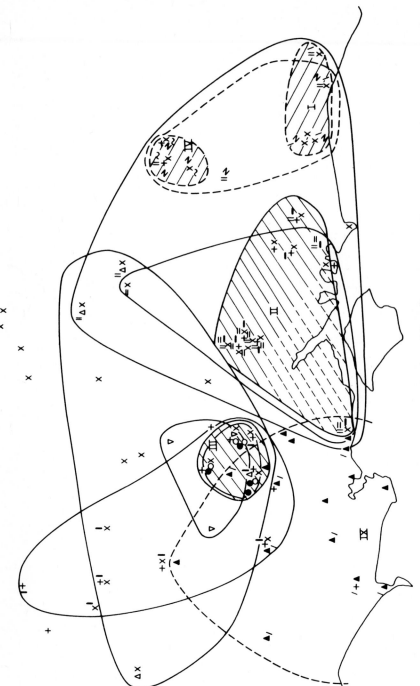

FIG. 48. The distribution of Iron Age pottery motifs.

than the central style zone. Indeed, Cunliffe acknowledged some difficulty in the allocation of assemblages to particular style zones. This difficulty arose because Cunliffe was, in effect, comparing assemblages on the basis of their associated types, and expecting distinct groupings to emerge. As has been seen, an alternative approach is to plot the distributions of individual styles or types and to examine their spatial relationship. It is possible to obtain this information from Cunliffe's data since, for each site, a list of associated decorative motifs is given. These motifs have been plotted in Fig. 48. All the decorative traits recorded by Cunliffe for this area are shown, except those which only occur at one or two sites. It should be emphasized that the number of sherds from any given site is often very small.

From the pattern in Fig. 48 it appears that there is a number of localized types (shaded areas). It is these areas on which Cunliffe based his style zones. However these areas can be seen as regions within wider areas where only some of the styles in the small groupings are found. This pattern can in fact be discerned in Cunliffe's own work. For example, his style zone III is very distinctive in a localized area in Wiltshire, and Cunliffe termed the sites here "main sites". He distinguished a number of peripheral sites in the same style zone where only a few comparable sherds were found.

● Zone of oblique lines between horizontal lines, bordered by rows of dots.

○ Continuous arcs with circular impressions at ends.

Δ Zone of cross hatched lines.

∇ Horizontal band of a line between horizontal rows of dots.

+ A continuous wavy line, sometimes doubled.

X Bands of 1−3 horizontal lines.

I Jar with horizontally perforated lugs.

− Single or several rows of dots (horizontal) below rim or above base.

‖ Band of oblique lines below rim, between horizontal lines.

= Oblique line zone bounded by horizontal lines of dots.

▲ Countersunk handles.

/ Indentations arranged in groups of two, three or four.

\ Pendant swags of groups of lines.

N Pendant swags of lines and dots.

~ Groups of lines or single lines arranged in rectilinear zones

Roman numerals indicate Cunliffe style zones, also shaded.

Key to Fig. 48.

The general pattern is now a familiar one. Central localized areas have a wide range of traits only some of which are found in the surrounding areas. With increasing distance from the main association groups the similarity of the site assemblages decreases.

Although the main concern of this study is to examine the structure of artefact distributions, it may be of interest to consider the possible interpretation of the pattern of Iron Age pottery traits. An initial point which must be made is that the differences in spread of the distributions are partly related to the level of specificity of definition of the traits. It is difficult to decide, from the definitions given in Fig. 48, which are more specific than others, but it often seems to be the case that the more widespread traits are more generalized.

Another factor which must be considered is Peacock's demonstration that the "Glastonbury" pottery (1969) and the stamped and linear tooled pottery (1968) were not made in the home but in restricted areas from which they were then distributed. Similar results have been obtained for the Dorset area (Peacock, pers. comm.) for the phase studied here, and it seems reasonable to suppose that much the same will be true for other areas. This pattern of production need not apply to all the pottery made in an area, but it can be supposed to have had some effect on the distribution of pottery stylistic traits. Peacock (1969) has shown that Iron Age pots made in the same area may have rather different distributions. Generally, the marketing pattern from pottery sources may be part of the interpretation for the distributions in Fig. 48. It cannot be a complete explanation, because particular style motifs are commonly found on very different types of pot in different areas. It seems that pots were sometimes made in different areas but were decorated with the same motif. The distributions of motifs might, therefore, give some indication of local traditions in the sense that in these areas certain ideas were held in common. It is of interest that there is some similarity between these association groups and the areas covered by late Iron Age inscribed coins and the Roman cantons (see below).

Distributions with spatial structures comparable to those already discussed are discernible in many other studies. The distribution, for example, of the Corded Ware in Saxony (Behrens and Schlette, 1969, pp. 30-36) can be divided into two groups of material which relate to the two areas of highest site density. Traits from each are, however, found outside the concentrations in lower density areas where there is some overlap of types (see also ibid., p. 108). In an earlier study of the east Prussian Corded Ware, Killian (1955) considers the distributions of traits in terms of a core area within a wider similar area. Laux's (1971) work on the Bronze Age of the Lüneburg area in north Germany shows quite clearly that, although the distributions of types overlap considerably, they have their modal centres in one or other of three distinct areas. The extent and pattern of dispersion around the modal centres depends on the constraints discussed in Section 4 for single artefact distributions.

C. DISCUSSION: THE STRUCTURE OF ARCHAEOLOGICAL CULTURES

There seems to be little evidence in the examples discussed in Section 5.B for patterns of random spatial association (Pielou, 1969). Rather, the modal centres of distributions within one area often show a tendency to cluster. The dispersion of a distribution around a modal centre often depends on the type of object and a range of other complex factors. Thus, the different distributions which make up an archaeological "culture" may be spread around the same modal centre to different degrees for a variety of reasons (Clarke, 1968, p. 248). Binford (1972, pp. 203-4) has made a more general point concerning the different meanings which should be attached to different distributions. According to Binford, a "tradition" or "style-zone" shows continuity through time in the formal properties of locally manufactured craft items. An "interaction sphere", on the other hand, is made up of socio-cultural relationships reflected in items that are widely exchanged and which occur in a context of social distinctiveness. The distributions of different types of object or of different traits may have different dispersions and may tell us different things about patterns of interaction. A distribution may also exhibit skewness around its mode and this often appears to be the result of the constraints discussed in Chapter 4.

A characteristic of many distribution patterns, and one which is especially clear in Bergmann's data and in the Iron Age pottery distributions, is that of a hierarchy of spatial groupings. Smaller, localized groupings are incorporated into larger regions by more widespread types and traits (cf. Struever and Houart, 1972). In addition, there appear to be many association patterns in which the core area of greatest overlap corresponds to the area of highest density of sites (for example Bergmann's data, the early Bronze Age data from the Carpathian basin, and the Corded Ware groups in Saxony). These denser areas may be seen as having the greatest opportunity for interaction (see Section 4.B), and this opportunity decreases with distance from the density clusters.

A discussion follows of some ethnographic evidence for the structure of material culture groupings, although, as Robbins (1973, p. 209) has pointed out,

> archaeologists are uniformly frustrated when they turn to the ethnographic literature because most of the reports do not approach the subject of material culture from the spatial dimensions most appropriate for primary archaeological site analysis.

Much the same can be said for studies of cultural groupings although, fortunately, there are some important exceptions.

A useful study is that by Klimek (1935) in which the distribution of cultural traits among Californian tribes was examined. Klimek was able to identify a number of cultural traits which were associated together in different areas ("cultural strata") and the distribution of these strata are shown in Fig. 49. In Fig. 49, the quantity of material culture elements of each stratum in each tribe is signified by the degree of shading. It is clear that in every case there is a central tribe or group of tribes associated with a particular range of cultural elements (a stratum), and that outside this area rather less of these cultural traits are found, producing a fall-off in similarity with distance. Each central cultural province was found (Klimek, 1935, p. 53) to have some relationship to a particular linguistic group. It will become clear, however, that there are a number of problems associated with the approach followed by Klimek.

In a further study of the Californian material by Milke (1949), the average similarity with a given tribe, for tribes at a particular distance from it, was quantified (Fig. 50; see also Clarke, 1968, pp. 368–388). The same process was also carried out for S.E. Melanesian peoples (Fig. 51). It is clear that there is a pattern of gradually decreasing similarity and this is also apparent in Fig. 52 where the only area having a steeper fall-off in similarity is to the northwest. Milke also noted that the parameters of the fall-off curves differed according to the material culture traits used.

A serious problem associated with ethnographic studies of tribal groupings and similarity is the difficulty of defining tribes and ethnic groups. It seems that both language and material culture often merge from one tribe to another without any clear break, while language patterns do not necessarily correlate with cultural or political organization groups (Fried, 1968). Fried (ibid., p. 5) discusses the Siuai tribe,

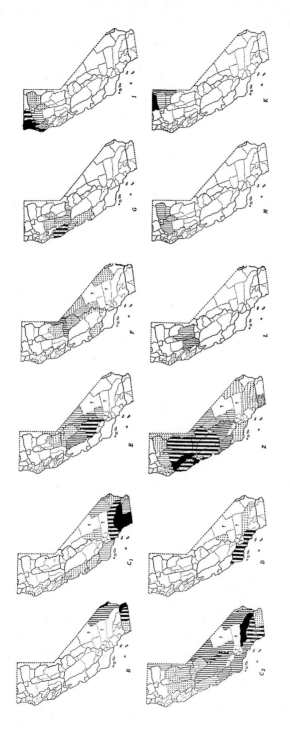

FIG. 49. The distribution of "cultural strata" (Klimek, 1935).

the members of which do not act together in land use, are fuzzy about boundaries and intermarry with people speaking another language. Some Siuai interact more frequently and regularly with non-Siuai than they do with Siuai. Dole (1968) in fact suggests that interaction is often

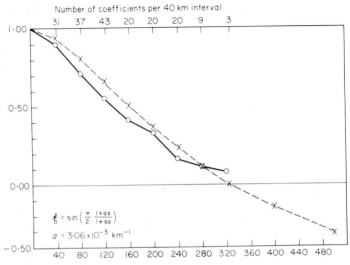

FIG: 50. Q_6-coefficients of 20 peoples of N.W. California (solid line by method of text; broken line by formula given in Fig.).

not based on cultural unity or similarity but on such factors as from where particular specialist craft products can be obtained. Dole also states (ibid., p. 86) that,

> like linguistic similarity, both economic and ceremonial interaction are very difficult to apply in classifying groups because these also may grade from one society into another indefinitely in a series of neighbouring groups.

A further difficulty is known as Galton's problem (see for example Naroll, 1961, 1970). Anthropologists have been concerned to discover which particular socio-cultural traits are functionally associated. The spatial distribution of a particular trait is partly the result of historical diffusion factors, and there has been considerable effort directed towards distinguishing functional relationships from those co-occurrences of traits which are results of cultural diffusion. Driver (1966), for example, has examined the distribution of "kin avoidances" in relation to variables such as language group, descent and residence patterns. He found that "historical factors seem to have as much or more to do with the occurrence of avoidances as do the other correlatives" (ibid., p. 141). A detailed historical study enabled him to isolate the cases in which diffusion had occurred by inter-tribal marriages, migration, or heritage from a proto-culture. In the

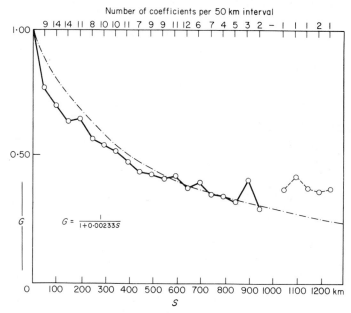

FIG. 51. *G*-coefficients of 19 peoples of S.E. Melanesia (broken curve by method of text; smooth curve by formula given in Fig.).

remaining cases, relationships could be examined as functional correlations. An example of the diffusion of a cultural trait is provided by Driver and Massey (1957) and is shown in Fig. 53.

It is clear then that it is difficult to interpret the patterns obtained by Klimek and Milke, as well as the archaeological patterns, without knowledge of the historical process of diffusion, although it certainly cannot be suggested that, as with Wissler's (1923) theories, more widespread traits are always those which diffused earliest. But it is possible that, to a certain extent, some of the patterning of ethnographic and archaeological distribution is the result of processes of spread from separate origins and core areas (e.g. the expansion outwards of the Ife culture in Nigeria discussed by Willett, 1971).

If considered at a very general level, what has been discussed in this study as the structure of cultures is:

1. Similar in a wide range of temporal and spatial contexts both in prehistory and ethnography, and may, therefore, not vary with different types of social organization.

2. Explainable in terms of a simple model based on distance and "value" factors. Patterns of interaction and the exchange of goods

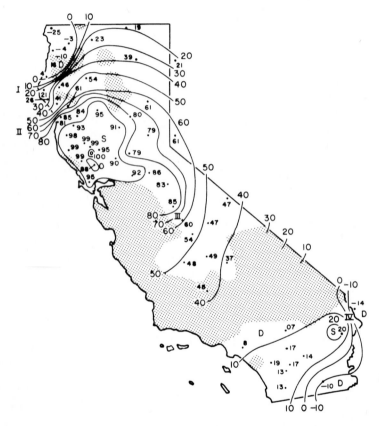

FIG. 52. California contours of cultural similarity. Coefficient: Q . Point of reference: Lake Miwok. Hatched areas indicate groups not analysed for lack of material (Milke, 1949).

and ideas depend, for example, on the type of artifact involved and are more intense with nearer individuals (see Section 4 for other factors involved).

Let us consider an ethnographic example which makes this point rather well. At the localized level of interaction among pottery manufacturers in Hopi villages, Stanislawski (1973, p. 121) states that

> there are a minimum of four ceramic teaching models in use, three of which involve cross-clan teaching of ceramic techniques, designs, and styles. . . . Women are

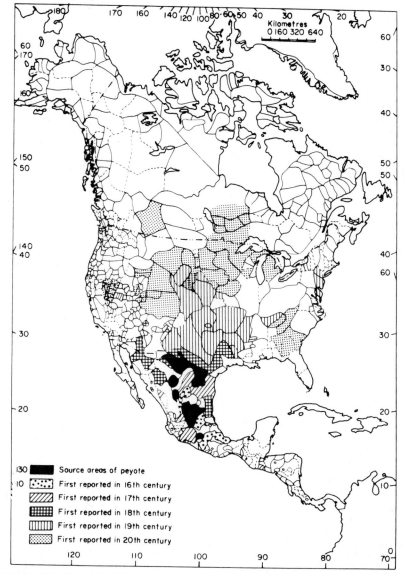

FIG. 53. The dispersal of the use of the narcotic peyote. The lack of occurrences to the west is due to the use there of a different narcotic (Driver and Massey, 1957).

known to make several wares and classes of design and 10 to 20 pottery types during their lifetimes; and individual women make quite different pottery types from their mothers. . . . They all agree that they can use any designs and styles they wish. They do not simply learn one type at one time from one source; and types are not associated with residence or descent groups. . . . In short, the localization of ceramic types in prehistoric and modern pueblos is more likely to be a matter of the localization of "ad hoc" work groups of neighbours and friends including both kin and non-kin.

Bunzel's 1929 study of the pueblo potter indicates that inspiration was obtained not only from the kinship or residence group but also from others in the vicinity with whom the potter had contact.

Thus

characterisations of tribes in terms of similarity in specified cultural traits, limits of interaction, or the possession of several traits in common are inadequate because they are based on an implicit assumption that human groups and their cultures are closed systems. . . . Actually, all human groups are open systems in that they interact with other groups. . . . It is apparent that there is no inherent reason why different traits should have coterminous boundaries (Dole, 1968, p. 88).

Hence, although the mechanisms of within-group and between-group exchange may be rather different (Sahlins, 1965), there is less evidence that one is more or less efficient than the other, or less used.

The two points made above, and the realization that many human groups are open systems, are of importance for they stress that archaeological cultures may define patterns of contact and interaction structured by distance constraints as much as by kinship sharing, although these two factors may be closely related.

Of considerable interest is the interplay between distance factors and kinship ties in determining patterns of interaction. Patterns of interaction evident in the archaeological material can be interpreted in terms of simple proximity constraints (p. 316) so that greatest contact is with nearest individuals or groups. Anthropologists have been little concerned with spatial controls on social systems (Canfield, 1973, p. 1522). "The role of kinship as a means of social unity appears to have been exaggerated and that of the 'territorial tie' underestimated" (Wiseman, 1966). Cultural identity is, however, often considered as being the main determinant of interactive behaviour. "Culture is the fabric of meaning in terms of which human beings interpret their experience and guide their action" (Geertz, 1957, pp. 33-34). According to this view it might be suggested, for example, that in many cases people live near each other because of kinship ties, rather than that kinship ties develop because of the patterns of interaction based on distance factors. Canfield (1973), however, in a study of rural ethnic groups in Bamian in central Afghanistan, has suggested that "effective distance" — a time-cost measure of the degree of separation and accessibility of different locations — controls the degree to which various local groups have been able to interact with each other and the outside. It is this pattern of interaction which Canfield suggests has resulted in the spatial distribution of the three religious sects in the area (Sunni, Imami and Ismaili). Thus groups whose material interests for locational reasons coincide with those of the central and dominant culture of Afghanistan have identified with Sunnism. But those whose material interests for locational reasons primarily conflicted with Sunni interests have identified with, for example, Imamism.

It seems possible to hypothesize, then, that in certain cases peoples' similarity to each other in their material culture is as much related to their spatial distance apart as to their tribal or linguistic affinity. This may seem an obvious point, but it seems seldom to have been explicitly considered by prehistorians and ethnographers. It is an important point because it implies that it may be possible to take the following path of study. First, models can be used and built of spatial interaction and for the similarity between locally-made items which do not take tribal nor linguistic affinity into account. These models, such as regression models and the gravity model, can be based on factors such as distance, size of settlement, geographical features and the "value" of an object. Tribal or linguistic affinity and variations in societal type might sometimes then be identifiable as having caused deviations from expected trends. Such effects may only be visible in certain circumstances. It has already been seen (p. 294) that the boundaries between "tribal" groups do not seem to have caused deviations from expected fall-off trends in the case of late Iron coin distributions. Much work, especially by ethnographers, needs to be carried out before one can determine the range of circumstances in which linguistic and tribal boundaries do affect material culture distributions.

However, one circumstance in which deviations from expected patterns may be found is when particular artefacts have been taken by past societies to identify certain spatial groups of people. Such artefacts might be found very rarely outside the area of an identity group and have a constant frequency within it. Sharp deviations from normally expected fall-off trends might, therefore, be found. The possible identification of such symbols of identity might be checked against other evidence — context of find in burials or position in settlements for example.

It has been suggested that archaeological distributions often reflect patterns of interaction, the structure of which is the result of spatial as well as kinship factors, and this will be examined further in the following section.

> Underlying all transactions are implications of social distance and, as well, spatial components which together specify the nature of exchange interactions. . . . Exchange distance is . . . a variable function of social and physical distance (Wilmsen, 1972, p. 2).

This suggestion is more clearly appropriate to moveable and exchangeable objects than it is to stylistic traits on non-moveable items. However, in the latter case, there seems to be some evidence (p. 318) that individuals may accept ideas or styles from many of those they are in contact with, rather than just from kin. In addition to local contact, trade and exchange contact may therefore influence the formation of styles so that a strong relationship exists between the distributions of moveable, exchanged objects and of styles or customs. This will also be apparent in the following study.

6. An analysis of some late Iron Age association groups

Having discussed a framework for archaeological cultures, it is appropriate to introduce a detailed analysis of one period and region where overlapping distributions of a number of artefact types can be obtained. Such a situation is provided by the late Iron Age in southern England, where the development of the pattern into the Roman period facilitates an understanding of the nature of the association groups.

It will often be difficult to demonstrate that the various distributions considered are exactly contemporary. All the distributions do, however, fall within a 100-150 year period. There is some indication that major changes in groupings did not occur within this period. The various inscribed coinages show little variation in distribution, and Cunliffe's (1966) grouping of Iron Age pottery found remarkable continuity from the earliest to the latest phase. However, it is necessary to interpret the distributions in the light of the probability of non-contemporaneity and of slight changes in pattern (see especially Spratling, 1972).

A. THE STRUCTURE OF THE EVIDENCE

In Fig. 58 are shown the distributions of some late pre-Roman Iron Age coin types. The coins include all inscribed coins as well as those uninscribed coins which have been included by Allen in his late tribal groupings (1944, 1958, 1961, 1962, 1963, 1968, 1970). For the Catuvellaunian area however only the Cunobeline coins are shown since there are sufficient of these to give a clear picture of the extent of this group (Allen, 1944, p. 21). The date of the minting of the coins is suggested by historical references to certain of the inscribed names (Commius, Tincommius and Verica for example). It is mainly by typological comparisons with these coins that Allen has been able to date other inscribed coins such as Addedomarus and Andoco . . ., while several coins occur in archaeological contexts which are dateable by other means (Allen, 1944, 1962, 1963, 1968, 1970, 1971). The coins mapped in the figures were thus probably produced in the period from the last quarter of the first century B.C. to the years around 43 A.D. and in a few cases probably rather after this date (Allen, 1968, 1970). In fact, the observed pattern of coins probably in part represents post-conquest behaviour due to continued use into the early Roman period. Crawford (1970) suggests that the coins buried during the destruction of Alesia covered a period of 100 years, as well as mentioning other examples of the long life of coins in the Roman world. In Britain, hoards of pre-Roman coins sometimes contain Roman coins of post-conquest date. These usually give a mid first century context for the Celtic coins, but a hoard of Durotrigian coins from Holdenhurst, Hampshire, contained second century A.D. Roman coins (Allen, 1968, p. 50), and a third century date for a Coritanian coin is provided by the Ashover hoard (Allen, 1963, p. 34). Pre-Roman coins are also found in Roman levels, for example at Verulamium, Peterborough and Camulodunum (Sheepen site).

That different patterns of exchange existed in southern England is suggested by the different character and range of denominations of the coins in each area. For example, a definite bronze coinage is confined to the Cunobeline and eastern Atrebatic area, while the Durotriges have a mainly silver coinage with no gold coins (which, however, are common in other areas), and an almost complete absence of coins actually inscribed with names. Minor silver denominations (half and quarter) are common only among the Coritani (Allen, 1963), Iceni (Allen, 1970) and Atrebates (Allen, 1968), while gold quarter staters are confined to the coins of Cunobeline and the Atrebates.

Even within particular coin-type areas some variation in the extent of distributions is apparent, and the gradual fall-off in density from the main centres has already been discussed (p. 294). In the Catuvellaunian-Trinovantian area it appears that certain coin types are more widespread than others. For example the earliest bronze coinage (British Lx) develops (Allen, 1958) in the central part of the area later covered by Tasciovanus and Cunobeline coins. In Fig. 54 is shown the distribution of bronze, gold and silver Cunobeline coins. There is some suggestion that bronze coins are found less in the peripheral areas of the distribution, especially the Oxfordshire region (encircled in Fig. 54). Collis (1971b, p. 79) has suggested that the distributions of the bronze and gold coins indicate two types and degrees of interaction with the production centres. The distribution of Welwyn type burials (Stead, 1967), shown in Fig. 54, defines a core area within the total coin distribution which will recur in a number of other distributions.

A very clear distinction between central and peripheral zones in the area of distribution of Dobunnic coins is seen in the wider distribution of Corio coins as opposed to the more central Bodvoc examples (Fig. 55). These two coin types were suggested by Allen (1961) to be very close to each other in date. Rivet (1962) has discussed the date of these two coin types and the interpretations which have been made of their distributions.)

Wider distributions have been found for the various types of iron bar mapped by Allen (1967), termed currency bars and plough shares and dated to the first century B.C. A westerly distribution of spit-shaped and sword-shaped bars is apparent in Figs 56 and 57, and this west/east division will be found in further distributions. The scanty distribution of tapered bars points to the Durotrigian area.

A further important source of information for spatial groupings within the Iron Age is provided by the distribution of pottery types. The pottery groupings for the late pre-Roman Iron Age have been taken where possible from Peacock's (1968, 1969) analyses of pottery fabrics since these provide a fairly objective method of defining types of pottery. Where this has not been possible the groupings have been taken from Cunliffe's (1966, 1974) regional zones for the Iron Age in southern Britain. The groupings in Fig. 58 are those in Cunliffe's latest horizon and an indication of the extent of the groupings is given by joining with straight lines the outer sites in each style-zone. These groupings are much the same as those in the preceding

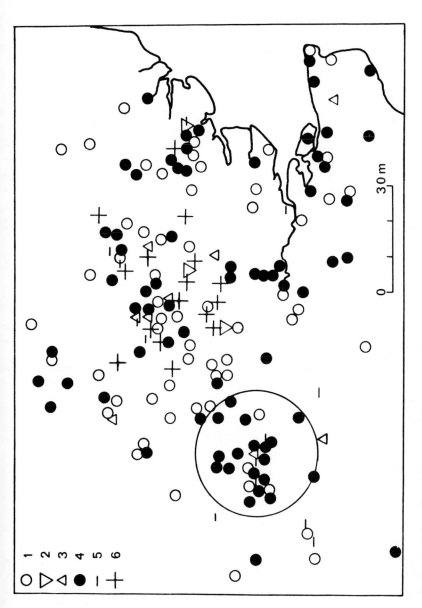

FIG. 54. Coins of Cunobeline and Welwyn-type burials. 1. Bronze coins; 2. Oppida with many bronze-major maricet. 3. Many bronze-minor maricet (2, 3, Collis, 1971a); 4. Gold coins; 5. Silver coins; 6. Welwyn-type burials (Stead, 1967) with addition of more recent finds.

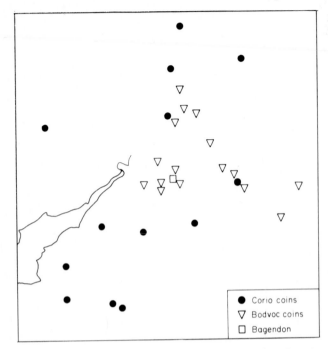

FIG. 55. The distribution of Corio and Bodvoc Dobunnic coins.

"saucepan pot continuum" analysed above (p. 308). Cunliffe suggests that they begin around 100-50 B.C. and continue into his proto-Roman Iron Age (10-43 A.D.).

Two empirical studies have forced a questioning of a purely cultural interpretation of late Iron Age pottery groupings. Peacock's work on the Glastonbury pottery (1969) and the stamped and linear tooled pottery (1968) has shown that these pottery types were not made in the home but in restricted areas from which they were then distributed. Similar results have been obtained for the Dorset area (Peacock, pers. comm.) and it seems reasonable to suppose that other late Iron Age pottery groupings will prove to be of like nature. Both Peacock (1968) and Bradley (1971) suggest that competitive marketing may explain the observed pattern of groupings. An analysis of early Romano-British hand-made pottery in the Malvern area (Peacock, 1967) shows a similar pattern of localized manufacture followed by distribution over a limited area. In the Roman period, exchange at markets seems the most likely way in which much pottery was distributed (Hodder,

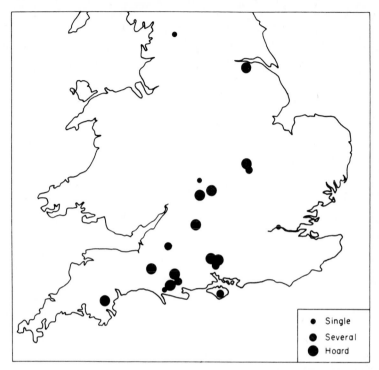

FIG 56. The distribution of sword-shaped iron bars (Allen, 1967).

1974d), and it is interesting that the Roman group studied by Peacock covers much the same area as the pre-Roman stamped and linear tooled wares produced in the same Malvern district (Peacock, 1967, p. 26). The pre-Roman and Roman Malvernian groupings are thus similar in character and distribution, and Peacock has argued for continuity in production (ibid.). Although this does not necessarily entail a similar method of dispersal, such a possibility must be considered.

A second study of importance is Jope's work on medieval pottery distributions. By plotting various types of pottery, Jope was able to identify restricted groupings. These localized groupings did not correlate with groupings of other evidence such as building styles, dialect variants and legal codes and did not represent cultural areas. "One thing is at least clear, integrated regional cultures do not seem to emerge crisply from medieval pottery distributions. This should dictate caution in postulating prehistoric cultures largely in terms of pottery styles" (Jope, 1963, p. 349). Rather, "medieval pottery was

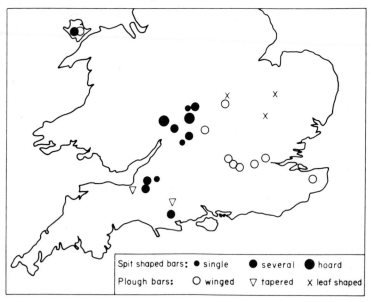

FIG. 57. The distribution of spit-shaped and plough-share iron bars (Allen, 1967).

probably marketed through fairs and weekly markets" (Jope, 1947, p. 52) so that the pottery distributions simply indicate the market or service areas around markets (Jope, 1963, p. 329). One distribution of medieval pottery "corresponds closely with that of Iron Age B Glastonbury type pottery; the medieval example could not be erected into a culture" (ibid., p. 349) and we must consider whether the same is not true of the Iron Age group. Posnansky (1973), in a discussion of some West African specialized production of pottery, states that

> these vessels are traded into neighbouring potting regions if such a pot is not made locally. The ancient trade in pottery was a complex matter, and the simplistic belief that different wares represent different groups of people can rarely be substantiated. A single Mo potter of the present day makes several distinct types of ware which are used by a variety of different linguistic groups, while a consumer, even before the advent of modern transport, would buy, or obtain by barter, specific types of vessels from relatively long distances (ibid., p. 159).

Peacock's and Jope's work raises the question of whether late Iron Age pottery groupings really indicate marketing rather than cultural areas. But Peacock's study of the Iron Age pottery, despite the suggestive similarities with the Romano-British evidence, need not necessarily indicate market exchange as the means of dispersal. Clearly other forms of distribution (by redistributive and reciprocal exchange

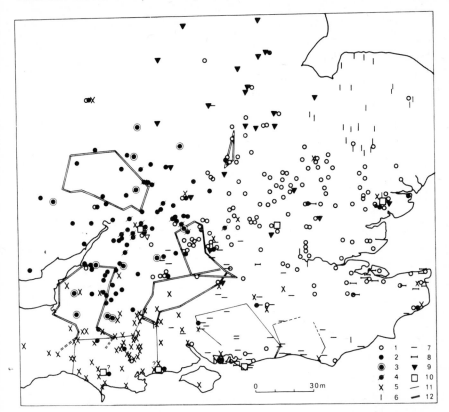

FIG. 58. Late pre-Roman pottery and coin groupings. 1. Coins of the Catuvellauni; 2. of the Dobunni; 3. of the Dobunni (Corio); 4. of the Dobunni (Bodvoc); 5. of the Durotriges; 6. of the Iceni; 7. of the Artrebates; 8. of the Kent Artrebates; 9. of the Coritani; 10. Possible tribal centres (oppida); 11. Central pottery groupings; 12. Other pottery groupings.

for example) may have been in operation. Whatever the mechanism of distribution, it remains a possibility that the impulse for pottery manufacture at a particular location and the style of the pottery, could have been partly a response to the needs of a particular settlement cluster or node of settlement. The pottery may also have been traded well outside this immediate area of distribution, but the total distribution may have some significance in terms of patterns of interaction directed towards some central or nodal area. This is indicated by those pottery distributions in Fig. 58 which have the same centres of distribution as the coin distributions of the Durotriges and Atrebates, although in each case the coin distribution is found over a wider area. The lack of a pottery grouping in the central Dobunnic area around Bagendon (Cunliffe, 1966) is due to the lack of excavation in the south Gloucestershire region, but it is of interest that this area is covered by the distribution of Bodvoc coins (Fig. 55).

A number of pottery groups do, however, occur at the peripheries of the coin groupings and cannot readily be assigned to any one coin type. A distinction between central and peripheral areas is, therefore, again apparent, with the range or dispersion of the distributions relating to the type of artefact involved.

Late Iron Age pottery distributions in the south-east of England have been studied by Birchall (1965). She suggested that the Aylesford-Swarling pottery types occurred in the first century B.C. She noted that pottery of pedestal urn type (Fig. 59) has a wide distribution in the southeast, but

> no other pottery type is quite so widely distributed and, in fact, the Aylesford-Swarling culture is found to be mainly concentrated in the three counties already discussed, Kent, Hertfordshire and Essex. However, some sporadic burials of Aylesford-Swarling type, and other material which relates to distinctive features of this culture as already analysed, should be noted. Such material is found mainly in Cambridgeshire and Bedfordshire (Birchall, 1965, p. 254).

Certain distributions of her pottery types cover a fairly restricted area (Fig. 60) in England while others are found rather more widely (Fig. 61). The latter distributions define a central area within the area covered by the pedestal urns, and the still wider distribution of coins of Tasciovanus and Cunobeline. It is of interest that fire dogs and shale vases are only found in burials in the same central area north of the Thames.

A comparable central area in eastern England is seen in the distribution of Dressel 1 amphorae (Peacock, 1971) dated to the first century B.C. The distribution (Fig. 62) includes the important oppida at Colchester, Braughing, Verulamium and Wheathampstead. Peacock (1971, p. 175) has suggested that these types indicate the extent of the Trinovantian tribe. This is difficult because it places the Catuvellaunian centre on its periphery while other, later, amphora types include this centre in their distribution. Since the area covered expands with time, it is difficult to assert that either the earlier or the later distribution relates to a tribal grouping. It is, perhaps, also difficult to identify a tribal area by the distribution of imported pottery. However, the area covered does seem to be identifiable as a core area within the distribution of, for example, Cunobeline coins. With the oppida, it may have acted as the nerve centre of a wide area. During the Romano-British period it contained the administrative centres of the Catuvellaunian and Trinovantian cantons.

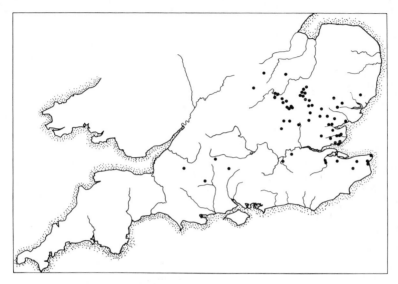

FIG. 59. Aylesford type pedestal urns (Dunning).

Another source of distributional information[1] is provided by late pre-Roman Iron Age decorated bronzes in the 50 year period up to about 50 A.D. (Spratling, 1972). Morphological differences between the bronze types were often found to have localized distributions in southern Britain. Other types are fairly widespread, but the difference in dispersion does not appear to relate to differences in function of these fine metalwork types. For example, among the terrets, some types have a wide distribution while others are fairly localized. It is likely that the pattern is the result of the level of specificity of definition of the types so that further work may make it possible to break down the widespread types into regional groups (Spratling, pers. comm.).

Although certain types have a distribution covering southern Britain, other types are restricted to the two "style-zones" identified by

---

[1] I should like to thank M. G. Spratling for allowing me to use these data, the analysis and interpretation of which he is currently re-examining.

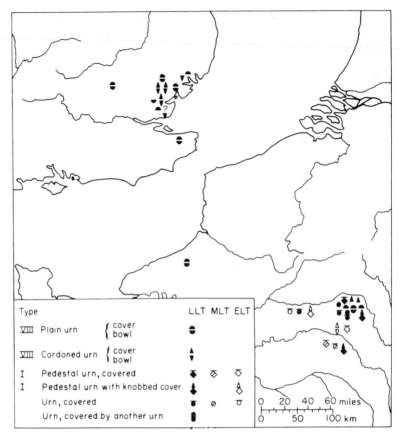

FIG. 60. Distribution map of pottery type VIII (a and b) and other urns with covers in Late, Middle and Early La Tène (Birchall, 1965).

Spratling (1972). The eastern style-zone is centred in East Anglia with extensions into the East Riding of Yorkshire, Surrey and Kent, while a western style-zone is centred in Dorset and Somerset. It is clear from the distribution maps provided by Spratling that further divisions of the style-zones can be made. For example in the eastern style-zone and in the latest phase identified by Spratling, kidney-shaped mirror plates, asymmetric mirror-back designs, IIB and IVB mirror handles are found in southern East Anglia, while IXB terrets are only found in northern East Anglia. In the western style-zone a number of types are found in the Dorset core area of the Durotrigian coins. These include late La Tène chapes. Other types are found mainly in Dorset and south Somerset with one peripheral example (such as "Hod Hill" hilts). In the

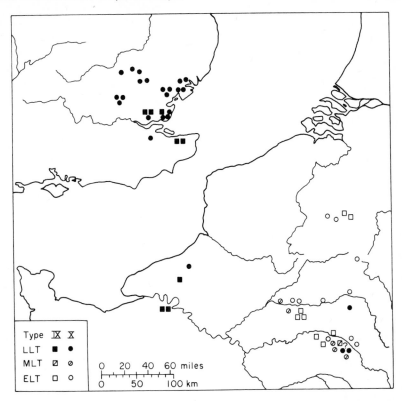

FIG. 61. Distribution of pottery types IX and X in Late, Middle and Early La Tène (Birchall, 1965).

South Wales/Somerset area is found the arc and ring-punching technique on certain types of object (see Peacock, 1969, Fig. 2, group 3, for Iron Age pottery types covering a similar area).

As with the distribution of decorative motifs on Iron Age pottery (p. 308), there seems to be a hierarchy of groupings with smaller association groups within larger groupings. It is important to assess the mode of manufacture of these metal items. The Gussage All Saints workshop should throw light on this (Wainwright and Spratling, 1973), but for the moment there is only one case in which objects from different sites are so similar that they could have come from the same workshop. These are the Group VI terrets from Rickinghall and Stanton in Suffolk (Spratling, 1972). There is a number of sites with evidence of workshop manufacture and these indicate that workshops existed at small settlements (e.g. St. Mawgan-in-Pyder) as well as at

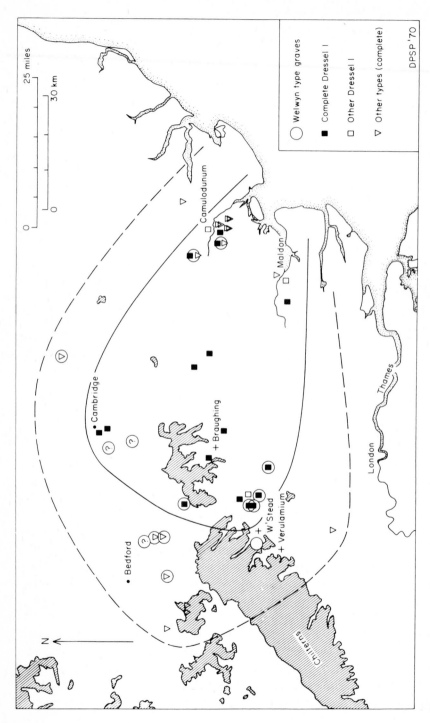

FIG. 62. Amphorae in East Anglia. The continuous line encloses Dressel 1, the broken line later types (Peacock, 1971, with added contours).

big centres (e.g. at Hod Hill and South Cadbury Castle). Further indication of very localized manufacture is seen in the local variation of types. For example Spratling (1972) refers to a mirror on the extreme western edge of the East Anglian style-zone which has similarities in certain aspects with East Anglia and in others with south-western England.

It would be difficult to undertake a more systematic analysis of these data because the sample size of most type groups is very small (often three or four objects) (Spratling, 1972). However the impression is that local manufacture was in accordance with local traditions and contacts. The modal centres of these local traditions can be seen to have a close similarity with the distributions of a range of other evidence already discussed.

The analysis so far has been concerned with moveable objects. In these cases it seems probable that the groupings have some relationship to marketing and workshop patterns. A better idea of cultural traditions, in that it is a matter of shared ideas, may perhaps be gained from the similarities between non-moveable objects. For example, when a more complete picture of late Iron Age burial rites has been obtained (cf. Collis, 1973), it will be of interest to compare this picture with the distribution of moveable items.

In south-eastern England are found a number of late Iron Age burials containing covered urns. Birchall's (1965) type VIII bowl has a rim-groove for a lid and is often found associated with lids. But in the same area other urn types are found with some form of covering. For example, a type Va urn at Heybridge has a lid which is an Arretine derived platter. The practice of covering urns (Fig. 64) may therefore be seen as a burial tradition in this area (although an urned cremation burial with a lid does occur outside the area at Owslebury (Collis, 1968, p. 27)).

Figure 65 shows the eastern extent of hillforts with widely spaced ramparts in the southwest of England (Fox, 1964). It is of interest for this study that these hillforts are not found in the area of the Durotrigian coins to which their distribution is adjacent.

In summary, it seems that certain core areas can be defined in which a large number of different types of objects and traits have their modal centres. In many cases, the range or dispersion around the mode varies considerably. In the Durotrigian area the distribution of pottery traits is less wide than that of the coins and decorated bronzes, while the area is included in a wider area of a type of iron bar. In southern East

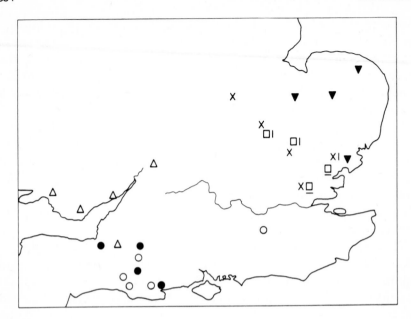

FIG. 63. The distribution of some late pre-Roman decorated bronze traits (Spratling, 1972).

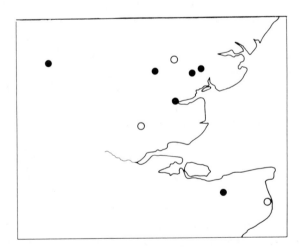

FIG. 64. Covered urn burials in eastern England. Open circles = uncertain examples (Data from Birchall, 1965).

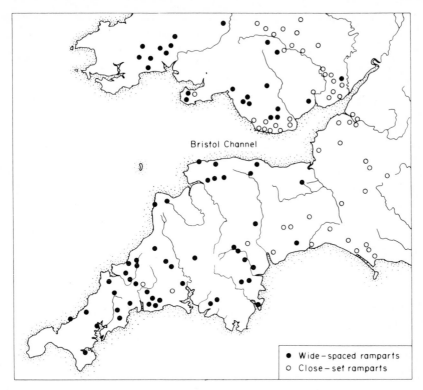

FIG. 65. Multivallate hillforts in the south-west (Fox, 1964).

Anglia a localized area is defined by a number of Aylesford-Swarling pottery types, the Welwyn burials with their imported amphorae, and by the distribution of types of decorated bronzes. Pedestal urns have a wider distribution while the Cunobeline and Tasciovanus coins are found even more widely. It might be suggested, therefore, that it is not possible to use the artefact distribution to define tribal areas as if these were similar to modern political groupings (see Rivet, 1964) in which institutionalized boundaries are of importance. Rather, the archaeological artefact evidence simply allows us to identify interaction patterns as seen in the presence of well defined central areas and surrounding regions having varying degrees of contact with the nodal centres. There is, however, evidence of a different sort that a hierarchy of smaller groupings which can be considered as tribes or sub-tribes did exist in late Iron Age southern England. Caesar (*de Bello Gallico*

5, p. 2) mentions a number of tribes which have no parallel in the coin distributions. Tacitus summarized the situation in Britain when he wrote

> once they owed obedience to kings, now they are distracted between the jarring factions of rival chiefs. Indeed nothing has helped us more in war with their strongest nations than this inability to co-operate. It is but seldom that two or three states unite to repel a common danger: fighting in detail they are conquered wholesale (Tacitus, *Agricola* 12).

Thus, in discussing the coin distributions, "the areas described . . . . as 'tribes' were no doubt loose confederacies of smaller and earlier tribal units, some of whose names, recorded in Caesar, do not appear thereafter" (Allen, 1944, p. 2; see also Rivet, 1964). There is some archaeological evidence, of a form not being examined in this study, for a pattern of small territorial groupings which were clearly defined. A number of Iron Age boundary dykes and ditches have been identified (Dyer, 1961), and extensive entrenchments may be related to the Colchester and Selsey oppida (Bradley, 1971b; Frere, 1967, p. 46). In north Oxfordshire, Grim's Ditch (Hawkes, 1961) encloses an extensive area which apparently does not contain an oppidum. Although such small units are rigidly defined, there seem to be no such boundaries related to the larger groupings which have been suggested from the artefact distributions.

However, that the scale of groupings suggested by the archaeological artefact material, and in particular by the coins, did come to have some significance is strongly indicated by the Romano-British evidence. It is in the pre-Roman core areas that the Roman cantonal capitals were located, either on the site of the pre-Roman centre (Verulamium or Silchester) or at an adjacent location (Cirencester nearby Bagendon for example). Also, the coin pattern does not contradict what little is known independently about the Roman civitas areas which, except perhaps for the civitas Belgarum, were probably based on the pre-Roman tribal areas. The Geography of Ptolemy mentions some of the towns found in each civitas in Britain, but the entries for the lowland area are very scanty. There is also some evidence from inscribed milestones, especially that from Kenchester, which helps to define the civitas areas.

The pattern of distribution of pre-Roman and Romano-Celtic temples is also of interest in its relationship to the pre-Roman groupings. There is some evidence that pre-Roman temples or sanctuaries played an important non-religious role in Britain and Gaul in attracting large periodic gatherings of people. Caesar, for example, when retelling Posidonius' (a generation earlier) account of the Druids in Gaul (*de Bello Gallico* 6, p. 13), records that they,

> at a certain time of the year, meet within the borders of the Carnutes, whose territory is reckoned as the centre of all Gaul, and sit in conclave in a consecrated spot. Thither assemble from every side all that have disputes, and they obey the decisions and judgements of the Druids.

Similarly in Ireland (Lewis, 1966, p. 5) there is a known tradition of

> sanctuaries where the gods were worshipped, the centres of the periodical 'Assemblies' for religious, legislative, judicial, and competitive (athletic and literary) purposes, which were perhaps the most important element in the pre-Christian social life of the country (Macalister, 1949, p. 310).

It has often been assumed that, in addition to the above functions, Romano-Celtic temples were associated with markets and fairs (Richmond, 1963, p. 138; Rivet, 1964, p. 134). "As in other civilizations, fairs were associated with ancient sanctuaries, where the god hallowed transactions and enforced a sacred peace on the market" (Lewis, 1966, p. 130). There is some archaeological evidence for markets or fairs at temple sites. At the Woodeaton temple the abundant small change (over 2730 coins) spread over the surrounding fields and "the wealth of small objects that lie outside the range of offerings . . . suggest the existence of periodic fairs which thronged Woodeaton with buyers and sellers as well as worshippers" (Richmond, 1963, p. 138; see also Milne, 1931, p. 102). Large numbers of coins have been found at other temple sites but Lewis (1966, p. 47) has suggested that they were votive offerings. At the Gosbecks temple the large associated ditched enclosure has been suggested (Lewis, 1966, p. 130) to indicate a fairground. Also "the presence at Gosbecks of Mercury, the guardian of trade and commerce, is quite consistent with the probable use of the site as a fairground" (ibid., p. 48). Caesar (*de Bello Gallico* 6, p. 17) records that the main divinity of the Gauls is Mercury whom they regard as "the inventor of all arts, the guide for every road and journey, and they deem him to have the greatest influence for all money-making and traffic". There is thus at least some independent evidence for a relationship between temple sites and fairs and markets.

In Gaul, where the civitas and earlier tribal areas are reflected fairly accurately in the medieval bishoprics (Holmes, 1911, p. 347), Romano-Celtic temples often occur on their boundaries (Lewis, 1966, p. 130; Stevens, 1940, p. 166). This is further supported for Britain by the pattern of temples in Fig. 66. Only those temples have been included for which there is reliable structural evidence (Lewis, 1966, with the addition of more recent discoveries). They occur either in or near the major civitas capitals (Dorchester, Cirencester, Colchester, St. Albans, Silchester, Wroxeter and possibly Chichester), or in the contact area between coin areas. Thus, if lines are drawn connecting all peripheral temples and all lesser walled towns (for the peripheral location of these towns see Hodder, in press), areas of fairly uniform coin type can be defined, with the civitas or tribal capitals at their centres. The pattern is less clear towards the north either because of the lack of coins (around Wroxeter) or their small number (in the Coritanian area around Leicester). In the south, Winchester and perhaps Silchester, which may not have had important late pre-Roman equivalents (Biddle, 1966, p. 320; Boon, 1969; Collis, 1971b, p. 80), possibly for this reason do not fit well into the overall pattern. Temples and towns are found half-way between St. Albans and Colchester, although these two centres are within the same coin area. This division could perhaps correspond to that between the Catuvellauni and the Trinovantes. It should be stressed however that the lines joining temples and lesser walled towns in Fig. 66 are only intended to clarify an interpretation of a rather complex picture. Several of the Romano-Celtic temples begin at a very early Roman date (such as Woodeaton) while others have pre-Roman structures beneath them (e.g. Frilford and Worth). The temple at Harlow has a large number of pre-Roman coins, and a pre-Roman temple has been identified at Heathrow (Grimes, 1948). Indeed the development of the pattern of temples may have begun in the pre-Roman period. The relationship of this pattern to the coin areas may indicate the growth of peripheral markets (Benet, 1957; Hodder, B. W., 1965; Menger, 1892; Vansina, 1962), or the temples may be related to the peripheries of the coin distributions in some other way. Whatever the interpretation, the pattern in Fig. 66 suggests that in the Roman period, at least, socio-cultural groupings at the scale indicated by the inscribed coin distributions may have had some significance, even though, in the late Iron Age, other aspects of the material culture of the central areas had more restricted distributions.

It seems then that some idea of the structure of archaeological groupings in Iron Age lowland Britain may be gained. The pattern is hierarchical with smaller groupings incorporated into larger groupings. At a high level of aggregation, although the central areas of the groupings are well defined, the broad peripheral areas have a

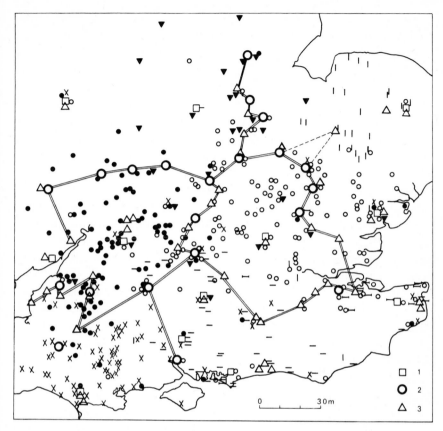

FIG. 66. 1. Cantonal capitals. 2. Lesser walled towns. 3. Temples. (Coin symbols as in Fig. 64.)

similarity and affiliation with the core region which decreases with distance. There is a centrified pattern of interaction in which traits and objects are spread outside the core to a distance depending on chronology (as in the case of the amphorae) and on the type of object or trait. Therefore, whether at the broad regional level actual boundaries were well described before the Roman period or not, boundaries are not clearly indicated by the artefact material. Patterns of interaction do not seem to have been structured or hindered by the presence of socio-cultural or political boundaries, but seem to have been structured rather by reference to a central area.

B. AN INTERPRETATION OF THE EVIDENCE

Having discussed the structure of the pattern, an interpretation may be suggested. Vance (1970), on the basis of medieval and early American examples, has suggested a model in which large regional centres grow up not through internal demand but through close external ties in long distance trade. Such centres may act as collecting points for the syphoning off of goods from internal networks and the articulation of these goods with external centres. They may also act as nodes for the redistribution of imports to surrounding areas (Rowlands, 1973). Thus, externally orientated trade at such centres involves local organization and exchange mechanisms. For example in pre-European sub-Saharan west Africa large states arose with a strong commercial power based on the trade flowing along the trans-Saharan caravan routes. "In these northern savanna lands arose a succession of often powerful indigenous states whose very life lay in their ability to trade across the Sahara with the Mediterranean world" (Hodder, B. W. and Harris, 1967, p. 4). Most of this trade was in luxury items. "Gold, slaves, ivory, ostrich feathers and hides moved northward across the Sahara in return for salt and luxury items" (Hodder, B. W., 1967, p. 223). The later European contact in west Africa was, before the late nineteenth century, almost exclusively in the form of coastal trading bases. This was because the hinterland trade was adequately organized by the African states. The main European interest was slaves and these were provided in large numbers by indigenous African states at or near the coast which acted as middlemen for European traders (Hodder, B. W. and Harris, 1967, p. 6). These states thus articulated the externally orientated trade.

The Vance model and the development of trade in west Africa may be of value for our understanding of the late Iron Age patterns in Britain. Strabo's Geography, derived from various sources from Pytheas to Caesar, records that pre-Roman Britain exported slaves, grain, cattle, gold, silver, iron, hides and hunting dogs. This list, together with the evidence of the amphorae (Peacock, 1971), indicates that much of the external contact was in luxury items. Cunliffe has noted that concerning social development in the late Iron Age, "a significant factor was the existence, after the mid-first century B.C., of an easily accessible Roman consumer market ready to absorb slaves in unlimited quantities" (Cunliffe, 1971, p. 63). It has been shown that the import of amphorae in eastern England was to a localized area which is associated with rich burials. This area also includes the three large oppida at Braughing, St. Albans and Colchester. It seems reasonable to accept the suggestion that this area articulated the internal and external trade for the surrounding region. If this is the case then this core area will have been a node of interaction, having some degree of functional relationship with the wider surrounding region. Other centres are also known to have developed in central areas (Bagendon, Selsey and Hengistbury Head for example) and these are again associated with a range of finer or luxury items (see also Rowlands, 1973). The patterns of interaction visible in the archaeological material may be seen as evidence of a functional relationship with nodal centres in which the centres articulated internal and external trade (see also Collis, 1971a, b). These economic centres can be assumed from the Romano-British pattern to have been, in addition, social, administrative and political centres to which interaction was attracted. This interaction decreased with distance, and the differing ranges of the artefact and trait distributions around the central areas indicate different types and levels of interaction (with some chronological variation) and show that it was not strongly confined by any boundaries. It would be difficult, with this perspective, to say that any particular distribution, whether of coins or of pottery, represented a tribal group on the artefactual evidence alone. However, the level of interaction indicated by the coin distributions does appear to be formally related to the later pattern of certain sites in the Roman period (Fig. 66).

This interpretative framework accounts for the complex distributional evidence rather better than a simple "tribal" explanation (Radford, 1954). Human groups form open and not closed systems, and the archaeological evidence, with its variety of differing distributions according to differing artefact types, relates to different patterns of interaction and participation rather than to simple socio-cultural or tribal groupings. In the late Iron Age we can envisage a number of small tribal groupings interacting with important nodal centres to a degree dependent on distance and on the reason for that interaction. Thus, rather than be considered an anomaly when compared with the pre-Roman distributional evidence, the Roman canton of the Belgae may not be such an "artificial creation" as has been supposed (Rivet, 1964, p. 140). This socio-cultural group may simply not be evident in the archaeological artefact distributions. In Belgium, Marien (1971) has been unable adequately to correlate the pre-Roman archaeological groupings with the Roman cantons although the archaeological groupings sometimes occur in their central areas. It may be the case that the framework offered in this study would provide a more fruitful approach.

Acknowledgements

I should like to thank Dr. A. D. Cliff for introducing me to many of the techniques used in this study, and Dr. D. L. Clarke for many stimulating and helpful discussions. C. R. Orton, M. Rowlands and M. G. Spratling have been kind enough to read and criticize an initial draft. I have benefited greatly from their comments.

Bibliography

Abler, R. Adams, J. S. and Gould, P. (1971). *Spatial Organisation.* Prentice Hall, Englewood Cliffs, New Jersey.

Allen, D. F. (1944). The Belgic dynasties of Britain and their coins. *Archaeologia,* **90,** 1-46.

Allen, D. F. (1958). The origins of coinage in Britain: a reappraisal. In *Problems of the Iron Age in Southern Britain* (S. S. Frere, Ed.). Institute of Archaeology, London.

Allen, D. F. (1961). A study of the Dobunnic coinage. In *Bagendon: A Belgic Oppidum* (E. M. Clifford, Ed.), pp. 75-149. Cambridge University Press, Cambridge.

Allen, D. F. (1962). Celtic coins. In *Ordinance Survey,* 19-32.

Allen, D. F. (1963). *Sylloge of Coins of the British Isles. Coins of the Coritani.* Oxford University Press, London.

Allen, D. F. (1967). Iron currency bars in Britain. *Proceedings of The Prehistoric Society,* **33,** 307-335.

Allen, D. F. (1968). The Celtic coins. In Richmond, I., *Hod Hill,* London, Vol. II, pp. 43-57. British Museum, London.

Allen, D. F. (1970). The coins of the Iceni. *Britannia,* **1,** 1-33.

Allen, D. F. (1971). British potin coins: a review. In *The Iron Age and its Hillforts* (M. Jesson and D. Hill, Eds), pp. 127-154. Southampton University.

American Ethnological Society (1968). *Essays on the Problem of Tribe.*

Ammerman, A. J. and Cavalli-Sforza, L. L. (1971). Measuring the rate of spread of early farming in Europe. *Man,* **6,** 674-688.

Ammerman, A. J. and Cavalli-Sforza, L. L. (1973a). A population model for the diffusion of early farming in Europe. In Renfrew (Ed.) 1973a, pp. 343-357.

Ammerman, A. J. and Cavalli-Sforza, L. L (1973b). Bandkeramik simulation models: a preliminary report. (In press.)

Anscombe, F. J. (1950). Sampling theory of the negative binomial and logarithmic series distributions. *Biometrika,* **37,** 358-382.

Atkinson, R. J. C. (1972). The demographic implications of fieldwork. In *Field Survey in British Archaeology* (E. Fowler, Ed.), pp. 60-66. C.B.A.

Barnard, G. A. and Pearson, E. S. (1947). In *Biometrika*, **34**, 123-138 and 139-167.

Barnes, J. A. (1972). Social networks. *Addison-Wesley Module*, **26**, 1-29.

Behrens, H. and Schlette, F. (Eds) (1969). *Die Neolitischen Becherkulturen im Gebiet der DDR und ihre Europäischen Beziehungen.*

Beloch, K. J. (1880). *Italisches Bund.* Teubner, Leipzig.

Benet, F. (1957). Explosive markets: the Berber highlands. In Polanyi *et al.*, pp. 188-217.

Bergmann, J. (1968). Ethnosoziologische Untersuchungen an Grab- und Hortfundgruppen der älteren Bronzezeit in Nordwestdeutschland. *Germania*, **46**, 224-240.

Bergmann, J. (1970). *Die ältere Bronzezeit Nordwestdeutschlands.* Elwart, Marburg.

Berry, B. J. L. (1961). City size distributions and economic development. *Economic Development and Cultural Change*, **9**, 573-588.

Berry, B. J. L. and Garrison (1958a). A note on central place theory and the range of a good. *Economic Geography*, **34**, 304-311.

Berry, B. J. L. and Garrison (1958b). Recent developments in central place theory. *Papers and Proceedings, Regional Science Association*, 1958, 107-120.

Bessac, F. (1968). Cultunit and ethnic unit — processes and symbolism. In *American Ethnological Society*, 58-71.

Biddle, M. (1966). Excavations at Winchester 1965. *Antiquaries Journal*, **46**, 308-332.

Binford, L. R. (1963). "Red Ochre" caches from the Michigan area: a possible case of cultural drift. *Southwestern Journal of Anthropology*, **19**, 89-108.

Binford, L. R. (1972). *An Archaeological Perspective.* Seminar Press, New York.

Birchall, A. (1965). The Aylesford-Swarling culture: the problem of the Belgae reconsidered. *Proceedings of the Prehistoric Society*, **31**, 241-367.

Blalock, H. M. (1960). *Social Statistics.* McGraw Hill, New York.

Bohannan, P. (1973). Rethinking culture: a project for current anthropologists. *Current Anthropology*, **14**, 357-372.

Bohmers, A., Bruijn, A., Modderman, P. J. R. and Waterbolk, H. T. (1959). Zusammenfassende Betrachtungen uber die Bandkeramik in den Niederlanden. *Palaeohistoria*, **6-7**, 225.

Boon, G. C. (1969). Belgic and Roman Silchester: the excavations of 1954-8 with an excursus on the early history of Calleva. *Archaeologia*, **102**, 1-82.

Bradley, R. (1971a). Trade competition and artefact distribution. *World Archaeology*, **2**, 347-352.

Bradley, R. (1971b). A field survey of the Chichester entrenchments. In *Excavations at Fishbourne* (B. Cunliffe, Ed.). Report of the Research committee of the Society of Antiquaries of London, **27**, 17-36.

Brandt, K. H. (1967). *Studien über Steinerne Äxte und Beile der jungeren Steinzeit und der Stein-kupferzeit Nordwestdeutschlands.*

Bretz-Mahler (1971). *La Civilisation de la Tene 1 en Champagne.* Centre National de la Recherche Scientifique, Paris.

Brown, L. A. and Moore, E. G. (1969). Diffusion research in geography: a perspective. In *Progress in Geography* (C. Board, R. J. Chorley, P. Haggett and D. R. Stoddart, Eds), **1**, 121-157.

Bylund, E. (1960). Theoretical considerations regarding the distribution of settlement in inner north Sweden. *Geografiska Annaler*, 1960, 225.

Canfield, R. L. (1973). The ecology of rural ethnic groups and the spatial dimensions of power. *American Anthropologist*, **75**, 1511-1528.

Catana, A. J. Jr. (1963) The wandering quarter method of estimating population density. *Ecology*, **44**, 349-360.

Childe, G. (1951). *Social Evolution*. C. A. Watts, London.

Clark, G. (1965). Traffic in stone axe and adze blades. *Economic History Review, 2nd Series*, **18**, 1-28.

Clark, P. J. and Evans, F. C. (1954). Distance to nearest neighbour as a measure of spatial relationships in populations. *Ecology*, **35**, 445-453.

Clarke, D. L. (1968). *Analytical Archaeology*. Methuen, London.

Cliff, A. D. (1968). The neighbourhood effect in the diffusion of innovations. *Transactions, Institute of British Geographers*, **44**, 75-84.

Cliff, A. D. and Ord, J. K. (1973). *Spatial Autocorrelation*. Pion, London.

Cliff, A. D. and Ord, J. K. (1974). The quantitative approach in human geography: a review, an interpretation and some new results. (In press).

Cliff, A. D., Haggett, P. and Ord, J. K. (1974). *Elementary Regional Structure: some Quantitative Approaches to the Spatial Organisation of Static and Dynamic Regional Systems*. Cambridge University Press, Cambridge.

Cohen, J. E. (1966). *A Model of Simple Competition*. Harvard University Press, Harvard.

Cohen, R. and Schlegel, A. (1968). The tribe as a socio-political unit: a cross-cultural examination. In *American Ethnological Society*, 120-149.

Collis, J. R. (1968). Excavations at Owslebury, Hants. an interim report. *Antiquaries Journal*, **48**, 18-31.

Collis, J. R. (1971a). Markets and money. In *The Iron Age and its Hillforts* (M. Jesson and D. Hill, Eds), pp. 97-103. Southampton University.

Collis, J. R. (1971b). Functional and theoretical interpretations of British coinage. *World Archaeology*, **3**, 71-84.

Collis, J. R. (1973). Burials with weapons in Iron Age Britain. *Germania*, **51**, 121-131.

Corcoran, J. X. W. P. (1969). The Cotswold-Severn group. In *Megalithic Enquiries* (T. G. E. Powell, J. X. W. P. Corcoran, F. Lynch and J. G. Scott, Eds). Liverpool University Press, Liverpool.

Cottam, G. and Curtis, J. T. (1949). A method for making rapid surveys of woodlands by means of pairs of randomly selected trees. *Ecology*, **30**, 101-104.

Crawford, M. (1970). Money and exchange in the Roman world. *Journal of Roman Studies*, **60**, 40-48.

Croxton, F. E. (1953). *Elementary Statistics with Applications in Medicine and the Biological Sciences*. Dover Publications, New York.

Cunliffe, B. W. (1966). *Regional Groupings within the Iron Age of Southern Britain*. Unpublished Ph.D. thesis submitted to Cambridge University.

Cunliffe, B. W. (1971). Some aspects of hillforts and their cultural environments. In *The Iron Age and its Hillforts* (M. Jesson and D. Hill, Eds), pp. 53-69. Southampton University.

Cunliffe, B. W. (1972). Saxon and medieval settlement-pattern in the region of Chalton, Hampshire. *Medieval Archaeology*, **16**, 1-12.

Cunliffe, B. W. (1974). *Iron Age Communities of Britian*. Routledge and Kegan Paul, London.

Curry, L. (1964). The random spatial economy: an exploration in settlement theory. *Annals of the Association of American Geographers,* **54,** 138-146.

Curry, L. (1967). Central places in the random spatial economy. *Journal of Regional Science,* **7** (supplement), 217-238.

Curry, L. (1972). A spatial analysis of gravity flows. *Regional Studies,* **6,** 131-147.

Dacey, M. F. and Tung, T. (1962). The identification of randomness in point patterns. *Journal of Regional Science,* **4,** 83-96.

Dacey, M. F. (1968). An empirical study of the areal distribution of houses in Puerto Rico. *Transactions, Institute of British Geographers,* **45,** 51-69.

Dacey, M. F. (1973). Statistical tests of spatial association in the locations of tool types. *American Antiquity,* **38,** 320-328.

Dalton, G. (1969). Theoretical issues in economic anthropology. *Current Anthropology,* **10,** 63-102.

David, N. and Hennig, H. (1972). The ethnography of pottery: a Fulani case seen in archaeological perspective. *Addison-Wesley Module,* **21,** 1-29.

de Blij, H. J. (1967). *Systematic Political Geography.* Wiley Interscience, New York.

Dole, G. E. (1968). Tribe as the autonomous unit. In *American Ethnological Society,* 83-100.

Doran, J. (1969). Systems theory, computer simulations and archaeology. *World Archaeology,* **1,** 289-298.

Driver, H. E. (1961). Introduction to statistics for comparative research. In *Readings in Cross-Cultural Methodology* (F. W. Moore, Ed.), pp. 303-331. New Haven.

Driver, H. E. (1966). Geographical-historical *versus* psycho-functional explanations of kin avoidances. *Current Anthropology,* **7.**

Driver, H. E. and Massey, W. C. (1957). Comparative studies of North American Indians. *Transactions of the American Philosophical Society,* **47,** 166-456.

Dyer, J. F. (1961). Dray's Ditches, Bedfordshire and early Iron Age territorial boundaries in the eastern Chilterns. *Antiquaries Journal,* **41,** 32-43.

Fox, A. (1964. *South West England.* London.

Frere, S. S. (1967) *Britannia.* London.

Fried, M. H. (1968). On the concepts of "tribe". In *American Ethnological Society,* 3-22.

Geertz, C. (1957). Ritual and social change: a Javanese example. *American Anthropologist,* **59,** 32-54.

Getis, A. (1964). Temporal land-use pattern analysis with the use of nearest neighbour and quadrat methods. *Annals of the Association of American Geographers,* **54,** 391-399.

Godlund, S. (1956). *The Function and Growth of Bus Traffic within the Sphere of Urban Influence.* Lund Studies in Geography, B. 18.

Gould, P. R. (1969). Spatial diffusion. *Association of American Geographers, Resource paper,* 4.

Gower, J. C. (1971). A general coefficient of similarity and some of its properties. *Biometrics,* **27,** 857-874.

Greig-Smith, P. (1964). *Quantitative Plant Ecology.* Methuen, London.

Grimes, W. F. (1948). A prehistoric temple at London Airport. *Archaeology,* **1,** 74-78.

Hägerstrand, T. (1953). *Innovation Diffusion as a Spatial Process.* (Translated by Pred, A. 1967. Chicago.).

Hägerstrand, T. (1967). On Monte Carlo simulation of diffusion. In *Quantitative Geography* (W. L. Garrison, and D. F. Marble, Eds). *Evanston: Northwestern University Studies in Geography,* **13**, 1-32.

Haggett, P. H. (1965). *Locational Analysis in Human Geography.* Edward Arnold, London.

Haggett, P. H. (1972). *Geography: A Modern Synthesis.* Harper Row, New York.

Hammond, N. D. C. (1972). Locational models and the site of Lubaantun: a Classic Maya centre. In *Models in Archaeology* (D. L. Clarke, Ed.), pp. 757-800. Methuen, London.

Hänsel, B. (1968). *Beitrage zur Chronologie der mittleren Bronzezeit im Karpathenbecken.* Rudolf Habelt, Bonn.

Harvey, D. (1968). Some methodological problems in the use of the Neyman Type A and the negative binomial probability distributions for the analysis of spatial point patterns. *Transactions and Papers, Institute of British Geographers,* **44**, 85-95.

Hawkes, C. (1961). The western third C culture and the Belgic Dobunni. In *Bagendon: A Belgic Oppidum* (E. M. Clifford, Ed.), pp. 43-74. Cambridge University Press, Cambridge.

Hawkes, C. (1973). Innocence retrieval in archaeology. *Antiquity,* **47**, 176-178.

Hill, J. N. (1966). A prehistoric community in eastern Arizona. *Southwestern Journal of Anthropology,* **22**, 9-30.

Hill, J. N. (1970). Broken K: prehistoric social organisation. *Anthropological Papers of the University of Arizona,* **18**, Tucson.

Hodder, B. W. (1965). Some comments on the origins of traditional markets in Africa south of the Sahara. *Transactions of the Institute of British Geographers,* **36**, 97-105.

Hodder, B. W. (1967). West Africa. In Hodder, B. W. and Harris (Eds), pp. 221-258.

Hodder, B. W. and Harris, D. R. (Eds) (1967). *Africa in Transition.* Methuen, London.

Hodder, I. R. (1971). The use of nearest neighbour analysis. *Cornish Archaeology,* **10**, 35-36.

Hodder, I. R. (1972). Locational models and the study of Romano-British settlement. In *Models in Archaeology* (D. L. Clarke, Ed.), pp. 887-909. Methuen, London.

Hodder, I. R. (1974a). A regression analysis of some trade and marketing patterns. *World Archaeology.* (In press.)

Hodder, I. R. (1974b). The distribution of Savernake ware. *Wiltshire Archaeological and Natural History Magazine.* (In press.)

Hodder, I. R. (1974c). The distributions of two types of Romano-British coarse pottery in the west Sussex region. (In press.)

Hodder, I. R. (1974d). Some marketing models for Romano-British coarse pottery. (In press.)

Hodder, I. R. (with Fulford, M.) (1974). A regression analysis of some late Romano-British fine pottery: a case study. *Oxoniensia.* (In press.)

Hodder, I. R. and Hassall, M. (1971). The non-random spacing of Romano-British walled towns. *Man,* **6**, 391-407.

Hodder, I. R. and Orton, C. R. (1974). The detection of competition among Mayan ceremonial sites. To be published as a note in an article by N. Hammond.

Hodder, I. R. and Orton, C. R. (1976). *Spatial Analysis in Archaeology*. Cambridge University Press, Cambridge.

Hodson, F. R. (1962). Some pottery from Eastbourne, the 'Marnians' and the Pre-Roman Iron Age in southern England. *Proceedings of the Prehistoric Society*, **28**, 140-155.

Hodson, F. R. (1964). Cultural grouping within the British pre-Roman Iron Age. *Proceedings of the Prehistoric Society*, **30**, 99-110.

Hodson, F. R. (1969). Cluster analysis and archaeology: some new developments and applications. *World Archaeology*, **1**, 299-320.

Hodson, F. R. (1973). Review of models in archaeology (D. L. Clarke, Ed.). *Nature*, **242**, 350.

Hogg, A. H. A. (1971). Some applications of surface fieldwork. In *The Iron Age and its Hillforts* (M. Jesson and D. Hill, Eds), pp. 105-125. Southampton University Press, Southampton.

Holgate, P. (1965). Some new tests of randomness. *Journal of Ecology*, **53**, 261-266.

Holmes, T. Rice (1911). *Caesar's Conquest of Gaul.* Oxford University Press, Oxford.

Hsu, S. and Tiedmann, C. E. (1968). A rational method of delimiting study areas for unevenly distributed point phenomena. *Professional Geographer*, **20**, 376-381.

Hudson, J. C. (1969). A location theory for rural settlement. *Annals of the Association of American Geographers*, **59**, 365-381.

Jacob-Friesen, K. K. (1959). *Einführung in Niedersachsens Urgeschichte*, **1**.

Jacob-Friesen, G. (1967). Bronzezeitliche Lanzenspitzen Norddeutschlands und Skandinaviens. *Veröffentlichungen der Urgeschichlicken Sammlongen des Landesmuseums Zu Hannover*, **17**, Hildesheim.

Jope, E. M. (1947). Medieval pottery in Berkshire. *Berkshire Archaeological Journal*, **50**, 49-76.

Jope, E. M. (1963). The regional cultures of medieval Britain. In *Culture and Environment* (I. L. Foster and L. Alcock, Eds), pp. 327-350. Routledge, London.

Jope, E. M. (1972). The transmission of new ideas: archaeological evidence for implant and dispersal. *World Archaeology*, **4**, 368-373.

Kariel, H. G. (1970). Analysis of the Alberta settlement pattern for 1961 and 1966 by nearest neighbour analysis. *Geografiska Annaler*, **52B**, 124-131.

Keesing, R. M. and Keesing, F. M. (1971). *New Perspectives in Cultural Anthropology*. Holt, Rinehart and Winston, New York.

Killian, L. (1955). *Haffküstenkultur und Ursprung der Balten.*

King, L. J. (1962). A quantitative expression of the pattern of urban settlements in selected areas of the United States. *Tijdschrift voor Economische en Sociale Geografie*, **53**, 1-7.

King, L. J. (1969). *Statistical Analysis in Geography*. Englewood Cliffs, New York.

Klimek, S. (1935). *The Structure of Californian Indian Culture*. University of California publications in American archaeology and ethnology, **37**, 1-70.

Kossack (1959). *Südbayern während der Hallstattzeit.*

Kruk, J. (1973). *Studia Osadnicze nad Neolitem wyzyn Lessowych*. Polska Akademia nauk Instytut Historii Kultury Materialnej.

Laux, F. (1971). *Die Bronzezeit in der Lüneburger Heide*. Hildesheim.

Lewis, H. S. (1968). Typology and process in political evolution. In *American Ethnological Society*, 101-110.

Lewis, M. J. T. (1966). *Temples in Roman Britain.* Cambridge University Press, Cambridge.

Longacre (1970). *Archaeology as anthropology.* Anthropological papers of the University of Arizona, **17**. Tucson.

Lynch, F. (1969). Megalithic tombs of north Wales. In *Megalithic Enquiries* (T. G. E. Powell, J. X. W. P. Corcoran, F. Lynch and J. G. Scott, Eds). Liverpool University Press, Liverpool.

Macalister, R. A. S. (1949). *The Archaeology of Ireland.* Methuen, London.

McNeil, J. (1972). The hierarchical ordering of characters as a solution to the dependent character problem in numerical taxonomy. *Taxon,* **21,** 71-82.

Marien, M. E. (1971). Tribes and archaeological groupings of the La Tène period in Belgium: some observations. In *The European Community in Later Prehistory* (J. Boardman, M. A. Brown and T. G. E. Powell, Eds). Routledge and Kegan Paul, London.

Meadows, D. H. *et al.* (1972). *The Limits of Growth.* Earth Island, London.

Medvedkov, Y. V. (1967). The concept of entropy in settlement pattern analysis. *Papers, Regional Science Association,* **18,** 165-168.

Meier-Arendt, W. (1966). *Die Bandkeramische Kultur im Untermaingebiet.* Habelt, Bonn.

Menger, K. (1892). On the origin of money. *Economic Journal,* **2,** 239-477.

Milke, W. (1949). The quantitative distribution of cultural similarities and their cartographic representation. *American Anthropologist,* **51,** 237-252.

Milne, J. G. (1931). Woodeaton coins. *Journal of Roman Studies,* **21,** 101-109.

Modderman, P. J. R. (1970). *Linearbandkeramik aus Elsloo und Stein.*

Morrill, R. L. (1962). *Simulation of Central Place Patterns over Time.* Lund studies in geography, B, 24.

Morrill, R. L. (1963). The development of spatial distributions of towns in Sweden: an historical-predictive approach. *Annals of the Association of American Geographers,* **53,** 1-14.

Morrill, R. L. (1965). Migration and the Spread and Growth of Urban Settlements. *Lund studies in geography,* B, 26.

Mountford, M. D. (1961). On E. C. Pielou's index of non-randomness. *Journal of Ecology,* **49,** 271-276.

Naroll, R. (1961). Two solutions to Galton's problem. In *Readings in Cross-Cultural Anthropology* (F. W. Moore, Ed.). Hraf Press, New Haven.

Naroll, R. (1970). What have we learned from cross-cultural surveys. *American Anthropologist,* **72,** 1227-1288.

Newall, R. (1970). *The mesolithic affinities and typological relations of the Dutch Bandkeramik flint industry.* Ph.D. thesis presented to the University of London.

Newcomb, R. M. (1970). The spatial distribution pattern of hill forts in west Penwith. *Cornish Archaeology,* **9,** 47-52.

Ord, J. K. (1972). Density estimation and tests for randomness, using distance methods. Draft for lecture to Advanced Institute on Statistical Ecology in the United States. The Pennsylvania State University.

Peacock, D. P. S. (1967). Romano-British pottery production in the Malvern district of Worcestershire. *Transactions of the Worcestershire Archaeological Society,* **1,** 15-28.

Peacock, D. P. S. (1968). A petrological study of certain Iron Age pottery from western England. *Proceedings of The Prehistoric Society*, 34, 414-426.

Peacock, D. P. S. (1969). A contribution to the study of Glastonbury ware from south-western Britain. *Antiquaries Journal*, 49, 41-61.

Peacock, D. P. S. (1971). Roman amphorae in pre-Roman Britain. In *The Iron Age and its Hillforts* (M. Jesson and D. Hill, Eds), pp. 161-188. Southampton University.

Peebles, C. S. (1973). The sites and their setting. In *Moundville: The Organisation of a Prehistoric Community and Culture*. University of Windsor.

Pielou, E. C. (1959). The use of point-to-plant distances in the study of the pattern of plant populations. *Journal of Ecology*, 47, 607-613.

Pielou, E. C. (1962). The use of plant-to-neighbour distances for the detection of competition. *Journal of Ecology*, 50, 357-368.

Pielou, E. C. (1969). *An Introduction to Mathematical Ecology*. Wiley Interscience, London.

Pierson-Jones, J. (1973). Undergraduate thesis presented to the University of Cambridge.

Polanyi, K., Arensberg, C. M. and Pearson, H. W. (1957). *Trade and Market in the Early Empires*. The Free Press, Glencoe, Illinois.

Posnansky, M. (1973). Aspects of early West African trade. *World Archaeology*, 5, 149-162.

Pounds, N. J. G. (1969). The urbanisation of the classical world. *Annals of the Association of American Geographers*, 59, 135-157.

Pounds, N. J. G. and Balls, S. S. (1964). Core-areas and the development of the European states system. *Annals of the Association of American Geographers*, 54, 24-40.

Pred, A. (1967). *See* Hägerstrand, 1953.

Radford, C. A. R. (1954). The tribes of southern Britain. *Proceedings of the Prehistoric Society*, 20, 1-26.

Renfrew, C. (1969). Trade and culture process in European prehistory. *Current Anthropology*, 10, 2-3, 151-169.

Renfrew, C. (1972). Patterns of population growth in the prehistoric Aegean. In *Man, Settlement and Urbansism* (P. J. Ucko, R. Tringham and G. W. Dimbleby, Eds), pp. 383-399. Duckworth, London.

Renfrew, C. (1972b). *The Emergence of Civilisation*. Methuen, London.

Renfrew, C. (1973a). *The Explanation of Cultural Change: Models in Prehistory*. Duckworth, London.

Renfrew, C. (1973b). *Before Civilisation. The Radiocarbon Revolution and Prehistoric Europe*. Jonathan Cape, London.

Richmond, I. A. (1963). *Roman Britain* (2nd edn). Penguin, Harmondsworth.

Rivet, A. L. F. (1962). Review in *Antiquity*, 36, 145-147.

Rivet, A. L. F. (1964). *Town and Country in Roman Britain* (2nd edn). Hutchinson, London.

Robbins, L. H. (1973). Turkana material culture viewed from an archaeological perspective. *World Archaeology*, 5, 209-214.

Rowlands, M. J. (1970). A study of the bronze working industries of the middle Bronze Age in southern Britain. Ph.D. thesis presented to the University of London.

Rowlands, M. J. (1973). Modes of exchange and the incentives for trade, with reference to later European prehistory. In Renfrew, 1973a, pp. 589-600.

Rowlett, R. M. and Pollnac, R. B. (1971). Multivariate analysis of Marnian La Tène cultural groupings. In *Mathematics in the Archaeological and Historical Sciences,* (F. R. Hodson, D. G. Kendall and P. Tautu, Eds), pp. 46-58. Edinburgh University Press, Edinburgh.

Sahlins, M. D. (1965). On the sociology of primitive exchange. In *The Relevance of Models for Social Anthropology.* A.S.A. monograph, **1,** 139-236.

Scott, J. G. (1969). The Clyde cairns of Scotland. In *Megalithic Enquiries* (T. G. E. Powell, J. W. P. Corcoran, F. Lynch and J. G. Scott, Eds). Liverpool University Press, Liverpool.

Sherratt, A. G. (1972). Socio-economic and demographic models for the neolithic and bronze ages of Europe. In *Models in Archaeology* (D. L. Clarke, Ed.), pp. 477-542. Methuen, London.

Sherratt, A. G. (1973). The interpretation of change in European prehistory. In Renfrew, C. (Ed.) 1973a, pp. 419-428.

Sielman, B. (1971). In *Acta praehistorica et Archaeologica,* **2,**

Sielman, B. (1972). Die frühneolithische Besiedlung Mitteleuropas. In *Die Anfänge des Neolithikums vom Orient bis Nordeuropa* (J. Lüning, Ed.), Vol. 5a, pp. 1-65. Institut für Ur- und Frühgeschichte der Universität zu Köln.

Simon, H. A. (1955). On a class of skew distribution functions. *Biometrika,* **42,** 425-440.

Skellam, J. G. (1952). Studies in statistical ecology. I. Spatial pattern. *Biometrika,* **39,** 346-362.

Skellam, J. G. (1958). In *Biometrika,* **45.**

Soja, E. W. (1971). The political organisation of space. *Association of American Geographers, Commission on College Geography,* Resource paper, 8.

Soudsky, B. (1962). The neolithic site of Bylany. *Antiquity,* 1962, 190.

Soudsky, B. (1968). Criteria to distinguish cultural phases—methods employed at Bylany. Institute of Archaeology, London, seminar paper.

Spratling, M. G. (1972). Southern British decorated bronzes of the late pre-Roman Iron Age. Ph.D. thesis submitted to the University of London.

Sprockhoff, E. (1930). Zür Handelsgeschichte der germanischen Bronzezeit. *Vorgeschichtiche Forschungen,* 7.

Stanislawski, M. B. (1973). Review in *American Antiquity,* **38,** 117-122.

Stead, I. M. (1967). A La Tène III burial at Welwyn Garden City. *Archaeologia,* **101,** 1-62.

Stevens, C. E. (1940). The Frilford site—a postscript. *Oxoniensia,* **5,** 166-167.

Stjernquist, B. (1966). Models of commercial diffusion in prehistoric times. *Scripta Minora,* **2.**

Struever, S. and Houart, G. L. (1972). An analysis of the Hopewell Interaction Sphere. In Wilmsen, 1972, pp. 47-79.

Taylor, C. (1971). The study of settlement patterns in pre-Saxon Britain. Circulated seminar paper, London.

Todd, M. (1970). The small towns of Roman Britain. *Britannia,* **1,** 114-130.

Toynbee, A. J. (1965). *Hannibal's Legacy,* Vol. 2. Oxford University Press, London.

Vance, J. E. (1970). *The Merchant's World: the Geography of Wholesaling.* Prentice Hall, Englewood Cliffs, New Jersey.

Vansina, J. (1962). Trade and markets among the Kuba. In *Markets in Africa* (P. Bohannan, and G. Dalton, Eds), pp. 190-210. Northwestern University Press.

von Merhart, G. (1952). Studien über einege Gattungen von Bronzegefässen. *Festschrift des Römisch-Germanischen Zentralmuseums in Mainz,* 2.

Wainwright, G. and Spratling, M. (1973). The Iron Age settlement of Gussage All Saints. *Antiquity,* 47, 109-130.

Warntz, W. and Neft, D. (1960). Contributions to a statistical methodology for areal distributions. *Journal of Regional Science,* 2, 47-66.

Webster, G. A. (1966). Fort and town in early Roman Britain. In *The civitas capitals of Roman Britain* (J. S. Wacher, Ed.). Leicester.

Webster, P. V. (1972). Severn valley ware on Hadrian's wall. *Archaeologia Aeliana,* 50, 191-203.

Weeden, J. S. (1965). Territorial behaviour of the tree sparrow. *Condor,* 67, 193-209.

Weiss, G. (1973). A scientific concept of culture. *American Anthropologist,* 75, 1376-1413.

Whallon, R. (1973). Spatial analysis of occupation floors: the application of dimensional analysis of variance. In Renfrew, 1973a.

Wheatley, P. (1971). Archaeology and the Chinese city. *World Archaeology,* 2, 159-185.

White, J. P. and Thomas, D. H. (1972). What mean these stones? Ethnotaxonomic models and archaeological interpretations in the New Guinea highlands. In *Models in Archaeology* (D. L. Clarke, Ed.), pp. 275-308. Methuen, London.

Whitworth, W. A. (1934). *Choice and Chance.* Deighton, Cambridge.

Willett, F. (1971). Nigeria. In *The African Iron Age* (P. L. Shinnie, Ed.), pp. 1-35. Clarendon Press, Oxford.

Williamson, E. and Bretherton, M. H. (1963). *Tables of the Negative Binomial Probability Distribution.* Wiley Interscience, New York.

Wilmsen, E. N. (Ed.) (1972). Social exchange and interaction. *Anthropological papers of the Museum of Anthropology, University of Michigan,* 46.

Wiseman, H. V. (1966). *Political Systems — Some Sociological Approaches.* Routledge, Kegan and Paul, New York.

Wiseman, T. P. (1970). Roman Republican road building. *Papers of the British School at Rome,* 38, 122-152.

Wissler, C. (1923). *Man and Culture,* Harrap, London.

Wood, J. J. (1971). Fitting discrete probability distributions to prehistoric settlement patterns. In *the distribution of prehistoric population aggregates* (G. J. Gumerman, Ed.). Prescott College anthropological reports, 1.

7

Some Observations on Medieval and Post-medieval Artefact Distributions: A Spatial Model at the Regional Scale (Macro)

PETER DANKS

King's College, Cambridge

This chapter is a multi-period study, based on the East Anglian region of Britain, the prime aim of which is to suggest methods of studying often complex systems of distribution and marketing. Although essentially spatial in character, it deals with temporal considerations and the evidence for continuity.

East Anglia is a loosely defined geographical area comprising the counties of Norfolk, East and West Suffolk, parts of Lincolnshire, Cambridgeshire and Essex. It is particularly useful for study in this context for several reasons. Paradoxically, although displaying the characteristics of Fox's lowland "invasion" and "replacement" (Fox, 1947) in the proto-historic and early medieval periods, its isolation from the main economic and cultural centres during the Industrial Revolution and after has resulted in a greater survival of settlement patterns and other cultural evidence than in most other moderately populated areas of Britain. Also, the early historical period of this area is comparatively well documented.

The "market days" which still exist in East Anglia are clearly vestigial traces of earlier markets (Berry, 1967) and the map which Berry illustrates, of which Fig. 1 is a more complete version, is still basically representative of the present-day pattern. Although the present-day periodicity may be of more consequence to the motorized

vendor of clothing or fancy goods than say the local producer of fruit
and vegetables, it still reflects the distillation of a former system of
markets and the factors which influenced its creation. However, some
caution must be exercised in producing deterministic arguments based
on contemporary evidence and due reference to temporal factors may
produce a more realistic view. For instance, Fig. 1 shows that the
larger centres have markets on a Saturday but this has only been so
since the end of the Middle Ages. Until that period, Sunday was the
most popular day for a market and resistance to the change seems to
have come partly from the market-owning clergy themselves. In fact,

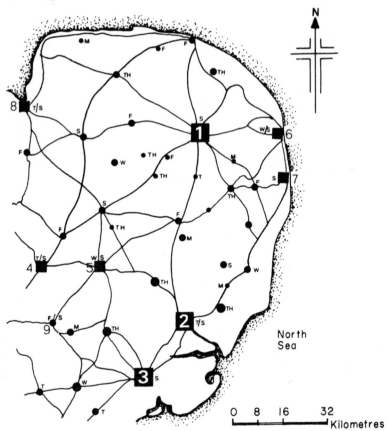

FIG. 1. Market days in East Anglia. 1. Norwich; 2. Ipswich; 3. Colchester; 4.
Newmarket; 5. Bury St. Edmunds; 6. Great Yarmouth; 7. Lowestoft; 8. King's Lynn;
9. Haverhill. It is interesting to note that Haverhill, which is the town with the greatest
population increase in East Anglia, has recently begun to have a market on Saturday,
in addition to the one held on Fridays.

the Church appears intricately linked with marketing not only with regard to time but also with place (Addison, 1953). Although beyond the scope of this paper, clearly if attempts to postulate the continuity of use of sites for religious purposes have any validity, then perhaps it may also have some significance too for the siting of early marketing centres.

Modifications to Fig. 1 can still be made; e.g. the market at Sudbury which is now held on a Thursday was, until 1829, held on a Saturday (Grimwood and Kay, 1953). Further evidence for factors influencing change is to be found in the Little Domesday Book (1088) as the following extract shows. It concerns the towns of Hoxne and Eye in Suffolk, which are only about three miles apart, and the effect of the coming of the Normans on the Church's estate at Hoxne.

> In this Manor there used to be a market and it continued after King William came. And it was a Saturday market. And William Malet made his castle at Eye. And on the same day as the market used to be held on the Bishop's Manor at Hoxne, William Malet established another market at Eye. And thereby the Bishop's market has been so far spoilt that it is of little worth; and is now set up on Fridays. But the market at Eye is held on the Saturday.

The competition from the neighbouring Norfolk town of Diss clearly affected both the markets at a much later date and indeed caused the market at Eye to change to its present day of Monday and the abandonment of a market at Hoxne.

Domesday book (1088) cites seven other markets in Suffolk:
1. Beccles (Wangford)   One market, three parts with the Abbey of Bury St. Edmunds and a fourth part with the King.
2. Sudbury (Thingoe)   One market.
3. Clare (Risbridge)   Then, as now, one market.
4. Thorney (Stow)   One market.
5. Blythburgh (Blything)   One market.
6. Caramhalla (Kelsale in Plomesgate)   One market.
7. Haverhill (Risbridge)   The third part of a market.

Compared with markets recorded for other counties (the Norfolk list contains only three) this is a long list, but it cannot by any means cover all the markets that must have been held in the county (Darby, 1971). However the Domesday evidence is summarized as it stands in Fig. 2, a map of Suffolk showing its division into hundreds and the larger territorial groups, the Liberty of St. Edmund and the Liberty of St. Etheldreda. A "hundred" was a territorial unit, the primary purpose of which was the levying of taxes but there are some

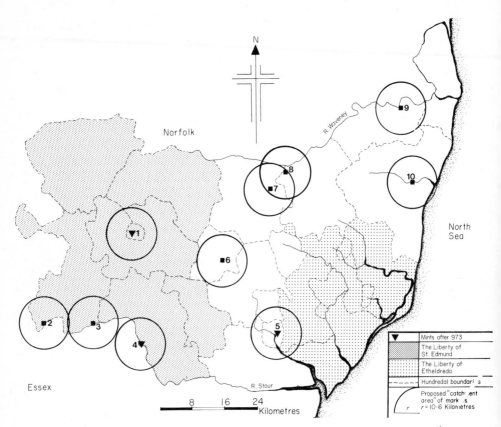

FIG. 2. Suffolk Domesday markets *c.* 1088. 1. Bury St. Edmunds; 2. Haverhill. 3. Clare; 4. Sudbury; 5. Ipswich; 6. Thorney; 7. Eye; 8. Hoxne; 9. Beccles; 10. Blythborough. Caramhalla is omitted from the map because of the uncertainty surrounding its location. Mints after 973: Bury St. Edmunds; a mint under Edward the Confessor (1042-1066); Ipswich, a mint of Eadgar (959-975); and Sudbury, a mint may have been at work from the time of Eadgar but coins are known only from the following years. (From Dolley and Metcalf, 1960; based on Scarfe, *The Suffolk Landscape.*)

indications of their earlier existence as tribal territories. Certainly there is good evidence that the hundredal territories were in existence from at least the time of Athelstan (928-939) and Edmund (939-946) (Davis, 1954).

The Liberty of St. Edmund consisted of eight and a half hundreds given by Edward the Confessor to the Abbey at Bury St. Edmunds in 1044. One form of the grant "gives the eight and a half hundreds soc as fully as Aelfric, son of Withgar held it to my mother's use, or as I myself held it since" (reference is to Queen Emma). The term liberty has a two-fold meaning in this case. It implies that the Abbot had sac and soc over the tenants on all the land, and signifies that the Abbey had jurisdiction over all men within the definite area of the eight and a half hundreds irrespective of the tenure of their lands (Redstone, 1848; Davis, 1909). One translation of sac and soc is as "cause and suit" (Stenton, 1967). A fuller discussion will be found on pp. 490-1 of that work. Incidentally as a case for continuity it is apposite to note that the Liberty of St. Edmund is the present-day unit of the County of West Suffolk (before amalgamation with East Suffolk, 1st April, 1974).

Returning to the Domesday markets, it will be seen that, within the Liberty, the Abbey was having tight control over marketing; the three markets which are named, Haverhill, Sudbury and Clare are as far away as is possible without being outside the boundary limit. However, the distance between each of these is far less and, perhaps significantly, similar; this is discussed more fully below. This control, which was made explicit by King John (1156-1216) who forbade the holding of any market or fair within the Liberty without the consent of the Abbot, continues until at least the middle of the 13th century. The overall lack of competing centres (Figs 2 and 3) is matched in part only by the pattern around the other regional centre — Ipswich. If the unconvincing translation of Caramhalla is discounted, it may be significant that no markets are mentioned for the Liberty of St. Etheldreda. The writer has been unable to find any reference to this situation.

The administrative control of markets began with William the Conqueror and in effect it meant that no markets could be held except in cities, walled towns or other secure places, i.e. around castles under the patronage of powerful land owners. This is in no way extraordinary and clearly a general factor in the establishment of markets has been security of law and order (Belshaw, 1965). One long term effect of this was to vest in some individuals a franchise which produced increasingly lucrative returns as towns developed (as another instance of continuity, the town of Bradford acquired market rights on lease from a private individual for a rent of £5000 in the 19th century, and even at that the market was held in the streets (Addison, 1954)). Another effect, a corollary of the first, was the regulation of establishing markets. Before a new market was granted, a jury was sworn to determine whether it was likely to affect either the King or a neighbouring owner. For instance in 1261 Richard, Earl of Cornwall, brought an action against Maurice, Lord Berkely, for damaging his market. The two places in question, Newport and Wenden in Essex respectively, were only one and a half miles apart and this was the main cause of the dispute. One criteria a jury used in reaching a decision was whether a proposed market was seven leucae, approximately six and two-thirds miles, away from its nearest neighbour (this law remains on the statute books to this day). This distance appears to have been based on the premise that, in present-day terms, 20 miles was a full day's walk and by dividing this by three, equal amounts of time and energy were allowed for those who lived on the periphery of the marketing area. It would appear from Fig. 3 that this was the ideal rather than the reality, and other factors such as communications and density of population must have modified the situation. For instance a linear

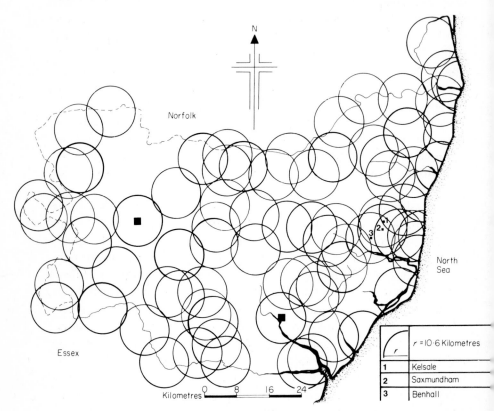

FIG. 3. Suffolk markets before 1300.

concentration between Ipswich and Lowestoft (Fig. 3) follows the line of the major coastal road, now the A12. But this "packing" must be offset against market failures for one reason or another. Kelton, shown as Benhall in Fig. 3, no longer exists in name. It was granted a market (and fair) in 1292 but Guy Ferre, to whom it was granted, died childless in 1323. His wife died in the year of the Black Death, 1349, and the Earl of Suffolk, who eventually took over the estate, seems not to have bothered with the market. Of the other markets crowding Saxmundham, which still has a market today, Kelsale seems to have been the victim of Edward the First's displeasure of the Bigods; he granted a market and fair to Saxmundham, just a mile away, in 1272 — the year he came to the throne. The other centre, Knodishall, is only recorded as having a "Friday Market Heath" in a survey of 1620, no other record of a grant having yet been found (Scarfe, 1972).

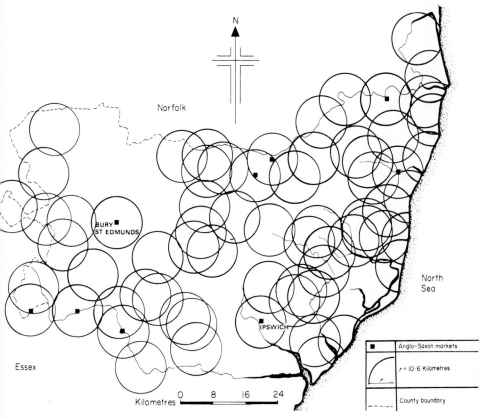

FIG. 4. Suffolk markets after 1300.

To revert again to Fig. 1, it is clearly misleading to assume (Berry, 1967) that all markets are involved in a similar activity. This emphasizes the need to recognize that settlement and distribution patterns are often an accumulation which can be modified, and incidentally made more useful and realistic, by temporal considerations. Figures 2, 3 and 4 show the "build up" of a marketing system which can be modified as indicated above. In the country as a whole, it is worth noting that from 1199 to 1483 over 2800 grants of markets were made by the Crown, more than half of which were made in the first 74 years of that period. In the period from 1700 to 1846, the number was 93 (Min. of Agriculture, 1927).

One further consideration necessary in this type of study is the nature of the exchange influenced by the form of the commodity which is being marketed. For instance markets are held at Bury St. Edmunds on Wednesdays, one cattle market, one corn market and one general market. Paradoxically, the latter is held in two locations, Buttermarket and Cornhill, and is still held by charter by the Borough. The corn and cattle markets are held some distance from the general market.

Economic historians have generally tended to distinguish markets from fairs in terms of size and long-distance trade, and whilst these factors may, in part, constitute the essential characteristic differences, it has resulted in undue emphasis on extreme and atypical examples. In consequence, the larger fairs, such as Sturbridge, St. Ives, Winchester and St. Bartholomew's, have become the models and, although important for long-distance/international trade and the large scale wholesaling of commodities, the attention they have received has tended to focus away from the real situation and the importance of fairs for the movement of artefacts, commodities and people within society on a much more intimate scale. Figure 5 makes this point graphically (also see Table 1 and Appendix A).

It may be more realistic and certainly more apposite from an archaeological viewpoint, to see fairs and markets as a binary marketing system (but not the only outlets); the markets dealing with local produce and domestic items and the fairs concerned with seasonal commodities and exotic or luxury artifacts. Significantly the number of commodity fairs decreased as some of the markets became more specialized. Apart from the other primary difference, markets held weekly and fairs held annually, the long distance journey to purchase large quantities of local seasonal material was another factor. The

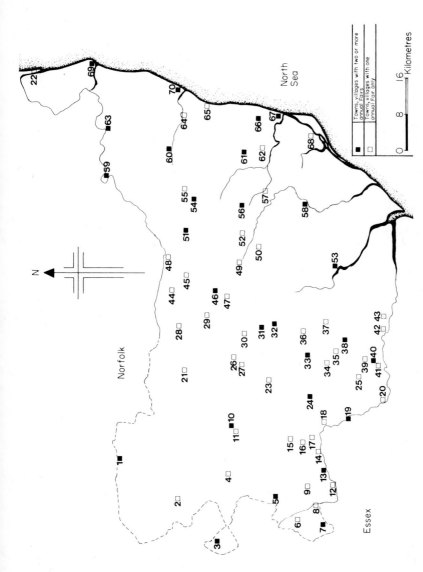

FIG. 5. Annual fairs in Suffolk c. 1800 based mainly on the list given in *The History and Antiquities of the County of Suffolk*, Vol. 1, 1846—Suckling.

TABLE 1. Fairs in Suffolk (key to Fig. 5; see also Appendix A)

1. Brandon	February 14th	(St. Valentine's Day)
	June 11th	(St. Barnabas)
	November 11th	(St. Martin)
2. Mildenhall	October 11th	
3. Newmarket	June 1st	(Whit Tuesday)
	August 24th	(St. Bartholomew)
	[Second Friday in August]	
4. Barrow	May 1st	(St. Philip and St. James the less)
	The Cathedral church at Bury St. Edmunds, about 6½ miles away is dedicated to St. James.	
5. Cowlinge	July 31st	
	October 17th	(St. Etheldreda)
6. Great Thurlow	October 10th	
7. Haverhill	May 12th	
	August 26th	
	[Second Monday in July—sheep and lambs]	
8. Kedington	June 29th	(St. Peter)
9. Hundon	April 8th	(Holy Thursday)
10. Bury St. Edmunds	April 12th	(Easter Tuesday)
	October 2nd	
	December 1st	
	formerly July 25th (St. James) and then September 21st (St. Matthew)	
	[Horringer Fair held 1st Tuesday in September]	
11. Horringer	September 4th	
12. Stoke by Clare	May 31st	**(Whit Monday)**
13. Clare	April 13th	(Easter Tuesday)
	July 26th	(St. Anne)
14. Cavendish	June 11th	(St. Barnabas)
15. Hartest	April 23rd	
16. Boxted	April 12th	(Easter Monday)
17. Glemsford	June 24th	
18. Melford	June 1st	(Whit Tuesday)
	[Thursday after Whit—horses]	
19. Sudbury	March 12th	
	July 10th	
	September 4th	
	June 29th	(St. Peter, prior to 1751)
20. Bures	April 8th	(Holy Thursday)
21. Stanton	June 1st	(Whit Tuesday)
22. Gorleston	May 31st	(Whit Monday)
23. Felsham	August 16th	
24. Lavenham	February 23rd	(Shrove Tuesday)
	October 11th	

TABLE 1 — *continued*

25. Boxford	June 1st	(Whit Tuesday)
26. Elmswell	November 1st	
27. Woolpit	September 6th	
28. Botesdale	April 8th	(Holy Thursday)
29. Finningham	September 4th	
30. Haughley	August 25th	
31. Stowmarket	July 10th	
	August 12th	
	[1st Friday in July]	
32. Needham	October 12th	
	October 13th	
33. Bildeston	February 24th	(Ash Wednesday)
	April 8th	(Holy Thursday)
34. Lindsey	July 25th	(St. James)
35. Kersey	April 12th	(Easter Monday)
36. Bricet	July 5th	
37. Elmsett	June 1st	(Whit Tuesday)
38. Hadleigh	May 31st	(Whit Monday)
	October 10th	
	[1st Thursday in July — lambs]	
39. Polstead	June 16th	
40. Stoke by Nayland	February 25th	
	May 31st	(Whit Monday)
	The first Wednesday after May-day	
41. Nayland	October 2nd	
42. Stratford St. Mary	June 11th	(St. Barnabas)
43. Bergholt	Last Wednesday in July	
44. Thrandeston	July 31st	
45. Eye	May 31st	(Whit Monday)
46. Thwaite	June 30th	
	November 26th	
47. Mendlesham	April 8th	(Holy Thursday)
48. Hoxne	December 1st	
49. Debenham	June 24th	
50. Framsden	April 8th	(Holy Thursday)
51. Stradbroke	third Monday in June	
	October 2nd	
52. Earl Soham	July 23rd	
53. **Ipswich**	first Tuesday in May	
	May 18th	
	July 25th	(St. James)
	August 22nd	
	September 25th	
	[First Tuesday in May	
	third Tuesday in May (Handford Fair — livestock)]	

TABLE 1. — *continued*

54. Laxfield	May 12th	
	May 13th	
	October 25th	(St. Crispin)
	October 26th	
55. Cratfield	September 16th	
56. Framlingham	May 31st	(Whit Monday)
57. Hacheston	November 12th	
58. Woodbridge	April 6th	
	October 11th	
59. Bungay	May 14th	
	September 25th	
	formerly May 3rd	(Invention of the Cross)
	September 14th	(Holy Cross)
	[May 14th — horses, cattle]	
60. Halesworth	June 1st	(Whit Tuesday)
	October 29th	
	[Second Monday in July — lambs and ewes]	
61. Saxmundham	April 8th	(Holy Thursday)
	September 23rd	
	[Third Friday in July]	
62. Snape	August 11th	
63. Beccles	May 31st	(Whit Monday)
	July 11th	
	Sessions	
	October 2nd	
64. Blythburgh	April 5th	
65. Dunwich	July 25th	(St. James)
66. Aldringham	October 11th	
	December 1st	
67. Aldeborough	March 1st	(St. David)
	May 3rd	(Invention of the Cross)
68. Orford	June 24th	(St. John)
69. Lowestoft	May 12th	
	October 11th	
70. Southwold	June 7th	(Trinity Monday)
	August 24th	(St. Bartholomew)
Not included on the map		
[Kesgrave	Third Thursday in July — lambs and sheep	
Melton	First Friday in June	
Barnham	First Monday in July]	

All entries in square brackets are from *Markets and Fairs of England and Wales*, Ministry of Agriculture, Fisheries and Food. Economic Series, 1927.

herring fair at Great Yarmouth, which flourished until the Dutch wars, is a good example of this.

For an aristocratic or aspiring aristocratic group living in the provinces and away from the principal areas of urban life, the fairs provided the opportunity to acquire the type of luxury, status-giving commodity which would have been readily available to their city dwelling cousins. Other social effects may have been the continuous circulation of travelling people, the lines of communication developed and the widening of cultural boundaries.

The periodicity of fairs may have been a direct result of a local seasonal commodity, such as the herrings at Yarmouth, but this is not so in every case. The earliest record of a fair in East Anglia is in the Little Domesday book (1086) and refers to a third part of a fair at Aspall in the Hartismere Hundred, but there is no indication as to the rest of the fair or the nature of its activity. "There must have been other fairs in the county but they are unrecorded" (Darby, 1971). The origin of fairs is obscure and as with markets their regulation appears to coincide with the coming of the Normans. They become chartered during the 12th and 13th centuries. Their early recorded history is inextricably linked with the church and many fairs fall on Saints' days or other religious festivals. It has been suggested that many were a translation of a pagan festival, the nearest appropriate Christian festival being chosen and, if the Edict of Gregory the Great to Bishop Mellitus in 601 A.D. (Bede's *Ecclesiastical History, Book* i c 30), and Raedwald's (died 624/25) adjacent pagan and Christian altars (Bede's *Ecclesiastical History, Book* iic 15) are remembered, it seems at least a possibility.

Apart from the practice of holding fairs and markets in churchyards (made illegal by Edward I in 1285, but continuing to at least the reign of Henry VI; his statute 27 demanded due observance of Sunday and the abolition of fairs and markets on Sunday and High Feast days), the churches were clearly not averse to profiting from them. A fair was granted by Henry I in 1135 to the Abbot of Bury St. Edmunds to assist in the building of St. James' Church, now the Cathedral. Appropriately enough, the day around which the fair was centred (they usually lasted for several days) was St. James' Day, July 25th but clearly this was not well chosen as it was in the middle of the harvesting. When a new charter was granted by Henry III, the date of the festival was changed to that of St. Matthew, September 21st. Henry I in fact granted fairs to many of the greater churches including Canterbury where, such was the appeal to pilgrims to the shrine of St. Thomas a Becket that the fairs of the neighbouring towns were altered in date to catch the pilgrims.

Some artefact distribitions and methods of study

The first example concerns the distribution of porcelain articles from the Lowestoft, Suffolk factory (1757-1803). There are no records, pattern book, etc. known to be extant from this factory, and so it is particularly suited to this type of analysis. The possible reasons for this lack of evidence has been discussed elsewhere (Danks, 1974).

In common with many others this factory produced not only normal table and decorative wares but also especially commissioned inscribed and dated pieces (Fig. 6.), and although naturally fewer in number,

FIG. 6. Lowestoft inscribed and dated wares. (a) A blue and white mug 4½ in. high, inscribed Edd. Amond, Wymondham 1768; one of a set of three bearing the sign of the Rising Sun Inn. (b) A blue and white mug inscribed John Harman, Beccles 1772; made for the Black Boy Inn. (c) A blue and white mug inscribed James and Mary Curtis, Lowestoft 1771; thought to have been painted by Thomas Curtis, a painter at the factory, for his parents. (By courtesy of Norwich Castle Museum.)

the writer suggests that in a local sense, i.e., excluding bulk consignments to warehouses outside the immediate area and exports, they will follow a similar pattern of distribution to the ordinary wares. If it could be demonstrated that the known inscribed pieces are a representative sample of all the porcelain produced, then the suggestion has more credibility and usefulness. To test this hypothesis the frequency of both blue and white and polychrome inscribed pieces was plotted against the date they bear, and the resulting histogram (Fig. 7) generally follows the assertions made by ceramic historians about the factory and the introduction of polychrome wares.

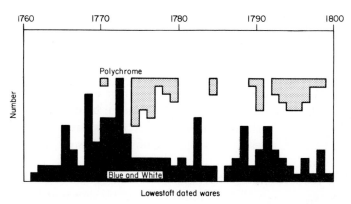

FIG. 7. Histogram of the frequency of blue and white and polychrome against the date they bear.

In 1771 the Lowestoft factory entered a new and intensive phase of production following the death of Robert Brown, Snr. In the previous year a London warehouse had been opened under the management of Clark Durnford in an ambitious attempt to compete in a wider market (Watney, 1963).

However, *The Public Advertiser* of 1st December 1768 carried a note: "Lowestoft China warehouse is removed from Mr. Mathews, Addle St., to Clark Dumford (sic) No. 4 Great St. Thomas Apostle, where all merchants and shopkeepers may be supplied at the usual prices" (Trans. E. C. C. Vol. 6, part 3, 1967). An earlier reference to Mathews is in Mortimers London Directory for 1763 and locates him at the "Loestoft warehouse, Ademanbury" (Adams, 1973). Was the transfer of the agency from Mathews to Durnford part of a general move to increase the factory's trading position?

From the histogram, it will be seen that there is a higher peak in 1772 and it is tempting to see the plateau which follows as reflecting a general lack of demand for blue and white wares resulting from the deterioration of the American market. Another possible measure of the fit of this histogram to the real situation is the dovetailing of the frequency of polychrome and blue and white wares. Although mutually exclusive in their subsequent firings, the wares are all fired together at the biscuit stage and this situation might reasonably be expected to produced a similar pattern to that which emerges in Fig. 7.

The inscribed pieces of Lowestoft porcelain have been well catalogued by A. J. B. Kiddell (Trans. E.C.C. No. 3, 1931), and G. L. Levine (1968), and it is this latter work which has been employed in this paper. The main distribution (Fig. 8) has been restricted to pieces bearing a full name, place and date, e.g. William and Mary Cobb, Harleston, 1790. Pieces bearing initials only, without place, armorial bearings and idiosyncratic birth tablets have been excluded since they might reasonably be expected to behave in a different manner or are without provenance. The only other inscribed pieces which fall within the category under discussion and are not included are:

1. A bowl which commemorates a ship's launching and which reads: "Captain Osbourne, from Colchester: success to 'The Frances' ".

2. A teapot: "Jane Wharton, Gainsborough, Lincs. 1776."

The distribution of the remaining pieces is shown at Fig. 8, and the incidence of pieces at one location is indicated by the number of dates shown. As might be expected, the three major towns, Lowestoft, Great Yarmouth and Norwich, are the three main recipients, and generally the pattern tends to elongate southwards down the coast but with a cluster around Norwich. The transportation of the pots to Norwich was probably by water since there was already considerable river traffic in other commodities and, in general, water is a favourite means of transporting pottery (Nicklin, 1971). The pots may have been carried along the River Waveney or shipped by sea to Yarmouth and then to Norwich along the River Yare (the cut which joins these two rivers was not constructed until 1883). The southerly distribution is not so easily explained but could be the result of two factors: first, transportation by sea in local fishing boats or barges from the Orwell, or alternatively, movement by the main London road which runs via Ipswich.

Over 80% of the Lowestoft pieces occur within a radius of 25 miles, and over 90% within 35 miles. There are a few examples, excluding the outriders already mentioned, which occur as far away as 45 miles.

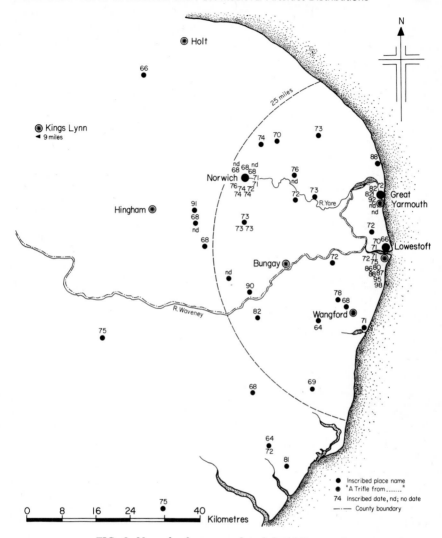

FIG. 8. Named, place-named and dated Lowestoft wares.

It is interesting to compare the pattern of distribution with the theoretical marketing areas of English porcelain factories illustrated in Figs 9 and 10 (see Appendix B). It is tempting to see a shift of emphasis to the south, suggested by the fact that no piece bearing a date later than 1776 appears in the Norwich area as confirming the change in theoretical distribution which occurs between figures *x* and *y*, and which was caused by the closing of the Bow factory in 1775 and the moving of Chelsea workmen and business to Derby in 1770.

FIG. 9. English porcelain factories hypothetical marketing areas before and up to
c. 1776.

The mugs, inkpots and other decorative pieces which bear the
legend, "A trifle from . . . ." (Fig. 11), form a typologically discreet
group and are, together with the birth tablets, peculiar to the
Lowestoft factory. In relation to the other inscribed pieces they survive
in sufficient numbers — by far the majority being, "A trifle from
Lowestoft" — to warrant consideration. Initially, their distribution was
quite speculatively plotted (Fig. 8) and immediately ruled out the
notion, suggested by analogy with Victorian examples and tacitly
followed by many writers, that they were the souvenirs of happy days
on holiday. Identifying the pot with a town or village in this manner
indicates that this would be the point of sale and the use of the word
"from" demonstrates that the recipient would be a visitor. Since it is

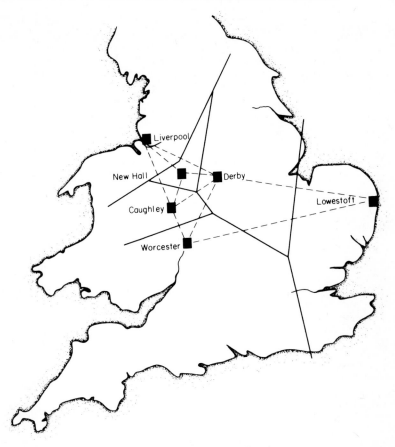

FIG. 10. English porcelain factories hypothetical marketing areas *c.* 1776 to *c.* 1800.

unrealistic to postulate either a flourishing holiday trade or a china warehouseman or trader in, for instance, Wangford, which in the year 1801 (the first year in which a census was taken) was a parish of some 2700 acres, supporting 593 people (V. C. H. Vol 1, 1907), some other explanation was sought.

The author suggests that these were made as trinkets to be sold at annual fairs and this explanation allows for the conditions already noted and the particular form of distribution. This hypothesis was then tested by reference to historical sources. Lowestoft itself is recorded as having two annual fairs, on May 12th and October 11th (Suckling, 1846), and the existence and renown of Yarmouth fair is adequately vouched for by the folk song of that name. The fair at

FIG. 11. A typical "Trifle" mug, decorated in a free, fluent manner in polychrome enamels. (By courtesy of Norwich Castle Museum.)

King's Lynn was originally granted a charter by King John and was later given another royal charter by Henry VIII, after which the fair was held, perhaps appropriately, on February 14th, St. Valentine's

Day. There were two annual fairs held at Bungay, on May 14th and September 14th and their origin may be traced from festivals of the early church.

> Although Hugh Bigod gave the King forty marks in 1199 for extending the privileges of his fair, which he was then holding twice a year, these fairs do not seem to have been granted a charter but to have originated from ancient wakes that were annually held on festival days observed by the church in honour of the Saints to whom the parish and other religious foundations were dedicated (Mann, 1934).

Fairs certainly were held at Holt as early as 1309 when a grant was made for a fair on the eve and day of St. Mathew, on September 21st; at the beginning of this century they were being held on the 25th of April and the 25th November. The fairs at Hingham were granted by Henry III and in the 16th century are recorded as being held on the 24th February and the 21st of September, these dates continuing to be observed until 1836 when they were transferred to the 7th March and the 2nd of October. The author has been unable to trace the existence of a fair at Wangford in the 18th century, but circumstantial evidence suggests that in fact one may well have been held there too.

From an archaeological viewpoint, this discussion has several implications. It indicates that marketing was a complex system with many agencies involved, for as well as an outlet at the fairs and markets and the more usual practice of supplying warehousemen, who in turn supplied retailers, the factory is said to have had two travellers employed in the area (Chaffers, 1874). The number of inscribed mugs bearing the name of an inn keeper and/or the sign of his inn may indicate a further specialized market and a situation somewhat analogous to the clay pipes bearing inn signs, which were available at hostelries in the 18th century, is suggested. Inns were of some importance for marketing and, even into the early part of this century, corn sales were effected in public houses in many small towns in the region (Dickinson, 1932). In 1927, corn and provender sales were held at 340 centres in England and Wales, of which 118 were controlled by municipal authorities, 62 by corn exchange companies and 160 held in inns, streets, cattle markets and other places (Min. of Agriculture and Fisheries, 1927).

The general distribution of Lowestoft "trifle" pieces is shown in Fig. 8, and the greatest number, as might be expected, originate from Lowestoft. Comparatively few are known from Yarmouth and this perhaps requires some explanation in view of Yarmouth's size and proximity. One may be the presence of a ceramic decorator working in

Yarmouth, at 25 Market Row, some time before 1790, who produced inscribed and gilded wares (Kiddell, 1960). This was William Absolon who purchased glass, earthenware and some porcelain and decorated them with flowers and local scenes in enamel colours. Most of his place inscribed pieces bear the legend, "A Trifle from Yarmouth," but there are other possible examples carrying an inscription such as, "A Trifle from Aylesham".

The majority of Lowestoft porcelain "trifle" pieces are generally dated, on stylistic grounds, to the period 1790-1800, and this would fit in well with the documentary evidence of Absolon's activities at Yarmouth. That the two concerned were exploiting an almost mutually exclusive marketing area is suggested and it is perhaps significant that of all the known pieces decorated by Absolon none had its origin in the Lowestoft factory, which, in view of its apparent convenience, is surely significant.

Perhaps of even greater consequence in terms of artefact distribution is the funnelling effect that this secondary processing causes. Factories from which it is known (mainly on the evidence of impressed factory marks) Absolon obtained his ceramic blanks are Turner of Lane End, Wedgwood of Etruria, Wilson of Hanley, Rogers of Burslem, Davenport of Longton, Shorthose of Hanley; all in Staffordshire, Leeds, Liverpool and Welsh potteries. Some porcelain to which gilding was added may have been obtained from Caughley and there is a reference to Wigan pottery (Church, 1911); but this cannot be substantiated. The total situation is summarized graphically in Fig. 12.

From an archaeological point of view it is interesting because it suggests that secondary processes, such as enamelling and engraving may not necessarily have been employed in the original workshops and, because of the influence of this second workshop, varied artefacts from widely scattered sources may achieve a local distribution which disguises the complex nature of the marketing system. For example, this could explain the distribution of the Anglo-Saxon square headed and cruciform fibulae on which red enamel has been used. As Fox first noted (Fox, 1923), this use of enamel on fibulae is practically confined to the area shown in Fig. 13 and Table 2. Although it has been suggested that the three from Little Wilbraham may represent the produce of a local workshop (Leeds, 1949), the list below shows the wide range of designs of fibulae involved, all of which may be parallelled elsewhere but without the use of enamel. For instance the

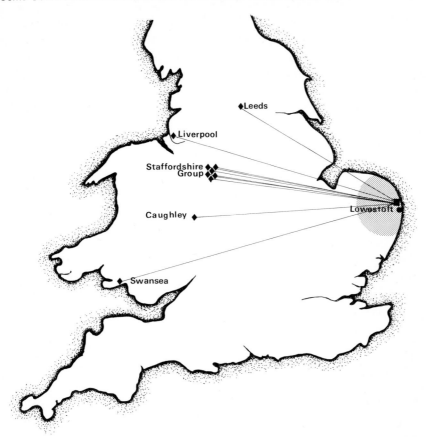

FIG. 12. Origins and redistribution area of wares of Absolon of Yarmouth, *c.* 1790.

example from Quy can be parallelled with one from **Ragley Bank, Warwicks** (Leeds, 1949). Some temporal and spatial affinity is perhaps suggested by Leeds' B group classification of the square headed brooches however. The author suggests that these factors indicate that the enamelling may have been simply a local survival of a Romano-British technique which was applied to artefacts coming into the area, and may have been the result of the activities of one workshop; the radius of distribution certainly does not preclude this thesis. Reference to the widespread general distribution of group B4, B5 and B8 and the late florid cruciform brooches, only serves to emphasize this impression.

In the case of Absolon's wares there was clearly a demand for an artefact which had a local relevance and a certain exclusiveness as a result of the decorator's modifications. That people were prepared to pay extra for this quality is amply demonstrated by Absolon's commercial success and by documentary evidence that the wares on which he was working were readily available to the general public in their original state and at their original price.

An interesting notice appeared in the *Norfolk Chronicle* on July 12th 1783:

> WILLIAM BELOE, CHINA-MAN, Market Place, Norwich, has just received from the India Company's Sale a large and regular assortment of useful and ornamental CHINA, Japanned Tea Boards, etc. He has also a large parcel of useful China from Commodore Johnstone's Prize Goods taken from the Dutch, which will be sold cheap. He is lately returned from Staffordshire with a very large and elegant assortment of that much improved Manufactory particularly some complete Table Services after the Dresden Manner and from their Patterns: and in consequence of his frequent Attendance on that Manufactory he will be able to supply his Warehouse in Norwich immediately with every new and improved pattern.

It is interesting to note that Beloe claims to have visited Staffordshire to select his merchandise — most other dealers mention only London as a source (Smith, 1974).

To add further complication to this secondary process of redistribution, it is interesting to consider the case of 18th century Chinese Armorial porcelain. In this instance it was not the wares which were being moved to be added to or modified, but the designs which were travelling to the original source of the pots. Drawings of British coats-of-arms were provided for the Chinese decorator who copied them on to the glazed porcelain wares. They were then exported occasionally bearing part of the original instruction, such as "paint this blue" or "party per pale", forever recorded in fired on enamel by some unknown non-English speaking Chinese painter. The confusion that hard paste porcelain bearing the most obvious signs of British aristocratic breeding on them caused Victorian antiquaries has been discussed elsewhere (Danks, 1974). That a Lowestoft origin for this class of ware could have been postulated and widely accepted on virtually no evidence, and even less logic, would seem astonishing.

Both this and the Absolon examples show clearly the dangers of attempting to construct typologies and of postulating centres of distribution on one attribute factor, whether it be method of manufacture or decoration. In general, the author suggests that apart from clarifying and testing hypotheses about the medieval and post-medieval periods, the value of this type of study is to suggest alternative models of artefact distributions in proto-and pre-history, and may prevent the

TABLE 2. Anglo-Saxon enamelled fibulae

1. Square headed fibulae — red enamel unless otherwise stated

	Leeds classification	References	Illustrated
i) Linton 21	B 4 Herpes type	A.J. XI, 100. Fox, 260. ASAA, 90 Leeds, 57.	Leeds Pl. 86.
ii) Linton 32	B 5 Linton Heath type	A.J. XI, 103. ASAA, 90 Fox, 260 Leeds, 60.	Leeds Pl. 91.
iii) Linton 39	This is a small square-headed brooch bearing blue enamel	Fox, 260. Archaeologia Vol. XCI f	Archaeologia, Vol. XCI, Fig. 34.
iv) Quy	B 5 Linton Heath type	Fox, 264. ASAA, 90 Aberg, 150 Leeds, 60	Leeds Pl. 92.
v) Little Wilbraham 3	B 8 Barrington type	Leeds, 69. S.O. Aberg, 34	Leeds Pl. 113.
vi) Little Wilbraham 40.	B 8 Barrington type, also bears blue enamel.	Fox, 262. Leeds, 69. Aberg, 35. S.O.	Leeds Pl. 114.
vii) Little Wilbraham 28.	B 8 Barrington type	Leeds, 69. S.O. Aberg. Fox, 262	Leeds Pl. 112.

2. Cruciform fibulae

i) Little Wilbraham	Fox, 262	
ii) Lakenheath	C.M.	Fox, Pl. XXIX.

N.b. A square headed brooch from Brooke in Norfolk may have carried enamel but its subsequent burning makes it conjectural (Leeds, 44).

Abbreviations:

Aberg	The Anglo-Saxons in England	Nils Aberg	1926.
ASAA	Early Anglo-Saxon Art and Archaeology	E. T. Leeds	1936.
A.J.	The Antiquaries Journal		
C.M.	Cambridge Museum of Archaeology and Ethnology		
Fox	The Archaeology of the Cambridge Region	Sir C. Fox	1932.
Leeds	Early Anglo-Saxon Great Square headed brooches	E. T. Leeds	1949.
S.O.	Saxon Obsequies	The Hon. R. C. Neville	1852.

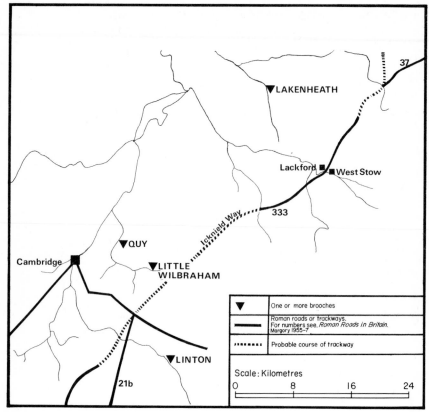

FIG. 13. Anglo-Saxon great square-headed and cruciform brooches bearing red enamel.

adoption of simplistic models because of restrictive frames of reference.

It is conceded that some of the conclusions in this chapter may be debatable and may be replaced as more evidence becomes available. Perhaps the most important aspect is that a study of this kind breaks the vicious circle caused by frequently repeated ideas, often based on a single tentative suggestion, which have achieved the status of an established fact.

Appendix

A. In the original list Saints' Days are not given — just dates and Holy Days such as Whit Monday and Holy Thursday. Saints's days have been included in the present list because although many may have been replaced at a later date there is some evidence for the continued use of the original charter dates. Where moveable feasts such as the Easter ones are indicated these have been translated into calendar dates and to avoid a further random element all these have been taken from *Time's Telescope for 1819* which contains *An explanation of Saints' days and holidays.*

It is tempting to seek some pattern within the network of fairs and perhaps the present-day circuit of the fairground showman has some usefulness. However, there are factors which make reconstructions of circuits difficult. First as has already been discussed many dates have changed, second some are on moveable feasts, third many fairs stretch over a period of several days and fourth it may be impossible to recover the date of many fairs; indeed some of the villages themselves may have disappeared.

Clearly the Suckling list gives a somewhat "late" picture but has the advantage of giving some indication of the extent of fair distribution at one point in time.

B. Figures 9 and 10 suggest what the effect of the American War of Independence may have been on English porcelain factories. In this context it is apposite to consider not only changes in location but also the alteration in the hypothetical marketing areas delineated by the use of Thiessen polygons. For instance, the continuing prosperity of the Derby factory is significant. "Unlike most English factories Derby made comparatively little blue and white" (Watney, 1963). No explanation has been offered but Fig. 9 indicates that non-participation in the American market, which appears to have been almost completely blue and white orientated, could have been one reason. This proposition is supported by the apparent lack of effect that the War had on the continuation of the factory and the apparent lack of competition over an area of high population. Figure 10 indicates a bow-wave movement towards London and this may be significant since effective competition in the production of the more decorative polychrome wares, which formed the bulk of its production, had been removed by the incorporation of the Chelsea works.

Significantly the distribution of inscribed and dated Lowestoft wares shown in Fig. 8 follows an area indicated in Fig. 9. Again the increase in the manufacture of polychrome wares at the Lowestoft factory, circa 1775, indicated by the histogram at Fig. 7 could be seen as reflecting the exploitation of the London marketing centre which was thrown open by the failure and closure of Bow and Chelsea. The existence of a Lowestoft warehouse in London at this time tends to confirm these observations.

Bibliography

Adams (Elizabeth), Personal communication.
Addison, W. (1954). *English Fairs and Markets.* Batsford, London.
Belshaw, C. S. (1965) *Traditional Exchange and Modern Markets.* Mod. of Traditional Socs. Ser., Prentice Hall, New Jersey.
Berry, B. J. L. (1967). *Geography of Market Centres and Retail Distribution.* Foundations of Economic Geography, Prentice Hall, New Jersey.
Bimson, M. *et al.* (1966). *Transactions of the English Ceramic Circle, part II.*
Chaffers, W. (1874). *The Collector's Handbook of Marks and Monograms on Pottery.* London.
Church, Sir A. H. (1911). *English Earthenware Made During the 17th and 18th Centuries.* H.M.S.O., London.
Danks, P. (1974). Chaffers and the Lowestoft Factory. *The Connoisseur,* (in press).
Darby, H. C. (1971). *The Domesday Geography of Eastern England* (3rd edn). Cambridge University Press, Cambridge.
Davis, H. W. C. (1909). The Liberty of St. Edmund. *English Historical Review,* **XXIV.**
Davis, R. H. C. (Ed.) (1954). *The Kalendar of Abbot Samson.* Camden 3rd Series, Vol. 84 Royal Historical Society, London.
Dickinson, R. E. (1932). Distributions and functions of the smaller urban settlements of East Anglia. *Geography,* **17.**
Dolley, R. H. M. and Metcalf, D. M. (1961). The reform of the English coinage under Eadger. *Anglo Saxon Coins Dedicated to F. M. Stenton* (R. H. M. Dolley, Ed.). Methuen, London.
Fox, Sir C. (1923). *Archaeology of the Cambridge Region.* Cambridge University Press.
Fox, Sir C. (1947). *The Personality of Britain: Its Influence on Inhabitant and Invader in Prehistoric and Early Historic Times* (4th edn). National Museum of Wales, Cardiff.
Grimwood, C. G. and Kay, S. A. (1953). *History of Sudbury, Suffolk.* The Authors, Sudbury.
Kiddell, A. J. B. (1913). Inscribed and dated Lowestoft porcelain. *Transactions of the English Porcelain Circle,* No. 111.
Kiddell, A. J. B. (1960). Absolon of Yarmouth. *Transactions of the English Ceramic Circle,* 5, 1.
Leeds, E. T. (*comp.*) (1949). *A Corpus of Early Anglo Saxon Square Headed Brooches,* (compiled by E. T. Leeds). Clarendon Press, Oxford.
Levine, G. L. (1968). *Inscribed Lowestoft Porcelain.* The Author, Brundall.
Mann, E. (1934). *Old Bungay.* Heath Cranton, London.

Ministry of Agriculture and Fisheries (1927). Economic Series. *Markets and Fairs of England and Wales.*

Nicklin, K. (1971). Stability and innovation in pottery manufacture. *World Archaeology,* **3**, No. 1.

Redstone, L. J. (1848). The Liberty of Saint Edmund. *Suffolk Institute of Archaeology and Natural History,* **XV**, 2.

Scarfe, N. (1972). *The Suffolk landscape.* Making of the English Landscape, Hodder and Stoughton, London.

Smith, S. (1974). Norwich china dealers of the mid 18th Century. *Transactions of the English Ceramic Circle,* **9**, 11.

Stenton, Sir F. M. (1967). *Anglo Saxon England.* Clarendon Press, Oxford.

Suckling, A. I. (1846). *The History and Antiquities of the County of Suffolk,* Vol. I. John Weale, London.

Victoria County History of Suffolk, Vol. 1 (1911). Oxford University Press, London.

Watney, B. (1963). *English Blue and White Porcelain of the 18th Century.* Faber Monographs on Pottery and Porcelain, Faber and Faber, London.

Index